The Invasion of Western Europe by Nazi Germany, May 10, 1940

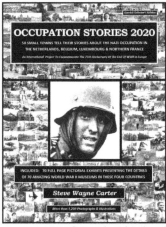

Cover Design © Dazzle Whitehead

Occupation Stories 2020

Remembering & Honoring the Sacrifices Endured By So Many

To my Parents, Bob & Jeanette, who instilled

in me the values and the music I enjoy today.

Discounted copies for resale at museum gift shops and other retail

outlets may be purchased by establishing an account with the

Ingram Content Group at https://getstarted.ingramcontent.com/

Digital & Limited Collector's Editions Are Available at:

https://www.occupationstories2020.com/

OCCUPATION STORIES 2020

Occupation Stories 2020

Remembering & Honoring the Sacrifices Endured By So Many

OCCUPATION STORIES 2020

An International Pictorial Project to Commemorate the 75th Anniversary of the End of World War II in Europe

Compiled & Authored By

STEVE WAYNE CARTER

Occupation Stories 2020

Remembering & Honoring The Sacrifices Endured By So Many

"Democracy alone . . . Is the most
humane, the most advanced, and, in
the end, the most unconquerable of
all forms of human society . . .
We would rather die on our feet
than live on our knees."

Franklin D. Roosevelt, 1941

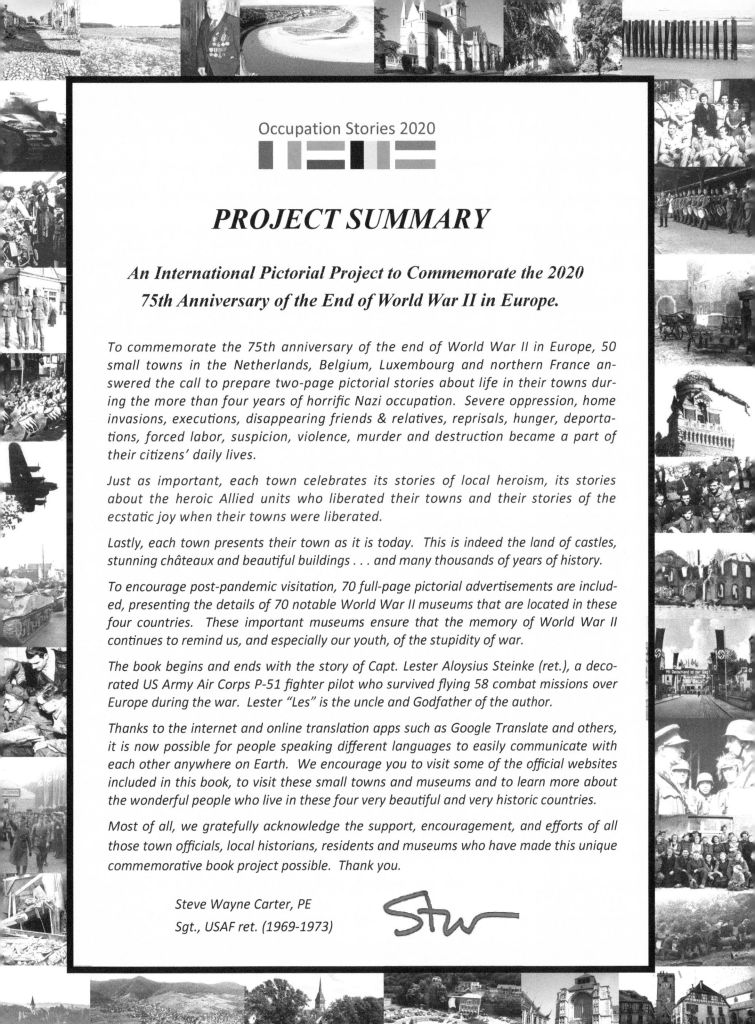

Occupation Stories 2020

PROJECT SUMMARY

An International Pictorial Project to Commemorate the 2020 75th Anniversary of the End of World War II in Europe.

To commemorate the 75th anniversary of the end of World War II in Europe, 50 small towns in the Netherlands, Belgium, Luxembourg and northern France answered the call to prepare two-page pictorial stories about life in their towns during the more than four years of horrific Nazi occupation. Severe oppression, home invasions, executions, disappearing friends & relatives, reprisals, hunger, deportations, forced labor, suspicion, violence, murder and destruction became a part of their citizens' daily lives.

Just as important, each town celebrates its stories of local heroism, its stories about the heroic Allied units who liberated their towns and their stories of the ecstatic joy when their towns were liberated.

Lastly, each town presents their town as it is today. This is indeed the land of castles, stunning châteaux and beautiful buildings . . . and many thousands of years of history.

To encourage post-pandemic visitation, 70 full-page pictorial advertisements are included, presenting the details of 70 notable World War II museums that are located in these four countries. These important museums ensure that the memory of World War II continues to remind us, and especially our youth, of the stupidity of war.

The book begins and ends with the story of Capt. Lester Aloysius Steinke (ret.), a decorated US Army Air Corps P-51 fighter pilot who survived flying 58 combat missions over Europe during the war. Lester "Les" is the uncle and Godfather of the author.

Thanks to the internet and online translation apps such as Google Translate and others, it is now possible for people speaking different languages to easily communicate with each other anywhere on Earth. We encourage you to visit some of the official websites included in this book, to visit these small towns and museums and to learn more about the wonderful people who live in these four very beautiful and very historic countries.

Most of all, we gratefully acknowledge the support, encouragement, and efforts of all those town officials, local historians, residents and museums who have made this unique commemorative book project possible. Thank you.

Steve Wayne Carter, PE
Sgt., USAF ret. (1969-1973)

Occupation Stories 2020

Remembering & Honoring The Sacrifices Endured By So Many

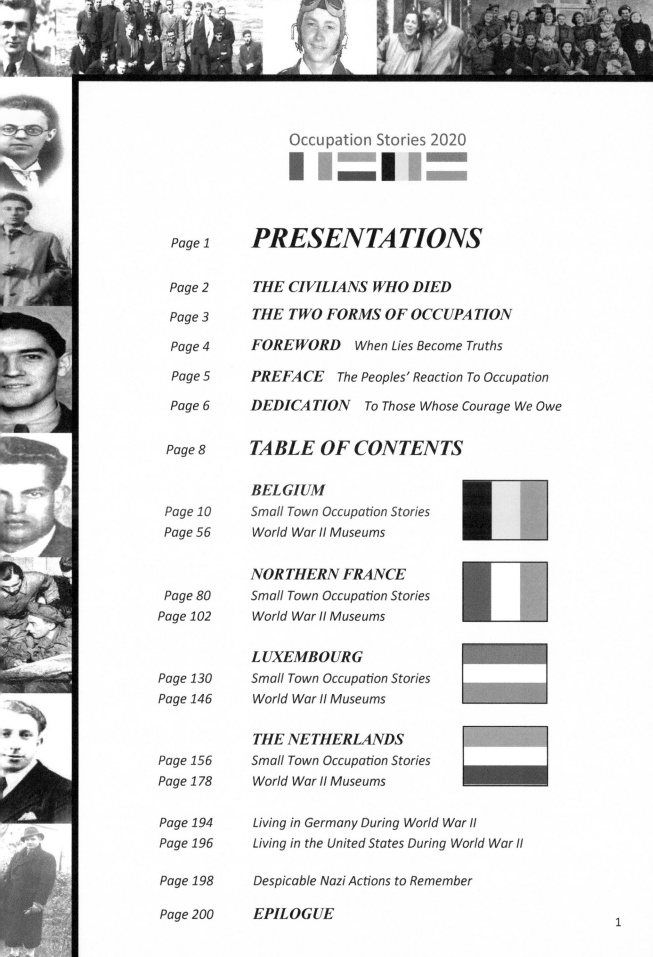

Occupation Stories 2020

Page 1   # PRESENTATIONS

Page 2   **THE CIVILIANS WHO DIED**

Page 3   **THE TWO FORMS OF OCCUPATION**

Page 4   **FOREWORD**   When Lies Become Truths

Page 5   **PREFACE**   The Peoples' Reaction To Occupation

Page 6   **DEDICATION**   To Those Whose Courage We Owe

Page 8   # TABLE OF CONTENTS

BELGIUM

Page 10   Small Town Occupation Stories
Page 56   World War II Museums

NORTHERN FRANCE

Page 80   Small Town Occupation Stories
Page 102   World War II Museums

LUXEMBOURG

Page 130   Small Town Occupation Stories
Page 146   World War II Museums

THE NETHERLANDS

Page 156   Small Town Occupation Stories
Page 178   World War II Museums

Page 194   Living in Germany During World War II
Page 196   Living in the United States During World War II

Page 198   Despicable Nazi Actions to Remember

Page 200   # EPILOGUE

Occupation Stories 2020

Remembering & Honoring The Sacrifices Endured By So Many

"Let us be firm, pure and faithful; at
the end of our sorrow, there is the
greatest glory of the world, that of
the men who did not give in".

Charles de Gaulle

THE CIVILIANS WHO DIED

The Number of Civilian Deaths in the Netherlands, Belgium, Luxembourg and France During World War II Was Staggering.

 In the **Netherlands**, nearly 300,000 civilians died during the war. This would be equivalent to nearly 13,000,000 people dying in the United States.

 In tiny **Luxembourg**, as many as 6,000 civilians died during the war. This would be equivalent to nearly 7,000,000 people dying in the United States today.

 In **France**, more than 600,000 civilians died during the war. This would be equivalent to nearly 5,000,000 people dying in the United States today.

 In **Belgium**, nearly 90,000 civilians died during the war. This would be equivalent to nearly 4,000,000 people dying in the United States today.

Most all of them civilians prior to the start of the war, another 250,000 men and women from these four countries died as soldiers and airmen, fighting to rid their homelands of the brutal and ruthless Nazi invaders and occupiers.

*In **Germany**, nearly 800,000 civilians died during the war.*

We honor the memory of all who died and suffered at the hands of the Nazis.

The Occupation Stories 2020 Project

Occupation Stories 2020

Remembering & Honoring The Sacrifices Endured By So Many

THE TWO FORMS OF OCCUPATION

Many occupations have occurred since nations began establishing national military forces and in fact, all occupations are military occupations. In the simplest analysis, occupations can either be classified as morally-just occupations or immoral, unjust occupations. Morally-just occupations are those occupations necessary to restore peace and ease the suffering of the people whose lands are occupied. Immoral, unjust occupations are those occupations that are not necessary and are not desired by the people in the lands being occupied.

The best historical example of a morally-just occupation was the Allies' military occupation of Germany following the end of World War II. This occupation was not only necessary to prevent the reemergence of those forces responsible for Germany's unjust war actions but necessary to help the people of Germany recover from the severe economic conditions and physical devastation they suffered and help them again become welcome members of global society.

The best historical example of an immoral and unjust occupation was the four-year-long occupation that is the subject of this book. Not only were there no moral justifications for Germany to invade and occupy these four countries, there were no needs that would have been satisfied. Instead, the people of these four countries were facing a future of permanent occupation, facing integration into a brutal, autocratic regime and facing the disappearance of their centuries-old countries from the future maps of Europe. Fierce and widespread resistance to the German Nazi occupiers was therefore inevitable.

Fortunately, global society places a great deal of importance on morality and therefore moral and just occupations can be expected to be successful, as was the case of the Allies' post war occupation of Germany. Conversely, immoral and unjust occupations will always be rejected by global society and will always fail, especially when the world unites to fight and prevent them from being successful, as was the case when Germany attempted its brutal occupation of these four countries.

As you will see in the 50 small town occupation stories in this book, resistance to the occupier began soon after the May, 1940 German invasion, growing in intensity and becoming more and more coordinated with a world that had become united to fight Germany's Nazi brutality. Hitler's attempt to incorporate these countries into the Third Reich was doomed to fail.

As this book is being published, the world is again facing an attempt by a depraved man to force an immoral occupation onto the people of Ukraine. History and the world's demand for morality are certain to be repeated and this attempt will fail. Unfortunately, this time the people of Russia are not likely to benefit from a postwar moral occupation and thus will have to bear their wartime costs alone.

Occupation Stories 2020

Remembering & Honoring The Sacrifices Endured By So Many

FOREWORD

WHEN LIES BECOME TRUTHS

The tragedies of World War II in Europe were the direct result of a ruthless use of power by one man, Adolf Hitler, arguably the most evil human being to ever live on our earth.

Hitler's rise to power and his control over the German people was the result of many factors. At the end of World War I, the Versailles Treaty, written by the winning Allied countries, forced many punitive economic restrictions on Germany and the payment of large amounts of reparations, greatly reducing Germany's global stature throughout the 1920's. In 1930, the Great Depression arrived and the already poor German economy collapsed even further. The 1930's were a period of desperation in Germany.

These conditions were exactly what Adolf Hitler needed; an already anti-Semitic audience desperate for a leader that would promise them a way out of their misery. A gifted speaker, Hitler spoke eloquently and often about Germany's return to global prominence and economic strength, emphasizing his desire for Germany to live in peace with the rest of the world. Unknown at the time, he was indifferent as to whether or not what he was saying was a truth or a lie.

He then added his biggest lie: squarely putting the blame for Germany's miserable conditions on the Jews and justifying the need to rid Germany of all Jews and Jewish influence. The already anti-semitic population allowed the lie to become a truth. Any dissent was treated brutally, mostly at the hands of Hilter's Brown Shirts who were free to beat, imprison or even murder. The Nazis called any dissent expressed by the few German newspapers that were still in existence "Lügenpresse". The literal translation: "Fake News", a phrase intended only to turn their truths into lies.

Hitler and Geobbels

Hitler and his Propaganda Minister, Josef Goebbels, are famous for their belief that "if you repeat a lie frequently enough, people will sooner or later believe it". Hitler and Goebbels used radio speeches and printed propaganda to spread their Nazi lies. Imagine if the internet and social media had been available to them.

Today, social media does exist and because of that, we now live in a world where lies can be easily and quickly spread to literally millions of people. If the lie aligns with someone's own personal bigotries, they want to believe it and it suddenly becomes the truth, justifying their bigotries, empowering and emboldening them to even commit verbal terrorism. An even greater danger, these same communication platforms allow people with similar bigotries to form groups; sometimes dangerous, violent groups.

Social media has enhanced our ability to stay in touch with those close to us, but we must never accept allowing lies on social media to become truths. The stories in this book testify to what can happen when lies are allowed to become truths and each of us must constantly do our part to guard against it.

The memory of this terrible man, his Nazi cult and this horrific war demands just that.

Occupation Stories 2020

Remembering & Honoring The Sacrifices Endured By So Many

PREFACE

THE PEOPLE'S REACTION TO OCCUPATION

In the following pages there are a great many stories about the resistance and local resistance heroes. These stories are important stories to be appreciated, commemorated and they can be a source of pride today. It is a historical necessity however, to point out that there was collaboration in the occupied territories as well.

There was indeed both active and passive resistance but there was also active and passive collaboration. Existing research on the distribution of resistance and collaboration within the populations of the occupied territories is limited, however, based on several examples, one can assume that the number of people active in the resistance throughout the occupied territories was likely relatively equal to the number of people who overtly collaborated with the Occupier. Some estimates suggest that each represented roughly only 5% of the population.

In fact, the overwhelming portion of the civil population in the occupied territories tried, sometimes through courage, or selfishness, often through pain and sorrow, to simply keep themselves and their families intact during the more than four years of Nazi occupation. They merely tried to get through war time by submitting to the new realities of each day, staying free from harm, trying to avoid being identified as a part of either of the two camps and trying to maintain their immediate standing in society. Furthermore, the feelings and actions of people evolved over time, changing as the war and the oppression situations changed or their sense of what the outcome of the war would be.

Since the war, particularly in Europe, there has been a questionable general feeling, sometimes deliberately inflated, that the majority of the French, the Belgians, the Dutch, the Luxembourgers, (and so on) were somehow overtly against the occupier. It is important to understand that the majority of the people simply did what they thought they and their families had to do "to get through it".

This is in no way different from today's war and oppression scenarios.

Over the last 15 to 20 years, many reputable historians, especially the Germans (in search of their "Vergangenheitsbewältigung"[1]), have been earnestly working on this question and many other aspects of World War II, researching material and interviewing both victims and perpetrators to better understand the many aspects of the war including the Holocaust, racial superiority, the postwar Nurnberg trials, the responsible Nazi personnel and importantly, the impact of Nazism on German society. Providing ever better historical insights, these insights help us define the challenges we face today.

We hope these efforts will continue to be encouraged and supported in the coming years.

---

[1] *Working through the past.*   *Contributed by: Albert Dondelinger, Luxembourg*

A DEDICATION TO THOSE WHOSE COURAGE WE OWE

Four long years of terrible violence and fighting were necessary to defeat the Nazis. The liberation of these four countries was only made possible by the actions of the many local resistance fighters and the many millions of individual fighting men and women, from many countries around the globe, who united to achieve a common goal. Each and every one of them has a story, different from all others, but together, those millions of individual stories defeated the Nazis.

Very few of these millions of men and women achieved fame and glory so we especially want to recognize the courage and determination of the local resistance fighters and the millions of men and women who volunteered to serve in the armed forces of the many countries fighting Fascism. Most were merely patriotic individuals who felt a need to serve their country.

A good example is the story of Capt. Lester Aloysius Steinke of the US Army Air Corps, a P-51D Mustang Fighter pilot who flew 58 combat missions over Europe during the last two years of the war. During the Great Depression, "Les" grew up on a self-sufficient small farm in rural northwest Ohio with his widowed mother and 11 brothers and sisters, each with their own set of responsibilities needed by the family to survive their spartan living conditions. After graduating from high school, Les was able to find work at the Cadillac automobile factory in Detroit where his older sister lived.

Les & his mother
Philomena

That changed when the Japanese bombed Pearl Harbor and America entered the war. Les enlisted in the Armed Forces, qualified for pilot training, and because of his high scores in flying school, was trained as a fighter pilot, flying the P-47 Thunderbolt, the standard fighter of the US Army Air Corps at the time. When it was introduced in 1944, Les was trained to fly the new P-51D Mustang, the greatest fighter of World War II. At the age of 22, Les boarded a ship to begin 28 days at sea to arrive at a 15th Air Force Fighter base located in Madna, Italy along the Adriatic coast where he was assigned to serve with the 4th Squadron of the 52nd Fighter Group, the longest serving active Fighter Group in the Mediterranean Theatre.

A new 21-year-old
fighter pilot

The Distinguished Flying Cross Mission. On his 31st mission on 12 October 1944, 1st Lt. Steinke led the 4th Squadron of the 52nd Fighter Group in a strafing mission to attack a vitally important German airdrome at Seragelyes, Hungary. This mission earned him the Distinguished Flying Cross.

The Citation reads: *"Lt. Steinke displayed outstanding courage and skill in making nine (9) separate passes at the enemy airdrome, and in so doing destroyed one (1) Ju88, one (1) JU 87, one (1) DO 217 and one (1) unidentified single engine aircraft on the ground, observed strikes on at least four (4) more and inflicted considerable damage to hangers and other ground installations on the airfield."*

Lt. Steinke's P-51 Mustang "*Vicious Aloysius*"
15th Air Force, 52nd Fighter Group - Madna, Italy

"Lt. Steinke has displayed a high order of courage, leadership and professional skill throughout nine (9) months of hazardous missions against the enemy, and in leading the squadron he has been particularly successful at the times when, because of extremely bad weather, navigation was most difficult. Lt. Steinke has participated in more than fifty-five (55) successful missions and has unfalteringly showed great combat spirit and aggressiveness."

"The Yellow Tails"

THE REST OF THE STORY - By Capt. Les Steinke, US Army Air Corps. Paul Harvey, a radio commentator, had a segment called "The Rest of the Story". The Distinguished Flying Cross Citation cites the damage inflicted on the enemy but fails to tell the whole story.

On the first strafing pass, which is just above the tree-top level and at about noon time, you see personnel lined up outside what must be a mess-hall and you have just about two seconds to decide what to do. Right after that you see a square building on the right so you pull up a little then back down to give it a short burst to see it there is anything flammable inside. Then up ahead you see the silhouette of a Stuka dive-bomber parked under some trees so you have to sieve-icate it. But as you pass over it you get a glimpse of a line of airplanes hidden under the trees. So you think "good grief we have to check that out".

The Rest of the Story--continued

Well, we did check it out by making nine strafing passes over that airdrome. On the third or fourth pass my wingman was probably thinking "Come on Aloysius, let's go home." That sounds like it would have been a good idea but we had found some great targets and that was the purpose of the mission. After each pass you stay low until about a mile away then loop around low for another pass. As you approach the target area again you pull up to 300 to 400 feet, find the target, then you dive down again as you fire on the target.

As we started to loop around after the eighth pass, my wingman calls and says that "Aloysius" is streaming glycol coolant from the tail section. We made some shallow turns to check out the leak. It did not seem to be too bad. We were headed east and had to turn west anyway to go home, and there was a Donier bomber target still there, so why not. We made the ninth pass and did another "sieve-ication."

Group Leader, leading three squadrons (48 planes) on a B-17 bomber escort mission over Europe - at age 22.

"Vicious Aloysius" taxiing and ready for the take-off signal.

Ollie's (my sister Berniece's nickname for Aloysius) coolant temperature was going up as we finished the ninth pass. My wingman flew in close on both sides to look for damage but could see none. We reached the base and more or less glided down to a landing. We taxied about half way to the parking area when the engine temperature gauge said "Shut me down!" Michael, my crew-chief, came out to pick me up and we gave good ol' Ollie the once-over.

We found a large two-inch hole, slightly elongated, on the left side ten to twelve inches behind and below the wing. On the right side we found a similar hole except that it was elongated to three or four inches, about a foot higher on the fuselage, and about two feet behind the other hole. Apparently a shell had passed through the plane hitting the corner of the radiator but thankfully it did not explode. We saw that the shell had passed only about two feet from the 75-gallon gas tank just behind the pilot's seat. Ollie is towed to the repair area and you go to the debriefing area.

THE GRAYEST OF DAYS. The grayest of days was when my tent-mate and his entire flight of four planes failed to return to base. His operational status was the same as mine – Flight Commander. He led "B" Flight and I led "A" Flight. The weather was socked in. We hit the clouds at about 3,000 feet and did not break out on top until about 18,000 feet but when we did break through the clouds, we could see no other planes. We climbed about 5,000 feet more but saw no one. Cumulus type clouds were billowing up all around. No radio contact was tried because the anti-aircraft could home in on you. We circled maybe another five minutes then headed home back through the clouds.

When we thought we were back over the Adriatic Sea we started down until we saw water or a shoreline. We followed the shoreline to near our base then circled to spread out and land. The overcast was still at about 2,000 feet. My tent-mate and his Flight did not show up. While flying on instruments the flight leader does the instrument flying and the three wing-men fly on him.

Lt. Steinke interrogated by the 4th Squadron Intelligence Officer after a mission to Klagenfort, Austria

While flying on instruments, many times you feel as though you are in a turn or bank so you want to make a small correction to get rid of the feeling. However, if you let your feelings take over, the airplane stays in a slight turn, loses altitude, picks up speed and goes into a downward high speed spiral that gets tighter and tighter and there is no way you are going to recover. We could only assume that he failed to believe his instruments. That is what happened to John F. Kennedy, Jr.

We lived three men to a tent. The loss of that Flight Commander reduced the occupants in my tent to one, me, since we had already lost one tent mate three months earlier and it remained that way until this pilot went back to the USA. I guess I ended up the sole owner of that tent.

AFTER THE WAR. Like so many others around the world, Les returned to civilian life and, with the help of the GI Bill, obtained a degree in Electrical Engineering from Purdue University in Indiana. He then joined the NASA Lewis Research Center in northeastern Ohio for both the initial construction and then the operation of the Plumbrook Nuclear Reactor Facility. As the Head Electrical Engineer for the facility, Les conducted the radiation resistance testing of all spacecraft components that would have to travel through the earth's Van Allen Radiation Belt during space flights. When the reactor was shut down in 1973, Les moved to Phoenix, Arizona to become the Chief Facility Electrical Engineer at the Honeywell Large Computer Division facility.

Today, recently celebrating his 100th birthday, Les happily lives the good life on a golf course in Scottsdale, Arizona, though he is still sadly haunted by his wartime experiences. The world and I

Thank You, Uncle Les. Steve Carter, Author, Nephew & Godson, Friend

Lester Steinke, 2020

TABLE OF CONTENTS

Occupation Stories From Belgium

Page	Town	Province
12	Antoing	Hainaut
14	Arendonk	Antwerp
16	Bastogne	Liuxembourg
18	Beaumont	Hainaut
20	Beauvechain	Wallon Brabant
22	Bullingen	Liège
24	Chaudfontaine	Liège
26	Dalhem	Liège
28	Diest	Liège
30	Lichtervelde	West-Vlaanderen
32	Limbourg	Liège
34	Nandrin	Liège
36	Opwijk	Vlaams-Brabant
38	Peer	Limburg
40	Peruwelz	Hainaut
42	Putte	Antwerpen
44	Ravels	Antwerpen
46	Soignies	Hainaut
48	Thuin	Hainaut
50	Trois-Ponts	Liège
52	Trooz	Liège
54	Wielsbeke	West-Vlaanderen

Occupation Stories From France

Page	Town	Department
82	Albert	Somme
84	Brebières	Pas-de-Calais
88	Corbie	Somme
90	Dives Sur Mer	Calvados
92	Hazebrouck	Nord
94	Laon	Aisne
96	Oye-Plage	Pas-de-Calais
98	Ribeauville	Haut-Rhin
100	Villers Bretonneux	Somme

Germany invaded all four countries on May 10, 1940. Belgium, Luxembourg and northern France were overrun by greatly superior, fast-moving mechanized forces (the 'Blitzkrieg') whereas airborne landings and severe bombing characterized the invasion of the Netherlands.

World War II Museums In Belgium

Page	Museum	Municipality
58	101st Airborne Museum	Bastogne
59	Ardennes American Cemetery	Neupré
60	Atlantic Wall Museum	Oostende
61	Bastogne War Museum	Bastogne
62	Baugnez 44 Museum	Malmedy
63	Canada Poland Museum	Maldegem
64	December 1944 Museum	La Gleize
65	For Freedom Museum	Knokke-Heist
66	Fort Aubin Neufchâteau	Dalhem
67	Fort Breendonk Nat'l Memorial	Willebroek
68	Fort Eben-Emael	Bassenge
69	Fort Embourg	Chaudfontaine
70	Fort Huy Museum	Huy
71	Henri-Chapelle American Cemetery	Welkenraedt
72	Kazerne Dossin Memorial	Mechelen
73	La Roche En Ardenne Museum	La-Roche-en-Ardenne
74	Lommel German Military Cemetery	Lommel
75	Manhay History 44 Museum	Manhay
76	Mons Memorial Museum	Mons
77	National Resistance Museum	Brussels
78	Remember Museum	Thiminster-Clermont
79	Wolfsschlucht (Wolf's Ravine)	Couvin

World War II Museums In France

Page	Museum	Municipality
104	Airborne Museum	Sainte-Mère-Église
105	Atlantic Wall Battery Tody	Audinghen
106	Battle of Normandy Museum	Bayeux
107	Blockhaus D'Éperlecques	Éperlecques
108	Bunker of Hatten Museum	Hatten
109	Caen Memorial & Museum	Caen
110	Crisbecq Battery Museum	Saint Marcouf
111	D-Day Experience	Canentan les Marias
112	Falaise Memorial	Falaise
113	Fort Hackenberg Museum	Veckring
114	Fort Schoenenbourg	Hunspach
115	Fort Simserhof	Siersthal
116	Grand Bunker Museum	Ouistreham
117	Juno Beach Center	Courseulles-sur-Mer
118	Merville Battery	Merville-Franceville-Plage
119	MM Park France	La Wantzenau
120	Museum Dunkirk 1940 `	Dunkirk
121	Normandy American Cemetery	Colleville-sur-Mer

World War II Museums In France (Continued)

Page	Museum	Municipality
122	Normandy Resistance Museum	Forges-les-Eaux
123	Normandy Victory Museum	Forges-les-Faux
124	Omaha Beach Museum	Sainte-Laurent-sur-Mer
125	Overlord Museum	Colleville-sur-Mer

Page	Museum	Municipality
126	Pegasus Memorial Museum	Ranville
127	Picardy Resistance Museum	Tergnier
128	Somme Trench Museum 1916	Albert
129	Utah Beach Landing Museum	Sainte-Marie-du-Mont

Occupation Stories From Luxembourg

Page	Town	Canton
132	Bertrange	Luxembourg
134	Bettembourg	Esch-sur-Alzette
136	Diekirch	Diekirch
138	Esch-sur-Alzette	Esch-sur-Alzette
140	Ettelbruck	Diekirch
142	Niederaven	Luxembourg
144	Petange	Esch-sur-Alzette

World War II Museums In Luxembourg

Page	Museum	Commune
148	9-44 WAX Museum	Pétange
149	Deportation Memorial & Museum	Hollerich
150	General Patton Museum	Ettelbruck
151	Luxembourg American Cemetery	Luxembourg
152	Museum of the Battle of the Bulge	Clervaux
153	National Museum of Military History	Diekirch
154	National Resistance Museum	Esch-sur-Alzette

Occupation Stories From The Netherlands

Page	Town	Province
158	Baarlo	Limburg
160	Beesel	Limburg
162	Midden-Delfland	Zuid-Holland
164	Nieuwkoop	Zuid-Holland
166	Noord-Beveland	Zeeland
168	Oostburg	Zeeland
170	Reusel-De-Mierden	Noord Brabant
172	Strijen	Zuid-Holland
174	Woendrecht	Noord Brabant
176	Zuidplas	Zuid-Holland

World War II Museums In The Netherlands

Page	Museum	Municipality
180	Airborne Museum Hartenstein	Oosterbeek
181	Anne Frank Museum	Amsterdam
182	Arnhem War Museum	Arnhem
183	Betuws War Museum "The Island"	Heteren
184	Eyewitness Museum	Beek
185	Frisian Resistance Museum	Leeuwarden
186	Kamp Westerbork	Midden-Drenthe
187	Liberation Museum Zeeland	Borsele
188	Museum 1940-1945	Dordrecht
189	Museum De Bewogen Jaren 39-50	Reusel-De Mierden
190	Overloon War Museum	Overloon
191	Vrijheidsmuseum(Freedom Museum)	Berg en Dal
192	Wings of Liberation Museum	Best
193	Wolfheze Glider Museum	Wolfheze

Page 194   **Germany During The War. Voltlage, Germany**   The Common Thread Between Two Courageous Men
Page 196   **The United States During the War. Sidney, Ohio, USA**   The Impact of the War On An American Town
Page 198   **Despicable Nazi Actions To Remember**   Page 201   **Epilogue**

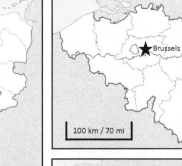

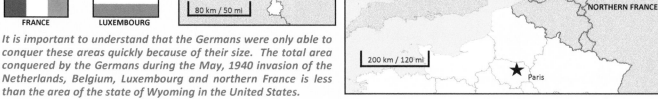

It is important to understand that the Germans were only able to conquer these areas quickly because of their size. The total area conquered by the Germans during the May, 1940 invasion of the Netherlands, Belgium, Luxembourg and northern France is less than the area of the state of Wyoming in the United States.

WORLD WAR II IN BELGIUM

No match for the German Panzer tanks, two French "Meuse" tanks lie in ruins in the small town of Beaumont along the border with France, a common scene repeated throughout Belgium.

Across the entire country, Belgian civilians were forced to flee the invading German army, each family having to determine their own safest destination.

German soldiers being welcomed in Eupen-Malmedy, an area of Belgium that was part of Germany before the World War I Treaty of Versailles of 1919 was signed.

A Belgian forced to work in the Siemens Factory in Berlin. 145,000 Belgians were deported to work in Germany. 200,000 went into hiding.

Shortly after the invasion, marching German soldiers and members of the calvary parade in front of the Royal Palace in Brussels. May, 1940.

After entering Belgium on September 2, British tanks arrived to liberate Brussels on September 4, 1944. The Belgium government returned to power 4 days later.

THE SMALL TOWN OCCUPATION STORIES OF BELGIUM

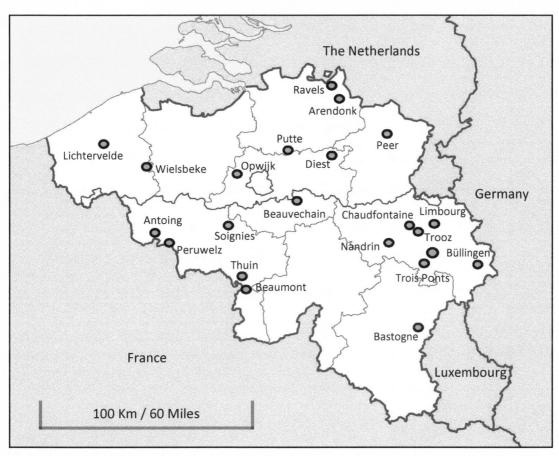

Belgium and World War II.

Prior to the start of World War II, Belgium and its colonies and possessions in Africa were neutral states, wanting to avoid a repeat of World War I. In spite of this, on May 10, 1940, Belgium's entire eastern border with Germany was viciously and voraciously attacked, catching most citizens by surprise, causing much fear and causing the residents of the majority of small towns to evacuate to wherever each family thought best. The Belgian forces were soon driven into a small pocket in the northeast part of the country, surrendering to the Germans after only 18 days of fighting on May 28th.

The unilateral surrender by King Leopold III was a political controversy after the war but fortunately, a great many Belgians were able to escape to the United Kingdom where an army-in-exile was being formed on the side of the Allies. Notably. during the entire war, the people of the Belgian Congo remained loyal to the Belgian government, contributing greatly in terms of providing both material and human resources.

Many Belgians became actively or passively involved with the work of many notable resistance organizations throughout the country but there were also some who chose to collaborate with the Germans, especially members of the right-wing VDB political party. Those collaborating political factions allowed the Germans to deport citizens to work in Germany, allowed the German army to recruit two divisions of the Waffen-SS from Belgium and allowed the Nazis to persecute Belgian Jews. Ultimately, 25,000 Belgian Jews were killed by the Nazis.

Following D-Day, most of Belgium was liberated by the Allies between September and October 1944, although areas in the far eastern part of the country remained occupied until early 1945, primarily because of the Battle of the Bulge. All told, nearly 90,000 Belgians died during World War II, equivalent to 4 million people dying today in the United States.

ANTOING BELGIUM

Province: Hainaut   Pop. 1940: 9,000   Pop. 2019: 7,760

SITING & HERITAGE

Mentioned as early as 868 as Antonium (Antonius' estate), Antoing is located on the river Scheldt near the French border. Known as the capital of the *pays blanc* (White Country), an area where limestone has been quarried since the Roman times, Antoing is surrounded by rich agricultural areas.

During the Middle Ages, the town had strategic value because of its location along the Scheldt River near what was known as the Antoing hole where the river suddenly drops more than one meter. This required all boats to be unloaded and reloaded, for which the local lords levied tolls in money or goods. First mentioned in the 12th century, the town's Neo-Gothic castle is one of Belgium's best known castles to visit.

GPS Coordinates: N50.5676 E.4513

War damage on the Place du Préau, Antoing

Damage on the Grand Rue, Antoing

The Liberation of Antoing, 2 September, 1944

OUR TOWN'S OCCUPATION STORY

When Nazi Germany entered Antoing in May 1940, the German Army immediately occupied Antoing Castle, turning the castle into a hospital to treat their wounded.

From then on, the Nazis imposed a very restrictive way of life onto the residents including a curfew in the evening which had to be strictly observed. No resident was allowed to disregard the curfew unless they possessed a signed work certificate giving them permission to be outside their homes during the curfew. This was the case with Louis Dujardin and Sylvain Noisiez who were employed at the Société Nationale des Chemins de Fer Belges (National Belgium Railways Company who were authorized to return home on foot or by bicycle during the curfew; however they were required to take a specific (the shortest) route.

The Nazi occupying authority also banned church bells from ringing. To make sure they were silent, the Germans either removed or destroyed them. The bell was removed from the village church in Maubray and the bell tower was destroyed on the village church in Bruyelle. These actions greatly angered the local residents.

The Nazis were also careful not to be visible to Allied planes, hoping not to be overflown and observed by the Allies. If there was a plane sighted they did not know, the Germans fired upon the plane to destroy it as quickly as possible. This happened several times in the skies over Antoing. First, on May 18, 1940, three Allied planes were flying over the area when the aircrews saw tanks in the Antoing area. As they approached to get a better view, the Germans began shooting at them with machine guns. One plane crashed 20 minutes later in a field but one aircrew member was able to survive by managing to get off the plane and find help from local resistance fighters.

The second crash took place four years later. When the landing of the Allied forces began on June 6, 1944 in Normandy, one of the primary missions of the Allies was to destroy the main land transportation modes in order to delay the movement of German reinforcements to the front, especially targeting bridges and stations. On July 18, 1944, a British bomber was assigned to bomb the Aulnoy railway junction. The crew, from a Royal Air Force base, consisted of 7 airmen including 2 Australian officers, one Canadian officer and four British sergeants. Once the mission was completed and their plane was over Valenciennes, it was intercepted and strafed by a Luftwaffe night fighter, diverting it from its route. At 1:15 a.m. the plane crashed in flames into the Forêt Domaniale in the territory of Maubray, on the border between Laplaigne and Flines. Today, a monument at that location pays homage to those aviators.

The limestone quarries in the area were very important, allowing residents to have a job and not be subject to being deported to a concentration camp.

During the war, the town of Antoing was able to count on both its resistance fighters and the Allies to survive. Léonard Faisdherbes was one of those local resistance fighters. In May 1940, he blew up the Kain Lock, slowing the German advance.

TWO LOCAL STORIES OF HEROISM

Marie-Louise Bonnet Memorial
Photo: Luc Van Waeyenberge

Marie-Louise Bonnet, A Courageous Nurse. Marie-Louise Bonnet was born in Antoing and was passionate about her nursing profession. Living in Brussels, she accepted numerous Jews and Communists into her home who were being hunted by the Gestapo, and she did not hesitate to take on assignments that a resistance intelligence group offered her.

While she was unaware that she was being watched by the Germans, the Germans decided to go to the home of her parents, to whom they introduced themselves as friends of Marie-Louise, to obtain information. On September 16, 1942 she left Brussels to visit her parents in Antoing. When Marie-Louise arrived at the Antoing railway station, she was arrested by the two Germans.

She was beaten by the Nazis, but she said nothing. She was tried on June 23, 1943 and given a death sentence which was commuted to forced labor in a concentration camp. Throughout her detention, although physically weakened and ill, she became known for encouraging others with her smile, her words and for treating the wounds of other prisoners. Marie-Louise died on January 27, 1945, on the eve of the arrival of the Russians and at the dawn of liberation.

Lucien Delrue. On September 2, 1944, the town of Antoing was liberated. That day, at the stroke of 9:00 p.m., Lucien Delrue and Edouard Marlière, two local resistance fighters, entered the city with a German prisoner. As they pass through the town near the bridge over the Scheldt, they run into a man dressed like an American soldier.

As they walk past him without saying a word to him, they tell each other that after all the Allies have done to liberate the territory, this man deserves to be saluted so they decide to go back to see him. The man then shouts in German and immediately two other soldiers come from the bridge they were about to blow up to shoot at the two resistance fighters. Edouard Marlière is killed instantly while Lucien runs to reach the house of his fiancée, located about a hundred meters away.

When he arrives at her house he realizes that he is bleeding from his stomach. Fortunately, Lucien was able to be treated by the Americans and then able to convalesce in a hospital. He is considered to be the miracle of the Antoing Bridge.

RETRIBUTION & LIBERATION

On August 19, 1944, at around 10 a.m., the Mayor of Maubray, Gaston Fontaine, was killed by two hooded men as he was walking on his way home from work. The killers knew the habits of their target because they had been waiting and keeping watch nearby. After firing at and wounding the Mayor, they went to finish him off with two bursts of machine gun fire. Gaston Fontaine, known to be a far-right, anti-communist Rexist, had been chosen by the occupier to replace the former Mayor, which was the method used by the Nazis. During that time, violence against Rexist mayors increased dramatically and they were often the target of the resistance.

The Liberation. When the city of Antoing was liberated, it did not happen without material and human loss. Several women, accused of having seduced the enemy, were shaved on the Place Bara. Other people accused of complicity with the Nazis were shot dead in the Lime Kilns at Crèvecoeur.

Photos courtesy of the municipality of Antoing.

The town of Antoing, seen from the banks of the Scheldt

ANTOING TODAY

Today, the town of Antoing has rebuilt from the damage caused by the 1940-1945 war, and it has never stopped developing since then. Whether you are athletic, whether you come to love nature or the beauty of the town, Antoing is made for you.

Come and sail by boat on the Scheldt, and moor at the Grand Large Marina in Péronnes, which will soon be redeveloped and enlarged to allow more ships to come and enjoy the city. Also discover the many sports activities and the 100% sustainable Your Nature accommodation, located in the Péronnes woods next to the Grand Large. You can also follow the city's many routes to discover, on foot or by bike, Antoing and its surrounding serenity.

Thanks to the permanent exhibition "The White Triangle, Stone and Men", you can learn more about the interesting history of extracting limestone in the Tournaisis area, and you must not miss visiting Antoing's impressive 12th century Château des Princes de Ligne to see and hear the history of the city and the de Ligne family since Medieval times.

The Neo-Gothic Castle of the Princes de Ligne in Antoing

The Grand Large in Péronnes

*To learn more about Antoing, please visit the town's official website: **www.antoing.net** and to find out more about the tourism of the area please visit: **www.antoing.net/loisirs/tourisme/office-du-tourisme.***

The city of Antoing would like to thank Mr. Nicolas and Mr. Claude Cordier who lent documents, old press articles or period photos; Miss Mélanie Kerskens, student, who gave her time to do the research; Mrs. Colette Bocage, Alderman; and Mrs. Marie-Line Masquelier, Guide who has contributed to the city's participation in this project by sharing her knowledge of the city during the 1940-1945 war.

ARENDONK BELGIUM

Province: Antwerp   Pop. 1940: 7.000   Pop. 2020: 13,300

SITING & HERITAGE

A rural village, in 1212 Arendonk was proclaimed 'Stad en Vrijheid' (Free City), and as such it was among the main municipalities of the region for many years. The falconers of Arendonk were renowned in several European royal houses.

Always an agricultural village, in later years the manufacture and trade of stockings brought reasonable prosperity. By 1900 many men and women were employed in cigar factories, locally as well as across the border. Several beautiful municipal houses still testify to the village's former cigar factory prosperity as do the imposing Church of Our Lady and the Town Hall.

GPS Coordinates: N51.3222 E5.0864

English soldiers in Arendonk
(From the 'Doei en despotie' Hendrik Van Gorp)

The Hotel De Kempen damaged by the Germans

Destroyed Arendonk houses on the Dutch border

The Hooper and Williams soldiers burial site

OUR TOWN'S OCCUPATION STORY

The Invasion. May 1940. On May 13 1940 the Belgian 3rd Carabiniers, the 3rd Grenadiers, the 39th Regiment de Ligne and the French 4e Régiment de Dragons Portés fought the Germans at the Dutch-Belgian border. 14 Belgian casualties and 5 French casualties were buried in Arendonk at Voorheide, before their exhumation and reburial in several military cemeteries in Belgium later on. During World War II seven military men from Arendonk were killed in battle.

Oppression. During the period of occupation food was restricted. Since Arendonk was a rural community, people tried to grow their own crops - at least the part that was not confiscated by the Germans. Inspection of identification papers occurred frequently and any infractions were severely punished. After some time, prisoners of war were allowed to return home from the camps.

On the other hand, young men were ordered to go to work in Germany. Some refused and submerged into the woods, stables and hay lofts. Frequent surprise raids took young men out of their homes or work places. Using whistle sounds, a villager in a wheelchair tried to warn the boys when the Feldgendarmerie or Gestapo was in the neighborhood. The hidden men did not receive food coupons, which complicated their ability to obtain sufficient food supplies.

Smuggling. Situated at the Dutch-Belgian border, Arendonk has always been seduced to smuggle. In the dark, across little paths along the border, wheat and soap were brought home and sold on the black market.

Recreation. Villager Rik Van Steenbergen brought some distraction during the years of occupation by winning several cycling competitions, becoming the Belgian cycling champion in 1943. Festivities were organized to celebrate his victory, despite the prohibition of gathering imposed by the Germans. Flowers were laid down at the WWI remembrance monument at the market place and a ball was organized in the pub near the Van Steenbergens house, a pub that later on was burned by the Gestapo in September 1944. This brave act brought some distraction to the suppressed town.

Deported villagers. In the night of July 21st 1944, the SS arrested 27 people as political prisoners, who were deported to concentration camps in Germany. Amongst them were veterans of the First World War, being accused of resistance activity. Mr. Dincq, the director of the dynamite factory who hid a Jewish girl, died in Dachau. Marguerite Walravens was a condemned WWI British spy who had obtained the medal of Officer of the British Empire. She was executed together with her daughter, in Ravensbrück. Only 10 deported persons returned to Arendonk after the war, after having witnessed cruel atrocities.

September 3, 1944. During the retreat of the Germans, a column of German soldiers and civilians stopped at the Belgian-Dutch border in Arendonk. They asked for some milk to drink. What followed was a shooting of eight civilian men near the border (Grens) and houses were burned down.

There were various airplane crashes here (11 are known); German as well as British and American planes came down. During the Operation Market Garden (Battle for Arnhem), the villagers hid some pilots and airmen from September 17th 1944 until the liberation was completed.

Laat de kleinen tot Mij komen, want
hunner is het rijk der hemelen.

TOT ZALIG AANDENKEN AAN

**GERARDUS JOANNES MARIA
KONINCKX**

Lid der H. Kindsheid en der Broederschap van den
H. Cornelius, geboren te Arendonk den 13 Mei 1944
en aan de liefde zijner familieleden ontnomen den
29n September 1944.

zoontje van

HENDRIK en OCTAVIE KONINCKX-VAN REUSEL.

Onschuldig Gerarke, toen een oorlogsstorm vijf da-
gen lang rondom uw vredig wiegsken dood en ver-
nieling met daverend geweld had uitgespat en hij
uwe beangstigde huisgenooten voortdurend hulpe-
loos met U hield samengedrongen in eenen kleinen
killen kelder, toen heeft het O. L. Heer behaagd U,
als een onschuldig oorlogsslachtoffer op te nemen
in Zijnen schoot van eeuwige vrede en liefde.
Heer aanvaard uit de handen van Uwe Goddelijke
Moeder ons lief Gerarke als een vlekkeloos offerlam-
meke tot verzoening met het zondig menschdom.
Lief Gerarke, blijf nu als eene ster die vooral de
familieleden leidt, zoodanig dat geen enkel hunner
zijne eindbestemming misse eenmaal bij U in de eeuwige glorie.
Heer niet onze wil, maar uw wil geschiede.
Mijn Jezus barmhartigheid.
H. Maria, Koningin van Vrede, bid voor ons.

Arendonk, drukk. J. Alf. en Alb. Lavrijsen

Funeral card for little Gerard Koninckx
Family archive Louis Koninckx

AN INNOCENT VICTIM

During mid-September 1944, Arendonk was in the middle of the front line. The town centre on the southern bank of the canal was almost free of Germans. Armed resistance fighters marched in the streets.

On the other side of town, the German occupier was still present and his artillery frequently attacked the town. On September 24th, British troops of the 53th Welsh infantry division mounted an attack on the German forces on the northern canal bank, arriving from the town of Postel, located 2 km southeast of Arendonk on the northern canal bank.

When they arrived at Voorheide on the north side of Arendonk, they were attacked by the Germans and the battle was difficult since the towpath was filled with land mines.

Even though the battle was difficult and a number of British soldiers died, the division was able to enter the town. At night, the Germans would counterattack, forcing the residents into their basements and cellars.

The beautiful Church of Our Lady

These attacks lasted for days and residents were amongst the lethal victims. One family was Hendrik and Octavie Koninckx and their nine children. During the fights, they hid in the basement of their home. For days they stayed in the dark without food.

The situation became fatal for their youngest son, Gerard. On the 29th of September, the fifth day of the battles, the four-month old child died because of the hardship. A pillow case serving as a white flag, the family ran, carrying the dead child with them through the battle area. Impressed by this deeply sad vision, the Germans allowed them to pass, allowing the family to bury little Gerard in an improvised soldiers cemetery near the canal. Only a few days later, Arendonk was liberated. In remembrance of the war, the liberation, and little Gerard, a memorial sign is now planted on the site.

Windmill with 'Teljoorlekker'
Photo Peter Stusz

LIBERATION & RECOVERY

During the period of Market Garden, on September 21, 1944 a plane crashed on the site of the dynamite factory, an important factory at the time in the region. The two pilots, Dorville and Ades, died on the crash scene. The other members of the crew were able to escape and were hidden in a barn across the border in Holland.

A few days later, the British 2nd BN, the Monmouthshire Regiment, arrived in Arendonk. At Voorheide, near the crash scene of the plane mentioned above, they buried 18 British soldiers who had been killed, and the two pilots, together with little Gerard Koninckx, in an improvised cemetery at Voorheide. The final resting place of these military men lies in Valkenswaard, approximately 5 km south of Eindhoven.

These days, peace & serenity   Photo Peter Stusz

OUR TOWN TODAY

Today Arendonk is a modern community. The inhabitants are known for their somewhat peculiar, self-willed character and open minds towards the future.

Arendonk provides its residents with extensive social services, several primary schools and a secondary college. Our Academy of Arts attracts not only local pupils but also many from the Netherlands.

Arendonk provides lots of opportunities for business and recreation. Many youth, sports and cultural clubs form a lively community able to fulfill anyone's desires.

Situated near the old 'Toremansmolen' (windmill from 1809) is the Museum of Local History, recently modernized. Arendonk is proud of the town's enjoyable atmosphere in the market square, with people shopping and others tasting the local beers and food.

Arendonk's most attractive feature is its rural character and natural scenery just a few steps from the town centre. Let yourself be submerged in an invigorating bath of peace and silence and admire the fauna and flora of the area's wonderful nature reserves. Both walkers and bikers will be pleasantly charmed by a visit to Arendonk, a simply surprising village.

*For more information about Arendonk, visit: **www.arendonk.be**. For more information about Arendonk's very interesting historical heritage visit **www.heemkringarendonk.be**.*

This information was prepared by the volunteers of our institution for local history "Als Ince Can" and the Arendonk tourism association. Photos courtesy of the Arendonk municipality.

BASTOGNE BELGIUM

Province: Luxembourg   Pop. 1940: 4,500   Pop. 2020: 16,500

SITING & HERITAGE

Because of the important role Bastogne played during the Battle of the Bulge, Bastogne is now the best known small town of World War II. The basis of untold numbers of historical films including *The Band of Brothers,* life in Bastogne was considerably different prior to World War II.

Bastogne is a semi-rural town with an economy historically oriented towards trade and agriculture. Situated on the heights of the Ardennes plateau a few kilometers from the Grand Duchy of Luxembourg, and at an important crossroads since Roman times, Bastogne has flourished for centuries as a center of attraction for local villagers and merchants who came here to sell their livestock and produce or, on the contrary, to buy products on the markets or in the stores in the town center. The events of World War II radically changed Bastogne forever.

GPS Coordinates: N50.0007 E5.7153

Hitler parades past his troops in Bastogne, 17 May, 1940 Photo Jean-Marie Doucet

BASTOGNE UNDER THE OCCUPATION

The history of the German offensive in Bastogne begins when the words "General alert" sounded on the morning of May 10, 1940 in the Heintz barracks. The troops of the Belgian army were gradually mobilized at their posts. The men of the 2nd Regiment of Ardennes Chasseurs, posted near Bastogne, were the first to see the advance of German infantrymen in Belgium.

While the squadrons of German planes were flying over Belgian soil, the first skirmishes took place on the ground, near the entrance of the town on the road to Clervaux. Corporal Emile Cady (5th Company of the 2nd Regiment of Ardennes Chasseurs) lost his life at the small fort at the entrance of the town under the bullets of the Germans and under the eyes of his comrades.

Panic quickly set in among the population following the noise of the fire and explosions approaching. The first refugees from the Grand Duchy of Luxembourg and the Belgian border villages further reinforced this feeling of fear and proved that a massive invasion was indeed taking place from the east. Part of the inhabitants of Bastogne fled the city, while people learned with dismay that the Belgian army was also on the run towards the west.

Postcard of the monument to the war veterans and resistance fighters after the war. Photo: Bastogne War Museum

On May 17, Hitler disembarked in person in Bastogne and crossed the main street, triumphing and reviewing his troops in order to reach the HQ of General Von Rundstedt, located at the Avenue de la Gare. A little later in May, English planes flying over the city dropped bombs that destroyed many buildings and killed German soldiers.

This renewed tension in the city once again pushed the "Bastognards" to flee, on foot, by bicycle or by wagon, to cities in the west of the country or, on the contrary, to the south to reach France. Some will stay there for the duration of the war but others will return, once the fighting is over in Belgium at the end of May. In the city of Bastogne the population decreases drastically, it goes from 4500 inhabitants to only a few hundred.

Those who remain or return to the city must resign and submit to the new precepts in force. While captured soldiers were gradually transported to labor camps or farms in Germany, the civilians of Bastogne had to comply with the instructions the new administration put in place by the Germans. Bastogne, like the rest of the country, passed on German time. Life was punctuated by requisitions, supplies and the fight against the looting by soldiers and destitute civilians.

Liberation of Bastogne by the U.S. Army and the Secret Army, September 10, 1944 Photo Jean-Marie Doucet

Public and private life was also controlled by Reich militias through their intelligence networks. As early as 1942, some of the men had to leave to contribute to the Compulsory Labor Service. Civilians who were resistant to order were sometimes also deported, like the Mayor himself, Pierre Renquin, who in 1944 was deported to Germany for refusing to set up a civil guard on the Route de Marche.

While the large Belgian cities suffered the full brunt of supply problems, Bastogne did not fare too badly, thanks in particular to the products directly from nearby local agriculture, which supplied the citizens with fruit and vegetables, meat and dairy products. But some goods are in short supply, such as coffee, leather and coal traditionally used as fuel. The population of Bastogne and the surrounding area rapidly became poorer and some can no longer meet their basic needs.

SPECIAL BASTOGNE STORIES WE REMEMBER

The Organization of Aid to Refugees, the Wounded and Prisoners of War. In the city, the care and assistance services for the most precarious are gradually being organized. Yvonne Olivier set up a reception center for refugees. Under the supervision of Renée Gerardy, meals are served there every day and care is provided. In addition, the center is in charge of finding housing for the newly homeless or foreigners passing through.

The beautiful and vibrant Bastogne Town Center– Photo by Author

The Red Cross is also mobilizing even more to take care of sending parcels to extradited soldiers and political prisoners held in Germany. Mrs. Olivier, supported by Henriette Mortehan, receives parcels for prisoners in Bastogne and the surrounding regions. During the years of occupation, the Winter Relief Organization even organized the transfer to Bastogne of hundreds of children who had come from Liège to temporarily lodge them with host families. A forward post of the Passive Air Defense Medical Service will also be created at the Institute of the Sisters of Notre Dame to provide immediate help and relief in case of an air attack.

Our Resistance Fighters. At the same time, some citizens of Bastogne do not hesitate to secretly enlist in resistance networks at their own risk and peril. People suspected of resistance and arrested in the streets by German intelligence services are often brought to pass through the Kommandantur to undergo intense interrogation. In 1942, the lawyer Joseph Renquin joined an organization under the aegis of the British, the stationmaster Pierre Thomas enlisted as an intelligence agent, while the carrier Gustave Delperdange supplied the resistance with explosives stolen from the Germans. All three were arrested and shot by the Germans during this period of the occupation. Their names will remain famous in Bastogne, memorialized by the renaming of streets in the city, forever embodying the cause of all the men and women in the shadows, martyrs of the war and of the resistance in the face of the invader.

The Mardasson Memorial to the American soldiers involved in the Battle of the Bulge. © Erwan Nicolay

Several inhabitants of the Bastogne region, whose identities were sometimes never known, were also approached and employed by the British Office of Special Services (OSS), particularly for missions related to the security or intelligence of agents working as spies for the Zero Network. There were also the existence of clandestine radio broadcasts, often in Morse code, that came from the resistance campaign.

Setting Up a Clandestine Newspaper: Three inhabitants of Bastogne, the Ardennes hunter Marcel Guiot, Joseph Bossard and Marcelle Koeune founded, at the beginning of 1941, the clandestine newspaper *Bastogne Gazette*, which later became *La Hure*. With the help of small financial funds, these improvised shadow journalists were able to print a bi-monthly newspaper distributed until 1943 at the price of 1 franc.

The incomparable Bastogne War Museum site (see page 61).

In addition to a review of the facts of war on the current fronts, the publication showed a certain optimism and promised the people of the Ardennes a final victory over the enemy. The motto under the title of the newspaper reflected this optimism shared by many patriotic Belgians: "*The struggle will be hard and the hardships will be considerable, but no one can doubt the final success. The cause of Belgium is pure, with God's help it will triumph*". To support his words, the newspaper service also reproduced photographs of parachuted leaflets or scenes from the life of the occupation. The daily newspaper *La Libre Belgique* also included a few pages of *La Hure* in several of its editions. If certain distributors of the newspaper were suspected or questioned by the occupier, the authors were never arrested.

TWO LIBERATIONS ARE NECESSARY

It was first thanks to the radio that a wind of hope was born in Bastogne, as elsewhere, in the summer of 1944, when messages explaining that the Allies had liberated Paris and then Brussels, resounded in clandestine radio station broadcasts.

The city of Bastogne had to wait for its liberation until the afternoon of September 10. That day the inhabitants took to the streets and waved flags and pennants in Belgian and Allied colors as the American liberating troops and the Belgian resistance, represented by a detachment of the Secret Army, passed through.

Once the German troops returned to their borders, several American units settled in the region setting up tent hospitals to care for wounded soldiers and provide care and medical equipment to civilians in the towns and villages of the southeast of the country.

These same Americans, liberators of the occupied territories, had no idea that they would have to face the enemy again in Bastogne and across the Ardennes in a new offensive in the middle of December. The city will be terribly marked by the five years of war and particularly by the Battle of the Bulge which took many human lives, not only American and German soldiers but also civilians, all victims of the harsh fighting in the winter of 1944-1945.

BASTOGNE TODAY

Today, numerous monuments and traces of the Battle for Bastogne are located throughout the commune, telling the story of these difficult times to the general public. The best known of these is the Mardasson Memorial located on a hill northeast of the town which pays tribute to all the American soldiers involved in halting this German offensive during the winter of 1944/1945.

Presented on Pages 58 and 61 of this book, two renown WWII museums exist in Bastogne; the 101st Airborne Museum and the Bastogne War Museum.

In addition to these war-related aspects, Bastogne remains a city focused on leisure, commerce and its beautiful natural heritage visible in its countryside and throughout the many villages of the entity. Bastogne is the perfect place to stay during any visit to our area to experience and enjoy the beauty of the Ardennes.

*For more information about Bastogne, visit: **www.bastogne.be**. For more information about Bastogne war museums, see pages 58 and 61. We appreciate the efforts of Pierre Lhote, historian of the Bastogne Memorial WWII Reference Center asbl.*

BEAUMONT BELGIUM

Province: Hainaut   Pop. 1940: 4,500   Pop. 2020: 8,000

SITING & HERITAGE

Beaumont is located in the south of Belgium in Botte du Hainaut. Located on a rocky outcrop, Beaumont has always held a strategic position. During the 11th century Richilde, the Countess of Hainaut built the Salamandre Tower which her successors would surround with 2,400 meters of ramparts.

The Golden Age of Beaumont occurred during the 16th & 17th centuries with the Lords of Croÿ. Charles de Croÿ, an extensive property owner and a reknown collector of paintings and art pieces, entrusted painter Adrien de Montigny to prepare an inventory of his extensive land holdings that resulted in a very famous and valuable series of landscape paintings.

GPS Coordinates N50.2374 E4.2394

A French "Meuse" tank before the battle

Destroyed French "Meuse" tanks after the battle

Beaumont after its capture by German troops

STORIES ABOUT BEAUMONT RESIDENTS

At The Beginning. Léon Albessart owned a large house adjoining the railway line. Before the invasion, Léon had dug a large pit on his property to shelter his family in the event of bombing. On May 14, 1940, the neighbor, Georges Gillet, insisted that the Albessart family come to spend the night in his cellar on the pretext that the bridge over the railway near the Albessart house was threatened. The Albessart family reluctantly accepted and no doubt rightly so, because, just 2 hours after they entered the Gillet family cellar, a bomb fell on their house and the facade was completely destroyed.

The two Delbèque sisters lived together in their house located on Rue Rouge Croix. They had bought a small goat to maintain their land. When the German planes bombed Beaumont, the sisters got scared and went outside to put their goat under cover. Unfortunately, while they were out, a bomb fell near their house. One sister died there and the other died the day after of her injuries at St. Joseph's Hospital.

Jules Joret, a postman, lived at the Porte de Binche in small house below the pastry shop. Following an explosion by Beaumont resistance fighters at a pile of gravel stored near the Beaumont train station, the Germans required all residents of Beaumont to stay in their homes and to not go out. The postman Jules, who wanted to go and get milk from the Palisarde farm, was turned back into his house by the Germans. His furious wife Emilie sent him back out to get the milk. Braving the German ban, Jules went to the farm to get her milk. No doubt he feared his wife more than the Germans!

At The End. On September 3, 1944, an American infantry patrol arrives in Barbençon, five km southeast of Beaumont. They are in constant contact with a small reconnaissance plane called "Dragonfly" which flies above them continually, observing the ground. The plane pilot warns the American troops that a German car is traveling from Beaumont towards them. The Americans set up an ambush with a machine gun placed on an embankment, covering the entire roadway.

Arthur Derenne, a young resistance fighter, and his young friends surround the place where the soldiers hide. The German car appears. There is one burst, the officer is killed and the car nose-dives into the ditch. The driver is taken prisoner.

Arthur and his comrades take possession of the Volkswagen vehicle, pull the car out of the ditch and decide to go see what is going on in Beaumont. During the whole journey, they are continually flown over by the Dragonfly reconnaissance plane pilot who is wildly waving his wings at them. To the boys, it's the day of glory for Arthur and his friends: a car taken from the "Boches" and being overflown by an American plane!

At the entrance to Beaumont, an American GI stops them and dresses them up and down. "*You are stupid!*" comes up many times. Arthur and his friends do not understand what the American is saying until when, coming up from the embankment of the railway bridge, an American soldier, in impeccable French, shouts at them: "Boys, you have just escaped a beautiful death. Without the Dragonfly flapping its wings, we were going to chop you to pieces ". *In their euphoria, Arthur and his friends had forgotten that the car was still German with its distinct "black crosses"!*

To avoid any misunderstanding in the future, the American soldiers brought out some paint and, in a few minutes, splendid white stars covered the sides, top and rear of the Volkswagen.

A STORY OF LIBERATION

Dominick Gatto. The only American soldier killed during the liberation of Beaumont was Private Dominick Gallo. Dominick was born in Bound Brook, New Jersey into a family of 9 children. He is one of 4 children in his family who signed up to fight during World War II.

Dominick Gatto

Dominick was part of the 47th regiment, an American fighting unit that began its fight against the Germans at Normandy and famously became the first American unit to cross the Remagen bridge over the Rhine.

On September 3 at 10:00 am, arriving by jeep at a place call "Le Pavillon" Dominick was killed by shrapnel from a German cannon fired at the crossroads of the Beaumont-Leugnies-Grandrieu roads.

After the battle had ended, his body was brought back by the population to the town hall of Leugnies. On September 4, 1944 at 3 pm, a funeral mass was celebrated by an American military chaplain, the parish priest Guillaume Meters de Leugnies and the Reverend Father Bonaventure Feuillen.

First buried in the American cemetery of Fosses, his body was repatriated in 1949 to the military cemetery of Bridgewater in New Jersey. Inaugurated on September 4, 1994, a monument was erected by the organization R.S.L. (Recognition, Souvenir, Liberation) at the Pavillon in Leugnies to honor the fiftieth anniversary of the death of Dominick Gatto.

BEAUMONT ON FIRE

On May 16, 1940, around 1 p.m., chased by the German army, six French tanks surviving from the 125 RI unit entered Beaumont, which was almost deserted. The few civilians remaining were hiding in the cellars.

Pressed by the Germans of the 5th Panzer Division, the tankers were forced towards rue Madame. Running out of fuel and trapped in the narrow streets where they can't maneuver or hide, the French decide to scuttle their tanks. The tanks explode and set fire to rue Madame and rue Félix Dutry.

Due to the lack of firefighting resources, and especially the lack of firefighting personnel because most of the population had fled, the fire spreads throughout the neighborhoods surrounding these two streets. The huge blaze will not burn out the following day. After the fire ended, the tanks remained there for several days.

On Sunday May 19, around 8:00 p.m., a resident of Beaumont, Mr. Arthur Pauporté, was killed by shrapnel from an explosion at the threshold of his house. About fifteen meters away, a group of German soldiers had been inspecting one of the French tanks.

One of the soldiers inadvertently activated the tank's 75mm firing mechanism. A loaded shell was already in the barrel and the shell ricocheted off an electric pylon and exploded. Mr. and Mrs. Destraix, who were having a conversation with Mr Pauporté, are injured and Mr. Pauporté is struck in the stomach. He died on the spot.

Overview of the Salamandre Tower and the town ramparts

The Salamandre Tower overlooking lovely Beaumont

OUR TOWN TODAY

Grea Beaumonth is a thousand-year-old city, preserving its old cobbled streets and its mansions from the 16th, 17th and 18th centuries. A walk around Beaumont is a walk through history combined with the comforts of welcoming people and wonderful local food & drink.

There are many things to visit and experience in Beaumont. Beaumont has retained part of its ramparts and a few towers, including the Tour Salamandre keep (shown above). Restored in 1955, it is accessible to the public during the good seasons.

Great historical figures including Charles V, Charles de Croÿ and Napoleon marked our city and their marks on the city continue to this day.

For example, Charles V, when on a visit to Beaumont, was attacked by 3 Auvergnats from France. Arrested on the spot, they were tried and hanged in less than an hour, resulting in the local saying: "City of Beaumont, City of Doom! Arrived at noon, hung at one o'clock". Every 5 years, a colorful procession called "Ommegang" reproduces the event and celebrates the life of the medieval 1500s.

Beaumont has many gastronomic specialties including macaroons, the praline-making shop of the chocolate factory Bressant and Beaumont Poularde, the recipe of which was bequeathed by the cook of Napoleon to the Ladies of Beaumont. We invite you to come and share these delights with our local residents.

For more information about Beaumont, visit: www.beaumont.be. For more information about Beaumont's tourism opportunitites, visit: www.visitbeaumont.be.

This information was prepared by the Beaumont Tourist Office, Grand-Place 10—B-6500 Beaumont. @officetourismebeaumont. Photos courtesy of the municipality of Beaumont.

BEAUVECHAIN BELGIUM

Province: Walloon Brabant   Pop. 1940: 5,000   Pop. 2020: 7,200

SITING & HERITAGE

The municipality of Beauvechain has ancient roots. Inhabited since Neolithic times when flint was first discovered nearby, our villages were colonized by the Romans and a main Roman road between Boulogne-sur-Mer and Cologne passed through Beauvechain. Beauvechain owes its name to the words "bavo" and "heim" meaning "Bavon inhabitats". At the end of the 9th century, Beauvechain was devastated by the Normans who came from a camp at Louvain, 25 km to the northwest. Since those ancient times, Beauvechain has been the site of many conflicts and battles, suffering devastation numerous times.

Beauvechain is located in an area that transitions from gentle hills to the northeast and south-west to extensive agricultural areas that comprise three-fourths of the land around the town. North of the town lies the Meerdael Forest, known for its tall majestic beeches and the Roman Air Force Base lies just south of the town.

GPS Coordinates: N50.7806 E4.7739

OUR TOWN'S OCCUPATION STORY

The Invasion. When France and England declared war on Germany, Belgium declared a policy of neutrality, proclaimed a general mobilization, and launched an emergency process of rearmament. Belgium also increased its defenses, in particular by creating the famous KW line, an anti-tank barrier installed between Koningshooikt (province d'Anvers) and Wavre which passed through Beauvechain.

To reach France, the Netherlands and Luxembourg, Germany invaded Belgium on May 10th and led the nation into a conflict that would last only 18 days. On May 28, 1940, after trying to negotiate a cease fire, the Belgian King, who was Commander-in-Chief of the armies, capitulated unconditionally.

Some 112,500 Allied soldiers managed to escape to England via Dunkirk where many Belgian soldiers were able to join the famous Belgium 1st Infantry "Piron" Brigade. Others found ways to return to their homes, but many were sent into captivity in Germany and most of them would not be released until 5 years later. During the invasion, the two Belgium military aerodromes in the Beauvechain area became targets of the German Luftwaffe and most of the Belgian planes were destroyed on the ground.

Joseph Trotoir
19 years old in 1940

Joseph Trotoir - Taken Prisoner:
"We surrendered and I was taken prisoner of war, putting our weapons on the ground, one by one, in front of the Germans. We were then marched to a train to Germany and put into cattle wagons, 50 of us in a wagon. We had nothing to eat or drink until our arrival."

The Occupation. The occupier made life difficult for the population in two main areas. First, the Nazis exploited any local resources of their choosing, especially those agricultural, livestock and taxes needed to support the Wehrmacht operations. Secondly, to support the German war industry, the Germans established compulsory labor in 1942 and thousands of workers were deported to Germany. Some refused and fled or joined the resistance. Some, a minority, chose collaboration.

On a daily basis, the first concern of the population was to survive, to eat! The German regime required rationing and distributed ration supply stamps. The black market develops and becomes a parallel economy. At first, the Germans strive to give a positive image but the relationship between the residents and the Germans becomes more and more strained. Denunciations, resistance, threats, executions and deportations to concentration camps will mark a good number of destinies.

The Beauvechain Aerodromes. During the war the Germans used and expanded the Beauvechain air bases to house Luftwaffe long-range bombers which were continuously used to bomb England. Beginning in January 1944, the Beauvechain air installations were regularly bombarded by the Allied planes, pushing the local residents to make an exodus, notably to Hamme Mille (M'lin). On July 5, the heart of the village of La Bruyere suffered the consequences of the bombing and had casualties. The bombardment of August 15, 1944 remains in everyone's memory as the most heavy and most destructive. After the war, the Beauvechain air base was renamed after Lieutenant Colonel Aviator Charles Roman, housing the Belgium 1st Fighter Wing. Today the base still hosts the Belgian Air Force pilot school as well as the Wing Historical Center.

Simone Van Meerbeck
16 years old in 1940

Simone Van Meerbeck: *"I never had a youth during the war. I had nothing. I didn't have dances. Because of the military presence, our parents didn't want to let us go out for fear that we would get pregnant because there were many fighting men without women. There were many rapes."*

Luis Kruijfhooft
23 years old in 1940

Luis Kruijfhooft: *"I had a group of buddies and we passed much of our time together. At that time we had small 5-cent coins with a small hole in them and we would play the game where we would draw a line and then each of us would toss the 5-cent coins to see who could get the closest to the line.*

We were playing this game when suddenly a chic Mercedes drove up, with a small Nazi flag, belonging to a fat German officer. He demanded that I give him directions to Bourg-Leopold. I told him to first go to Éghezée, then to continue to Huy and at Huy, ask for the remaining directions there. I had sent him on a Greek Calendar [a wild goose chase.] We laughed long and loud about it, but we thought it best to get off the street after that."

Note: Personal quotes of residents from *40-45 Expressions & Impressions,* The Municipality of Beauvechain, 2017

THE BELGIUM 1ST INFANTRY BRIGADE

The Belgian Army didn't stop fighting after Germany invaded and occupied the country. In fact, many Belgian soldiers played an important role during the liberation of France, Belgium and The Netherlands as members of the Belgian 1st Infantry Brigade which was formed after a call by Belgian Prime Minister Pierlot, in exile in London, for all Belgians to join in the fight to liberate the country.

Jean-Bapiste Piron

This call to arms resulted in the recruitment of a wide range of fighters that included Belgian and Luxembourg soldiers who survived the 1940 evacuation at Dunkirk, volunteers from the African Belgium colonies and Legionnaires from North Africa. In command of the Brigade was Colonel Jean-Baptiste Piron, a veteran of World War I and an illustrious officer in the Belgian army.

These troops were then trained in Great Britain and Canada and in 1942 the 1st Belgian Brigade was formed with a mix of infantry, artillery and reconnaissance units. Their training continued through 1943, adding beach landing training in early 1944 and, by the time of the Normandy invasion, the force had grown to more than 2,200 men. Since the fighters had arrived from around the world, thirty-three languages were spoken in the Brigade in 1944.

The D-Day landings took place without the "Piron Brigade" to the great disappointment of its 2,200 men but the British preferred to reserve them for the liberation of Belgium. Colonel Piron lobbied the exiled Belgian government to send the Belgian troops to the front to reverse the declining morale of his troops. He soon got his wish.

Beginning on 17 August 1944, the Belgian 1st Infantry Brigade participated in clearing the Germans from the Normandy coast and, on 2 September, the Brigade was ordered to move as quickly as possible to the Belgian border to allow the Brigade to lead in the liberation of their homeland. On 3 September the Brigade arrived at the French–Belgian border and during September the Brigade specialized in liberating small towns, guiding British soldiers and providing aid to resistance fighters. During their advance through Belgium, the Belgian troops were sometimes mistaken for French Canadians since local people did not expect that their liberators would be fellow Belgians.

Belgians greeting the Piron Brigade

The Brigade continued fighting the Germans and liberating Belgian towns until November, 1944 when the Brigade was relieved from the fighting at the front and ordered to take a reserve position in Leuven, just west of Beauvechain. The Brigade was a great source of pride for the Belgian people.

LIBERATION & RECOVERY

The liberation of Belgium by the Allied forces began in September 1944 when the Allies, led by the American Army and the Piron Brigade, entered Belgium. Beauvechain and the other villages of the municipality were liberated on September 6 with great celebrations and joy.

Denise Menada
17 years old in 1940

Denise Menada: "They shaved the heads of the ones who had been with the Germans. There was one they did not catch who should have had his head shaved so instead they shaved his dog. The Americans who were at the chateau gave us cigarettes - Camels - and played cards with us but I didn't continue smoking after that; I didn't have enough money."

The Beauvehain municipal building © Julien Deper

St-Martin in Tourinnes-la-Grosse © Julien Deper

The Beauvechain field of 36 pagodas by Judos
Photo By Laurence Latour

OUR TOWN TODAY

Located on the edge of the Meerdael forest and watered by the Néthen, the Beauvechain entity includes the villages of Beauvechain, Hamme-Mille, L'Ecluse, Nodebais and Tourinnes-la-Grosse. It is a land known for its beautiful churches and the municipality's exceptional natural heritage, its gently rolling country landscapes, and its horizons as far as the eye can see make the Beauvechain area an ideal destination for green tourism.

The Beauvechain municipality has experienced a renewed conviviality, making it one of the most active localities in Walloon Brabant in terms of the quality of local life. Art enthusiasts will enjoy the surreal field of pagodas created by the famous singer and songwriter Judos and the Beauvechain Air Base Museum is a must-see for military history and aviation enthusiasts.

The diversity of our ancient villages and neighborhoods contribute greatly to Beauvechain's charm. The villages of Beauvechain, Nodebais, L'Ecluse, Tourinnes-la-Grosse, Hamme-Mille and their various hamlets each have their unique heritage of ancestral homes, rural paths and gently rolling countryside, all worth visiting.

For more information about the Beauvechain municipality, visit: www.beauvechain.be. For more information about the local tourism opportunities in the Beauvechain area visit: www.beauvechain.be/loisirs/tourisme.

We appreciate the assistance provided by Mathieu Bertrand of the Beauvechain Memory and Citizenship Service in preparing this commemorative document. Photos courtesy of the municipality of Beauvechain.

BÜLLINGEN BELGIUM

Province: Liège   Pop. 1940: 2,200   Pop. 2020: 5,500

SITING & HERITAGE

Büllingen has ancient roots. Inhabited since Mesolithic times (prior to 4000 B.C.) and first known as Büllingen during the 1st century, Büllingen has been tied to Germany and the Germanic languages since the 8th century A.D. Even today, German is the primary language spoken in our municipality.

Not only is Büllingen located within the beautiful Ardennes and Eifel mountain range, Büllingen has the second largest surface area of any municipality in Belgium and the second highest point in Belgium called "Weißer Stein" is located in the Büllingen municipality. Tourism, nature and agriculture have played important roles in the Büllingen municipality for many years and Büllingen is known for its many protected heritage sites, especially the many protected churches and chapels that exist throughout the municipality.

GPS Coordinates: N50.4074 E6.2575

BÜLLINGEN'S OCCUPATION STORY

The Eupen & Malmedy Cantons integrated into the Third Reich

Before the Invasion. Prior to 1920 and prior to the end of World War I, Büllingen had been a part of Germany. When World War I ended, both of the Eupen-Malmedy areas (East Cantons), including Büllingen, were ceded to Belgium under the terms of the Treaty of Versailles.

During the following years, having been a part of Germany since 1815, many residents felt the area should be returned to Germany. In fact, the "Heimattreue Front", a pro-Nazi party, won majorities in all of the Eupen-Malmedy election districts during the elections of 1936 and 1939 and, prior to the German invasion, many locals could be seen wearing Nazi armbands in public.

Thus, when Germany invaded Belgium on May 10, 1940, the Germans considered the occupation of Büllingen as the retaking of German land and, on May 18, Hitler announced that the Eupen-Malmedy area had been "reintegrated" into the Third Reich. However, the Belgian government, in exile, refused to recognize the annexation. As a result of the annexation of the East Cantons, 8,000 local men were conscripted into the German armed forces. Of them, 2,200 were killed on the Eastern Front during the Germans' invasion of Russia.

Locals greeting German troops with the Nazi salute

The forced conscription of the local men into the German Wehrmacht and the brutality of the Nazi regime soon made it clear to the residents that ideological attachment to Germany was a mistake and they became more and more suspicious and fearful of their occupiers.

THE BATTLE OF THE BULGE DESTRUCTION OF BÜLLINGEN

As the Allies pushed the Germans east after D-Day, the Büllingen municipality was first liberated on September 13, 1944. However, more fighting was expected so the Americans evacuated all civilians (except for a few cattle keepers) on October 7, 1944, first to Malmedy and then to other areas. Then, completely surprising the Allies, on December 16, 1944, the Germans launched a major counter offensive on a broad front, hoping to recapture the port of Antwerp and divide the Allied forces. Becoming known as the Battle of the Bulge, on December 18, 1944, the Germans reached the Büllingen municipality which was viciously defended by the Americans for two days before, on the night of December 20, the German troops finally secured the area, driving the last Americans from our municipality.

Captured American GIs

SS Lt. Col. Joachim Peiper

As it turns out, the main spearhead of the German offensive had passed through the Büllingen area and sadly was led by the infamous, ruthless and murderous SS Lt. Col. Joachim Peiper, killing both civilians and American POWs in his path, including the Massacre at Malmedy where he machine-gunned a large group of American POWs on December 17. On that same day, his murderous methods were employed again when he murdered several dozen American POWs after capturing a small fuel depot in Büllingen. Heavy tank and house-to-house fighting continued until the end of January and finally the last of Büllingen's villages was liberated on February 4, 1945.

When the residents of the Büllingen villages returned to their homes, they found their villages almost completely destroyed and their houses looted. In the end, of the 2,200 residents of the municipality of Büllingen, 372 were conscripted into the Wehrmacht of which 140 were killed and 38 residents were killed during the Battle of the Bulge. Thanks to the help of the Belgian authorities, makeshift barracks were built for the population and only when the first war compensations began to arrive in 1947 was it possible to slowly build up an existence again.

Condemned to death at the Dachau war criminal trials, Peiper was released from prison in 1956. Finally settling in France, his location was exposed during June of 1976 and on July 14, 1976 his house was mysteriously set on fire and he died of smoke inhalation.

THE BATTLE FOR LANZERATH: THE FIGHT OF 18 AMERICAN SOLDIERS, DECEMBER 16, 1944

The historical stories about the Battle of the Bulge generally focus on the battles in the Ardennes forest areas (Bastogne, St. Vith, etc.) however the primary goal of Hitler was to control the Losheim Gap, a long, narrow valley through which large volumes of equipment could be moved for the push to recapture Antwerp.

In the northern portion of the Losheim Gap lies Lanzerath, a tiny hamlet southeast of Büllingen, where 18 men of the Intelligence and Reconnaissance Platoon of the 394th Regiment, 99th Infantry Division had been occupying two- and three-man foxholes since December 10th to observe the open valley. Their foxholes were covered with six- to eight-inch pine logs and fresh snow had fallen several times, camouflaging the positions beyond detection. A sharp wind, gusting from the north, drove a freezing fog across the area.

Little did they know that more than 115 tanks were headed directly towards them, led by the dreaded SS Lt. Col. Joachim Peiper. Commanded by a 20-year old lieutenant named Lyle Bouck Jr, of Missouri, this handful of soldiers, positioned on a hilltop outside Lanzerath, successfully halted the movement of Peiper's division for a full day after a nearby friendly tank destroyer unit had retreated. Bouck's men obeyed their orders to hold at all costs.

Lt Lyle Bouck Jr., commander of the I&R Platoon: *"Suddenly, without warning, a barrage of artillery registered at about 05.30 hours and continued until about 07.00 hours. The artillery was relentless and frightening, but not devastating. Much landed short, wide and long of our position, and mostly tree bursts. At any rate, our well-protected cover prevented casualties. The telephone lines were knocked out, but our one radio allowed us to report to regiment. I called regiment and told them, 'The TDs are pulling out, what we should do?' The answer was loud and clear: 'Hold at all costs!'*

"The next hour or so, nothing happened. Then suddenly we spotted a column of troops marching toward Lanzerath. This was reported to regiment, and I asked permission to withdraw and engage in a delaying action. Regiment said, 'Remain in position and reinforcements from the 3rd Battalion will come to support you.'(they never arrived)."

The German soldiers deployed and attacked up the hill, but the heavy fire of Lyle Bouck's men made it impossible for the Germans to get up the hill, and they retreated.

Lt Lyle Bouck Jr.: *"Sometime in mid-afternoon, a second attack was made and repelled, but left its mark on the I&R Platoon. The communications were out, ammunition was running low, the wounded increasing, and apprehension running high. Our evaluation was not impressive. A third attack was directed on the platoon later in the afternoon; this was also repelled. Our ammo was not out, but it was low."*

"All of a sudden, and no one knows from what direction, our entire platoon was infiltrated with Germans. Some firing, screaming, and running. As I ducked back into the hole, automatic small arms fire ripped into our emplacement. Just then, the end of a burp gun barrel pointed into our hole. At this time, everything seemed quiet, with just small amounts of sporadic rifle fire. A voice asked calmly, 'Who is the commandant?' I informed him it was 'me.' He wanted to know what my men were going to do. I told him I would call them from their positions if he would have his men to stop firing. This was accomplished and we were searched."

The Battle for Lanzerath was over. The men of the I & R Platoon left about 60 dead and wounded German paratroopers on the fields surrounding the tiny hilltop. For 18 hours the 18 Americans held off an entire German parachute battalion (1st Battalion of the 9th Infantry Regiment of the 3rd Parachute Division). Not until their ammunition was exhausted, their radio had been destroyed, and Bouck himself and most of his men had been wounded did the GIs capitulate.

Thus, a small group of men, including four men of the 371st Artillery Forward Observation Team that had earlier been in the town and helped Lyle Bouck and his men, was responsible for holding off a 500-man strong battalion a whole day. The I & R Platoon was later decorated for valor with the Presidential Unit Citation.

A Lanzerath memorial to those who fought

OUR MUNICIPALITY TODAY

The Büllingen Municipality includes 27 villages and hamlets, each with their own identities and local histories. Known for its many beautiful churches, the Municipality's exceptional natural heritage, its gently rolling country landscapes and its horizons as far as the eye can see, make Büllingen an ideal destination for green tourism.

The Büllingen Municipality has experienced a renewed conviviality, making it one of the most active localities in the Liège province in terms of the quality of local life. A popular tourist destination, a visit to the tourism section of the municipal website shows the variety of the amenities and activities available to visitors in the Büllingen area, ranging from equestrian, hiking and cycling trails to skiing. Of course, the Büllingen Battle of the Bulge monuments are a must-see for military history enthusiasts.

The diversity of our ancient villages and neighborhoods contribute greatly to Büllingen's charm. The 27 villages and hamlets of Büllingen are surrounded with beautiful scenery, full of medieval and military history and populated by people who are ready to welcome visitors to see and experience the exceptional hospitality Büllingen is known for.

An aerial view of Büllingen today

*For more information about the Büllingen municipality, visit the municipality's website: **www.bullingen.be**. For more information about the interesting local history of the Büllingen area visit: **www.rocherath-krinkelt.be/**.*

We greatly appreciate the assistance provided by Marcel Vaessen, a tourism guide in Büllingen, in the preparation of this commemorative document. Photos courtesy of the Municipality of Büllingen.

CHAUDFONTAINE   BELGIUM

Province: Liège   Pop. 1940: 9,400   Pop. 2020: 20,800

COMMUNE DE
CHAUDFONTAINE

SITING & HERITAGE

Chaudfontaine is a spa town near Liège. Criss-crossed by forest roads, Chaudfontaine is a major link to the Ardennes. Set in a wooded setting of green hills surrounding two winding rivers, Chaudfontaine possesses the only warm mineral water source in the BENELUX region and in 1983, hydrologists discovered that the water makes a 60 year journey through protecting and purifying rock layers from a depth of 1,600 metres before emerging at the surface at 36.6°C. The Coca-Cola company now takes advantage of this pure source of water.

Chaudfontaine is the location of two of the twelve forts that formed the "Fortified Position of Liège" (namely Chaudfontaine and Embourg), built at the end of the 19th century. The Fort of Embourg is today a museum that recounts the two world wars through a unique collection of arms, uniforms and military equipment (see Page 69).

GPS Coordinates: N50.5866 E5.6394

American liberators with a family In Embourg
September 1944

OUR TOWN'S OCCUPATION STORY

The forts in the villages of Chaudfontaine and Embourg, rearmed and consolidated in the inter-war period, could count on the assistance of ten other forts in the "Fortified Position of Liège", forming what was thought to be a very efficient barrier against the German troops who crossed the Belgian borders on 10th May 1940.

The Fort of Chaudfontaine was defended by two groups of 200 men. At the start of the hostilities, the second group and the infantry defending the forts received the order to retreat to the Meuse River. On 13th May, the German army bombarded the fort, weakening it and enemy soldiers attacked the fort during night time, using shell craters as shelters. Then, on the morning of 17th May, the Luftwaffe pounded the fort and its defenders sent out an S.O.S. to the other forts who responded by firing towards Chaudfontaine to disrupt the enemy artillery. At approximately midday, a German grenade, followed by a shell fired at the entrance archway, exploded inside the fort, seriously injuring several soldiers. Any further resistance would put the lives of the men in ultimate peril so the fort was abandoned that evening.

The Fort of Embourg was one of the smallest forts in the "Fortified Position of Liège" with a garrison of 153 men. As with the Fort of Chaudfontaine, the two groups were separated during the night of 10th to 11th May. The fort of Embourg resisted whilst also assisting the Fort of Chaudfontaine. On 14th May, the enemy had completely surrounded the fort, making any attempt at escape impossible. The Luftwaffe joined the combat on 15th May, destroying part of the fort's weaponry. On 16th May, the bombardment continued however the fort could no longer count on the help of the forts in Boncelles and Flémalle which had been overrun.

Allied troops in Vaux-sous-Chèvremont
September 1944

When the Fort of Chaudfontaine called for help and the Fort of Embourg deployed its artillery in support, the enemy bombardment destroyed it. The fort's defenders transmitted an S.O.S. which was met with no response at all. The fort was therefore alone and unarmed while the enemy continued to attack. The garrison had to choose to either perish in the bomb blasts or cease fighting. The commander decided to lay down arms.

The surrender of the forts marked the start of German occupation, accompanied by a curfew, requisitioning, forced labour, shortages and distribution of ration tickets. The lack of foodstuffs and the long, tough winters drove the inhabitants to create their own vegetable gardens and farm smallholdings. Some even cut down the trees on one of the village squares to grow potatoes in their place. Whilst daily life continued and a theatre troupe was even created, the beginnings of resistance started to emerge.

The church of Vaux-sous-Chèvremont before
its destruction in December 1944

Underground newspapers started to appear with the aim of supporting the Belgians or inciting them to rebel against the occupier. They came from a clandestine printing press installed by the resistance movements in the manor of Jules Hennekinne, who was arrested and then deported to the Buchenwald concentration camp where he died in 1944. The Germans captured almost twenty resistance members, among whom was teacher Regnier Elias, arrested in July 1943 in front of one of his pupils aged 10 years old. All of these prisoners were either sent to concentration or extermination camps in Germany or to Liège to the sinister Block 24 of the Citadel where the prisoners were executed by firing squad, as was the case for Félix Trousson.

WE REMEMBER THE OCCUPATION

The Stalag 1A Memorial in Chaudfontaine

Chaudfontaine attaches great importance to the memory of its heroes as well as its inhabitants who were children or teenagers during the occupation. Three examples are Charles Labalue, Jacques Renwa and Paul Van den Brûle. Other accounts ls can be consulted in the towns' libraries or at the Centre for Information and Documentation in Chaudfontaine.

Charles Lablue. *A teenager during the occupation, Charles has clear memories of the liberation and the bombardment of the Palace Hôtel (now the Urban Lodge) which could have killed his father. Later in life, Charles contributed to political and community life in the town, occupying the positions of councillor and chairman of a patriotic association. His testimonial is published in a booklet written for the purpose of explaining the occupation to children.*

Jacques Renwa. *Jacques was 12 years old and had just received his first communion when the church in Vaux-sous-Chèvremont was bombarded. Later, he took charge of his parents' undertaking business and still lives in Vaux-sous-Chèvremont. A member of the FNC in Chaudfontaine, Jacques recounted to us the destruction of the church in Vaux-sous-Chèvremont by the German V1 rockets on December 19, 1944.*

Paul Van den Brûle. *Aged only 5 years old at the start of the war, Paul has written a moving account about the day-to-day life of the inhabitants during the occupation. Initially intended for his grandchildren, his text is distributed as a booklet to the town's schools.*

LIBERATION AND RECOVERY

On 7th September 1944, German vehicles attempted to cut a breach in the column of Allied troops that was approaching. American Sergeant Tony Ross, leading the column as a scout, was cut down by the bullets of the enemy, whose brief attempt to counter-attack failed. The Americans repulsed the Germans while the inhabitants flew the nation's flag from all their windows. Chaudfontaine was free, but the war was not over.

On 19th December, Chaudfontaine was bombarded by the Germans when the Battle of the Bulge began. A V1 rocket fell on the church of Vaux-sous-Chèvremont, killing the priest and vicar. All that was left standing was the bell tower and even the surrounding houses were flattened by the blast. The Basilica of Notre-Dame de Chèvremont was severely damaged, while other bombs killed several people and injured many others.

On the same day, the Americans set up their headquarters at the Hôtel des Bains as well as the Palace Hôtel. On 20th December, Lieutenant General Hodges received a visit from Field Marshall Montgomery in order to coordinate efforts to halt the German counter attack and resume the offensive. On 23rd December, just after the military chiefs had left Chaudfontaine, enemy planes bombarded the Palace Hôtel, killing three resistance members and an American Colonel.

Chaudfontaine underwent rebuilding until the 1960's and paid homage to the memory of its defenders through the streets which bear their names, as well as via the monuments built in their honour, including Sergeant Tony Ross and the prisoners deported to Stalag 1A, who were, for the most part, captured during the surrender of the two forts.

OUR TOWN TODAY

Today, the Chaudfontaine Municipality consists of six villages and towns: Chaudfontaine, Beaufars, Embourg, Mehagne, Ninane and Vaux-sous-Chèvremont. Chaudfontaine is a dynamic town that has built its reputation on its spa water, its mineral water and the town's rich natural, architectural and cultural heritage.

Just 7 minutes from the international railway station in Liège, the station of Chaudfontaine is immortalized by works by the painter Paul Delvaux. Just outside the station is the Esplanade du Casino and its superb illuminated fountains, the Parc des Sources and two museums for children and adults alike: The WaterHouse museum reveals the mysteries of water while The ArtHouse museum addresses Modern Art.

The Esplanade du Casino in Chaudfontaine

Further on, the Parc de Hauster plays host to the Festival of the 5 Seasons, a unique event in Wallonia, with art works tucked away amidst nature. This park is next to the Château des Thermes spa, which has become the spearhead of a new spa sector in Belgium focusing on tourism, well-being and relaxation.

The outstanding green setting, as well as the soft mobility network, make it possible to go on wonderful walks, bike rides or horse rides, for both the sporty and less sporty. Chaudfontaine is a town that rhymes with easy living, beautiful scenery and wonderful people.

The beautiful Chaudfontaine riverfront—Wikipedia

*For more information about Chaudfontaine, visit Chaudfontaine's official website: **www.chaudfontaine.be/**. For more information on tourism in Chaudfontaine, visit the town's tourism website: **www.chaudfontaine.be/decouvrir-chaudfontaine/**.*

This information has been prepared by the services of the Town Hall, Tourism and Culture in the town of Chaudfontaine with the valuable help of the Royal Tourist Board, Mrs. Claudine Marichal (a town inhabitant) and Mr. Jean-Marc Lebrun (Chairman of the Former Fortified Position of Liège non-profit making association), as well as on the basis of work by Mrs. Bernadette Lognard and Mr. Fernand Michel from the Centre for Information and Documentation. Except as noted, photos courtesy of the municipality of Chaudfontaine.

DALHEM BELGIUM

Province: Liège   Pop. 1940: 4,700   Pop. 2020: 7,550

SITING & HERITAGE

The municipality of Dalhem, which has 7,550 inhabitants, is comprised of eight villages: Berneau, Bombaye, Dalhem, Feneur, Mortroux, Neufchâteau, Saint-André and Warsage. Located halfway between Liège and Maestricht in the Ardennes, Dalhem is a farming community rich in cultivated land (wheat, corn, beets & potatoes), livestock (cows & pigs) and fruit (apples & pears).

Dalhem lies within an area rich in medieval history. The Counts of Dalhem, who erected a castle in 1076, possessed land from Liège to Maestricht. The Dalhem "old town" area is a historically classified site that today continues to attest to the vestiges of this glorious past and the Fort of Aubin-Neufchâteau *(Page 66)* is a permanent reminder of the vicious invasion by Germany on May 10, 1940.

GPS Coordinates: N50.7134 E5.7230

The battered Fort d'Aubin-Neufchateau

The local surrender to the Germans, May, 1940

11 September 1944—liberation in Mortroux

The return of Belgium Army prisoners

OUR TOWN'S OCCUPATION STORY

The Exodus. The population of several villages near the Fort of Aubin-Neufchâteau had been warned that they would have to evacuate if war was declared. May 10, 1940 began an exodus of hundreds of families on foot, by bicycle or by cart either to the Netherlands or to Flanders. The few people with a car left for France. Many returned a few days or weeks later to avoid the looting of their property.

The Invasion. Built from 1935 to 1940, the Aubin-Neufchâteau fort was intended to block access to Aachen-Visé-Liège. It was part of the first line of defense of the fortified part of Liège along with the forts of Eben-Emael, Battice and Tancrémont on the Maginot Line. On Friday May 10 the fort was completely surrounded and on the next day had to repel more than 20 assaults. The fighting continued for 10 days during which three requests for surrender by German parliamentarians were refused. Finally, on May 21, after 11 days of heroic resistance, the fort fell to the Germans. The 550 soldiers were taken prisoner and went into captivity.

Oppression and Reprisals. To make up for the enormous losses of the German army resulting from the invasion of Russia and the shortages in labor at the German factories, in March of 1942 the German "Werbestelle" began requiring local men between 18 and 51 years of age, and single women between 21 and 35 years of age to work for the German Reich. In case anyone refused, the worker became an "Arbeidverplichtet" and was sent either to a labor camp or directly to companies in Germany where the living conditions and discipline were very harsh, always under the constant threat of fines and being sent to disciplinary camps and of course, the risk of Allied bombing was always present. Many of these local people hid from the authorities, even being declared "deceased" to escape compulsory labor. In addition to this, many civilians paid with their lives for acts of resistance as was the case on September 5, 1944 when an explosion at the Berneau crossroads (next to the church) killed two Germans. In retaliation, four civilians were shot.

The Resistance. Resistance movements under the command of "Jacques de Dalhem" were organized at the start of the 1940-1941 football season during matches and meetings, notably at the Café des Sports Monami. The out-of-service Dalhem railway tunnel was used by the resistance fighters as a hiding place for weapons that had been parachuted in by the Allies, hiding the weapons between the masonry and the shale rock walls. The resistance fighters had a wide variety of missions: gathering intelligence, gathering and aiding downed Allied airmen, hiding Jews and escaped prisoners from Nazi prisons and camps, helping those who resisted compulsory labor and organizing escape routes to neutral countries and England.

Meteorological Observations. Allied bomber aircrew losses throughout the continent often became intolerable because of bad weather conditions. It was therefore decided to create an underground network of meteorological observation stations in Belgium. One of the observation posts was established in the Dalhem village of Berneau in September 1943 and was successfully hidden from the Germans.

The 749th Tank Battalion. On November 8, this US Army tank battalion installed its headquarters in the Dalhem villages of Mortroux and Neufchâteau, remaining there until the battalion was called to participate in the Battle of the Bulge on December 19. Fighting continuously until the end of January 1945, the battalion suffered numerous losses before progressing towards and into Germany.

A Special Story. *Born in Verviers on October 29, 1897, Oscar D'Ardenne studied at the University of Aachen and spoke fluent German. From 1935 to 1940 he directed the construction of the Fort of Aubin-Neufchâteau, a part of the Maginot Line.*

On 10 May, 1940 Colonel D'Ardenne had 14 officers and 545 soldiers when the Fort was violently attacked by the invading German forces. Despite the fierce fighting, the fort only fell on 21 May after the fort's heavy artillery had been completely destroyed.

Belgian Army Colonel
Oscar d'Ardenne

D'Ardenne then met with the German commander Colonel Rünge and laid three conditions for surrender: that the dead could be given a burial, that the wounded could be cared for and that the garrison could rest 24 hours before leaving in captivity.

Thanks to the resistance of the brave Belgian soldiers, the Fort slowed down and restrained the enemy forces needed by the Germans on other fronts. Their bravery contributed in an important way to the ability of the British to rescue the hundreds of thousands of English, French and Belgian troops surrounded in Dunkerque.

Oscar d'Ardenne left in captivity with his men and returned to Dalhem almost blind near the end of 1942. Fortunately the care he received after his return allowed him to regain his sight. His sight restored, he then served with the resistance until the end of the war.

After the war, he was appointed Colonel and resumed service in Germany with the Belgian army. He died on July 19, 1968 in Dalhem, at the age of 71 years, and was buried in Verviers.

The beautiful Chateau Francotte Castle in Dalhem

The Le Wichet de la Rose Castle entrance to the lower town

LIBERATION AND RECOVERY

The Liberation. On Saturday, September 9, 1944, a reconnaissance patrol of the American 113th Mechanized Cavalry Group, nicknamed "The Red Horse Cavalry", attached to the 30th Infantry Division, entered Dalhem including jeeps, light armor on wheels, cannon and machine guns.

Led by members of the local resistance and briefed by the members of the resistance on the positions of the Germans, the Americans took positions in various places around the town and attacked the Germans. Many Germans fell, but also, unfortunately, did several local civilians. Dalhem was finally liberated, soon followed by the liberation of the other surrounding villages.

On 16 December the town's liberation ended when the Germans launched the counter offensive known as the Battle of the Bulge whose strategic objective was to recapture the port of Antwerp. During this time the 749th Tank Battalion from Mortroux and Neufchâteau continually distinguished themselves in battle. On 29 April, 1999 a monument was inaugurated in the village of Neufchâteau in the presence of families of missing American soldiers, commemorating this bloody winter victory.

On February 18, 1945, Lieutenant General Omar Bradley, commanding officer of the 12th American Army Group visited the headquarters of the 83th Infantry Division in Dalhem to visit troops who were being allowed to rest for three weeks in Dalhem before having to return to the front.

Reconstruction. Many war damages occurred in the Dalhem area and fortunately the population was able to benefit from compensation from the ORD (Office of the Devastated Regions). Several houses still carry the acronym "ORD" on their façade. The badly damaged Fort of Aubin-Neufchâteau is now accessible to the public several weekends a year. (See page 66).

OUR TOWN TODAY

The Dalhem Municipality of 7,550 inhabitants includes the eight surrounding villages of Berneau, Bombaye, Dalhem, Feneur, Mortroux, Neufchâteau, Saint-André and Warsage.

Located in the beautiful forested hills of the Ardenne area of eastern Belgium and covering more than 3,600 hectares, Dalhem is a well known destination of nature enthusiasts. Dalhem's hiking maps offer fifteen different walking and cycling circuits through the woods, fields, rivers and many other sites, and along the way excellent restaurants welcome tourists in a bucolic environment.

There are many classified (designated) historical sites to discover in Dalhem including "the old town" ramparts, the Wichet de la Rose (1620), the Chapel of the Tomb in Bombaye, the organs of Mortroux and Berneau and the Valley South of Neufchâteau.

The beauty and tranquility of Dalhem's villages also makes it an ideal residential municipality. Known for its festive spirit and many public events, the municipality welcomes all who come to visit.

For more information about Dalhem, visit the town's website: www.dalhem.be. For more information about the area's tourism and recreational opportunities, visit the tourism website: www.paysdeherve.be. For more information about the Fort of Aubin Neufchateau, visit www.fort-aubin-neufchateau.be. (See Page 66).

This information was prepared by Chrystel Blondeau, Echeviant of the Culture of the Municipality of Dalhem under the supervision of Eschevine Daniela Crema-Wagmans and Bourgmestre Arnaud Dewez. Photos courtesy of the municipality of Dalhem.

DIEST BELGIUM

Province: Flemish Brabant   Pop. 1940: 15,000   Pop. 2020: 26,000

SITING & HERITAGE

Diest is a small provincial town about 30 kilometers northeast of Leuven. Founded in 1229, the city has a long and rich history. From the 16th till the 18th century the city was under the rule of the house Oranje-Nassau and Prince Philip-William of Orange is buried in the beautiful Sint-Sulpitius church. This church, built between the 14th and 16th century in the Gothic style known as Demergotiek, dominates the city center Grote Markt with its beautiful historic step gables just steps from Diest's neoclassical town hall.

The city also has a former convent for lay women, known as a Beguinage, which was established during the 13th century. Located in a largely agricultural area interspersed with forests, over the years Diest has gained a reputation for beer brewing, its preserved ramparts and military fortresses from the 19th century that include the Citadel of Diest, and many historic buildings in its city center.

GPS Coordinates: N50.9902 E5.0502

Bombardment of the arsenal in Diest

Diest boys and Allies at Schaffen airfield after the liberation

Parade for the victims of WWII in Diest

OUR TOWN'S OCCUPATION STORY

Scarcity. During the occupation there was a shortage of all kinds of goods, but that did not prevent the people of Diest from getting what they needed to survive. While moving German railway cars at the railway station, resident Rik Saenen would open the hatches of the coal wagons with a number of friends to obtain this most valuable commodity. Rik and his friends also helped other people who had a hard time keeping warm during the cold winters.

The basic needs of the residents could be partly covered with ration stamps but it was the café of the parents of local resident Guy Vandermeulen where residents could get what they needed for cash or exchange, from frog legs to tobacco.

Bombing. One morning 10 year-old Guy Vandermeulen suddenly heard "tuf tuf tuf"... the characteristic sound of a Flying bomb that landed in the Speelhofstraat area. A number of windows broke and a gas pipeline caught fire. The nearby Schaffen airfield was heavily bombed in May 1940 and April 1944, with dozens of casualties and a lot of material damage.

The Diest station on the strategically important Leuven-Hasselt-Liège-Germany railway line was also bombed in April 1944. Rik Saenen experienced it while he and a friend were collecting horse manure from the paved roads for fertilization.

Suddenly planes appeared. Rik and his friend sought cover in a ditch. After a while however, his friend got frightened and crawled out of the canal to flee home. At that moment however, a bomb fell on him. Only one piece of his ear was recovered afterwards.

Resistance. Marie-Thérèse Haesevoets witnessed the brutal murder of fellow villager Hilaire Gemoets, who was a member of the resistance. He was arrested by the Germans and taken to a remote place on the countryside of Diest. There he was forced to dig his own grave.

Once the grave was ready, the Germans shot him. Hilaire fell into the grave and the Germans buried him under the earth. The mother and aunt of Marie-Thérèse Haesevoets, who also witnessed the murder, dug him out as soon as the Germans were out of sight but they were too late. Hilaire was already dead.

Mischief. Guy Vandermeulen often went to play with the Hanegreefs family at the "De schaapskooi" in the Hasseltsestraat area. This building opened onto the Arsenal where German soldiers were stationed. On a hot summer day, one of the boys hit a bottle of eau de cologne with his slingshot that was next to a German soldier who was sun-bathing. The boys had to go to the soldiers' barracks to explain what happened but luckily they weren't punished.

A FOUNDER OF BELGIAN RESISTANCE

Frans Neyskens was born in Diest on February 9, 1898. During WWI he went to England as a 16-year-old via the Netherlands to join the Belgian army being formed there. After the war he stayed in the army, becoming a part of the occupying army in Germany. In 1929 he returns to Belgium. After residing in a number of places Frans finally returns to Diest via Beringen, where he first becomes a sub-commissioner and later a commissioner.

At the outbreak of WWII, Frans Neyskens was one of the founders of the local Resistance. He becomes commander of the Secret Army and an assistant in the intelligence service. In this position he helps hide countless citizens so that they can escape deportation to work or punishment camps.

Frans Neyskens was arrested on May 20, 1944 and deported on June 19, 1944 to Mittelbau-Dora, a slave labor sub-camp of Buchenwald. Two other inhabitants of Diest, Louis Van Brabant and Leopold Smolders are also part of the same deportation convoy.

Frans Neyskens dies there on December 16, 1944. On Monday, June 25, 1945 the solemn funeral is held in Diest. A memorial stone is dedicated to Frans and is placed on the side wall of the town hall, which is now located in the atrium of the town hall.

LIBERATION & RECONSTRUCTION

Resident Arthur Van Eechaute met his best friend on the day of the Liberation watching the passage of the British tanks. His friend asked him to come with him to the Metropole café but Arthur did not go. Suddenly, at the end of the Koning Albertstraat Arthur heard a major explosion. A bomb from a German plane had fallen in front of the Lakenhalle at the Metropole café killing 10 bystanders, including his friend. Another classmate of Arthur's was hit hard by shrapnel that would later regularly come out of his skin.

Guy Vandermeulen's older brother also died in this bombardment. This, of course, put a damper on the joy of the family, in contrast to the other town inhabitants who were ecstatic about the impending Liberation of Diest.

The Liberation was also a special day for Gust Clement. Gust had refused to work for the Germans and had gone into hiding day and night in different places for a long time. During the night before the Liberation, the Germans fled, using all possible means of transportation. After it became quiet on the street Gust heard someone scream: "The English are here"! For Gust this was the first moment he could again go outside without the risk of being arrested.

Everyone was exuberant, people climbed on vehicles and people sang and danced. After living under the German occupation with a curfew at 10:00 pm, a new life immediately began with parties and music by the Allies' jazz orchestras. Life had returned to Diest.

The 17th Century Beguinage Convent in Diest

The Neoclassical Diest City Hall

OUR TOWN TODAY

Diest is a beautiful municipality that cherishes its rich, long heritage and its historic city center. The city parks in the center of the town and the nature reserves on the outskirts of the city make Diest a very pleasant place to live and relax.

The beautiful Beguinage, the St. Catherine's Church, the St. Sulpitius' Church with the Museum of Religious Art and the City Museum of De Hofstadt are attractions that attract thousands of visitors to the community every year. In the many shopping streets, small shops and large stores provide something for everyone. The Grote Markt in the city center is the place to sit down and relax with a drink on the pleasant terraces between the historic facades.

The Provincial Domain Halve Maan is located on the outskirts of the city. With playgrounds, an outdoor swimming pool with a sandy beach, mini golf, water bicycles and the surrounding nature reserve, it is the perfect day trip for the whole family.

The 15th Century Gothic Church of Sint-Sulpitius

For more information about Diest and the local tourism opportunities in the Diest area, visit the municipal websites: ***www.diest.be and www.toerismediest.be***.

*The Municipality of Diest would like to give special thanks to the Friends of the City Museum and Archive vzw (**www.vsmad.be**), the Diest WWII eyewitnesses Rik Saenen, Guy Vandermeulen, Marie-Thérèse Haesevoets, Arthur Van Eechaute and Gust Clementt, and filmmaker Raoul Dirix.*

LICHTERVELDE BELGIUM

Province: West-Vlaanderen   **Pop. 1940: 6,500**   **Pop. 2019: 9,000**

SITING & HERITAGE

Lichtervelde is a small municipality in the province of West Flanders (West-Vlaanderen) in an area that has been inhabited since before Roman times.

The oldest record of the town name, from 1127, appears in the description of the murder of Charles the Good by the chronicler Galbertus of Bruges and, until 1794 the town was part of a feudal domain managed by the House de Lichtervelde. For many years Lichtervelde was the center of a major peat cutting area and over the years Lichtervelde has also been part of the Netherlands and France.

Lichtervelde is known for its cult of Saint Margaret. The church is devoted to Saint Jacob and lies on a pilgrimage route to Santiago de Compostella, Spain. The famous Callewaert accordions were produced here until 1940. The common language is West Flemish.

GPS Coordinates: N51.0278 E3.1439

A local boy interested in the German defensive weapons

LICHTERVELDE'S OCCUPATION STORY

On May 10th, 1940 the village awakened with the nasty news that the Germans had invaded Belgium. On the radio there were warnings of what to do and what certainly not to do. Good news for the kids: schools were closed. Belgian and French troops came and went. Bunches of refugees trailed west towards the French border. Now and then a couple of Stukas showed in the blue skies, exploring or unexpectedly attacking a suspicious target.

The weekend of May 25th and 26th was threatening; there was a strong feeling that Lichtervelde would soon be in the line of fire. Monday, May 27th was a frantic day: Belgian troops were caught in an air attack with seven casualties as a result. In the afternoon there was the sound of gun fire, at first from afar, then closer. In the evening everything turned calm again. Calm before the storm of tomorrow? The night was spent in the air raid shelters and lost Belgian soldiers and fleeing civilians tried to sleep in the garden in front of the church and in the front yards of houses.

On the morning of May 28th a lieutenant came to wake the neighborhood with the announcement that the King had capitulated and that the Germans might already be in the village within the next hour, which is what happened.

A large limousine with German officers, swastikas everywhere, and a group of young foot soldiers appeared in the marketplace which, in no time, got filled up with all kinds of war material. Trucks with food, clothing, leather and shoes were continuously driven in – and scarcely guarded. So they were soon marauded by the villagers.

They were neat and clean boys, those "Fritzes" with shining boots; they were considerate and decent. A textile shop with a huge stock of skirts, blouses, summer and winter dresses was immediately bought up by the Germans. Everything was directly sent to the Heimat for the Mutter, Schwester or das liebste Mädchen. Apparently, there was not so much wealth across the Rhine.

Belgian weapons collected on the market

Occupying troops came and went for long or short periods: for rest, reorganization or preparation of a new attack. "Einquartierung" of soldiers in schools and halls was common. The soldiers behaved reasonably well, apart from the odd excess or orgy. Pubs with young daughters behind the bar were very much in demand. The better ones were reserved for the Officers, the poorer ones for the common soldiers. The "Dreimädchenhaus" establishment was the place to be. The girls that worked there had to pay dearly for their unseemly behavior after the war. The local cinema, at that time not accessible to civilians, provided soldiers with recreation in the evening while others relaxed with the families they were billeted with. Friendships grew and after the war many of them returned to Lichtervelde.

Nevertheless, the people saw on it all sadly: Germans remained Germans, occupiers with a hellish list of "New Order" measures. The forced provisioning by the occupiers made bad blood and the black market flourished. Every week hordes of people came from Brussels to Lichtervelde by train to buy a little stock of food for a lot of money, but often their acquired treasure was seized and confiscated in random searches, not by the Germans but by civilians working for the provisioning service. Even a German soldier took part in the black market. Weekly he went with his company to Ghent for swimming and every time he took in his bag a small stash of bread, meat and the likes to provide the friends of his friends.

Lichtervelde had an important railway station with connections in four directions. Of course it was busily used by the German army, especially for transport to the coast and the Atlantikwall. This had not escaped the attention of the RAF and as regularly as clockwork the station was under attack from the air and by machine gun fire. Frequently there were civilian casualties: passengers, travelers or local residents. Deep fear for what might yet have to come was an incentive for the renewal of an intense religious life. Churches were filling up and at the many neighborhood chapels there was daily singing, praying and begging to be saved from greater evil. If this had any effect we cannot know but the fact is that the invasion in 1940 and the liberation in 1944 went rather smoothly after all.

THE TRAGIC DEATH OF MAYOR CALLEWAERT AND TWELVE COMPANIONS

In the first weeks after the invasion it seemed as if nothing would be put in the way of the invader. Yet, slowly some resistance, inspired by uneasiness about the imposed regime, was cropping up. Passive resistance would turn into fighting resistance from sabotage to military operations. The local resistance, started in secret in December 1941, was also looking for weapons and guns and pistols were bought and traded underhand. Careless talk and shrewd undercover agents often led to tragic results.

Thirteen citizens, including Mayor Callewaert, were accused of illegally possessing fire arms and ganging up against the German state and were sentenced to death. The sentences were executed by guillotine on June 15th 1944 at the prison of Wolfenbüttel, Germany. The death of thirteen executed fellow villagers together with that of five NN-prisoners who perished in various concentration camps made deep wounds that have not been forgotten.

A 1945 memorial to the residents who died
during the war or were taken to prison

The Lichtervelde town hall

LIBERATION AND RECOVERY

It had been brewing for months: the Allies were coming. Since the successful landing in Normandy, old, withered Michelin maps of France were dug up, glued onto a plank or some cardboard and pricked with needles which were connected by red threads to visualize the advancement of the Americans and the British but it took quite a while before Brussels and Paris were liberated.

At the beginning of September 1944, things sped up. German troops marched over the market place moving east, a shabby army on the run, on foot, on stolen bikes, on old creaking carts drawn by decrepit stolen horses. Was that all that was left of the proud "Heer" of four years ago?

On September 7th 1944, before noon, booming of guns was heard, coming from the southwest, just as in 1940. At nightfall the booming stopped. It got creepily still. Families and neighbors spent the night together in the shelters, providing themselves with bread and water in case things might last longer.

The next morning, a young man came to the marketplace with the big news: tanks with soldiers in khaki uniforms had been seen 2 kilometres from the town centre; the English had arrived! Afterwards, they appeared to be Polish. Never mind, nobody cared. An hour later, the first British tank showed on the marketplace, followed by another one, and then another one . . . The liberation was a fact!

Joy all over the place. The marketplace got crowded. Local resistance groups took control to start the long awaited cleanup. Those who had collaborated or were suspected of having collaborated with the enemy would have to bear the consequences. The arrests, just or not, were countless. After four years of bitter grief, justice had to be done.

An aerial view of the village

OUR VILLAGE TODAY

Recently the population of Lichtervelde has noticeably increased, growing to 9,000 residents today. Mainly a residential town, this growth has to do with Lichtervelde's central location, in the immediate proximity of important traffic arteries and the railway station at which two significant railway lines cross.

Lichtervelde is a town with a bustling social life and many fairs and festivals are enjoyed by residents and visitors alike. Important are the Margaretha Fair in July and the Kermes and biennial Folklore Festival, both in September. Lichtervelde also boasts of having one of the last surviving town cinemas in Belgium which has existed since 1924.

Tourism is also growing importantly, owing to the reforesting of the Huwijns woodlands in the 1990s where there are B&Bs, a camp site for youth and a dairy farm.

Since 2007 the municipality has twinned with the C.C.R.A. (Communauté de Communes de la région d'Audruicq) in France, bringing a new dynamism to the community.

*More info about Lichtervelde can be found on the town's official website: **www.lichtervelde.be**. For more information about Lichtervelde's many attractions, please visit **www.lichtervelde.be/contact-toerisme**.*

These texts were prepared by Modest Maertens, the translations by Werner Cornil and supervised by officials Mayor Ria Pattyn and heritage official Luc Haeghebaert. The photos are from library and local history society collections.

The liberation of Lichtervelde by Polish soldiers

LIMBOURG BELGIUM

Province: Liège   Pop. 1940: 6,000   Pop. 2020: 6,000

SITING & HERITAGE

Limbourg sits on a hill close to the German border between the agricultural boccage area of Herve and the beautifully-forested hills of the Ardennes massif region. Because it was the capital of the Duchy of Limburg it was the source of the name for the Belgian and Dutch provinces of Limburg. Victor Hugo was impressed with our valley which, after visiting, he called 'the most beautiful one I have ever seen in the world'.

Indeed, today Limbourg is classified as an Exceptional Heritage of Wallonia and holds the title of Most Beautiful Village. Limbourg has a long and storied medieval history and many centuries-old stories. The villages of Bilstain, Dolhain, Limbourg, Goé and Hèvremont form the municipality of Limbourg. Dolhain retains its history of the wool industry and Bilstain, Goé and Hèvremont equally preserve their authenticity as well as their wonderful natural settings.

GPS Coordinates: N50.6204 E5.9419

Mes années de guerre, Raymond Lejeune

Bilstain Tunnel. The body of M. Marcel Hendrick, voluntary firefighter, was buried under the ruins.

Chronique de la Libéation de Goé Roger PROPS

Exodus of the inhabitants, May 1940

Customs office at the Rue des Écoles in Dolhain

OUR TOWN'S OCCUPATION STORY

The Invasion. On the 10th of May, 1940 many plane flights flew over the villages and during the early hours, the bridges of the locality were destroyed so as to prevent, or at least slow down, the enemy arrival. This is also the exodus time for many civilians.

A New Border. On the 6th of June 1940, a border cuts Bilstain in two territories: the first one remains Belgian but the other one is annexed to Germany. The village has to adapt to that new organization: a part of the population is "on the other side." The church and the school stay in Belgium and some farmers note that their fields are situated on both sides of the border. The new German citizens stand up to directives and face diverse pressures.

Another frontier is also set up at the Béthane bridge, annexing a part of Goé. The third border is Rue des Écoles in Dolhain, at the limit with the locality of Baelen.

Incorporation Into the German Army. The Germans started the mandatory enlistment of men from annexed territories into the Reich army. All of them were against it and tried to cross the border to find shelter in Belgium. At the risk of their lives, smugglers led at nights numerous young people intended to be incorporated into the Wehrmacht.

Rationing and the Food Supply. Life doesn't offer the same advantages on each side of the border. On the Belgian one, food is very scarce, incredibly expensive and with severe rationing. The civilians get organized to face restrictions, create a black market and cross borders in order to get help from the annexed villages. In order to coax villagers and get their sympathy, the Germans give the inhabitants extra rations and white bread.

Life gets slightly better thanks to the "Winter Help". In Goé, soup, coal and biscuits supply took place in the Thibert Castle in exchange of stamps given by the town hall.

A dilapidated house in Bilstain (once situated at the crossroads "La Grappe" and the so-called place "Les Hayettes") had been turned into a depot to stock the potatoes seized from the smugglers by the German customs officers. Villagers kept an eye on this stock and organized the removal and transportation of the precious tubers before a German lorry would be able to take them away.

The Resistance. In spite of the potential risks, many of the local inhabitants join the Resistance to help with the transport of escaped military and civilian war prisoners, the sabotage of German machines and equipment, the delivery of underground mail and efforts to gather information that would be valuable to the Allies, anything to slow down the enemy.

TWO SPECIAL LIMBOURG STORIES

A Heroine from Dolhain Gets the Cross of the Legion of Honour.

The resistance networks count on numerous vital actors at each stage of the process including those residents who hide the runaways for one night, those who find clothes and food during these harsh times, those that can provide papers and those that can provide supply cards. If any of these contributors are exposed, terrible consequences are likely. Resistance member Jeanne Herquet was especially at risk.

Mrs. Jeanne Herquet particularly distinguished herself, earning the Cross of the Legion of Honour in 1946. This heroine from Dolhain and her collaborators Mr Henri Van Brackel, Mr Camille Pyre (both of them from Dolhain) and Mr Julien Delaval, helped by all the agents of the organization from Dolhain, Goé, Baelen and Welkenraedt, planned the escape and repatriation of 1,187 war prisoners who were held in camps, the network reaching as far as France. After the war, in 1946, to reward the organization's many acts of bravery, Mrs. Herquet and her organization were decorated with France's highest distinction, the French Legion of Honour medal.

The First Wedding Between Two American Soldiers.

On the 8th of December 1944, Limbourg was the witness of probably the first wedding between two American soldiers on Belgian soil. Russell Weisse of New Jersey, a First Lieutenant of the 207th Engineer Battalion, and Katherine Wright, a native of Kentucky and a First Lieutenant of the 5th Semi-Mobile Evacuation Hospital, got married in Limbourg.

The bride & groom

Aged about twenty, far from their relatives and immersed in the war atrocities, the fiancés exchanged their vows at the town hall on Saint-Georges Square, surrounded by the inhabitants of Limbourg who joined the event. The young couple was given a picture of the building upon which "Best Wishes" text had been written in English.

LIBERATION & RECONSTRUCTION.

The percentage of damaged buildings amounted to 42% in Goé, 9% in Limbourg/Dolhain and 8% in Bilstain. Many bridges had to be rebuilt.

The Cockerel of the Dead Memorial. Created in 1920 by the architect Charles Vivroux and the artist Gaspar to commemorate the victims of the First World War, the monument (which was one of the first inaugurated in Belgium) showed a proud cock standing on a German helmet, looking towards the East.

The proud cock symbol was amputated by the German army during the Second World War. To replace it, a temporary wooden cockerel was sculpted by and set on the stele by Alexis Springuel from Dolhain.

It is true that the sculpture had a lesser aesthetic value but the move was strong and symbolical. It wasn't until 1957 that, thanks to the help and the generosity of the population, a concrete cockerel replaced the wooden one and in 1959 a bronze replica was installed.

The three phases of the monument during the war

The original monument   *The amputation*   *The wooden cock*

OUR TOWN TODAY

A perfect balance between charm, history, nature, discoveries and oddities, the city of Limbourg is a top-grade destination to escape from everyday life. The specific richness of each village in the municipality has been preserved, including an intact nature, a rural and peaceful character and a very important association life.

Photo: Bernard Delhez

The church of Limbourg on its rocky promontory

The beautiful Limbourg countryside

The Limbourg area has always been dynamic, creative and enterprising. In the past, the Limbourg area developed thanks to the wool and the wood industry. Today, many companies have emerged, such as the firm Corman, globally known in the agri-food field.

One of Limbourg's welcoming streets

The Limbourg area has numerous festive events throughout the year such as the carnival, the night jogging, the Dolympiades, the flowers market and many more worth experiencing. Well-funded sports and cultural activities are also important for our residents.

The annual Carnival

*For more information about Limbourg and the local tourism opportunities in the Limbourg area, visit the municipal website: **www.ville-limbourg.be**.*

The City of Limbourg wishes to thank all who helped with the writing of these articles. We especially thank Mrs. Arlette Bebronne for her precious archives revealing forgotten stories; Mrs. Françoise Heine for her help in our search for our young American bride and groom; Mrs. Caroline Grotenclaes for her English translations and Katleen Van den Broeck for her Dutch translations. Photos courtesy of the Municipality of Limbourg.

NANDRIN BELGIUM

Province: Liège   **Pop. 1940: 2,800**   **Pop. 2020: 6,000**

SITING & HERITAGE

Nandrin is a rural community located in a region called Condroz, derived from the name of a Celtic tribe quoted by Julius Caesar in his work *The Gallic Wars*. Situated at an elevation of about 230 m and located 25 km from Liège in eastern Belgium, the language of the population is French. Nandrin is composed of four villages: Nandrin, Saint-Séverin, Villers-le-Temple and Yernée-Fraineux, all of which are still mainly agricultural although many new residential areas have been created since the end of the 20th century.

Most of the farms consist of imposing buildings of chalky stones dating from the 17th century. The farmers raise Holstein cows and cultivate sugar beets, corn, wheat and rapeseed, whose luminous intensity of the flowers make the fields absolutely magnificent in the spring. Villers-le-Temple is well-known as the location of the remains of an important Commandry of the Knights Templar and Saint-Séverin is famous for its Roman church of the 12th century.

GPS Coordinates: N50.5072 E5.4198

OUR TOWN'S OCCUPATION STORY

When the Germans invaded Belgium, on May 10, 1940 some inhabitants left the village to seek refuge in France. Resident Louis Delrée of Villers-le-Temple was 12 years old when the first German soldiers arrived in Nandrin where they established their quarters in a quarry called La Forge, in Villers-le-Temple.

Mr. Delrée remembers that in all of our villages, the Germans requisitioned the schools and rooms in the inhabitants' homes to shelter their soldiers, that the Germans commandeered many cows and horses and that soon all decisions made by the local authorities had to be approved by the Germans.

The houses after the reprisal of 6 September 1944

Mrs. Odette Lamer of Nandrin remembers that the inhabitants avoided contact with the German army as much as possible because they feared them, and that the local authorities were compelled to establish a list of the young men the Germans could send to Germany as compulsory workers, which they often did. The Mayor of Nandrin had false identity cards made up for young male residents to prevent them from being sent to Germany as compulsory workers.

Getting food was the main worry of the inhabitants because food was rationed. As soon as 1941 the population received food stamps from the Germans for very meager amounts of bread, meat, sugar (1 kg), butter (250 gr) per month per person, forcing the villagers to take whatever measures were necessary to obtain the food they needed.

Local compulsory workers under close surveillance

Residents would even raise pigs in their cellars for fear the Germans would confiscate them for their own use. Residents grew potatoes and vegetables in their gardens and bred chickens and rabbits, often using them to barter for things they needed. A black market progressively developed and the prices of food and other supplies increased dramatically.

The farmers suffered less from shortage of food and the local farmers made a major effort to supply milk to the schools during the entire occupation. Many city people came to our villages to buy foodstuffs from the farmers because they couldn't find them in the city shops or because they had become too expensive to purchase on the black market. They took many risks doing this.

A German observation post in Villers-le-Temple

The Germans regularly searched the passengers of the streetcars for illegally purchased food. One day there was a serious clash between the passengers and a German soldier on a streetcar because the soldier had been too zealous while searching a woman for illegal food. The local authorities as well as rich local farmers organized patrols to protect the crops and the cattle in the meadows from the thieves.

The local residents interviewed for this project generally stated that the Germans usually behaved correctly as long as they were not in danger. On the other hand, when the SS arrived they behaved badly and aggressively toward the residents.

Our residents interviewed for this commemorative book project remembered that local plays were performed in the Walloon dialect in order to raise money to buy wool that could be knitted into socks for prisoners in Germany.

RESISTANCE AND MEMORIES

The resistance in our villages occurred in secret. Numbers of Allied airmen were taken care of and provided with identity cards stolen from the town hall. One day the resistance members blew up an electric power tower. Our residents remember other things:

Jean-Marie Delmotte says that, on their own initiative, he and his brothers put sugar into the tanks of German vehicles and, though it was forbidden by the Germans under threat of death, people listened to the news broadcasts from London in spite of the Germans jamming the signal.

Louis Delrée from Villers-le-Temple states there was no major ill-treatment of the population because the mayor was a collaborator, even though he fought against the Germans during WWI. His two sons served at the Eastern Front and his daughter joined the German Red Cross. The mayor was shot dead by the resistance.

Odette Lamer from Nandrin states that a few, mostly poor women had love affairs with German soldiers. They were victims of despicable reprisals after the war. Mrs Lamer's husband, who was a member of the local resistance, tried to join the allied forces in England via France but was exposed by a supporter of the Vichy government. He was then sent to a prison camp but succeeded in escaping, returning to Nandrin.

LIBERATION & RECOVERY

On Tuesday 5 September 1944, a few members of the local resistance, lying in ambush along the road to Esneux, shot at a German military car and killed an officer. The driver however succeeded in escaping, unharmed. The next day, a column of soldiers accompanied by armed vehicles and light tanks returned to the scene of the shooting. It is not known whether they belonged to the dreadful division "Das Reich" or to a brigade in charge of repressing attacks which the Germans called terrorist attacks. They headed to the nearest hamlet of the attack which was called "Le Tombeu" and started first to shoot at the houses with their artillery and finally blew them up with dynamite.

They did not limit themselves to wrecking the houses after letting the inhabitants come out. They chose four men at random and forced them to go into a meadow. Because they dreaded what might happen, they tried to run away and were shot dead in the back. Another man was shot on the doorstep of his house while his aunt was killed as she was sitting in her kitchen.

Two days later, as the six coffins were lying in the church, a moving and solemn funeral was held and the first American soldiers were arriving in Nandrin. A monument was erected not far away from the spot where this tragedy took place in memory of these victims of barbary and human stupidity.

When the Americans arrived, the villagers gathered along the main streets and the children waved small Belgian and American flags. Everybody felt intense joy and relief deeply. The soldiers would throw instant coffee bags, chocolate, American cigarettes, oranges and chewing gum which was the most surprising discovery for the children.

J.M. Delmotte remembers the soldiers were very kind towards children. He also remembers that an American Indian soldier taught him how to clean and dismantle a gun which was very useful to him later when he became an officer candidate.

He adds: "When the Americans were quartered in our villages, the children were particularly surprised to meet colored people because they had never met any before".

The houses which had been destroyed at the time of the reprisal due to the killing of a German officer were only partly rebuilt. Today new modern houses have been built in the neighborhood and the owners perhaps wonder why their street refers to martyrs.

A tower of the ancient commandery in Villers-le-Temple

The 12th century Roman church in Saint-Severin

OUR TOWN TODAY

Our villages have many medieval and natural attractions for tourists and visitors. Villers-le-Temple owes its name to a powerful commandery built on the remains of a Roman villa by the knights Templar in 1257 of which two imposing towers and a part of the high walls can be admired. Inside the church is the impressive black tomb stone of the Great Commander Gérard de Villers, founder of the commandery.

Saint-Séverin proudly presents a beautiful 12th century Romanesque church which was built by Benedictine monks from Cluny. Inside there is an extraordinary baptismal font.

In Nandrin, opposite an ancient farm with a castle tower from the 12th century remains of an ancient castle, the town has constructed its beautiful town hall in present day style.

All of our villages provide the opportunity to discover our region by strolling along many sign-posted routes. At last, but not least, only one mile away from Nandrin, visitors will be deeply moved by the immense American cemetery of La Neuville (Pg.59) where thousands of young American soldiers lie who were killed in action to rid us of the Nazi tyranny. May they rest for all eternity.

For more information about the municipality of Nandrin, please visit the municipalities' official website: www.nandrin.be. For more information about the local area's tourism opportunities visit en.liegetourisme.be and www.eauxetchateaux.be.

This information was prepared by Andre Matriche, president of Patrimoine du Pays de Nandrin and approved by Mr. Michel Lemmens, Mayor of Nandrin. Photos courtesy of the municipality of Nandrin.

OPWIJK   BELGIUM

Province: Vlaams-Brabant   Pop. 1940: 9,500   Pop. 2020: 14,500

SITING & HERITAGE

Opwijk is a residential and rural municipality just northwest of Brussels in the northwest part of the province of Flemish (Vlaams) Brabant. The merged Municipality of Opwijk consists of the center, the hamlets of Nijverseel and Droeshout and the Submunicipality of Mazenzele. In the 12th century Opwijc is first mentioned as a part of the county of Flanders.

St. Paul's Church, (Sint-Pauluskerk), in the city center, holds some important cultural treasures such as the Gothic "kalvariegroep" and paintings by Gaspar de Craeyer and Hendrick De Clerck and sculptures by Antoon Faydherbe. More than 200 years ago agricultural Opwijk changed with the construction of provincial roads and in particular with the arrival of the Brussels-Opwijk, Kontich-Aalst and the legendary Leireken railways in 1879.

GPS Coordinates: N50.9717 E4.1869

OUR TOWN'S OCCUPATION STORY

The rationing office at the Liberation rally

The Invasion. On May 17, 1940 the first Germans reached Opwijk, preceded by light motorized reconnaissance units. Columns of refugees moving west passed through the village.

The Nazi Oppression. After the capitulation on May 28, 1940, the chaos subsided and life normalized under German occupation as much as possible. Refugees and Belgian soldiers returned and people learned to live with the scarcity of food and fuel, many requisitions, constant pass checks, stealing and sporadic investigations. On June 26, 1943 three heavy bells from St. Paul's Church were removed and taken away by the Germans, greatly upsetting the residents.

Being a rural municipality, an agricultural census was performed. To minimize the control and the requisitions of the occupiers, the land made available for agriculture suddenly shrank in surface area and food shortages occurred. The local population became inventive in smuggling the food necessary to make up for the draconian food shortages.

The Bombing of the Local Railways. During 1944, with the expected Allied invasion and the arrival of the liberation army, the Allied Air Forces, with the help of the local resistance, began concentrating on targeting the local railway network which was heavily used by the Wehrmacht. The Allied Air Force bombarded the Dendermonde -Brussels line at least four times from April 1944 until the time of the liberation.

The scenario was the same each time: a fighter plane circled the train to allow travelers time to get to safety and then the locomotive was repeatedly shot with on board guns. The Aalst-Londerzeel section was not spared either. In the evening of July 19, 1944, four fighter planes dove at a train and the locomotive was riddled and put out of service. Fortunately, there were no casualties or injuries to the residents. However, a few residents were killed on June 6, 1944 on "Steenweg" in Mazenzele after a few salvos were fired from a British plane.

KSA drummers at the Liberation rally

The Local Resistance. The local resistance was active, especially in sabotaging the railways. On 2 June 1944, a bomb exploded on the Aalst-Londerzeel railway line while two locomotives were passing each other, and on June 30, 1944 the same railway line was interrupted by explosives. On 4 June, 1944 service on the Brussels-Dendermonde railway line was interrupted because of two unexploded bombs and on 7 July, 1944 a bomb exploded during the passage of a passenger train. A second unexploded bomb on the parallel track was discovered and taken away. Fortunately, no reprisals followed these actions.

A key figure in the local organized resistance was Jean Meysman, born in Opwijk in 1908. At the outbreak of the war, Jean was a professional soldier with the rank of Assistant Lieutenant in the 13th Battalion of Fuseliers. During the 18 days of the invasion Jean became a prisoner of war but was able to return home on June 10, 1940. Jean then started the local branch of the Secret Army resistance organization, the largest resistance group in Belgium, becoming commander for the Londerzeel-Merchtem-Opwijk area for the remainder of the war. His remote home became a store of weapons, ammunition and explosives and importantly, Jean provided support to many people using his home, in particular downed Allied aircrews. **The story of Jean Meysman is told on the following page.**

The liberation procession on the 'Marktstraat' in Opwijk

A RECOGNIZED HERO OF OPWIJK

Jean Meysman

This story is told by Willy Meysman, the son of Jean Meysman, a courageous local resistance fighter and member of the Secret Army national resistance organization.

On the night of 27 August, 1944 the Gestapo carried out an extensive surprise raid on several houses in Opwijk. Eight residents are arrested along with two American pilots, Eugene Dingledine and Dick D'Nuncio Streett who were being hidden and assisted by Jean Meysman at his remote residence.

During the arrests, Jean was shot trying to escape and his residence was looted and badly damaged. Jean and the two American pilots were transported to Ghent where they were separated. Jean was soon sentenced to death at the Gestapo headquarters and transported to the Beverlo military prison in northeast Belgium, approximately 15 miles from the Holland border.

Soon afterwards, on 13 September, one day before the American liberation, a mass execution was scheduled and amid the chaos, Jean was able to escape, flee and hide with the locals in the area.

Following the liberation by the Americans, Jean was able to return home but physically severely damaged. Since the war had not yet ended, on 5 February, 1945 Jean returned to the regular Belgian Army, the Brigade Piron, where he continued to serve honourably until the May, 1945 surrender of Germany.

After the war ended, Jean Meysman received high English and American awards for his dedicated actions, some of which were personally presented to him by General Eisenhower. Jean is truly one of Belgium's great heros of WWII. After the war, Jean kept in touch with Eugene Dingledine and Dick D'Nuncio Streett. The correspondence between Jean, Eugene and Dick is now maintained in the local municipal Archives. Willy still vividly remembers the visits of pilot Eugene but Eugene hasn't been heard from since the Korean War.

LIBERATION AND RECOVERY

On 3 September, 1944 a retreating German army column in the area was heavily machine gunned by Allied fighter aircraft and Army trucks were attacked. German soldiers were hurt and a few local houses caught fire and burned.

On 4 September 1944, the first British soldiers passed through Opwijk, liberating the municipality. Tricolor Belgian flags immediately appeared on the building facades, and resistance fighters finally became visible and known. Unfortunately though, there were still a few scattered building facades with swastikas.

On September 17, 1944 the city council and the K.S.A. planned a liberation party that included solemn thanks and a procession. A week later, the football season was opened with a match between S.K. St. Paul (S.K. St.-Paulus) and the English Army R.A.S.C.

It wasn't only London that was terrorized by the German Vergeltungswaffe 1, the flying V1 bomb. Liège, Brussels and especially Antwerp also got their share. During the period November '44 to January '45, seven flying bombs struck Opwijk, luckily in an uninhabited area in Droeshout, Nijverseel and Eeksken. There were no casualties, but there was damage to homes.

On July 25, 1948 the Opwijk St. Paul's Church received three new bells, paid for by the village community. During the 1950s and 60s, new stained glass windows for St Paul's Church were provided with the recovery payments received for the stolen bells.

© Wim Robberechts/Municipality of Opwijk

Park Hof ten Hemelrijk

© Wim Robberechts/Municipality of Opwijk

De Dries in Mazenzele, owned by the "Sint-Pietersgilde"

OUR TOWN TODAY

Opwijk is a vibrant community with strong trade and manufacturing including the Affligem Brewery and the New Manta.

Opwijk is known and recognized for its wide range of schools serving a variety of various educational networks. In particular, the monastic order of St. Vincent de Paul (St. Vincentius à Paulo), founded in Opwijk in 1848, was the origin of the concept for normal schools all over the country and was important to the development of Catholic education in Opwijk.

Special initiatives such as the Saint Paul's Horse Procession (Sint-Paulus Paardenprocessie) and the Nijdrop Youth and Music Center also contribute to this.

Opwijk has a very active community center and a rich social association life, offering the residents many opportunities for socializing and relaxation. These facets, together with a good location near Brussels, have led to significant population increases, especially becoming popular with Brussels commuters who are looking for rural tranquillity Opwijk offers.

Residents can go to the beautiful Hof ten Hemelrijk Municipal Park where a tourist information point provides information about the area's extensive, well-marked hiking and cycling routes along a number of beautiful nature reserves such as Kravaalbos, Dokkenevijver and the ecologically framed waiting basin. An especially interesting tourist cycling route, known as the Leireken, crosses Opwijk.

*For more information about the municipality of Opwijk, please visit the town's official website: **opwijk.be**. For more information about the area's recreational opportunities, visit* **https://groenegordel.toerismevlaamsbrabant.be/catalogus/ gemeenten/opwijk.**

This information was graciously prepared by Nancy Meersman, Opwijk Archives Administrative Assistant and the volunteers. Except as noted, photos courtesy of the municipality of Opwijk.

PEER BELGIUM

Province: Limburg   **Pop. 1940: 6,000**   **Pop. 2020: 16,500**

SITING & HERITAGE

The city of Peer is a small rural municipality in the province of Limburg. The area has been inhabited since prehistoric times, a large site recently discovered from the Iron Age. Originally, in the 5th & 6th centuries Peer belonged to a Frankish (Germanic) domain and a triangular market square, typical of Frankish towns, is preserved to this day.

During the 14th century Peer grew due to the local cloth and wool industry and was designated a "Good Town" and walls and a town hall were built, the oldest in the Limburg province. However, during the 15th century a civil war claimed the lives of many of the town's residents and the town continued to suffer from war and plundering up to the 18th century. Peer experienced significant growth again during the 20th century when coal mining began in the Limburg province. Always a rural community, Peer has retained its rural charm to this day.

GPS Coordinates: N51.1331 E5.4535

The City of Peer around 1940

Members of the Resistance in Peer

Liberation of Peer by the British 2nd Army

OUR TOWN'S OCCUPATION STORY

The Invasion: The speed with which Nazi Germany conquered Belgium caused fear and panic. On the 11th of May the Germans met little resistance in Peer. The Germans first arrived around noon from Peer in Wijchmaal. They drove through the village by bicycle, "borrowing" bicycles of the people in exchange for a statement on paper. These first Germans were disciplined and friendly. They were soon followed by a large column of motorcyclists that had been held up by the Bollisserbeek bridge which had been blown up by Belgian soldiers.

In the afternoon, heavy trucks arrived as well as large numbers of wagons and carts pulled by horses. By evening, the population heard a frightening rumor that the Germans were coming around to "take all the men". Indeed, around seven o'clock PM, Feldgendarmen went from house to house and took out all the men yelling: "Come with me! The bridge must be repaired."

The next morning, Pentecost Sunday, a large mass of German infantry arrived singing marching songs. Everyone was scared and felt unsafe. The experience from the 1914-1918 war was still fresh in our memory, so the people took precautions and began to hoard. All stores were bought empty and food, clothes and anything available was stored in safe places, for later. The war to end all wars had arrived again.

A Military Administration: The Mayor, Aldermen, the Municipal Secretary and Police Commissioners had to resign their office permanently and were replaced by collaborating War Mayors. There was an 11 PM curfew for citizens, and the cafes and restaurants had to close at 10.30 pm. Only the Commander could grant exceptions to these rules. Houses and all other buildings had to be darkened so that no light could be seen, not even on the sides of windows and doors. Patrols went around the town to control the civilians. Designated shelters were installed in case of a bomb attack.

Mandatory Employment and Raids: The occupiers first promoted "voluntary employment" in Germany, but had little success in getting volunteers. On 6 September, 1943 an Order was issued requiring Service Duty by everyone, and all men were summoned by age group. The Military Police could no longer control the large mass alone, so a civil investigation service was set up, the Zivilfahndungsdienst. Manned by volunteers from the New Order, not in uniform but armed, they were called the Belgian Gestapo.

They would raid cafes, sports events, fairs, and other places where men assembled. All men were checked to see if they were working, or if they were a "job refusal." The largest Limburg raid took place on the 13th August 1944 in and around Peer. Three hundred suspects were brought into custody in Peer for investigation. Most were allowed to return home, but those who were "job refusals" were put on transport to Germany, and most never returned.

Bell Harvesting: In March 1943 the Germans started the the "Glockenaktion," taking bells from town buildings. Peer residents protested by ringing the church bells constantly, but that didn't help. One bell was removed in Wijchmaal, one in Linde-Peer, and two in Peer. After the war only one bell was found in Wijchmaal. The stealing of church bells was widespread with more than 175,000 church bells stolen throughout the occupied countries, of which 150,000 were destroyed.

A SPECIAL PEER STORY

Lt. Freddy Limbosch
Belgian SAS Paratrooper

Freddy Limbosch *was a Belgian Officer during World War II, serving with the Belgian SAS Paratroopers participating in the battles in Normandy.*

On 5 September 1944, during Operation Caliban, a squad of SAS Paratroopers, led by Lieutenant Limbosch, was parachuted behind the enemy lines at Peer to gather intelligence about the enemy.

On 8 September, Limbosch noticed that the Germans had sent considerable reinforcements to the front, and he decided to inform the Allied Command of this. He sent two SAS Parachutists towards the British lines, but when important new developments occurred shortly thereafter, he decided to inform the Allied Command himself, and left in full daylight, with a guide.

During this trip he stumbled upon an organized German position and tried to travel around them along their flank. However, he was discovered and decided to break through the enemy lines while firing his rifle. In the attempt, he was hurt and chased by the enemy. At the point where he was going to be overtaken, he told his guide to run away.

Limbosch refused to surrender but was only able to stop the enemy temporarily. After he had emptied his last cartridge holder, he was hit in the chest by a machine gun. In his memory a monument was erected with two granite plates with the inscriptions: LIMBOSCH / MELSENS, between which two wings with parachute: CAPTAIN FREDDY LIMBOSCH/KILLED IN ACTION/ 8TH-9-1944.

LIBERATION AND RECOVERY

Liberation. On September 10, 1944, the English came from Hechteren to surround the Germans, who were still fighting in Hechtel. Fierce fighting occurred, especially at 't Heike and at the railway station, but the western part of Wijchmaal was liberated. Several Germans were killed, as well as an English officer.

That same day, the first ten reconnaissance vehicles of the English arrived in Kleine-Brogel. On September 11, Peer, Grote-Brogel and Kleine-Brogel were liberated without any notable resistance.

Recovery. At the end of the war, the Allies installed a temporary airfield in Kleine-Brogel with the code name 'B-90'. The site, which did not yet have a paved runway, was used as a base for military operations during the last months of the war. After the war, the Allied forces transferred the air base to the Belgian army, which in 1953 accommodated the 10th Tactical Wing of the Belgian Air Force.

Today, "The Base", as it is popularly called, houses the Belgian Air Force's famed 31st Tiger Squadron. When the squadron was formed after the end of the Nazi war, the first flights of the Squadron were flown using the legendary World War II British Spitfire. For more information about the 31st Tiger Squadron visit: www.31tigersqn.be/.

Bicycle street passing by Peer's 1637 town hall

OUR TOWN TODAY

Today, Peer is a thriving rural community of around 16,500 inhabitants. Because of the charming historic city center, the Erperheide Holiday Park and the extensive network of walking, cycling and riding trails, Peer is one of the most important tourist destinations in Flanders for both the adventurous and families alike.

Tourists visit Peer for the peaceful charm, the beautiful landscape and especially the cosiness that is typical of this region. Snow Valley is an important local attraction. It has one of the largest indoor ski slopes in the region, with a total length of 300 meters. The largest blues festival in Europe, Blues Peer, has been held in Peer since 1985. For more information visit: www.bluesfestival.be/en/.

The 31st Tiger Squadron of the Belgian Air Force

Many rural bicycle routes exist around Peer

*For more general information about Peer, please visit Peer's official website: **www.peer.be**. To learn more about Peer's long and interesting history please visit **www.widdenog.be**. For more information about Peer's tourism opportunities please visit **www.peer.be/thema/3141/toeristisch-onthaal***

This information was prepared by the Peer Local Historical Circle (Heemkundige Kring Peer) and the city of Peer. Special thanks to Thomas Schonkern for his coordination efforts. Photos courtesy of the municipality of Peer.

PÉRUWELZ BELGIUM

Province: Hainaut   Pop. 1940: 8,100   Pop. 2020: 17,000

SITING & HERITAGE

A city with a rich economic past, Péruwelz is located along the Verne Noire river which flows west to join with the Schedlt on its way to Antwerp and the North Sea. First mentioned as Pereweis during the 11th century, throughout the middle ages the border town of Péruwelz experienced many tumultuous times. Lying on an important road axis linking Ghent to Valenciennes, industrialization at the end of the 18th century resulted in the creation of more than 20 woolen stocking factories, tanneries and dressmakers. Today the municipality consists of nine towns and villages.

The medieval village has a local bourgeoisie area exhibiting past wealth through sumptuous residences which generally have a landscaped park with a water feature and settings that blend in well with the surrounding nature, including the Bonsecours forest, wetlands, ponds and marshes.

GPS Coordinates: N50.5107 E3.5936

A group of resistance fighters in Péruwelz
(private source)

Ceremony for two members of the Secret Army who died during an operation
(Private Source)

Arrival of the Allies in Wiers (Private Source)

OUR TOWN'S OCCUPATION STORY

Resistance. The proximity to the French border allowed the Péruwelz region to be developed into an area for accessing England, and networks were soon woven in the area to provide accommodations to help people reach their destinations and to take actions against the occupier. Soon the resistance operations grew to become some of the most aggressive and organized resistance units in all of Belgium.

In August 1941, a regional group first calling itself "Houbar-Lelong" and then "La Phalange Blanche" decided to go further in the fight against the occupier by organizing punitive actions against Rexists who were Nazi collaborators. During one of these actions, two German police officers are killed which leads to the dismantling of the resistance network and the hunt for its members who almost all lose their lives.

Now cautious, resistance fighters structure themselves and become more organized. From then on, three groups worked in Péruwelz: the Armed Partisans, the Secret Army and the War Office (Group G). Even though their missions are very different from one another, their common point is the establishment of escape chains intended for prisoners (Belgian and Russian) or downed airmen (American, English and Canadian) fallen to the ground, and the accommodation of resistance fighters, refractories and Jews. They also publish an underground press (*Le Barbelé, Le Bon Combat* and *L'Union Fait la Force*).

The Body 21 group of the Armed Partisans retaliates hard against the occupier and the collaborators, detonating their properties and executing several Péruwelz Rexists. Some of the members are then forced to live in hiding and several members of the group are arrested and deported or executed. They also participate in sabotage activities ordered from London. On the eve of liberation, the British instruct them to destroy a German vehicle repair shop.

The "War Office", also known as Group G (Sector 31 - Péruwelz-Leuze-Renaix region), specialized in the evacuation of downed airmen and organizing itself into an important intelligence network, directly targeting the economic interests of the Nazis. They are aggressively targeted by the Germans and their members pay a heavy price. Seven are killed during the liberation of Péruwelz.

Their missions consist in gathering information on the movements of German troops and in providing assistance to the resistance. In 1944, they carried out sabotage operations on the German communication routes including the destruction of locks, high-voltage boxes, locomotives and railroads and even the destruction of a railway hub at the Péruwelz railway station.

In early 1944, the network lost several resistance fighters during an operation in Menen which had become infiltrated by the Germans and about 20 members are arrested. Some will not return from their deportation. In June, the Secret Army is told officially to support the arrival of the allies in Belgium and to disarm the other resistance networks. "Group G" is also placed under the sole command of the Secret Army to further coordinate all resistance activities against the Germans.

Cohabitation is however less harmonious with local Armed Partisans who, for example, do not hesitate to seize parachuted cargoes that were intended to supply the Secret Army.

HELP FOR A DESTROYED VILLAGE

During the Ardennes offensive (Battle of the Bulge), municipalities in the region of Malmedy and Saint-Vith were heavily damaged. Receiving no official aid, the delegate of Nives, Mr. Tasiaux, requested assistance from the mayor of Péruwelz on March 31, 1945.

The situation in Nives was catastrophic. Located just south of Bastogne, Nives was at the center of the German offensive. Previously liberated, American troops retreat from Nives and the Germans again occupy the village from December 22 to 25. On Christmas Day, the advance of the Nazi troops towards Neufchâteau is stopped and Nives became the first village to start the American offensive to liberate Bastogne. The fighting was terrible.

Cattle die in the flames, 23 houses are completely destroyed, 40 houses are severely damaged and many buildings are set on fire. In the town the inhabitants have no supplies and need everything (linen, dishes, kitchen utensils, pocket money, etc.).

The climatic conditions are very harsh during the 44/45 winter. The inhabitants are cut off from the world and they have to live in cellars and stables without fire for heat, without light and there was no correspondence between towns and villages because all of the roads were destroyed to not allow the movement of trucks.

Sensitive to this call, the City of Péruwelz "adopted" the small town of Nives with its 125 homes and its 545 citizens. On April 25, 1945, the Peruwelz subscription of 62,804.95 francs was given to the town of Nives and a large truck from Peruwelz heavily loaded with furniture, crockery, clothes and food reaches the town of Nives. The 458 eggs will arrive, in good condition for the preschool children of Nives.

LIBERATION AND RECOVERY

On Saturday September 2, 1944 the 5th US Armored Division (Victory) arrived from Valenciennes and took up position in the near-by Bonsecours Forest at Condé-sur-l'Escaut. With the organized withdrawal of German troops from the area towards the east, the Americans reached the Franco-Belgian border too quickly and had to wait for authorization to cross it.

At the end of the day, the resistance fighters already think they have been liberated and are arresting those wearing the uniform of the Rexist party who collaborated with the Nazis and the prisoners are brought to the Town Hall. To the contrary, during the night, three resistance fighters from the War Office resistance group will be shot dead by about fifty German soldiers and the shootings will continue in the municipal park and around the railway station.

In the morning, several resistance fighters and Germans were killed at Bonsecours and at the Barrière de Bury. At around 10 am, the 5th Armored Division (Victory) received authorization to cross the border to secure the surroundings and prepare for the arrival of the 2nd US Armored Division (Hell on Wheels) entering Rumes.

The first American motorcycle enters the city to the exhuberent and delirious cheers of the inhabitants. The Americans position an artillery battery at the Mont de Péruwelz just south of the town in order to pound a German entrenchment located in the wood of Beloeil.

The next day (September 4), threatened by a German column, the American soldiers, still deprived of their infantry, fell back to Valenciennes but then, to the relief of the inhabitants, English troops arrived from the north with significant resources (tanks, supply trucks and troops) and the territory is finally liberated. The residents now know that this terrible war and occupation are over.

The Neo-Gothic Basilique Notre-Dame de Bon-Secours Basilica, Peruwelz

OUR TOWN TODAY

Located in the south part of the Belgian area known as Picardy Wallonia with 17,000 inhabitants, Peruwelz is centrally located between Valenciennes, Tournai and Mons. Its particularity as a border town is reflected in its culture and customs. Even today, the proximity of France strongly directs the local economy.

In terms of heritage, the city contains large wealthy residences decorated with carefully designed parks. One of the main arteries of Peruwelz leads to the Bon-Secours Basilica, the silhouette of which can be seen from a great distance. This impressive neo-Gothic basilica houses a statue of the Virgin Mary which has been a pilgrimage destination since the 17th century.

A sanctuary overlooks the National Forest of Bonsecours, a former part of the great forest massif of Hainaut covering 1,200 hectares. Nowadays, hikers still enjoy using the eight large trailway systems laid out in 1753 by Emmanuel de Croy which is now managed by the Maison du Parc Naturel organization.

Another asset of the territory is the richness and extent of its unique wetland areas, The entire landscape around Peruwlz is shaped by pristine marshes and waters that include clear rivers and excellent fishing ponds. These beautiful natural areas are known for their large numbers of birds, both migratory and sedentary.

*For more information about Péruwelz, please visit Péruwelz's official website: **http://www.peruwelz.be**. For more information about the Péruwelz tourism opportunities, visit **http://www.plainesdelescaut.be/**.*

We appreciate the efforts of all those who prepared the information and provided photos for this commemorative event. The town of Péruwelz greatly appreciates their contributions. Photos courtesy of the Municipality of Peruwelz.

PUTTE BELGIUM

Province: Antwerpen   Pop. 1940: 8,000   Pop. 2020: 18,000

SITING & HERITAGE

Putte is located in a transition area between the region of Mechelse Groentestreek and the Zuiderkempen. The area of Putte has been inhabited since 1008. During the Municipal mergers of 1977, Beerzel and Peulis are added to Putte. Today Putte encompasses the sub-municipalities of Putte-Centre, Beerzel, Peulis and Grasheide.

For centuries, the Knights of Pitsemburg, a Christian order at the time of the Crusades, gathered together in Putte to hunt. The former town hall of Putte, a protected monument in rococo style, was built in 1748 and was used as hunting lodge by the Knights. The building was sold during the French Revolution, after which it served as a notary's residence. Later on, it was bought by the municipality, serving as the town hall from 1943 to 2010. Today, wedding ceremonies are still held there.

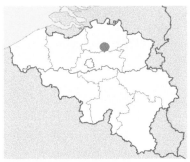

GPS Coordinates: N51.0549 E4.6287

A lonely man in a bombed Putte

The former town hall completely in ruins

The bells go back to the church

OUR TOWN'S OCCUPATION STORY

The Invasion. The construction of the Koningshooikt—Waver (KW) Line in 1939 puts Putte along the eastern and therefore hostile side of the "Iron Wall". Shortly after the German invasion, the Belgian army occupied this line to protect Brussels and fired artillery at Putte because the town was packed with Germans. The damage to the village was considerable.

The Church Bells Robbery. Not only food is claimed by the enemy during the war. Church bells are also wanted to melt them into weapons. The Saint Nicholas church in Putte counts three bells of 550 kg, 750 kg and 970 kg. In spite of the weight of these bells, the partisan resistance corps makes plans to hide them from the Germans. Their action on the night of 10 to 11 September 1943 will go down in history as the "De Klokkenroof", a fine example of guts.

But how can the partisans remove such heavy bells from the church tower unnoticed? The brothers Jules and Jozef Pauwels are familiar with the mechanism of timepieces in church towers so, with some allies, they figure out a method and a plan to remove and hide the bells.

On 10 September 1943 a truck with German soldiers entered the village. Several spectators approach and show their dissatisfaction with caution. The Germans open the lifting holes in the church tower, but stop their work in the afternoon temporarily.

Bell robbery memorial

Resistance. Now it must happen! At the first darkness and despite the imposed curfew, there is movement in the village. Shadows sneak past the houses to the church tower. Others dig a large hole behind the Forum room in the Poststraat. Still others are picking up a cart with rubber tires at Sus Corluy's. A last group is armed and on the lookout.

Everything runs perfectly, until a detached bolt falls down from the tower and hits Fonske Dockx in the face. Doctor Jules Cornil takes care of him while the action continues. The noise from the clattering metal can be heard from afar. (Today you can still see a damaged tile under the clock hole.) An alarmed "black" approaches the noise, but flees from the shots of the partisan guards.

The partisans succeed in silently hoisting the two bells onto the cart and transporting them to Poststraat, where they hide the bells in the pit and cover them with camouflaging crops. The theft of the bells was successful, but what will the reaction of the Germans be?

Reaction. The next day the German truck enters the village and stops at the church entrance. The men look surprised at the broken lock of the church door. Their mouths open even further when they only find the small bell in the tower. The Germans quickly take action and imprison a few people. The not always gentle interrogations do not have the desired result; nobody knows anything useful.

The German troops patrol the village; soldiers search in ponds and old loam wells. They find nothing, no offenders, no bells, nothing! The small bell, however, goes to the melting furnaces and never returns to the church. *Today however the bells hang back in the church tower where they belong, and they still sound the song of freedom.*

A BELOVED DOCTOR & RESISTER

Jules Cornil Death Card

Doctor Jules Cornil is born on January 17, 1907 in Lier. After his medical studies in Leuven, he marries Maria Theresia Vercammen in 1930; they have four children. In February 1934 the family settles in Beerzelhoek. Cornil is soon much loved and his Doctor's practice attracts many patients.

During the occupation, he dares to criticize the German presence in public which is not appreciated by everyone. Work refusers and people in hiding are hidden in Cornil's home. He also takes care of sick or injured partisans.

Following the killing of a "black" of Putte, a revenge action takes place by the Security Corps Verbelen, a group of Nazi collaborators. Some important people from Putte are put on the death list, including Dr. Cornil. They have to pay for their German aversion.

On May 1, 1944, Dr. Cornil takes care of hundreds of people after a bombing in Mechelen. The conscientious doctor returns home the next day, where he still continues to assist his own patients.

The following night the assassins of the Security Corps Verbelen stop in front of the Jules Cornils house. His wife looks through the window when she hears them kicking at the door and calling out "Aufmachen, Sicherheitspolizei!". She wakes up her husband, who calls the police before opening the door.

Three men enter the home; the latter has a machine gun. They order the doctor to get dressed to go to Brussels. His eldest son, Paul Cornil, then 12 years old, wakes up and looks straight into the machine gun. It is the last time he sees his father alive. The next day someone finds the lifeless body of Dr. Jules Cornil along the Mechelbaan.

LIBERATION AND RECOVERY

Liberation. Sunday morning 3 September, 1944. A few young people and members of the resistance lift the Belgian tricolour on the tower of the St. Nicholas Church in Putte. This is not without danger because German soldiers are still moving through the village towards "Heimat" (home). In the afternoon a few Putte inhabitants go to Sint-Katelijne-Waver because they hear that the Tommy's are on their way! *"They are already in Mechelen,"* it appears. The nervous murmur changes into an increasingly louder *"They are here!"*

And indeed, the first British motorcyclists and scouts enter the nearby village. The swelling crowd surrounds the soldiers and treats them to beer as they knock the dust off their clothes. Everyone is crazy with joy. Suddenly a crying out: *"Tanks, tanks!"*. In the distance the first colossi come rolling in; they were the famous "Desert Rats" with the image of a rat on the sleeve badge. The motorcyclists and scouts take the road to Putte and look for a bivouac place.

They will enter Putte on the 4th of September. The Belgian tricolour flies proudly over the village for the second day. Now it is official *"We are free!"*.

Yet for many families the liberation brings with it a double feeling, because many members of the resistance are still in German camps and prisons. They will not all return.

Recovery. The destruction will gradually disappear from the streets. People try to erase the memories with power and effort: rebuilding damaged houses, repairing bullet holes in the church, replacing the small missing bell. But what about mentally? Until today, the events of 75 years ago remain a sensitive topic of conversation. Pro and contra lived next to each other. Only the bullet impacts in the grille of the town hall will "survive" as silent witnesses.

The former Putte town hall

Aerial view of the Saint Nicholas church & the church square in Putte

OUR TOWN TODAY

Nowadays Putte is a lively municipality with more than 18,000 inhabitants. As a rural municipality, Putte can play a number of trump cards: farmhouses and farmlands, picturesque nature reserves, a fascinating cultural life, sports and recreational opportunities, a thriving middle class, playgrounds and much more.

To get to know the beautiful places in Putte, walking and cycling routes have been mapped out. Every year, a series of events takes place that draw attention to Putte's established values. Heemmuseum Het Molenijzer, which bundles numerous heritage aspects of the municipality and the old town hall are just a few of the many interesting locations that Putte has to offer.

The church square in the heart of the municipality, with the St. Nicholas Church in the centre, was renewed in 2017 and transformed into a cozy square, where both summer and winter events take place every year. In a very unique geological area of Belgium, the Beerzelberg nature reserve rises 51 meters above sea level, making it the highest point in the province of Antwerp.

As a bustling municipality, Putte works hard to bring its inhabitants together by promoting those common community values held by all residents. There is something for everyone; neither adults nor children will ever be bored in Putte. We invite you to visit our lovely community and meet our welcoming residents.

*For more information about Putte, visit the municipal website **www.putte.be/** and the official municipal Facebook page: **www.facebook.com/ GemeentePutte-189268428091266/**.*

With special thanks to Eddy Liekens for writing the texts, to Florent Van Vlasselaer for the fitting pictures, and to Sylvia Silvester for checking the translations. Photos courtesy of the Municipality of Putte.

RAVELS BELGIUM

Province: Antwerpen   Pop. 1940: 8,000   Pop. 2020: 15,000

SITING & HERITAGE

Ravels is a municipality in the north of the Belgian province of Antwerp. This municipality consists of three villages: Ravels (including Eel), Poppel and Weelde (incl. Statie). Within the Ravelian municipality three patron saints are visible: St. Servatius (Ravels), St. Micheal (Weelde) and St.Valentine (Poppel).

Originally, the way of life in the three villages was farming and agriculture remains important in Poppel and Weelde. In Ravels, a considerable amount of industrial development occurred because of its location along the major canal between Dessel and Schoten. Extensive archeological finds prove that the area of Ravels has been continuously inhabited since 4,000 BC when humans first became farmers. Ravels is famous for the many burial mounds in the area dating back to 1500 BC.

GPS Coordinates: N51.3712 E4.9938

OUR TOWN'S OCCUPATION STORY

The Phony War. Before the invasion, the people of the Antwerp province were unsure of what was going to happen next. Belgium was a neutral country but England and France had declared war on Germany soon after Germany invaded Poland on September 1, 1939. Called the "Phony War", things were relatively quiet until the morning of May 10, 1940.

The bridge of Ravels over the Potty River, readied for demolition

The Invasion. On May 10, 1940 the German bombing of Belgium and Holland began. The bombing lasted for days, causing much fear and the mass evacuations of many towns as the Germans advanced west towards the Belgian coast. On May 10 the bridge of Ravels was dynamited by the Belgian Forces to delay the German Forces. On May 11 evacuees on crowded roads were shot by German airplanes and bombs were dropped on schools and houses. On May 12, Pentacostal Sunday, heavy bombing devastated the Ravels hamlet of Weelde-Statie. The inhabitants of the village fled south to the nearby city of Turnhout.

French troops entered the area to fight against the approaching Germans with the Belgian army but the Belgian and French forces were not prepared for such a surprise, unparalleled attack. The Battle of Belgium was soon over.

The Occupation. From May 13 on, German soldiers occupied the area and the occupation began. The press was censored, Nazi propaganda and signs were everywhere, German soldiers appeared everywhere and the freedoms of the people were restricted. Soon, distrust of the occupier turns into avoidance, personal withdrawal and fear, the residents living their lives not knowing that their conditions would become worse each passing day. Life would become very difficult for our residents facing 4 years of constant fear and severe shortages.

The winter of 1941/1942 was incredibly harsh and very cold and many people had difficulty because of shortages of coal and food. In the spring, people learned that they could be told to report to any mandatory job the Germans demanded. During the summer, Jewish people were required to wear the yellow star and banned from public places. By the end of the summer Jews were being deported.

The Pain Before The End. Great anticipation and hope arrived with the news of the D-Day landings. When the Allies began the concentrated bombing of the Germans and their infrastructure to support the advance of the armies, it caused great harm to many small towns including Ravels and a new type of fear gripped the residents. The residents of Ravels prayed their liberation would come quickly.

The church tower in Poppel, damaged by English bombs

The destruction of the tile factory roof in Ravels

TWO WHO RISKED THEIR LIVES

Jef Vrijsen

*In the remote forests north of Poppel, in the hamlet of Nieuwkerk, stood a white farmhouse. Here lived **Jef Vrijsen**, his wife and six children.*

At great personal risk, Jef received refugees at his home and sometimes they spent the night at his farm when it was impossible to move on. When the situation was safe, Jef took them to The Burcht, a pub in the centre of Poppel. Most were French prisoners of war, Jews and crashed Allied pilots.

Miel Heykants

***Miel Heykants** was a farmer in Nieuwkerk. His farm was just a few yards from the Dutch border. He carefully developed a network of people he trusted who were able to deliver the refugees in hiding to their destinations, especially Portugal. At great risk, Miel was an especially important link in the rescuing, hiding and smuggling of downed allied aircrews back to England. From Miel's attic English spies observed German activities and in London Miel was known as a reliable link between the Netherlands and Portugal.*

LIBERATION AND RECOVERY

The western part of Ravels was liberated by the Polish under the command of the Polish General Maczek and the eastern part of Ravels was liberated by Canadian soldiers.

General Maczek

On October 1, 1944 there was heavy fighting at Weelde-Statie and houses were destroyed as a result of the Allied bombing of the Germans. Soon Polish tanks were seen approaching from the west.

On October 3 Weelde was liberated by "Polish Tommies". They brought bread, rice and raisins and there was great rejoicing in the streets. Then, along the canal, the first English soldiers, called the Polar Bears, were spotted with captured German prisoners of war, resulting in further joy and jubilation.

We were so happy and thankful and shared what we had. The soldiers gave us bread and chocolate and we gave them our last eggs and milk. Unfortunately the village of Poppel and the industrial areas were again damaged and destroyed by the fighting necessary to drive the Germans out of Ravels . . . But we were free again!

Canadian soldiers in Ravels after the Liberation

One of the local restored prehistoric burial mounds

The beautiful museum at the border, "T Kaske"

OUR TOWN TODAY

Ravels is a very green and rural place to live. About 30% of its almost 15,000 inhabitants are Dutch people who enjoy the tranquility here in Belgium.

In addition to the burial mounds, there are monumental buildings from more recent history, for instance: the castle of the estate "De Schrieken", the villa of the family de Jamblinne de Meux, the Carmel monastery Emmaus, the six Catholic churches and of course, "'t Kaske", the town hall of Poppel until 1977. Nowadays it's the local historical museum, run by a historical association, named after the Catholic saint Nicolaus Poppelius (canonized in the 19th century) who was born here in the 16th century.

Ravels is known for its extensive trailway systems for hiking, cycling and horse riding amidst the forest and meadows and Ravels has many modestly-priced accommodations and excellent local restaurants. We invite you to come and meet our friendly residents.

*For more information about the town of Ravels, please visit the municipal website **www.ravels.be/**. For more information about the tourism opportunities in the Ravels area, visit **www.toerismeravels.be**.*

Special thanks to Frank Konings and his collaborators of the Heritage Association Nicolaus Pollelius for their assistance in the preparation of this commenorative document. Photos courtesy of the municipality of Ravels.

SOIGNIES BELGIUM

Region: Hainaut   Pop. 1940: 16,000   Pop. 2020: 28,000

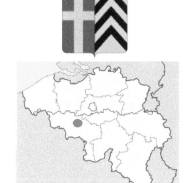

SITING & HERITAGE

A Francophone town in Belgium, located in a lovely green setting (Hainaut Province), between Brussels and Mons on the old Roman road, Soignies is home to more than 28,000 people and covers 110.3km². Recognized as a "European Centre of Bluestone", its history is profoundly linked to the mining of bluestone, whose roots date back to antiquity, examples of which can be found along every street and alleyway in Soignies.

A thousand-year-old town with a well-preserved historic centre, 11th century Romanesque church, fortifications and houses with classic façades, it is also packed with châteaux, farms and an idyllic countryside. Soignies maintains strong ties with its twinning city, Hazebrouck, France.

GPS Coordinates: N50.5766 E4.0706

© "Passeurs de mémoire"

Soignies railway station bombed

© "Passeurs de mémoire"

German units in retreat at the foot of the viaduct and the castle Savoye

© "Passeurs de mémoire"

SS units escaping from the Poche de Mons station at Place Verte

OUR TOWN'S OCCUPATION STORY

The Invasion. On 18 May, 1940 the Germans entered Soignies. The châteaux and mansions in the town centre became officers' homes and the main decision-making centres. The first Kommandantur moved into part of the Collège Saint-Vincent, while the Feldgendarmerie was based on Rue de la Station. The Athénée, on Rue Léon Hachez, became a German barracks. On the site of the current swimming pool, the occupiers set up a shooting range.

Oppression. Basic goods (like coal and bread) were rationed, wages were capped and assets were seized. Bread, stretched out with bran, became inedible. Shortages and rationing meant that all sorts of administrative processes were necessary, like queuing up every month to get stamps. Basic products (like butter, flour, potatoes and coffee) became prohibitively expensive, and hunger became the norm.

Although the occupying forces were very kind to the locals to start with, they became increasingly nervy. Fear took hold and the noise of boots would stay in the collective memory for a long time. Many workers from Soignies were deported to work in Germany. Some would never return.

The Resistance. Before long, the locals started to make plans to resist the Occupation. The Armée Secrète (AS or Secret Army) and the Front d'Indépendance (FI or Independent Front), the main active groups in Soignies, were very aggressive, disrupting German road and rail traffic, setting fire to crop transports, destroying telephone poles, attacking convoys, industrial espionage, surveillance of the Chièvres airport, developing escape channels and passing on the results of bombing attacks to the Allies. The local AS took delivery of more than 40 tonnes of military equipment parachuted into Saint-Marcoult between late 1943 and the Liberation.

The FI published an underground newspaper, *La Brabançonne,* printed on the same premises as the *Secours d'Hiver*, on the Place Verte. Actively involved in housing illegals and contributing to sabotage, from 1943 onwards, the FI coordinated its activities with the Partisans Armés (Armed Partisans.)

Two divisions of the Partisans Armés were formed in 1942 in the Soignies, Braine-le-Comte and La Louvière region, calling themselves the Corps 0/23. Their efforts included the theft of official documents and municipal government stamps from the Kommandantur in Soignies by members of the resistance dressed in German uniforms. They also stole food vouchers between Neufvilles and Soignies, by faking an armed attack with the collusion of our police officers.

Our Jewish residents. Some of the lesser known acts of resistance involved welcoming Jewish families or children known as "Enfants Cachés" (Hidden Children) who were often presented as young Spanish children who had fled the Civil War. Living typical family lives, they indirectly received support from the municipal authorities who drew up realistic false papers for them.

This dangerous activity often remained discreet and went under the radar. Risking their lives, some families (the Baucqs in Horrues, the Minors in Neufvilles, the Hosts in Chaussée-N-D-Louvignies), as well as the Franciscan Sisters, saved Jews and carried out the necessary formalities with the municipal authorities.

Bomb Attacks. As was the case for all Belgian towns, Soignies was bombed, but its historic centre was thankfully preserved, as the attacks mainly targeted the Chaussée du Roeulx, the areas around the railway station, Rue P.J. Wincqz and Rue Emile Vandervelde.

Marie Pilette

Marie PILETTE was 14 when war broke out. Her home in Horrues was used as a "postbox", a meeting venue for the Resistance and as a place to hide resistors. Marie soon became a courier for a major resistance network in Saint-Marcoult where her fiancé, Raymond Cappette, took part in the Saint-Marcoult air drops until his arrest. When Raymond was arrested, the Germans found a picture of Marie in his wallet. When they went to her family home, they discovered two deserters that she was hiding.

The Germans gave them the choice of sending Marie or her mother to go and see the Kommandantur in Soignies. Marie was 18 years old when she decided to go, because she had a younger brother who was 5. A solider reassured her, promising that she would be able to go home that evening. After being interrogated, Marie is arrested and sent on a truck to Mons Prison.

In Mons, Marie was then ordered onto one of 25 rail cars of prisoners and, after 3 days of travel, arrived in Germany September 1, 1944 at the Ravensbrück concentration camp for women. Known for the terrible cruelty at the camp, Marie was forced to work 12 hours per day at Siemens, making aeroplane parts. Several times a day, female prisoners are called out and made naked and humiliated, treated like animals, even receiving injections to suppress their periods so they could continue to work without having to wash. She continually sabotaged the work she was forced to perform.

In January 1945, the camp was bombed and the prisoners were sent on a death march towards the east during which they were liberated by the Russians. French & American soldiers then helped her return to Belgium. When Marie returned home on 15 May 1945, she was so thin that her mother did not recognize her. Two days later her fiancé returned home and they were married in 1946. After receiving many awards for her bravery, Marie lived a happy life with Raymond and their children. Marie passed away in 2015.

The Naast Bell

Stealing the Bells. On 10 May, 1940 the church bells rang every five seconds for three minutes to tell the people that the country was once again at war. Prohibiting the use of bells on 25 May, by 1943 the German arms industry had run out of raw materials and our churches' bells were removed to be melted down to make shells in spite of the residents' objections and resistance efforts to disrupt the requisitions.

The bells of Soignies and its 6 villages were removed from their churches and the villagers were saddened. In Naast, the bell was removed using a rope via the outside but the rope gave way and the bell fell to the ground. When the bell was replaced in 1948, the villagers were so excited that the bell was adopted by the boys' school who wrote a poem about it: "Le retour de notre cloche" ("Our bell is back"). After the liberation it was learned that more than 175,000 church bells had been stolen from the occupied countries.

LIBERATION & RECOVERY

Liberation. The Liberation of Soignies would last 3 days. On 3 September 1944, Allied reconnaissance units from the 1st American army and the British X XXth corps arrived in Soignies, the former from Mons and the latter from Enghien.

The next day, motorcyclists, Sherman "Firefly" tanks from the 2nd Household Cavalry British Regiment (Guards Armoured Division) and units from the American 113th Cavalry Group made their way through Soignies towards Braine-le-Comte.

5 September, 1944 would mark the Liberation of Soignies. The British came from Enghien and met the Americans in the Grand-Place, before leaving together to make their way towards Braine-le-Comte. There was chaos, indescribable jubilation, a moment of intense public joy! Everyone ran to the Hôtel de Ville, shouting "They're here!" The noise of the tanks rang out. Families had been making flags to put up in their window for 3 days. Their pride crushed, and surrounded by the Allies, the Germans beat a retreat. Many of them were practically children!

During this time, members of the resistance gathered in town. The tension was palpable. Skirmishes broke out. On 2 September, the last Germans to leave shot two youngsters from the Secret Army, Albert Plaetens and Victor Dupont.

On 3 and 4 September, two Resistance fighters from the Front de l'Indépendance, Georges Forton and René Baguet, were killed. Their companion, Edouard Vandercappelen, was killed fighting on 5 September.

Reconstruction. The victim of extremely aggressive bombing until just before the Liberation, leaving enormous craters, it took Soignies years to rebuild itself and even now, the scars remain.

The Town Centre with the Collegiate Church Saint-Vincent

OUR TOWN TODAY

Soignies and its 6 villages are home to all sorts of delights that are crying out to be discovered. A well-known rural town with a fantastic way of life, its main attractions continue to be its historic centre, its fortifications and its thousand-year-old Collegiate Church. Its façades bear witness to its rich past, with listed churches, châteaux (including the one in Louvignies adorned with its landscaped park), its quarries and its Bluestone Centre.

Alongside these stunning monuments, there are some authentic treasures for visitors to explore along various tourist routes. Walks and bike paths in the open areas make Soignies the perfect place for a wander.

Renowned for its vibrant and intense cultural activities, throughout the year, Soignies puts on all sorts of popular events, like its historic procession at Pentecost, its agricultural show, its Août en Eclats family festival, its Simpélourd procession and its Christmas onderland Féeries de Noël.

For more information about visiting the municipality of Soignies, please visit www.soignies.be.

Our sincere thanks go to the Protocol Department, from the Ville de Soignies, with the assistance of the Office Communal du Tourisme of Soignies, as well as the members of the "Associations Patriotiques Réunies de l'Entité Sonégienne" (A.P.R.E.S., patriotic organizations brought together by Soignies and its surrounding area), without whom these synopses could not have been compiled. Except as noted, photos courtesy of the Municipality of Soignies.

THUIN BELGIUM

Province: Hainaut   Pop. 1940: 6,500   Pop. 2020: 5,900

SITING & HERITAGE

Between Charleroi and the French border, the picturesque medieval city of Thuin is situated on a rocky spur at the confluence of the Sambre and Biesmelle rivers, a location that has been occupied since the Neolithic period. Following recent archaeological excavations, Thuin is now considered to be a major protohistoric site in northern Gaul.

Thanks to its favorable location, the city became a shelter for the Lobbes Abbey, an influential monastery in Belgium throughout the Middle Ages later the westernmost fortress (thanks to Notger-Prince Bishop) of the Principality of Liège, to which it belonged until the French Revolution. Taking advantage of the canalization of the Sambre River in the 19th century, an important ship-building industry flourished, which however was declining in 1940.

GPS Coordinates: N50.3408 E4.2873

OUR TOWN'S OCCUPATION STORY

The Invasion. Due to its proximity to the French border, Thuin saw French motorised convoys arrive on May 10th, later on followed by French colonial troops. That same day the first German bombs fell on the Maladrie hamlet in the early evening. During the following days, alarming news was received from the front by the first refugees from the eastern part of the country and by withdrawing French units. This news, and the closer and closer overflight of German airplanes, increased the tension among the population. The disorder in the city was beyond description. Many services (telephone, telegraph, trains) no longer operated properly.

The *coup de grace* was delivered on the 14th of May. After bombing evacuation trains in Lobbes (49 victims), around 6 pm, the area of the North station of Thuin was also destroyed. 5 people were killed, about 20 houses collapsed and some barges were sunk. These bombings, along with memories of the massacres of 1914 and orders to leave the city given by French units (preparing a new battle of the Sambre which, fortunately for the city, did not take place), those who had not yet left decided to join the cohort of refugees on the paths of the Exodus. By the arrival of the 'Boches' (nick name given to the Germans) on May 17th, 95% of the population had left the city.

A photo taken on 19 May, 1940.
The ruins are still smoking.
Elisa Colot Collection

Daily life. While some people were able to reach the South of France, most were quickly blocked by the advancing panzers, returning back to Thuin in the following days. On his return, the MP-Mayor Paul Gendebien was removed from his office on the pretext he had abandoned his post in May. He was replaced in October 1940 by a war Mayor of Rexist obedience. However, because he was surrounded by aldermen and a communal secretary concerned about the population, he had no harmful influence. He was too busy practicing the black market, the reason why he was finally arrested by the Germans themselves in 1943. Being near the frontlines, an Orstkommandatur was established in Thuin until the end of 1940. Afterwards only occupying troops would remain.

The black market was popular because everything was rationed and food was, as everywhere else, the main concern. Since they lived in a rural area and had the possibility of having a garden or marauding in the fields, the Thudinians only suffered marginal levels of starvation. The winters of '40-'41, '42-'43 and the summer of 1944 were nevertheless difficult periods due to poorer harvests and the increasingly harsh requisitions of the occupiers. It should also be noted that the folkloric Saint-Roch march in Thuin was suspended during these years of war.

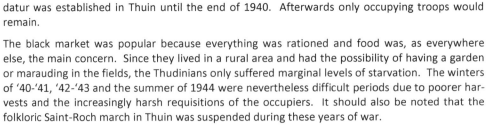
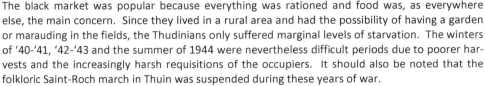

The Ville-Basse ('Lower Town'),
Thudinian's inland navigation paid a
heavy price during the war.
Elisa Colot Collection

Resistance. The Thudinians considered the occupation to be a burden and they complied without saying a word in order to avoid any trouble with the invader. However, as soon as the Reich imposed the *Service du Travail Obligatoire - STO* (mandatory work service), the resistance, essentially passive until then, would rise. Their focus was to hide the recusants to the STO and to help them by supplying them with food in their hideouts, thanks to stolen food coupons, etc.

Some Allied aircrews downed during their missions were also exfiltrated and some Jewish children were hidden by private individuals. The name of Victor Bohain is frequently mentioned when the resistance in Thuin was raised. As a communal secretary and founding member of the Secret Army in the region, he took part in several operations ordered by London, notably Othello, which consisted of reorganizing the Belgian agricultural sector as a resistance movement to supply food to the Belgian population.

Collaboration. Apart from the case of the mayor, and despite a lecture given by Degrelle in February 1941, few cases of collaboration were reported in Thuin. The most notable were those of a denouncer who was shorn at the Liberation, a Rexist family of which some members joined the Walloon Legion and a member of the National Corporation for Agriculture and Food, close to the Gestapo, found to be a killer commando of the right-wing OAS. The other cases opened after the Liberation mainly concerned economic collaboration or the black market.

A SINGULAR CATHOLIC PRIEST: FATHER WALLEZ

Father Wallez, living in the Aulne Abbey near Thuin since 1934 and a native of Pays des Collines, he was successively a teacher and reporter-journalist, ideologically close to the far right wing Action Française and their leader, Charles Maurras. He was the director of the influential Catholic newspaper Le XXe Siècle *(20th Century) between 1924 and 1933.*

Wallez also mentored the famous cartoonist Hergé, whom he commissioned for the Le XXe Siècle *newspaper's youth supplement,* Le Petit Vingtième, *where Hergé developed the cartoon character that would make him famous: Tintin. When he was dismissed from his duties, Wallez applied for and obtained the parish of Aulne where he invested himself in the restoration of the ruins of the abbey.*

During the war, he couldn't help but came back to the forefront. In 1942, on behalf of the Walloon Cultural Community, an organization close to the occupiers, he gave a series of lectures entitled "Dons et Torts des Wallons" (Gifts and Wrongs of the Walloons), in which he declared the Germanic origin of the Walloons and called on his audience, in a barely disguised way, to collaborate with the Germans.

Some people even argued that Wallez was national Rexist leader Leon Degrelle's silent and invisible partner during the war, the abbot having promoted Degrelle in Le XXe Siècle, in 1928. Degrelle was sentenced to prison for collaboration in 1947.

Wallez was arrested on the 4th of September 1944, convicted in 1947 and again on appeal in 1948 and he was finally sentenced to 5 years in prison. His health deteriorated from 1948 and, despite the support of Hergé and his wife, who remained faithful friends, Wallez died in 1952.

LIBERATION & RECONSTRUCTION

Liberation. After June the 6th 1944, the date of the D-Day invasion, the number of recruits joining the various resistance movements (Secret Army, Group G and Independence Front mainly in Thuin) increased and acts of sabotage of communication routes, railway lines and locks multiplied in the region. In the context of famine, with supplies being very low since May 1944, a pre-insurrectionary climate emerged in the town: several barges filled with grain, blocked by the sabotage of locks, were looted during the summer.

On the 21st of July, the Belgian flag was raised at the top of the Belfry. The massacres perpetrated by Rexists in the region, in retaliation to the attacks by the resistance, nevertheless caused fear until the day before the arrival of the Americans. On the 3rd of September, a German armoured vehicle was targeted by a gendarme who killed one of its occupants. Buildings were then machine gunned and set on fire by this armoured vehicle, which had brought in two other vehicles. A woman and her child were taken hostage by the Germans to save themselves. The woman and her child were finally released later in Marchienne, near Charleroi, northeast of Thuin.

The Americans arrived in Thuin on the 4th of September at about 6 p.m. by the Anderlues road. Jubilation, as everywhere else, was everywhere. The last unfortunate event of the war was in November 1944 when a V1 rocket landed at the crossroads of Biercée, approximately 2 km south of the Thuin town centre.

American trucks parked on the Place de la Ville-Basse during the liberation. Elisa Colot Collection

Reconstruction. It is essentially the area around the Gare du Nord that had to be rebuilt after the war. The industrial and commercial school, built nearby, saw its first classes given in 1950. For the rest, like the other Belgians, the Thudinian victims of war damage made reparation requests to the Ministry of Reconstruction, with different degrees of success.

The Hanging Gardens, an exceptional real estate heritage of Wallonia © Olivier Silveri

The high silhouette of the Belfry dominates and symbolizes the City of Thuin © Olivier Silveri

OUR TOWN TODAY

Situated at the heart of Thudinie, the territory of the Haute Sambre, sometimes called "Petite Provence" Thuin has managed to preserve its medieval character with its *postys* (ancient gates of the fortified city) and its paved narrow streets that wind through the Hanging Gardens, partially transformed into vineyards. The Belfry, classified as a UNESCO World Heritage Site, is its main symbol.

Another pride of the Thudinians is the escorted procession in honour of Saint Roch every third Sunday in May, a folkloric march that brings together some 2,500 walkers in uniforms from the 17th to the 20th century.

In the nearby region, you can stroll on the site of the ruins of the Aulne Abbey or at the medieval castle of Le Fosteau, or travel along the Ravel in an old tram or sail on the Sambre in the Vallée de la Paix (Peace Valley).

Nor should you miss Ragnies, one of the "most beautiful villages in Wallonia", and its square-shaped farms. Finally, you can taste wonderful mouth-watering products made by its craftsmen. In Thuin, you can recharge your batteries, discover and vibrate to the rhythm of folklore, and take the time to live!

*For more information about Thuin, please visit the official website of the town (in French): **www.thuin.be** or the website of the Tourist Office **www.tourismethuin.be/**.*

This information has been gathered by the C.H.A.T. (Centre d'Historie et d'Art de la Thudine) - Thudine History and Art Center. We appreciate their efforts to create this commemorative document. Photos courtesy of the municipality of Thuin.

TROIS-PONTS BELGIUM

Province: Liège   Pop. 1940: 2,200   Pop. 2020: 2,500

SITING & HERITAGE

Trois-Ponts is a small wooded commune in the south part of the province of Liège. It is located at the confluence of the Salm, the Baleur and the Amblève rivers, and this junction of three rivers is the origin of the village's name (Three Bridges). Nestled in the heart of the Ardennes, the Trois Ponts area lies in a forested, hilly landscape with clear, winding rivers dotted with renaissance castles and beautiful churches.

Historically, traces attest to the presence of Celts in the municipality. A post house for travelers existed during the 1700s, however the earnest development of the village did not occur until 1860 because of its privileged location at the crossroads of major roads, and the commissioning of its railway station in 1867.

GPS Coordinates: N50.3718 E:5.8703

The center of Trois-Ponts in May 1940

The village of Aisomont after the Battle of the Bulge

The village of Wanne after the Battle of the Bulge

TROIS-PONTS. — Pont de l'Amblève

The important Trois-Pont bridges over the Amblève river

OUR TOWN'S OCCUPATION STORY

The Rural Guard. During the difficult times of the German occupation -- times of food shortage and restrictions of all kinds-- the warehouses, attics, orchards and surrounding crops were the targets of night thieves. Vagrants, hungry townspeople, needy or simply unscrupulous villagers sometimes came from as far away as Verviers and even Liège. They often came on bicycles and did not hesitate to come and take what they could. To counter this stealing, rural guards and villagers were put in charge of guarding the village and its crops.

Livestock. During the 1940s, the winters were particularly harsh. Livestock who had suffered the hardships of war were sometimes reduced to such a state of exhaustion that, if the spring was not early, they died or were simply slaughtered. Some were so weak they had to be loaded on a sledge to be taken to slaughter.

The distribution of milk. The distribution of milk continued but, of course, was rationed via stamps. However, from time to time, a *rawette* (small portion) was granted to the farmer, but he had to keep careful accounts, because the Nazis knew well, by the number of his cows, how many liters of milk the farmer should produce. If the quantity of milk did not correspond to the number of cattle, the cows went to the slaughterhouse.

Horses. Despite the objection of the owners, every year, the Germans took a large portion of horses from our stables, leaving just a few for breeding.

Schools. The schools were forced to close from May 10, 1940, until mid-June. When they reopened, the teachers had to deal with the damage caused by the invasion of the Germans: the damage to the buildings and the disappearance of books and various objects necessary for teaching. A list of forbidden books was issued. Teachers had to take care to prevent any act of sabotage by students, including any inscriptions of "V" (for Victory) or any inscriptions offensive to the Nazis. The teaching staff would be held personally responsible for any offenses.

Work for the invaders. Many young men were conscripted to perform forced labor for the Germans. Those who were exempted were still assigned to certain tasks to help German interests, such as guarding the Trois-Ponts railway.

Single women: The women whose husbands were taken as soldiers or laborers had to take on the care of fields and crops. From time to time, "people of the city" came to buy food they could not get elsewhere.

The Battle of the Bulge. Even though Trois-Ponts was initially liberated by the American Army in September, like many other small towns and villages in eastern Belgium, Trois-Ponts found itself directly in the path of the German mechanized counter-offensive known as the Battle of the Bulge.

Even worse, the German spearhead headed directly towards Trois-Ponts was the 6th Panzer Division led by the dreaded SS Lt. Col. Joachim Peiper who had just murdered several hundred American soldiers near Malmedy and whose method was to kill, burn and destroy everything in his path. He was later condemned at Nuremburg for crimes against humanity.

Edmont Pirotte   Charles Gaspard

A Special Story. A Patrol Mission To The German Lines.

Before the main Allied attack on the retreating Germans, these two local civilian men were given the mission to inspect villages in the Trois-Ponts (Wanne) area, and report back to the Americans the positions of the Germans. They started out in the early evening of January 6, 1945 a cold and clear night with a fairly deep snow covering the ground.   Because of German infiltrators, their password was "J2 Colonel Jack".   The plan was for each man to proceed a few tens of meters then conceal himself and signal to the next one, who passes the first, and so on.   Silence was necessary and the two men each carried a revolver.

They cross Aisomont, go towards the mill of Wanneranval, then to Somagne, Hénumont, Wanne, La Vaux and Grand-Halleux before turning back, and along the way they had to constantly fear American artillery. In addition to finding abandoned machine guns and some civilians who were left to care for cattle remaining on isolated farms, they also discovered two Volksgrenadieres (German soldiers), a German battery with 6 pieces of artillery, a fleet of German vehicles and a machine gun nest before turning around.

Upon their return to the American lines, they were apprehended, neutralized, searched and disarmed by wary US soldiers, who marched them into a cellar with their hands in the air, before taking them to the headquarters of the company, where they were recognized and reported their information. Mission accomplished.

THE PRICE OF LIBERATION

Monday December 18, 1944, Wanne. During the Battle of the Bulge, no fewer than twenty-eight German tanks appeared, quickly joined by dozens more.   Hungry and dressed in mismatched uniforms and rags, German soldiers crisscross the village, machine guns in hand, demanding much food from the inhabitants.   Refusal results in ransacking the house.   In a short time the looting of farms and houses was complete.

Machine gun bursts sound, the men of the village are gathered near the church and murdered by soldiers.   Months later, witnesses still tell of the terrible smell that emanates from the village, where bodies, cows, horses decompose.

Tuesday December 19, 1944 Trois-Ponts.   Driven by the thirst for blood and the pleasure of seeing suffering, the Germans rush into houses and drive out all the inhabitants.   Gathered in the middle of the road, they are coldly machine gunned.   Like real barbarians, slaughtering the children they meet on their way, the Germans spread terror in their path.   Witnesses speak of unprecedented, relentless killing and inhuman sadism.

The Germans only occupied the center of Trois-Ponts for two days but the town will remain a long time a "no man's land", undergoing the numerous artillery shots of the belligerents posted on the heights on both sides of the city. Of the 240 houses in Trois-Ponts, 74 were destroyed by shells, 80 damaged and 25 burned. The passage of the Germans at Trois-Ponts leaves a bloody picture that will forever be impossible to quantify.

Trois-Ponts: first commune of Wallonia, where life is good

The natural beauty surrounding Trois-Ponts

OUR TOWN TODAY

Nestled in the heart of three magnificent valleys, Trois-Ponts is one of the least populated municipalities of Wallonia, with some 2,500 inhabitants. Located in the heart of the Ardennes, the countryside surrounding Trois-Ponts delights everyone with its calm and enchantment. 200 km of hiking, cycling or horseback riding will take you through mountains and valleys to discover charming villages and hamlets, beautiful landscapes, breathtaking views and unique forests filled with pretty streams. Also well known for its ski slopes, the town has become a favorite destination in winter.

Vibrant to the rhythm of local festivals and rich in many non-profit organizations of all kinds, Trois-Ponts has become a prosperous village where life is good; and just a short distance from many famous tourist sites such as Coo, Stavelot, Francorchamps, Spa, etc.

Many visitors return time after time to experience the charm of the village, the charm of the region, the friendliness of the reception of the Trois-Pontois, the numerous craftsmen, and the cuisine based largely on local products.

Military enthusiasts can witness the World War II tragedies of Trois-Ponts by visiting the well-known Wanne Museum in the nearby municipal village of Wanne. Trois-Ponts can assure you unforgettable memories when visiting our beautiful and historic town.

*For more information about Trois-Ponts, please visit the town's official website: **www.troisponts.be.** For more information about the town's recreational & nature opportunities, please visit: **www.troisponts-tourisme.be***

This information was prepared by: Claude Legrand, Trois-Ponts Alderman with the assistance of our town's dedicated historians and witnesses.

TROOZ BELGIUM
Province: Liège   Pop. 1940: 6,000   Pop. 2020: 8,600

SITING & HERITAGE

Trooz is a French-speaking commune in the Province of Liège, located in the deep valley of the Vesdre, which was greatly appreciated by Victor Hugo, the famous French writer. The commune consists of the villages and hamlets of Prayon, Trooz, Nessonvaux, Péry, Trasenster, Fraipont and Forêt-Village. Situated some ten kilometres from Liège and fifteen kilometres from Verviers, Trooz is a key stopover on the way to the heart of the Ardennes.

Trooz is proud of its prestigious metallurgical past. Trooz has a highly diverse natural and industrial heritage and Neanderthal remains have been found in its caves. We still remember the sound of the engines of the famous Imperia cars on the rooftop test track here. The Fenderie site in Trooz with its historic iron forge and its magnificent, well-preserved 16th century castle now hosts cultural events.

GPS Coordinates: N50.5788 E5.6737

The yard of the farm where the massacre took place

The bodies of some of the victims

The Resistance had been photographed in groups shortly before the tragedy.

THE TRAGEDY OF FORÊT-TROOZ

In September of 1944, while Allied forces were liberating Belgium, the Nazis carried out their final atrocities. For the hamlet of Forêt-Village, hostilities ended in one of the most tragic ways possible. Terrible reprisals were inflicted on a local group of Secret Army resistance fighters, in breach of all rules of war.

At the end of 1944, following the Normandy landings, Allied forces were making rapid progress thanks, in particular, to the support provided by a number of resistance networks throughout the country. The region surrounding the Vesdre river was no exception. In Trooz, there were other resistance groups but the largest and the most active resistance group was the Secret Army (SA).

Liberation approaches. As Allied forces neared Liège in several columns, more and more parachute landings and other operations to support resistance fighters took place around Trooz, including partisan attacks to support the actions of the Secret Army.

On September 5, at around 5 p.m., Germans attacked the Demonceau farm on the road from Prayon to Forêt-Village, where 100 members of the Secret Army had gathered, but the resistance members fought back and the Germans were pushed back. Five Secret Army members were killed, and their bodies were brought back to the castle at Forêt.

A parachute drop of weapons had been due to take place during the night of September 5-6, but it was canceled because of the attack and fighting. The officers of the Secret Army met at the castle and decided that unarmed men could return home.

The fateful day. The next morning, on September 6, at 7 a.m., the remaining men of the 100 SA members gathered in the courtyard of the Labeye farm and were told of the decision to send them home. At around 7:15 a.m., a sentinel sounded the alarm: 250 Germans had surrounded the castle.

The Germans attacked, using small arms and hand grenades, among other things. The battle raged for a while but, due to a lack of ammunition, the resistance fighters finally had to lay down their weapons, raise a white flag and surrender.

They held up their hands, but were punched, kicked and lined up against the walls. The Forêt massacre was about to begin. The castle of Forêt was set on fire. Most of the prisoners were thrown into trucks and taken to the Citadelle at Liège or to other places, where they were tortured and imprisoned.

Cowardly Slaughter. At the Citadelle the prisoners were shot in the back of the head at the Monsin Island dam in Liège. Those who could not escape or hide were cowardly gunned down and some were even burned alive in the stables. Many simply disappeared, leaving their families in total disarray. The next day, on 7 September, the city of Liège was liberated, and the Germans started fleeing back to their country.

A TOO COMMON STORY OF THE WAR.

Jacques Patureau *was born in 1920. He was just 20 years old when war was declared and he had no idea if he would survive it. At the end of 1944, in the hills around Trooz, he was one of those local men, driven by truck to an unknown location, to their death at the hands of the Germans. The tragedy for Jacques Patureau was all too common because his body was never found, resulting in years of suffering for his wife and son.*

Jacques Patureau

His wife Jeanne and their young son Jean-Claude, only found out several days later that he had been at the scene of the massacre. It was only in 1952, eight long years later, that his wife officially became recognized as the Widow Patureau.

Until then, life had been very unkind to her. Because of the absence of a dead body, she received no life insurance benefits, no widow's pension and none of the benefits granted to thousands of other collateral victims of the war.

She and her son therefore had to rely on family and friends: a coalman giving them scraps from the bottom of his coal bag, assistance from the local authorities and support from relatives who did what they could to help them out.

Later, Jean-Claude Patureau would, on top of his full-time job, hold political office in Trooz for 36 years, hoping thereby to "give back" part of the help he and his mother had received from the community.

His mother suffered for her entire life and died in 2008, having spent 64 years alone, refusing to start a new life because, to the very end, she was hoping and waiting for the return of her "missing" husband. Recognizing this tragedy, a street in Fraipont is now named for the victim: Drève Jacques Patureau.

REMEMBERING THE FALLEN

On 7 September, the city of Liège was liberated. Then, in December the Battle of the Bulge had to be fought just east of Trooz but fortunately the Allied forces were able to halt the German offensive before the battle reached Trooz. The region would now count its dead and begin the struggle of recovery.

Property and goods confiscated from Trooz's citizens were returned to their owners and peace finally returned to the village. Many commemorative plaques, including one located in front of the current town hall, pay tribute to all those men and women who thirsted for freedom.

After the liberation it was quickly decided that the Forêt-Trooz massacre should never be forgotten. "A people without a memory is a people without a future" was the call.

Money was raised through newspaper appeals. A booklet was also sold to support the building of a memorial in the village square of Forêt. This square, located near the farm and the farm's castle, was named Piscart after one of the resistance fighters.

In 1947, a memorial was built in Forêt-Village and, every year since then, a moving commemoration takes place on the first Sunday of September. The names of all the victims are engraved on the memorial and the remains of all the victims who could not be identified are contained in a crypt in its foundations.

The history of the names and faces will never be forgotten here!

The Forêt-Village monument where each year we commemorate the massacre that took place in the village.

The municipal park of Trooz, where a monument recalls the losses of the war among the population and the soldiers.

OUR TOWN TODAY

With its green countryside, the commune of Trooz is clearly looking to the future and a tourist office now welcomes visitors wishing to discover its many attractions.

Well known for its 7 major local trailways through nature offering hiking, biking and horse-riding trails, Trooz has become an important portal to discovering the beauty of the Ardennes forests and hills, and the many monuments and museums remembering the many local tragedies and triumphs occurring during World War II.

Trooz also takes great pride in supporting and presenting its museums and attractions such as the historic quarries of the Carrière de Trooz, the Château de la Fenderie castle, the Château de Forêt, the museum of radios, the Imperia Car Museum and the prehistoric caves of Fonds-de-Forêt.

Trooz is a dynamic commune hosting a wide range of various events for residents and visitors alike including many organized walks, conferences, exhibitions by artists from the region, flea markets and carnival processions.

For more information about the town of Trooz, visit the town's official website: www.trooz.be. For more information about the tourism opportunities in the Trooz area visit www.syndicat-initiative-trooz.com.

The text was written by Jean-Louis Lejaxhe, under the supervision of Fabien Beltran, Mayor of the Commune of Trooz, and Joëlle Deglin, Deputy Mayor for Culture, with the support of Isabelle Botterman and Sébastien Marcq.

WIELSBEKE BELGIUM

Province: West-Vlaanderen   Pop. 1940: 6,400   Pop. 2020: 9,700

SITING & HERITAGE

Wielsbeke is an important industrial municipality located alongside the river Lys that includes the communities of Ooigem, Sint-Baafs-Vijve and Wielsbeke. The river Lys in known as "The Golden River" because of the beautiful golden color its lime-laden water imparts to flax stems when soaked. This gave birth to a flourishing flax industry for which the region was renowned worldwide but the industry later declined. Today Wielsbeke is home to a number of multinational companies.

Wielsbeke's history dates to the middle ages and includes the 11th century Sint Brixius church in Ooigem and the 13th century Sint Bavokerk church in Sint-Baarfs-Vijve, one of the most valuable rural Romanesque churches of West Flanders. Many waterways and canals exist in the area, offering an abundance of scenic, peaceful natural beauty.

GPS Coordinates: N50.9100 E3.3724

Church Sint-Bavo in Sint-Baafs-Vijve, badly damaged during the German invasion

Wielsbeke town hall and village centre

Invasion damage to Ooigem

Wielsbeke deportees leaving for Germany

OUR TOWN'S OCCUPATION STORY

Ooigem on fire. On Friday 24th May, 1940, an order was given at 3:10 am to evacuate all civilians. At 6:00 am the German command "Feuer!" ("Fire!") resounded and more than 400 pieces of German heavy artillery started to besiege the Belgian military posts in the area who were forced to furiously defend themselves. Around noon the intensity of the assault finally diminished, mainly due to a German shortage of ammunition. In neighbouring Harelbeke and Stasegem, spy balloons were launched by the Germans to observe the Belgian positions. In Ooigem, the 1st Line Regiment came under heavy gun fire beginning at 14:00 and heavy German bombardments and countless mortars and shells were launched into the town. The centre of Ooigem was ablaze, the church tower was heavily damaged and there were numerous civilian casualties.

At approximately 17:00 the bombardments ceased and the first German ground assault wave was launched. The enemy's armoured vehicles reached our troops and succeeded in occupying the left bank on their second attempt, forcing our soldiers to retreat in panic behind the Ooigem-Roeselare canal. During this retreat, the beloved Second Lieutenant Auguste Marin was killed at the edge of the Leem forest. At approximately 22:00, buildings in the canal zone were assaulted during which Captain-Commandant Gustave Vincke of the 5th company was killed.

The decimated 1st Line Regiment regrouped in the neighbouring village of Oostrozebeke. The bloody battle resulted in more than 300 casualties within the 1st Line Regiment, and at least 60 soldiers were killed in the Ooigem countryside.

How I remember the 1940-1945 war *(Tale of Andréa Missiaen b.1931)*

The 18-day campaign began, culminating on 26 May with the battle of the River Lys. The Mayor and the village Policeman of Wielsbeke sent out a warning to the population: "Open all windows!" This was to protect houses from damage while the bridges of Sint-Eloois-Vijve, Wielsbeke and Desselgem were being blown up in an attempt to stop the advance of the German troops and mechanized forces.

May 26 was a sunny school holiday and many children were out in the fields, collecting tin-foil strips dropped by our airplanes to misguide the enemy. Masses of refugees were afoot, on bikes and with horses and carriages, fleeing from the east. We heard on the radio how the Germans were rapidly advancing towards the west. The 13th Line Regiment, led by Major Lamy, assured the defense of the river banks. Cannons roared all night and many mortars fell close to the houses. Civilians hid in their reinforced cellars and were joined by numerous refugees, all of them fearfully praying. The German occupation was a fact and would last for 4 years. German soldiers stayed in the girls' school, food was rationed. It was a harsh period for most people.

Deportation *(Tale of Daniël Vandenbussche b. 1924)*

Many young people were deported to Germany, forced to work for the occupier. Those who refused had their families threatened with harm. Also, those not willing would no longer receive any food stamps. Daniël Vandenbussche (then 16) was summoned, together with nineteen others from Wielsbeke, to go to work at an airplane construction facility in Dessau for 26 months. Daniël succeeded in coming back early by applying for an emergency leave for an allegedly sick family member. Upon his return he stayed in hiding and did not return home until liberation day.

A SPECIAL SERVICE FOR OUR TOWN

Valère Vindevogel

Valère Vindevogel (1905-1979) wrote an account of what happened in Ooigem in 1940. He was not a soldier but he had been asked by the Mayor to help during the after effects of the war. He was multilingual and his eyewitness reports are said to be very reliable. He compared his own experiences with the official written accounts.

He also corrected and complemented them with data from official documents from the Belgian, English, French, Canadian, German and US armies.

This represented a valuable and scientific asset for the local community. The events he experienced were clearly and appropriately worded and are still used by the local history group for their publications. We highlight a small fragment from his writings:

"10th May: around noon about 6 bombs were dropped next to the Desselgem Railway station, luckily without casualties.

Members of the civil defense were mobilised to fill sandbags and to reinforce windows by sticking paper strips on them, thus avoiding the fallout of glass shards. Meanwhile French troops entered Wielsbeke and a reconnaissance squad reached the bridge of the canal between Ooigem and Wielsbeke.

On May the 15th, around 6:00 pm, a squadron of 27 German bomber planes appeared against the sunny blue sky. Only 20 minutes earlier they were announced on the radio as a large squadron of German bombers, flying westward and approaching the city of Tongres.

We were eagerly awaiting the intervention of British fighter planes, when suddenly a French fighter plane appeared from behind the clouds. He destroyed a number of the bombers and vanished almost instantaneously . . ."

LIBERATION & RECOVERY

The following is taken from the writing of Valère Vindevogel about our experiences during the liberation days:

A few days before the liberation of Ooigem, on September the 3rd of 1944, we heard the news that the first British troops had crossed our country borders, south of Mons. A strong military force entered our country via the main road from Tournai to Renaix. People were convinced that the war was coming to an end.

The road from Courtrai to Ghent was heavily used by large columns of German military vehicles rapidly heading east. In the Lys region, people were convinced that the Germans would leave quietly and started expressing their joy.

On the other side of the river Lys, the situation was less clear and final liberation took some more time. Fleeing German military convoys were attacked by nose-diving American bomber planes. A group of Germans was heading towards our village to hide in the houses of residents.

The night before September the 8th, German officers were constantly on the phone while playing the piano, the same tune over and over again . . . until 5:00 pm. Suddenly there was a lot of commotion with loud and heavy footsteps, the piano went silent and they fled, leaving behind only cut phone wires, food leftovers, empty bottles and cigarette ends . . . the British were coming!

The natural beauty of Wielsbeke

The lovely Neoclassical 'Chateau Hernieuwenburg'

Photo by Monique Claerhout

The 12th century Sint-Bavo church in Sint-Baafs-Vijve

OUR TOWN TODAY

Today, the Wielsbeke communities are known for their numerous bicycle routes and hiking paths leading to interesting sites relating not only to its history, customs and traditions but also its rural character and industrial development.

The area's flax history is very apparent with a number of related buildings still existing. The neoclassical Chateau Hernieuwenburg is situated in the centrally located park and now serves as the Wielsbeke City Hall.

Located between the river Lys and the canal Roeselare-Lys, Ooigem is the ideal starting point for biking, hiking and kayaking trips. The Medieval (11th century) Saint-Brixius church in Ooigem is inspired by Romanesque architecture and includes some early Gothic elements (13th-16th centuries).

Other sites of interest in the Wielsbeke area include the restored, very unique three-staged lock on the canal (1872), the rural Sint-Baafs-Vijve area located near a meander of the golden river, the 12th century Roman church, the André Demedts house and the freely accessible cultural centre with new expositions every month. Internationally renowned is the yearly dog swimming event, a unique running and swimming contest for dogs.

For more information about Wielsbeke, please visit the town website: www.wielsbeke.be. For more information about the tourism opportunities in the Wielsbeke area please visit www.wielsbeke.be/toerisme or the local history group website: www.juliaanclaerhoutkring.be

This information was prepared by Monique Claerhout and members of the Juliaan Claerhout-kring/Wielsbeke historical group. Photos courtesy of the municipality of Wielsbeke.

Remembering & Honoring The Sacrifices Endured By So Many

Belgian King Leopold III (1901-1983)

As a young prince of 25, Leopold married Princess Astrid of Sweden, producing three children and a fairytale marriage adored by the people. When his father, King Albert, died in a mountaineering accident, King Leopold III became the 33 year-old King of the Belgians in 1934. One year later in 1935, Leopold lost control of his automobile on a winding road in Switzerland, crashing and killing Princess Astrid, resulting in a national period of mourning throughout Belgium.

Prior to World War II, King Leopold tried to insist on Belgium's desire to remain neutral but Germany ignored it. When the Germans suddenly invaded on May 10, 1940, they quickly overran Belgian's eastern fortifications and moving west, quickly overwhelmed the resisting Belgian, French and British forces. Leopold took command of the Belgian army and continued fighting the Germans in Belgium, concentrating on delaying the German advance through Belgium to give the British the time they needed to evacuate the 330,000 men of the French and British armies from the beaches at Dunkirk.

His Belgian army was soon overpowered by the Germans and he was forced to surrender, doing so without consulting the Belgian government-in-exile in England who, after the war, questioned his return to the throne for failing to consult them. In Belgium, Leopold refused to cooperate with the Germans and was thus held as a German prisoner of war at his château near Brussels. In 1941, as a German prisoner or war, Leopold secretly married Lillian Baels who remained his wife for life. In 1944, when the war began going badly for them, they were deported and held captive at a fort in Germany.

During his time in Germany Leopold wrote a 'Political Testament' critical of many of the decisions being made by the Allies and the Belgian government-in-exile, causing dismay and disappointment and further complicating his ability to return to the throne.

When the war ended, he moved to Switzerland to await the resolution of the "royal questions" about his right to return to sovereignty. In 1950 the people voted in favor of his return as king but soon after, continued internal opposition led him to abdicate in favor of his son, Baudouin, who then became King of the Belgians in 1951. After continuing to advise his son until 1960, Leopold pursed his passions in anthropology and entomology until his death in Brussels in 1983.

THE WORLD WAR II MUSEUMS OF BELGIUM

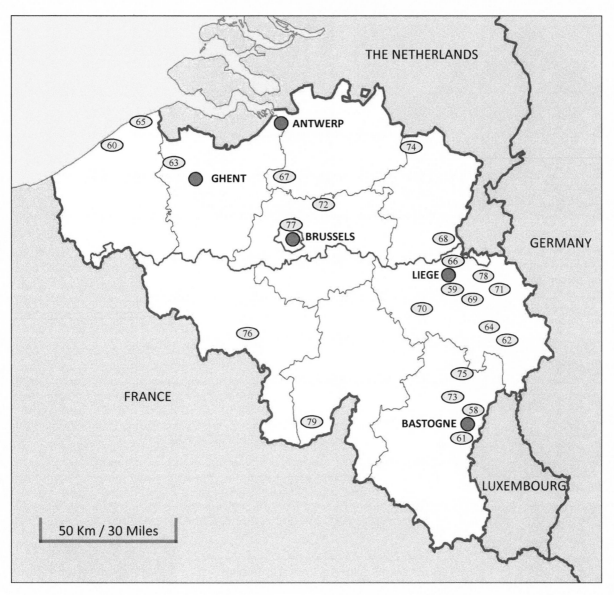

Page	Museum	Municipality	Page	Museum	Municipality
58	101st Airborne Museum	Bastogne	69	Fort Embourg	Chaudfontaine
59	Ardennes American Cemetery	Neupré	70	Fort Huy Museum	Huy
60	Atlantic Wall Museum	Oostende	71	Henri-Chapelle American Cemetery	Welkenraedt
61	Bastogne War Museum	Bastogne	72	Kazerne Dossin Memorial	Mechelen
62	Baugnez 44 Museum	Malmedy	73	La Roche En Ardenne Museum	La-Roche-en-Ardenne
63	Canada Poland Museum	Maldegem	74	Lommel German Military Cemetery	Lommel
64	December 1944 Museum	La Gleize	75	Manhay History 44 Museum	Manhay
65	For Freedom Museum	Knokke-Heist	76	Mons War Museum	Mons
66	Fort Aubin—Neufchâteau	Dalhem	77	National Resistance Museum	Brussels
67	Fort Breendonk Nat'l Memorial	Willebroe	78	Remember Museum 39-45	Thimister Clermont
68	Fort Eben-Emael	Bassenge	79	Wolfsschlucht (Wolf's Ravine)	Couvin

101ST AIRBORNE MUSEUM
Bastogne, Belgium

GPS Coordinates: N49.9993 E5.7122

This important and interesting museum concentrates on the Battle of the Bulge and more specifically, on the Battle of Bastogne when the "Battered Bastards of Bastogne" of the 101st Airborne Division held out, allowing the Allies to halt the German massive winter offensive at Bastogne.

Built in 1936, the 101st Airborne museum in Bastogne is located in a former officers mess building of the Belgian Army which was then used by the German army as an "Unteroffiziersheim" (NCO residence) during the WWII occupation of Bastogne.

Used after the war as a hospital by the Red Cross, this unique building with its rich history has been restored to its former glory and now displays the military history of the 101st Airborne Division and units involved in the Battle of Bastogne between December 1944 and January 1945. The 101st Airborne Division, commanded by General Anthony "Nuts" McAuliffe, was rushed to the small town of Bastogne in December 1944 to defend against the German winter offensive now known as the Battle of the Bulge.

The Battle of the Bulge comes to life in the museum in unique displays with realistic looking mannequins and large collections of original items from this dramatic battle. The museum, which stretches over 4 floors, focuses on the units that took part in the conflict in and around Bastogne, among them the famous 101st Airborne, immortalized in Steven Spielberg's *Band of Brothers* television series.

In addition to the museum's fine collection, visitors can immerse themselves in a frightening WWII experience in the basement, where the sound and vibrations of a bombing raid have been realistically re-created to give the visitor a realistic experience of the many civilians sheltering from the bombs in their cellars, not knowing what devastation they would find if and when they emerged. The constant danger faced by the town residents is not forgotten in this museum.

Would you like to visit the sites of the Battleground of Bastogne? Yes, It is possible! The museum offers the possibility to take a battlefield tour that brings you to the memorable places and actual scenes where the battles for Bastogne took place.

This museum is definitely worth a visit!

For more information about the museum, visit www.101airbornemuseumbastogne.com/. For more information about the local Bastogne area, visit www.bastogne.be/loisirs/tourisme/syndicat-dinitiative. Photos courtesy of the museum.

THE ARDENNES AMERICAN CEMETERY
Neupre, Belgium

The Ardennes American Cemetery in Belgium is the final resting place of 5,317 Americans who died in World War II.

GPS Coordinates: N50.5419 E5.4691

The American Battle Monuments Commission (ABMC) is responsible for maintaining this beautiful cemetery in the midst of the Battle of the Bulge area. Gazing across this meticulously-maintained cemetery conjures emotions that can only be felt at a cemetery such as this.

Designed by C. Paul Jennewein, a bronze figure, symbolizing American youth, looks out over the graves at Ardennes American Cemetery.

The approach drive at Ardennes American Cemetery and Memorial in Belgium leads to the memorial, a stone structure bearing on its façade a massive American eagle and other sculptures. Within the memorial is the chapel with three large wall maps composed of inlaid marble panels depicting combat actions, supply movements and other remembrance features.

Along the outside of the memorial, 463 names are inscribed on the granite "Tablets of the Missing." Rosettes mark the names of those since recovered and identified. The façade on the far north end, that overlooks the burial area, bears the insignia, in mosaic, of the major U.S. units that operated in northwest Europe in World War II.

This cemetery is unique among all ABMC cemeteries as it served as the central identification point for the entire European Theater of Operations from the last days of the war until 1960. The Ardennes American Cemetery is the final resting place for 5,317 Americans, with 65 percent of those being fallen airmen of the U.S. Army Air Forces. Their headstones are aligned in straight rows that compose the form of a Greek cross.

The inside of the memorial building includes a chapel area as well as large battle maps.

More than 400 Americans are commemorated on the Tablets of the Missing.

The meticulously-maintained cemetery covers more than 90 acres (36.6 ha)

For more information about the museum, visit www.abmc.gov/Ardennes#cemetery-info-anchor. For more information about the Neupre area, visit www.neupre.be. Except as noted, all photos by Warrick Page/American Battle Monuments Commission.

THE ATLANTIC WALL OPEN AIR MUSEUM
Raversijde (Oostende), Belgium

The North Sea Beach, Tram Line and Highway Along the Atlantic Wall

GPS Coordinates: N51.2035 E2.8507

The world's longest tram line runs for 70 km along Belgium's beautiful beaches that allows you to hop on and hop off at any of the 70 stops along the tram route where you can wander in and around many of the best-preserved Atlantic Wall German gun emplacements and fortifications in Europe.

The Atlantic Wall refers to the 2,000-mile-long system of defensive beach artillery positions and fortifications that were built by the Germans along the coasts of Europe, from Spain to Scandinavia, to repel any possible invasion by the Allies that might be launched from Great Britain. After Hitler ordered the construction of these fortifications in 1942, more than a million civilians were conscripted by the Germans to construct the entire system within a period of two years.

In the early part of 1944 it became apparent that an Allied invasion was likely so Hitler put Field Marshall Erwin Rommel in charge of further strengthening the Atlantic Wall defenses. Rommel was not convinced of the Atlantic Wall system's invincibility, adding hundreds of light and heavy artillery positions, millions of land mines and beach obstacles to increase its overall strength.

All told, more than 250 Atlantic Wall fortifications were built along the coasts facing England and after it was completed the fortifications were manned by hundreds of thousands of German soldiers. With the exception of only several air attacks by the Allies, the Germans occupying these positions enjoyed a relatively quiet assignment—at least until the D-Day invasion occurred.

Following the D-Day invasion, primarily because the system was designed to repel attacks from the sea, each of the fortifications were relatively easily defeated as the Allies moved north and east to liberate the coasts of France, Belgium and the Netherlands, proving that Rommel was right.

Following the Allied victory in Europe many of these fortifications were either destroyed or fell into disrepair as they were only seen as reminders of the four terrible years under Nazi control. It was only decades later that it was decided to preserve sections of the Atlantic Wall for future generations, one of these being the fortifications in the Oostende/Raversjide area where you can wander through the subterranean fortifications and see what life was like for the German soldiers who were stationed here.

For more information, visit www.raversyde.be/nl/atlantikwall. For more information about the Oostende beach areas, visit http://cheeseweb.eu/2013/10/10-reasons-visit-oostende-beach/. Except as noted, all photos courtesy of the museum.

THE BASTOGNE WAR MUSEUM & MARDASSON MEMORIAL
Bastogne, Belgium

GPS Coordinates: N50.6458 E5.7391

One of the best known WWII museums in Europe due to its location in the famous battle town of Bastogne, this museum has incorporated the latest technologies to make the visitor feel the intensity of the stories of four characters who were forced to live through the Battle of the Bulge.

The Ardennes town of Bastogne is a Walloon town in southern Belgium and it was the most important site of one of World War II's most notorious struggles, the Battle of the Bulge. Most of the town's military attractions relate to this landmark battle, including the Bastogne War Museum, the star-shaped Mardasson American War Memorial; the Wood of Peace, where 4,000 trees were planted on the 50th anniversary of the battle; and a Sherman tank that belonged to the US Army's 11th Division.

Opened in 2014 and housed in a striking contemporary building whose roof echoes the shape of the adjacent Mardasson memorial, the Bastogne War Museum begins with the backstory of the build-up to World War II, from the US stock market crash in 1929 that heralded economic depression across the world, to the emergence of Nazi fanaticism in Germany. A collection of modern, interactive exhibits pays homage to the 76,890 US soldiers, dead, wounded or missing in the Battle of the Bulge, through a series of personal testimonies, displays of uniforms, maps and weaponry, and graphic black-and-white footage of the battle's aftermath. Scenaristic shows allow visitors to experience bombardment in a Bastogne café and gunfire in the Ardennes forest.

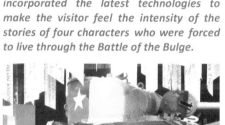

The Museum is located just a stone's throw away from the Mardasson Memorial, inaugurated in 1950 to bear witness to Belgium's gratitude to the American soldiers who risked or lost their lives on Belgian soil during the fighting with the enemy. The monument takes the form of a star.

Engraved in gold lettering, the story of the battle can be read on the walls of the open gallery. A viewing platform situated at the summit offers the visitor a panoramic view of the defensive positions held during the siege of the town. The Memorial is also endowed with a crypt, decorated with a mosaic by the French artist Fernand Léger.

For more information about the museum, visit www.bastognewarmuseum.be/en/home-en/. For more information about the local area, visit www.bastogne.be/loisirs/tourisme/syndicat-dinitiative. Interior photos by the author.

THE BAUGNEZ 44 MUSEUM
Baugnez (Malmedy), Belgium

GPS Coordinates: N50.4021 E6.0661

This museum is located at the road crossing near the village of Malmedy where, on December 17, 1944, the dreaded German SS Kampfgruppe Joachim Peiper murdered 84 captured American soldiers.

At dawn on the 17th December, armored vehicles of the 1st SS Panzer Regiment commanded by Lieutenant Colonel Peiper enter our region. The objective of this offensive is to seize bridges over the Meuse River then drive on via Liège to the port of Antwerp. The Battle of the Bulge had begun.

This same day, the US Army 285th Field Artillery Observation Battalion, under the command of Captain Roger Mills, arrives in Malmedy. Although warned about the presence of German armored vehicles in nearby Büllingen, Mills decides to follow his assigned route in the direction of Baugnez in order to link up with the 7th Armored Division's Combat Command B which was in St. Vith.

The column arrives at the Baugnez crossroads at the same time as the armored spearhead led by the infamous Kampfgruppe Joachim Peiper. A violent confrontation then occurs and some vehicles are destroyed whilst others must be pushed off the road in order to secure free passage of other vehicles. Mills understands that the situation of his men is beyond desperate so he makes the decision to surrender.

Thereafter follows the infamous "Malmedy Massacre" at Baugnez , in which 84 of these American prisoners are murdered. The reason for this remains unclear. This war crime, one of many carried out by the same unit the very same day and in the following days, resulted in many judgements being given at an international military court held in Dachau in 1946 to prosecute war crimes.

Authentic materiel, vehicles, photographs and films of the time take you back to the heart of the Battle of the Bulge and 15 dioramas depict the daily life of soldiers during the Battle of the Bulge. Two of these scenes, equipped with sound and light, are unique in Belgium and you will discover items that are unique in the world. Throughout your visit, an electronic multilingual guide provides you with a detailed, chronological commentary about the Battle of the Bulge and the Malmedy massacre.

Visiting the museum is facilitated by the use of an audio guide in four languages. Once you have visited the downstairs you will then go upstairs where a 25-minute cinema film in four languages awaits you.

Housed in the Baugnez 44 Historical Museum complex, with space to seat 75 people and a magnificent terrace that can accommodate a further 60 people, the popular "Five Points" brasserie-restaurant provides the visitor with an ideal opportunity to combine a gourmet experience with the discovery of an event that will live forever in the visitor's memory. "Five Points", is what the American GIs called this strategic crossroads location. The museum has a huge visitor parking area and all facilities at the museum are adapted to the needs of visitors with reduced mobility.

*For more information about the museum, visit **www.baugnez44.be**. Except as noted, all photos courtesy of the museum.*

CANADA-POLAND MUSEUM
Adegem (Maldegem), Belgium

CANADA-POLAND WAR II - MUSEUM

GPS Coordinates: N51.1890 E3.5000

The Canada-Poland museum houses two separate museums in one large building celebrating the Canadian and Polish armed forces that liberated this region of Belgium from the German occupiers.

Maurice Van Landschoot was a spy during the Second World War. On his deathbed, he told his son about how, all alone, without involving family or friends, he had hidden people from the Nazis and that he owed his life to the liberators. On his deathbed, Maurice asked his son Gilbert to give something back as gratitude to the Canadian and Polish liberators.

Gilbert opened The Canada Poland Museum on June 28, 1995 and its collections and popularity have grown ever since. The museum presents the mobilization, occupation and liberation of Flanders in a lively way. Dioramas show you lifelike military actions from WWII with 300 uniforms, weapons, transmitters, posters and equipment and includes films about the Battle of the Scheldt and the Katyn massacre of 22,000 Polish military officers and intelligentsia by the Soviet secret police in 1940.

On 7th September 2004 a new museum facility was inaugurated as "The Maple-Leaf" by the representative of His Majesty the King and many Canadian and Polish personalities. The museum includes an interesting collection of militaria miniatures in 1/35 scale, and depicts many battlefields of WWII with dioramas about the 1st Polish Armored Division and the Polish Air Forces that were responsible for liberating the local Adegem/Maldegem area.

The museum emphasizes the education of our youth so that they never forget that thousands of young soldiers died here for our peace and freedom.

*For more information about the museum, visit www.generalmaczekmuseum.com/. For a virtual tour, visit **https://goo.gl/maps/vPSdd**. For more information about the local area, visit **https://maldegem.be**. Photos courtesy of the museum.*

DECEMBER 1944 HISTORICAL MUSEUM
La Gleize, Belgium

GPS Coordinates: N50.4100 E5.8460

Located in the building used by the Nazi SS as a field hospital, this museum has one of the formidable German "Royal Tiger" tanks that fought in the Battle of the Bulge. Well worth visiting, the excellent museum website reveals a great deal of very interesting information about the museum's history and its collection.

It is exactly here that fighting took place resulting in hundreds of American, British and German deaths. In 1989, Philippe Gillain founded a cooperative society which, with the help of the Municipality of Stoumont, the Province of Liège and Gérard Grégoire, developed the museum in a building that housed a German infirmary during the fighting.

The first floor of the museum is devoted to the German counter-offensive led by tanks of the dreadful SS Kampfgruppe Peiper with multiple thematic windows full of thousands of objects of great historical value recovered in the field or donated by veterans. The detailed history of each object is included, like the Russian 120mm mortar, abandoned by the SS in their flight. Remaining in place for more than 40 years in the orchard of local resident Maria George, ill-intentioned criminals came during a dark night to tear the musical mortar from the ground and load it on a trailer. They were chased by a witness, the mortar was tipped onto the road, the thieves fled and the cumbersome tube was recovered!

The visit continues with the arrival of American troops, and in particular the 3rd Armored Division and the famous 82nd Airborne Division, which opposed Peiper's tanks. The route is dotted with windows and dioramas of striking realism, showing the richness of the collections kept at the Museum.

In the screening room, the film "La Gleize 1944" depicts the realistic sounds of automatic weapons and "Stalin's organs" (rocket tubes). Soldiers run under a deluge of iron and fire, prisoners are taken and march past before our eyes. The images are real, the sound too. It is in the midst of fights that the propaganda teams shot their films, providing gripping scenes for twenty minutes.

In other showcases, there are other remains. Helmets pierced by bullets or shrapnel; or the German ammunition box splashed with blood, or the coat of an SS found on the battlefield with holes from shrapnel at the collar as well as at the height of the legs. Sometimes, it is an unexpected object like the radio station thrown from a B-17 in trouble to lighten the plane and regain altitude! The package is so well padded that its contents are intact, including a kite antenna. Constantly changing and improving, this is a museum worth visiting!

*For more information about this museum, please visit **www.december44.com**. For more information about the La Gleize/Stoumont area, visit **www.stoumont.be/**. Photos courtesy of the museum.*

FOR FREEDOM MUSEUM
Knokke-Heist, Belgium

GPS Coordinates: N51.3135 E3.2520

Located near Belgium's popular North Sea beaches, this World War II museum is highly rated by visitors. The museum is especially well-known for its meticulous mannequin skin treatments resulting in the very realistic - looking soldiers presented in its extensively–detailed military dioramas.

No inhabitant of the Zwinstreek and West Zeeland Flanders area was spared repression and hardship between 1940 and 1944 during the four years of Nazi occupation. This dark period in our history is the museum's main theme. It is precisely this period of our local past that we want to pass on to our children and grandchildren in the hope that such war violence will never again be repeated.

Young people need to know that freedom has a price, a price our ancestors paid with hard currency so we must cherish Freedom. This important message of peace and tolerance is given daily in the For Freedom Museum.

To present our uniforms we chose to work with mannequins and 30 years of collecting has resulted in 100 of these creations. Most of the mannequin heads in our museum were made out of wax in the twenties and thirties. Their glass eyes and implanted hair give them a unique appearance. Wax heads sometime arrive at the For Freedom Museum in a wretched state but each is lovingly restored by the craftsmanship of curator Freddy Jones and mannequin stylist Jacqueline Bronneberg. This gives the mannequins a second life in our museum and results in them looking very real and life-like.

The For Freedom Museum is located in the old community school of the picturesque polder village of Ramskapelle (part of Knokke-Heist) where you can find the fine military collections by Freddy Jones, Patrick Tierssoone and the Belgian Aviation History Association.

From the moment you enter the museum you'll see how much attention has been paid to the details. Sometimes you will really see yourself in a plane, then in a U-boat, and suddenly you find yourself in a barn with a historic fact you can marvel about. The décor in itself is already something worth seeing in its own right. For Freedom is a living museum where the displays are continuously being developed further with regularly different vehicles to view. We look forward to seeing you when you visit Belgium's coastal region.

*For more information about the museum, visit **http://forfreedommuseum.be/en/home-en/**. For more information about the museum and the local area, visit **www.myknokke-heist.be/en/freedom-museum**. Photos courtesy of the museum.*

FORT AUBIN-NEUFCHÂTEAU
Dalhem, Belgium

Photo: Jean Herman Jun 2017 Google.com

GPS Coordinates: N50.7213 E5.7904

Manned mostly by teen-age soldiers, this Belgian fort is famous for its enduring, fierce and brave resistance during the May, 1940 German invasion. The battle scars have been preserved to honor their memory.

Fort d'Aubin-Neufchâteau was constructed during the 1930s as one of four major defensive fortifications built to protect the northern and eastern flanks of the city of Liège from a German attack. When German forces invaded on May 10 1940, the fort was surrounded by the Germans by the end of the first day.

However, instead of surrendering, the fort fought the Germans fiercely for 11 days, enduring serious losses, heavy artillery shelling, aerial bombing and repeated assaults before finally running out of ammunition and having to surrender to the Germans on May 21.

Guided tours of the fort occur every 3rd Sunday of each month between April and November in French, Dutch, English and German. Admission includes an above-ground walk around the massif where your guide will explain the fortifications and the 12 day battle. You will then enter and descend 160 steps into the tunnel network and galleries that include the cathedral-like munitions store, the machine and generator rooms, the shower block, the hospital, the chapel and the incredibly deep well.

Dominick C Oct 2017 Google.com

Along the way you will witness the devastation caused by the testing of new German secret weapons. Finally, you will exit the underground network where you will see the anti-tank defenses. The best tour end anywhere, the tour will end at the neighboring café, where you can pause for a coffee and a drink and reflect on your visit to Fort Aubin-Neufchâteau and the soldiers who fought and died there.

Photo: Berny Sijbers Nov 2019 Google.com

Photo: Robert Senders Oct 2017 Google.com

For more information about the museum, visit www.fort-aubin-neufchateau.be. For more information about the Dalhem area, visit www.dalhem.be/ and www.paysdeherve.be/ for more information about the region's tourism opportunities.

FORT BREENDONK NATIONAL MEMORIAL
Willebroek, Belgium

GPS Coordinates: N51.0581 E4.3417

The Fort Breendonk National Memorial is a very well-preserved example of the prison camps that were operated by Nazi Germany. Also a National Museum, it is a special place to visit and remember those innocent people who suffered here.

Wagon

Mirador

On 10 May 1940 at 8.30am, King Léopold III, the Commander in Chief, arrived at Breendonk, establishing the fort as the initial headquarters of the Belgian General Staff but, because of the onslaught of the German forces, by May 17th the General Headquarters had to be moved to the Ghent region.

On 20 September 1940 Nazi SS Sturmbannführer Philip Schmitt brought his first victims to Breendonk. The Fort officially became a transit camp and a major centre for the *Sicherheitspolizei-Sicherheitsdienst (SIPO/SD), the German political police.* During the first year of the Occupation, Jews made up half of the prisoners.

From 1942 onwards the camp gradually became a camp for political prisoners and members of the Resistance before they too were deported. Prisoners stayed on average three months at the fortress before being deported towards the concentration camps in Germany, Austria or Poland.

Breendonk hardly differed from an official concentration camp. The undernourishment, the forced labor and the ever-present physical cruelty at the hands of the SS guards sometimes caused the death of prisoners. In total, around 3500 persons, including around thirty women, were subjected to the "Hell of Breendonk", as Franz Fischer calls it in his memoirs. Half of these 3,500 did not come back from the camps alive.

In the spring of 1946 the Belgian SS men and the civilians and prisoners who behaved badly towards their fellow prisoners were put on trial. Two of the SS men were sentenced to death.

A visit to Fort Breendonk is more than a visit to a museum. The cruelty of bigotry and oppression is on display everywhere. A primary focus of the Memorial is youth educational programs. Each year more than 60,000 schoolchildren visit the Memorial and Fort. The artwork by former prisoners is particularly moving.

*For more information about the museum, visit **www.breendonk.be.** For more information about the Willebroek area, **visit** www.willebroek.be.. Photos courtesy of the museum.*

FORT EBEN-EMAEL MUSEUM
Eben-Emael (Bassenge), Belgium

GPS Coordinates: N50.7976 E5.6789

With three levels, barracks for 1,200 soldiers, 17 bunkers and 5 km of underground tunnels, Fort Eben-Emael is an excellent example of how the technological advances of the German army far outpaced the outdated and no longer effective defensive approaches along the German border.

Fort Eben-Emael, constructed between 1932 and 1935, was one of the largest fortifications in Europe and was thought to be impregnable. The spectacular and innovative attack on the fortress by an elite unit of German paratroopers in 10 DFS 230 gliders on 10 May 1940 marked the world's first-ever airborne attack and the tragic start of World War II for Western Europe.

Take a step back in time and visit the restored barracks, the museum, the immense system of galleries and the combat positions and then immerse yourself in the secret and innovative German plans for the attack on the fort.

Follow the museum guide through the maze of underground galleries to the command post and an artillery bunker. See the disastrous consequences of a new type of explosive (hollow charge), used for the first time in global military history during the attack on the fort.

Discover the huge roof with the bunkers and artillery cupolas. You will marvel at the 440-tonne cupola with a 360° firing arc and a range of up to 17 km. The two undamaged casemates, which can still be visited today, are each equipped with three rapid-fire 75mm guns. One of only three known German DFS 230 gliders is displayed.

This huge military complex was dug out of a limestone (sedimentary rock) hill, creating a floor plan measuring 700 m by 900 m. The Albert canal, alongside the fort, but 60 m below, forms the eastern perimeter of the fort on the side towards Germany. A moat with the ability to flood the area around the entrance protected the western perimeter and a dry anti-tank ditch was dug along the south side and re-enforced with anti-tank and barbed-wire fences.

Road signs were installed to show the soldiers in the garrison the way through the underground tunnel system. Today, tours in four languages keep visitors from becoming lost in the maze of tunnels. The museum has a pleasant café that is open during special occasions but drinks from a vending machine and a seating area are offered year round, allowing you to contemplate the expanse of what you have witnessed.

*For more information about the museum, please visit **www.fort-eben-emael.be**. For more information about the Bassenge area, visit **www.bassenge.be/**. Photos courtesy of the museum.*

FORT EMBOURG MUSEUM
Chaudfontaine, Belgium

The Entrance to Fort Embourg

The Lovely Town of Chaudfontaine

GPS Coordinates: N50.58444 E5.61589

This is one of 12 defensive forts built in the 1890s encircling the town of Liège. Bravely defended, they were no match for the vicious German Blitzkrieg invasion that occurred during May of 1940.

A visit to Fort Embourg includes enjoying the area's natural beauty and charm—and the excellent Chaudfontaine Belgian chocolates.

The Fort of Embourg is one of the 12 forts that made up the fortified position of Liège at the end of the 19th century in Belgium. It was built between 1888 and 1892 according to the plans drawn up by General Brialmont. It was made of non-reinforced concrete, a new material at the time, rather than in stonework.

The fort was heavily bombarded in the First World War during the Battle of Liège, and again at the start of the Second World War. It has been preserved and today is a museum to honor those who fought so bravely here in two wars.

After the initial contact on 12th May with German troops, the Fort of Embourg was surrounded on 13th May and the Fort of Chaudfontaine, its neighbor, provided artillery support against the German infantry which attacked at 10 pm. On 14th May, the Germans continued to bombard the Fort of Embourg while it was providing artillery support to the Chaudfontaine fort. On 15th May, the bombardment started at 2 pm and continued until nightfall.

The following day, with the bombardment unrelenting, the German infantry occupied the area around the fort. On 17th May, the fort was again attacked by the German artillery, infantry and air force. The fort's defenders requested assistance from its neighbors but they were unable to provide it. Its turrets were soon put out of action. After having sabotaged the fort, the garrison raised the white flag on 17th May at approximately 8 pm.

The Fort of Embourg museum was opened in 1973. The museum now recounts the history of the two wars and boasts a unique collection of arms, uniforms and equipment in a sobering structure that will make you feel the fear felt by those who have heroically fought and died here.

For more information about the museum visit www.en.liegetourisme.be/musee-du-fort-d-embourg.html#media. For more information about the town of Chaudfontaine, please visit the town's website at: www.chaudfontaine.be/. Photos courtesy of the museum.

FORT HUY MUSEUM
Huy, Belgium

Photo from Huy municipal website: huy.be

GPS Coordinates: N50.5174 E5.2371

An excellent example exposing the diabolical nature of the Nazi regime, this museum is well worth visiting. Located far above the River Meuse, the fort offers commanding views of Huy, the meanders of the Meuse, and the surrounding forests and hills of the beautiful Belgian Ardennes.

Built by the Dutch between 1818 and 1823 on the site of a castle that was destroyed in 1717, the fort was transformed into a detention camp and prison by the German army immediately after the invasion of May 10 1940. From May 1940 to 5 September 1944, the Germans used the fort as a prison camp that was guarded by the Wehrmacht and controlled by the "Geheime Staatspolizei" (the Gestapo). More than 7,000 political opponents, Jews, black marketers, those who refused to pay duties and resistance fighters of various nationalities were imprisoned there.

The fort was also used by the Germans as one of the central departure points for transports from Belgium to the Nazi concentration camps in the German Reich. Under the command of Field Marshall Wilhelm Keitel, prisoners were typically deported without their families being informed, a measure meant to prevent the population from supporting the resistance. After the war the fort was used as a prison for collaborators.

The interrogation rooms, detention rooms, and the testimonies of prisoners paint a sinister picture of the conditions faced by those held here by the Germans. A video presentation leaves the visitor with a life-long memory of what happened here during the war and special educational programs have been developed for schools and young visitors. Comfortable indoor and outdoor picnic areas and a conference room are also available.

For more information about the museum, visit www.en.liegetourisme.be/huy-fort.html. For more information about the Huy area, visit www.huy.be. Except as noted, all photos courtesy of the museum.

HENRI-CHAPELLE AMERICAN CEMETERY
Henri-Chapelle / Welkenraedt, Belgium

Photo: Philippe Vanderdonckt, Mar 2014

GPS Coordinates: N50.6974 E5.9010

The Henri-Chapelle American Cemetery contains burials from all the major battles in Northern Europe from September 1944 through March 1945, including the Battle of the Bulge. An overlook west of the highway offers an excellent view of the rolling Belgian countryside that was once a battlefield.

At the Henri-Chapelle American Cemetery and Memorial in Belgium, covering 57 acres, rest 7,992 of our American military dead, most of whom lost their lives during the advance of the U.S. armed forces into Germany. Their headstones are arranged in gentle arcs sweeping across a broad green lawn that slopes gently downhill below an impressive colonnade overlooking the cemetery.

The colonnade, with the chapel and map room, forms the memorial overlooking the burial area. The chapel is simple, but richly ornamented. In the map room are two maps of military operations, carved in black granite, with inscriptions recalling the achievements of our forces. On the rectangular piers of the colonnade are inscribed the names of 450 missing. Rosettes mark the names of those since recovered and identified. The seals of the states and territories are also carved on these piers.

The cemetery possesses great military historic significance as it holds fallen Americans of two major military operations: one covering the U.S. First Army's drive in September 1944 through northern France, Belgium, Holland and Luxembourg and into Germany; and the second covering the Battle of the Bulge. It was from the temporary cemetery at Henri-Chapelle that the first shipments of remains of American war dead were returned to the United States for permanent burial.

The repatriation program began on July 27, 1947 at a special ceremony at the cemetery when the disinterment began. The first shipment of 5,600 American war dead from Henri-Chapelle left Antwerp, Belgium the first week of October 1947. An impressive ceremony was held, with over 30,000 Belgian citizens attending, along with representatives of the Belgium government and senior Americans.

This cemetery, and all other major American World War II cemeteries in Europe are managed and maintained by the American Battle Monuments Commission (ABMC).

Photo: Jason Kahne, Feb 2011

Photo: Jason Kahne, Feb 2020

Photo: Frits Kruishaar, Nov 2011

*For more information about this cemetery, please visit **www.abmc.gov**. For more information about the Welkenraedt area, visit **www.si-welkenraedt.be/**. All photos from ABMC (American Battle Monuments Commission) website: **www.paysdeherve.be/**.*

THE KAZERNE DOSSIN MEMORIAL & MUSEUM
Mechelen, Belgium

GPS Coordinates: N50.4021 E6.0661

A very special part of this museum is the museum's effort to identify the behaviors in modern society that lead to discrimination, violence and the loss of freedom, stressing the importance of rejecting those behaviors.

Between August 1942 and July 1944, 25,483 Jews and 354 Roma and Sinti were deported from the 18th century Dossin military barracks to Auschwitz-Birkenau, only 5% surviving. Kazerne Dossin is an intense and unique place of commemoration that deals with the persecution of the Jews and Roma in Belgium.

The old military barracks is now a memorial to the unfortunate people who waited here in desperation and terrible fear before going on to die in unspeakable circumstances. The Memorial gives visitors an opportunity to silently remember those victims and, for their next of kin, this place has a special significance, evoking an almost tangible memory of the dramatic hours and days endured by family members and serving as the missing grave around which family and friends come together to mourn.

In the first room, photographs and video images paint a picture of Jewish life in Belgium before the war, showing an engaged and dynamic community with dreams and expectations. Each and every one of them has a story to tell. The Roma were a small and diverse minority group in Belgium and like the Jews, they were also victims of the Nazis.

Kazerne Dossin does not only deal with the "Belgian case" but it is also a museum about collective violence towards specific groups and races. Using the Holocaust as an example, Kazerne Dossin uncovers the timeless mechanisms of group pressure and collective violence that, under certain conditions, can result in mass murder and genocide.

This question touches the core of modern human rights, placing an emphasis on freedom and non-discrimination. The behaviors of the perpetrators and opportunists serve as the basis for alerting the visitor to the collective violent mechanisms among us, and to the need to say "No." For this purpose, the visitor starts by viewing a movie in which the museum and its disturbing questions are presented.

For more information about the museum, please visit www.kazernedossin.eu. For more information about the tourism opportunities in the Mechelen area, visit www.visit.mechelen.be. Photos courtesy of the museum.

MUSEUM OF THE BATTLE OF THE ARDENNES
La Roche-en-Ardenne, Belgium

With its well-preserved medieval hilltop castle, and tucked into a valley of hills and forests along the River Ourthe, La Roche-En-Ardenne is one of the most beautiful small towns in the entire Ardennes region. Totally destroyed during the Battle of the Bulge, the town has fully restored its charm and popular appeal. This museum is as beautiful as its hometown.

GPS Coordinates: N50.1833 E5.5760

The Museum of the Battle of the Ardennes tells the story of the battle and liberation of La Roche and nearby villages on the left bank of the River Ourthe during the Battle of the Bulge.

Starting 23 December, American warplanes bombed German positions in La Roche, and a bridge on the Ourthe that was still intact. During the battle more than 90% of the town of La Roche was destroyed and 114 inhabitants were killed. The museum is dedicated to their memory and to the liberators.

Founded in 1992, the La Roche Museum of the Battle of the Ardennes (Musée de la Bataille des Ardennes) places a particular focus on the roles played by British troops in the liberation of the Ardennes. A large museum, the museum spreads over three levels, with more than 120 mannequins of American, English, German and even Scottish soldiers with their equipment and armament, as well as uniforms donated by veterans of the Battle of the Bulge.

The visitor will also discover an important collection of light and heavy arms, personal objects and equipment found on the battlefield, some 20 military vehicles, and the famous Enigma decoding machine of Polish origin. The daily life of the soldiers during the battle is captured in a collection of photographs. The museum presents wall maps of the successive stages of the Battle of the Bulge and a film made with period pictures of the liberation of La Roche in January 1945.

The privately-run Battle of the Ardennes Museum is the brainchild of Michel Bouillon and his son Gilles. What started off as a modest hobby collecting artefacts relating to the battle just grew and grew; in the end, the two men had accumulated so many objects that in 1993 they decided to open a museum. This too has grown dramatically so that now it covers more than 1,500 square meters spread over three floors.

For more information about the museum, please visit www.batarden.be/laroche/. For more information about the La Roche-en-Ardenne area, visit www.la-roche-en-ardenne.be/. Photos courtesy of the museum.

LOMMEL GERMAN MILITARY CEMETERY
Lommel, Belgium

GPS Coordinates: N51.1907 E5.3048

This beautiful cemetery contains the largest number of fallen German soldiers of any military cemetery in Europe, including those in Germany. Impressive to visit any time of the year, each year the winter blooming of the heather entices thousands of visitors to pay their respects.

In Lommel, thousands and thousands of German soldiers of the Second World War have been led to rest. The German military cemetery is the largest European military cemetery for German soldiers of the Second World War outside of Germany, and tells the stories of the soldiers who died for their country. 39,111 German and Polish soldiers rest in this World War II cemetery attracting more than 30,000 visitors per year. After the majority had been buried in other Allied cemeteries, in 1946 and 1947 the soldiers' remains were brought to Lommel for interment. The initial inauguration of the graveyard took place in September 1959.

Covering a beautifully maintained park of 16 hectares (44 acres), 20,000 crosses remind us of the horror of the European 1940-1945 war. Thanks to the planting of heather, the site is bathed in an impressive purple glow during the months of January and February.

A walk along the endless rows of graves leaves no one untouched and you can learn the hidden story behind this German Military Cemetery by taking the guided tour. A cemetery building accommodates visitors with an information room, a monumental crypt and, on top of it, an immense statue in black lava rock forms the entrance to the graveyard.

Located along a Lommel cycling route, in the Residence Building you will find the Hof ten Vrede café that serves a variety of Belgian and European food, spirits and excellent desserts.

*For more information about the cemetery, visit **www.huisovergrenzen.eu.** For more information about the Lommel area, visit **www.lommel.be**. Photos courtesy of the cemetery website.*

MANHAY HISTORY 44 MUSEUM
Manhay, Belgium

GPS Coordinates: N50.2902 E5.6603

This new World War II museum is getting excellent reviews by those who have visited the museum. Located in the beautiful Belgian Ardennes, the museum is gaining notoriety for it's quality and for it's support and hosting of historical reenactments at the museum.

The new Manhay History 44 Museum vividly tells the story of the Battle of Manhay, a part of the Battle of the Bulge, that began on 23 December 1944, lasting until the liberation of the last villages of the region in January 1945.

The battle began with the defeat of the Americans in Manhay by the 2nd SS Panzer division, forcing the Americans to withdraw. In the following days, during Christmas, the Americans retaliated fiercely, and, with heavy losses, succeeded in pushing the German forces out of the area, liberating Manhay for the second time.

The museum puts you on board for a journey from New York to Europe in the boots of an American soldier who ends up fighting here, a story that will fully immerse you in the Battle of Manhay.

The museum collection includes many fascinating memorabilia, including full sets of uniforms and equipment donated by American veterans who fought at Manhay as well as many interesting local civilian objects such as two war-damaged church statues donated by the village of Odeigne, located 4 km away. The museum is continually increasing and improving its collection and exhibits.

Thanks to the meticulously-prepared decors and dioramas recreating iconic scenes of the battle precisely and a stunning 10-minute video with archived film, this museum will help you better understand this tragic part of World War II history and help us honor the many American soldiers who took part in this fierce battle to defeat the Nazis and restore our freedom.

For more information about the museum, visit **www.mhm44.be.** *For more information about the Manhay area, visit* **www.manhay.be/loisirs/tourisme/decouvrir-manhay**. *Photos courtesy of the museum.*

MONS MEMORIAL MUSEUM
Mons, Belgium

GPS Coordinates: N50.0393 E4.2200

This very beautiful modern museum encompasses the histories of the Mons territory during both WWI and WWII. The museum's extensive collection of more than 5,000 artifacts is artfully displayed with an impressive use of interactive technology.

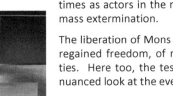

A museum of society, a place of reflection, a space for questioning . . . so many names to define the Mons Memorial Museum!

This new museum space invites visitors of all ages to question themselves about the multiple and complex realities of war. A vast permanent exhibition presents to the visitor the history of the Mons region and although the museum is focused on the two world war events, it begins with a Middle age history of the city.

Through the fateful stories of men and women who witnessed the events, the visitor is immersed in the daily life of soldiers and civilians in times of war. Their testimonies form the real common thread of the visit and bring the hundreds of objects presented to life. Through these letters, notebooks and interviews, a sensitive look is cast on the events by the Mons Memorial Museum.

Built from more than 5,000 artifacts in the military history collections of the city of Mons, the exhibits fundamentally reflect on the relationship between the civilian population and the military. Temporary exhibitions are regularly presented to complete the visitor's tour, many of which discuss societal issues.

The Mons Memorial Museum is transformed into a real place of questioning with new technologies (3D projection, "serious game" interactive table, etc.), used to shape the historical content; to bring it to life. The use of testimonials (interviews, letters, etc.) is at the heart of the concept transmitting history to the visitor.

The Great War inaugurated a cycle of violence which culminated in the Second World War when Mons is once again invaded by an armed force and is once again experiencing the throes of occupation. Civilians find themselves again at the center of the conflict, sometimes as actors in the resistance, often times as victims of harassment, deportations and mass extermination.

The liberation of Mons in September 1944 by American troops marked the beginning of a regained freedom, of reconstruction, but also the start of economic and social difficulties. Here too, the testimonies of the survivors of the time will allow visitors to take a nuanced look at the events that unfolded during the years after the war ended.

A museum for reflection, investigation and interaction, the museum includes a cafeteria with an ample capacity of more than 120 people. (No food or drinks are sold).

*For more information about the museum, visit **http://www.monsmemorialmuseum.mons.be/**. For more information about other attractions in the Mons area, visit **https://www.visitmons.co.uk/see-do/top-sights/mons-the-first-the-last**. Photos courtesy of the museum.*

NATIONAL MUSEUM OF THE RESISTANCE
Anderlecht (Brussels), Belgium

GPS Coordinates: N50.0018 E4.4591

This museum is located in the suburbs of Brussels near the Clemenceau metro station. In 1943 it was the site of one of the most dangerous resistance efforts undertaken in Brussels during the war. It gave people the needed hope that the unsustainable German occupation of Belgium would not endure.

The striking Belgian Resistance Museum exhibits a comprehensive collection covering the many resistance movements that operated throughout Belgium during World War II. Visitors often wonder why it doesn't look like typical museums and in particular why the unassuming museum entrance appears no different than the other buildings surrounding it.

It is because this building was the site of one of the most important resistance efforts carried out in Brussels during the war, designed not to destroy German assets but instead, to raise the hope of the beleaguered residents of this capital city.

During the war the Germans took over the national newspaper *Le Soir* to circulate Nazi propaganda. In 1943, a group of resistance members conspired to produce a satiric issue of this newspaper: while the format and layout appeared unchanged, the text used humor and derision to mock the Nazis.

National Museum of the Resistance © Hidden Raven

Under the leadership of Marc Aubrion, and under the threat of death, members of the Front de l'Indépendance wrote, printed and distributed more than 50,000 copies of this spook issue, commonly called the *"Faux Soir"*, taking the Nazis completely by surprise. The newspaper was widely read, significantly raising the spirits of the people and giving them hope at a time when they were experiencing the worst of Nazi suppression.

Inaugurated on June 6, 1972, the museum presents the actions and the personal peril faced by members of the various movements of the Belgian resistance grouped in the Resistance Action Committee (CAR-ARW). Their actions included taking part in underground press, armed resistance, aid to refractories, intelligence networks, escape lines, Jewish rescue networks and assisting victims of persecution.

The museum's collection is comprised of resistance armbands, typewriters, weapons, prisoner uniforms, many documents and photographs that together paint a picture of what life was like during the occupation.

The museum is especially active in educating primary and secondary school students. Its moral and civic goal is to pursue and transmit onto the younger generations the ideals and spirit embodied by the Resistance so they may be prepared for the present dangers of all forms of political extremism.

www/visit.brussels.be

*For more information about the museum, visit **www.museumresistance.be** and **www.visit.brussels/en/place/Musee-National-de-la-Resistance.** Photos courtesy of the museum.*

THE REMEMBER MUSEUM 39-45
Thimister-Clermont, Belgium

GPS Coordinates: N50.6688 E5.8840

This is one of those few museums where you feel the personal touch of the museum creators. A very special bond has developed between this museum and the descendants of the American 1st Infantry Division who convalesced here prior to suddenly having to leave to join in on the Battle of the Bulge.

Marcel Schmetz was seven years old when the area where he lived was annexed to the German Reich. Forced to attend primary school in the neighboring village where only German was allowed to be spoken, he and his family then lived for four years under perpetual restrictions and bad treatment until September 11, 1944 when the Plateau of Herve, and especially Clermont, was liberated. After the farm was liberated, his parents' farm was transformed into an enormous bivouac for one hundred and ten soldiers of the American First Infantry Division. It was like a vacation for a little boy who had been deprived of everything during the previous four years.

Then all of a sudden the G.I.s left in a hurry for the Battle of the Bulge with no time to pack so their many personal items and many pieces of equipment were left behind at the farm. Marcel kept them out of respect for and in memory of those who had left.

As an adult, Marcel taught himself to restore jeeps and motorcycles, opening his own body shop. In 1991, Marcel met Mathilde and the meeting would change both of their lives. Together they established a museum in the body shop with the goal of the museum being completed by 1994 for the 50th Anniversary of D-Day. After attending the D-Day ceremonies in Normandy, seventeen American WWII Veterans drove to Clermont for the inauguration of the museum, starting an everlasting friendship between the couple and these boys. The museum has continued to grow in size, quality and significance since then.

Touched and impressed by the respect that surrounds all of these items, many American WWII Veterans have donated their personal belongings to the museum and many veteran names are engraved on the wall outside of the museum and on the Red Ball Express truck that has also been transformed into a movie theatre. Guided tours are provided in French, Dutch, English, German and Walloon.

Today, many people visit the museum including school children, tour operators and especially the descendants of the 1st Infantry Division who have developed many close relationships with the museum. As proof, there are several hundreds of Christmas letters which Marcel and Mathilde receive each year . . . and to which they need to answer !

For more information about the museum, please visit www.remembermuseum.be. For more information about the Thimister-Clermont area, visit www.thimister-clermont.be/commune/services-communaux/tourisme. Photos courtesy of the museum.

WOLFSSCHLUCHT 1 (WOLF'S RAVINE)
Brûly-de-Pesche (Couvin), Belgium

Photo: Dirk Vanfraechem

GPS Coordinates: N50.0018 E4.4591

This bunker complex is where Hitler and his commanders met to devise and direct the Battle of France during June 1940. Located in a beautiful and remote part of the Ardennes forest, the visitor is forced to reflect on the realities of World War II.

Photo: Myriam Lanckmans

Photo: Bert Jans

Photo: Bert Jans

Lost in the middle of a sprawling forest, Brûly-de-Pesche could have forever remained just another spot on the map, but the events of World War II decided otherwise. The tactics and rapid advance of the German offensive through the Ardennes mountains on May 10, 1940 forced Hitler to find a headquarters further west. The village of Brûly-de-Pesche was chosen, and within one week a German General Headquarters was established and constituted as a prohibited access zone.

Hitler and his High Command came to Brûly-de-Pesche on June 6, 1940. He oversaw the Battle of France from this place, which he called the "Wolf's Ravine".

The site is still home to vestiges of Hitler's stay here, with two pavilions like those of 1940. One boasts a large collection of period photos and DVD films (FR-NL-EN), while the other one, located nearby, commemorates the local resistance efforts of Hotton Service Group D. An exhibition of the materials they used provides a glimpse of the tough day-to-day life of the resistance fighters.

Finally, the impressive Bunker awaits the visitor. Dive into the heart of the events that took place in Brûly-de-Pesche during the Second World War and live immersive experiences, including an immersive walk, animated site exhibits, film, and activities based on the themes of interculturality and youth and adult educational objectives. Educational panels and new interactive scenography equipment will enhance your visit and stimulate your reflections. A short film also offers various testimonies and documents relating the Nazi ideology, its devastating consequences and the commitment required for active Resistance.

You are strongly advised to book your visit by phone or via our website at least 24 hours in advance.

Photo: Myriam Lanckmans

For more information about the museum, visit www.bdp1940.be. For more information about the beautiful areas surrounding the museum, visit www.tourisme-couvin.be. Except as noted, photos courtesy of the museum.

WORLD WAR II IN NORTHERN FRANCE

After being driven north by the Germans to the coastal town of Dunkirk, more than 330,000 French and British troops were evacuated to Britain in 9 days by a flotilla of both Navy and private vessels.

On D-Day, June 6, 1944, more than 150,000 Allied troops and paratroopers landed on the Normandy coast involving nearly 7,000 ships and 2,400 aircraft. It was by far the largest invasion in history.

Throughout the war, the British Special Operations Executive (SOE) maintained radio contact with most all resistance groups to arrange weapon and equipment drops to support the resistance efforts.

Two of the most widespread, underground news-papers in France played a crucial role in giving the people hope that the oppression and suffering of the French people was only a temporary condition.

Women played an important role in the French resistance movements, comprising up to 20% of the total number of resistance fighters. Often used as couriers, women were less likely to be arrested.

After the liberation, more than 20,000 collaborating French women were stripped half naked, shaved, kicked, beaten, spat upon, smeared with tar, paraded through the streets and sometimes even killed.

THE SMALL TOWN OCCUPATION STORIES OF NORTHERN FRANCE

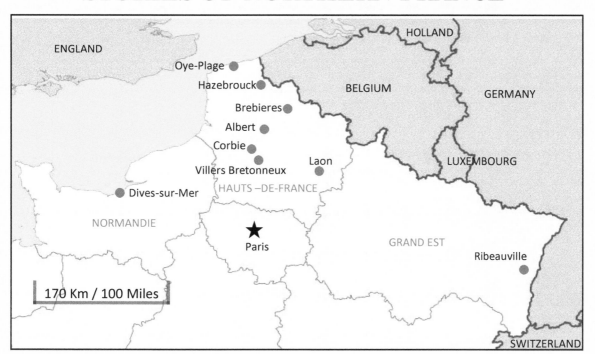

Northern France and World War II.

The Maginot Line and the Invasion. Prior to the start of World War II, France believed that their system of defensive forts along the Maginot Line would be sufficient to repel any attacks from Germany. Suddenly, on May 10, 1940, Germany invaded northern France with a deadly combination of mechanized and airborne assaults that quickly overwhelmed the defending forces, bypassing these defensive forts. Known as the Blitzkrieg, the Germans quickly penetrated deep into northern France and, on June 22nd, an armistice was signed, sealing France's defeat. Two million French prisoners of war were sent to camps in Germany.

The Occupation. The Germans immediately occupied the entire northern half of France and the entire French coastline. The southern half of France remained unoccupied under a puppet government in the town of Vichy until the Allies invaded north Africa in November of 1942. After that, the Germans occupied the entirety of France.

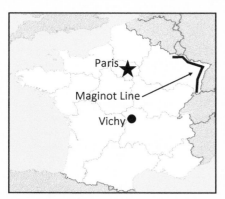

THE MAGINOT LINE OF FRENCH DEFENSIVE FORTIFICATIONS

After the occupation began, the Germans imposed more and more increasingly restrictive rules and regulations on the French population including food rationing, the deportation of hundreds of thousands of workers to work in Germany, strict curfews, travel restrictions, extreme taxations, the confiscation of agricultural goods, the registration of all Jewish citizens and the subsequent deportation of the Jewish residents to the Nazi death camps.

The worsening oppression resulted in the formation of resistance groups throughout France, especially in northern France. By 1942, the resistance groups had become organized, working in concert with Charles de Gaulle's Free French forces in England. Bolstered by airborne weapon and communication equipment drops from England, the resistance groups sabotaged the German occupiers in many ways, disrupting railway movements of German war equipment, printing and distributing resistance papers, disrupting German communication equipment, performing assassinations, performing reconnaissance for the Allies, hiding and helping downed Allied airmen return to England and helping those hiding from the Germans, including many Jews. Often times the German reprisals were severe, even including the random murdering of innocent civilians in the communities where the acts of resistance occurred.

The Liberation of France. On June 6, 1944 the D-Day liberation invasion occurred and the Allies began their unrelenting pursuit and destruction of the German army across northern France, reaching most of the eastern German border areas by September. By the end of the war, 600,000 French citizens had died, including more than 70,000 Jewish citizens. This would be equivalent to nearly 5 million people dying in the United States today.

ALBERT FRANCE

Region: Hauts de France   Pop. 1940: 9,300   Pop. 2019: 10,200

SITING & HERITAGE

The town of Albert is located in Northern France, in the Somme Department. The origins of the town date back to the Gallo-Roman Era. At that time, a small town called Ecrembatis was built on the so-called "Chaussée Brunehaut", an important trade route in Northern France.

In the beginning of the 17th century, the lands belonged to an Italian adventurer, Concino Concini, Marquis of Ancre (new name of the town). After Concini's assassination, Louis XIII, passionate about birds and hunting, gifted the town to one of his favourites, Charles Albert Duc de Luynes, Head Falconer of the King. In 1620, Charles Albert de Luynes changed the name of Ancre into his own name: Albert. Before WWII started, Albert had already been destroyed 7 times, but rebuilt every time.

GPS Coordinates: N50.0017 E2.6516

Underground shelters in Albert, which are now a part of the Somme Muséum 1916

Two views of the Potez aircraft factory in Méaulte

Damage to the Basilica Notre-Dame de Brebières

OUR TOWN'S OCCUPATION STORY

The invasion. Because of its location, the town has always been close to the frontier or on the invasion route. Located at only 3km from the front line during WWI, the town witnessed numerous battles between the Allies and the Germans. 90% of the town was destroyed: the city centre, the station and the factories were in ruins.

People in the city had started digging underground shelters in the Middle Ages, to protect themselves from frequent armies and invasions. After the experience of WWI, and at the approach of WWII, the municipality saw the importance of restoring its 13th century tunnels to be able to use them as air raid shelters. In 1938, the municipality strengthened the undergrounds with reinforced concrete. In case of an alert, kids were to go in first and families could stay inside for several hours. Indeed, those underground shelters were useful since the Potez airplane factories in Méaulte (the village next to Albert) became a target of German bombardments.

The 1st Panzer Division, an armoured division of the Wehrmacht, arrived in Albert on May 20th, 1940. The German Air Force, the Luftwaffe, commandeered the airfield between Albert and Bray-sur-Somme. A war committee was created in the Municipal Council in July 1940.

Oppression. Numerous buildings were commandeered by the Wehrmacht, starting with the town hall. Schools were occupied; among them the Collège Moderne (now Collège Pierre et Marie Curie) which was used for quartering soldiers. Hotels had to keep a register with the identity of all their guests, which then had to be approved by the Vichy government's Police Station. The landlord or proprietor could be considered responsible and penalized if the register was invalid or an opponent to the 3rd Reich was found.

In July 1940, several jobs were suppressed, in particular in the Police where the German Kommandantur placed its own people. The Germans used the aeronautic factories to create their own bomber, the Heinkel. To prevent the German army from using this facility, the Allies organized 11 bombardments of the factories, which resulted in numerous dead and wounded.

Resistance. Six inhabitants of Albert were in the "Convoy of the 45,000." This was the 1st Nazi convoy sent to Auschwitz on July 6, 1942, among which 90% were Communist activists deported following the first armed actions led by resistance fighters. None of them came back. In the following years, several resistance fighters, including members of the Municipality, were arrested and deported to camps in Germany and Poland.

On July 23rd, 1943 the trial of the "Groupe Michel" began at the German Military Court in Amiens. Groupe Michel was a resistance group in Northern France which had done a lot of sabotage, such as derailments and attacks. Among them were two inhabitants of Albert, Henri Wilgos (20) and Jacques Wilgos (18). Both were shot on August 2, 1943 in the ditch at the Amiens citadel, with 9 of their comrades.

AN IMPORTANT RESISTANCE LEADER

Léandre Deflandre

Léandre Joseph DEFLANDRE was born on September 26, 1901 in Fontaine-sous-Montdidier (Somme). He was an oil and fuel trader who became part of the Resistance movement, becoming the leader of the "Groupe Arthur".

Their main role was to collect information and give it to the Allies. They also helped escapees of Stalags and Allied pilots whose planes had crashed in the area. The Groupe Arthur was part of a bigger group called Libération Nord.

He was arrested by the Gestapo on July 23, 1944 and died soon after. The circumstances of his death are still unclear. One version says he managed to escape running through the Public Garden but was fatally wounded (a commemorative plaque can still be seen in the street nearby, close to the place of his supposed death). But another version testifies he was arrested and tortured in the prison of Amiens and was then buried alive in the Aveluy wood.

LIBERATION & RECOVERY

On August 31, 1944, after joining the resistance, the police and gendarmerie mercilessly fought all day long against an SS company. At 22:00 the British entered the town and took 300 prisoners. The next day, on September 1, 1944, Albert was liberated.

Albert was selected as one of the "affected localities" due to the large amount of destruction caused by the bombardments. Mainly residential buildings were destroyed, which led to a shortage of housing. A few months after the Liberation, some families were resettled in shelters that were transformed into apartments.

The Municipality had to make claim for war damages to stimulate the local economy and to provide for the inhabitants. In 1947, food was still shared through ration tickets and the portions were small. There was a lack of sugar, cacao, rice, cloth and working shoes and only limited quantities were available for a few years after the war. The unemployment rate after the war was high.

The town asked for the help of the Government to revive the airplane factories, which were already employing 6,000 people before the war in 1939. This helped a lot of local workers who were already qualified and specialized in aeronautic tasks before and during the war to find a job after the war.

An aerial view of Albert Today

OUR TOWN TODAY

Albert has always been surrounded by agricultural land, but since the 19th century, the strength of the town lies in its industry: metallurgy, machine tools, aeronautics. Today, Albert is a charming little town, full of history, where Remembrance Tourism and aeronautics industries contribute greatly to the economy. Albert is less than a two hour drive from Paris with a train station on the Paris-Lille railway line.

The welcoming heart of downtown Albert

The Reconstruction of the 1920's created more than 250 Art Deco façades that people can discover in the city centre through guided tours.

A main attraction, the Basilica Notre-Dame de Brebières built in the neo-Byzantine style, whose bell tower is topped by a statue of the Virgin Mary that is covered by 40,000 gold leaves, is a must see in Albert.

The Basilica Notre-Dame de Brebières

Not only history but nature is also very present in the town. The Public Garden, crossed by the river Ancre and its waterfall, is an arboretum classified in 2009 and the Ponds of the Velodrome are a Heaven for fishermen. To start your tour, you can visit the Tourist Office located in the former Public Bath of the town.

The Albert Town Hall

*For more information on the town of Albert, visit the town website : **www.ville-albert.fr/**. For more information about visiting Albert, visit the tourist office website : **www.tourisme-paysducoquelicot.com/***

This information was contributed by Flora Devillers and Perrine Chovaux, Office de Tourisme du Pays du Coquelicot. Photos courtesy of the Municipality of Albert.

BREBIÈRES FRANCE

Region: Hauts de France   Pop. 1940: 2,000   Pop. 2020: 5,000

SITING & HERITAGE

Brebières is located in the Scarpe valley between the towns of Arras and Douai on the edge of the Nord and Pas-de-Calais departments, at the base of rolling foothills. Archaeological research has established that the area has been inhabited from prehistoric times (before 1000 BC). Breeding and raising sheep was one of the first activities in the village, and the name Brebières came from sheep. The Municipal coat of arms shows two sheep facing a water mill wheel to symbolize the first activity of the village.

Le Chateau Pilat is an old farm of the Pilat family, dating from the 17th century. The Pilats were an influential family of farmer-breeders. They gave the municipality 7 Mayors, 1 General Councilor and 1 Deputy Mayor. The Pilat castle has been the property of the town since 1938 and was converted into the town hall in 1949.

GPS Coordinates: N50.3380 E3.0224

OUR TOWN'S OCCUPATION STORY

The Invasion. After eight months of the "Phony War", the Germans entered France on May 10, 1940 and from May 24 on, Brebières was occupied. The Germans settled down and appropriated all of the communal buildings. The authorities of Brebières were very quickly obliged to put themselves under German authority with its combination of requirements, rationing, denunciations, and arrests.

Oppression. Over time, the occupiers became more and more defensive to the obvious fact that most of the Brebièrois had a hostile attitude to German authority. The Germans decided that the population must face their arrogance and the demands of the invader, and the residents' hostile attitudes, increased.

Resistance. Despite the efforts of the Germans to control all aspects of the city, passive and active resistance was organized and developed. Patriots included many women joining secret resistance organizations but, beginning in 1943, the Germans began to dismantle the resistance organizations in the Brebières / Vitry sector. There were 33 arrests recorded, without counting those of nearby Arras and Douai. 28 people were deported. (See the "Special History" section on the next page for stories of local FTP Resistance members Pierre Moreau and Emile Mocq who died at the hands of the Nazis).

German soldiers at the Brebières railway station

Bombardments. Brebières was a military location of prime importance to the Germans. There was an airfield located partly on the territory of the commune; it also had the locks and the Levis bridge on the Scarpe, the railway station and railroad tracks. Brebières looked like one huge barracks. In 1941 nearly 5,000 German soldiers were housed in the village. Because of these, Brebières became a prime target for Allied bombing.

There were around thirty bombings between August 15, 1943 and September 1, 1944, the date of Liberation. The whole town was hit by bombs, and the damage was considerable. The railroad tracks were cut; the collapse of the bridge on the national road blocked traffic; the river locks were destroyed so navigation on the Scarpe became impossible. The main target, the airfield, was hit many times. Among the townspeople, 13 were dead and 8 were wounded.

Liberation. In front of the Allies' advance, at the end of August, the German retreat became more precipitous. For two days they had been destroying their airfield facilities, ammunition depots, batteries, and their quarters. Before leaving the city, they decide to shoot the 4 Russian prisoners being held. Two were killed in the prison. The two others escaped, to be hunted by the soldiers. Of those, one was fatally injured in a field; the other, though injured, managed to escape. (The victims were buried in the municipal cemetery.)

On September 1, 1944, Brebières was liberated. At 18:20h, an English armored tank was in Brebières and the joy was great. The flags came out of their hiding places, the people kissed, the cries resounded, "Vive les Allies, Vive la France!" The tanks followed one another on the national road towards Douai. On September 3 at 15:00h there was a Liberation parade. The crowd went to the war memorial, and after singing La Marseillaise they visited to the tomb of the Russian soldiers killed by the Germans.

English armor on the National road

Liberation, September 1944

THREE LOCAL RESISTANCE HEROS

Pierre Moreau: 1896-1944, died in deportation. In 1941 he was inter-municipal manager of the resistance network, head of the cantonal sector of Vitry, and Lieutenant in the FTP (Francs-Tireurs et Partisans) resistance organization. He was denounced, and was arrested by the Vichy police on May 8, 1943 and delivered to the enemy. He was transferred in February 1944 to Eyssa prison, where he participated in the prisoners revolt.

Pierre Moreau

On June 1, 1944 he was transferred to Compiegne prison and in early July he was sent to the Dachau concentration camp. On August 27, 1944 he was sent to the Flossenburg concentration camp in Germany near the Czech border where he died on December 2, 1944.

Emile Mocq

Emile Mocq: 1914-1945, died in deportation. Resistance member of the FTP network in the Vitry sector, he was arrested by the Feldgendarmerie on July 20, 1944, interned in Arras prison, then transferred to Loos les Lilla prison and deported to Germany by "Loos Train" on 1 September 1944. He was imprisoned at Ravensbruck camp, transferred to Bergen-Belsen camp on January 24, 1945 dying on February 20, 1945.

Maurice Debout: 1914-1944, prisoner of war, shot dead in Germany. Mobilized, he joined his Army corps at Rethel before the war and was wounded and taken prisoner at Charleville on May 15, 1940. Transferred to Germany's Stalag VII A, in the Munich region, he formed a core of resistance inside the camp and tried to escape, but without success.

Maurice Debout

After the escape attempt he was brutalized by the Germans. When he rebelled he was shot dead by a cowardly German sentry. After the liberation, he was chosen, by lot, to represent those who died for a repatriated France. He rests at the Memorial de la France Combattante at Mont Valeriaen, near Paris.

A TRIBUTE TO THE LORRAINE GROUP

The famous Lorraine Group, a bomber unit of the Free French Air Forces (FAFL,) participated in the operations of Koufra (in Abyssinnia,) Eritrea, and Libya commanded by General Leclerc. On April 1, 1943, in England, Lorraine was re-formed as a French unit, attached to the Royal Air Force and named "Squadron 342".

After participating in the D-Day landing operations of June 6, 1944, they were moved to liberated France on October 15, 1944 to occupy the airfield of Brebières-Vitry and from this base they continued bombing operations across the Rhine into Germany.

On April 20, 1945 the group left Brebières for Holland where they continued operations on Germany until the end of hostilities.

The Brebières Town Hall, the former Chateau Pilat

An aerial view of Brebières today

OUR TOWN TODAY

Brebières lives, moves, evolves and develops. Today it has become the capital of the Canton with more than 5,000 inhabitants. Brebières benefits from an ideal geographic location, in the heart of northern Europe with dense communication networks, major motorways, the SNCF line Paris-Lille, a TGV cross-channel link and the Scarpe river, which will be canalized as a navigational waterway and linked to the future Seine Nord Europe canal.

Some of the interesting things to see in and near Brebières include the Town Hall in the old Château Pilat with its Bell Ringer; the Château Prevost, a beautiful example of the architecture of the 17th-18th centuries and a tribute to the power of the old families; St. Vaast Church with its beautiful baptismal font and its three old columns; the Chappelle des Chartreux built in 1614; the World War I British Cemetery; and of course, Siquidgar and Radbodirode, a couple of millers who are immortalized as giants and are essential figures of Brebièrois folklore.

Anyone interested in seeing important and well-preserved archaeological and medieval sites should plan a visit to our beautiful and friendly town where everyone is welcome.

For more information on Brebières, please visit the city's official website: www.brebieres.fr.

This information was prepared by Jean-Pierre Bremard, a passionate collector of local history, with the help of Jocelyne Cieslak and Jean-Pierre Hecquet, Mayor of Brebières. We greatly appreciate their assistance in preparing this commemorative document. Photos courtesy of the Municipality of Brebières.

BREBIÈRES   FRANCE

Région: Hauts de France   Pop. 1939 : 2026   Pop : 2016 : 4908

SEE AUTHOR'S NOTE BELOW

SITUATION ET PATRIMOINE

Brebières est situé dans la vallée de la Scarpe entre Arras et Douai à la limite des départements du Nord et du Pas de Calais, au pied des premières collines de l'ère tertiaire de l'ostrevent. Des recherches archéologiques ont permis d'établir que le territoire était habité dès la préhistoire, (1000 ans avant JC). L'élevage de brebis et de moutons fut l'une des premières activités du village.

C'est de brebis qu'est issu le nom de "BREBIÈRES"
Le château Pilat : ancienne ferme datant du XVIIᵉ siècle de la famille Pilat, famille influente de cultivateurs-éleveurs. Elle a donné à la commune 7 maires, 1 conseiller général et 1 député du Tiers-Etat. Le château Pilat est propriété de la commune depuis 1938, il sera aménagé en hôtel de ville en 1949.

les allemands en gare

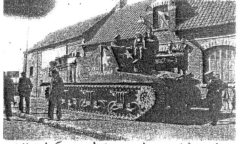

L'ancien café Terminus bombardé

blindé anglais route nationale

et convoi des libérateurs sept. 1944

OCCUPATION - LIBERATION

L'invasion : Après huit mois de drôle de guerre, les allemands pénètrent en France le 10 mai 1940, dès le 24 mai Brebières est occupé. Les allemands s'installent et s'approprient tous les immeubles communaux. Les autorités de Brebières ont été très vite tenues de se mettre sous autorité allemande avec son cortège de réquisitions, de rationnement, de dénonciations, d'arrestations.

L'oppression : Au fil du temps les occupants deviennent de plus en plus coercitifs au fait évident de l'attitude hostile des Brebièrois à l'autorité allemande. La population doit faire face à l'arrogance et aux exigences de l'envahisseur.

La résistance : Malgré les efforts des allemands pour contrôler tous les aspects de la ville, la résistance passive et active s'organise et se développe. Des patriotes comprenant de nombreuses femmes rejoignent des organisations secrètes de résistance dépendant l'organisation de résistance du secteur de Brebières / Vitry sera démantelé à partir de 1943. 33 arrestations enregistrées sans compter celles d'Arras et Douai, 28 personnes seront déportées. A noter pour Brebières (voir histoire spéciale) page suivante Pierre MOREAU Résistant lieutenant FTP mort en déportation le 2/12/44. Emile MOCQ Résistant FTP mort en déportation le 20/2/45.

Bombardements : Le champ d'aviation situé en partie sur le territoire de la commune, les écluses et le pont levis sur la Scarpe, la gare et les voies de chemin de fer constituent des objectifs militaires de première importance, de plus Brebières ressemble à une immense caserne (en 1941 près de 5000 soldats allemands sont cantonnés dans le village.)

Brebières devient une cible de choix pour les bombardiers alliés, au final une trentaine de bombardements entre le 15 Août 1943 et le 1ᵉʳ septembre 1944 date de sa libération. Toute la bourgade est touchée par les bombes, les dégâts sont considérables, les voies de chemin de fer sont coupées, l'effondrement du pont sur la route nationale bloque la circulation, les écluses de la haute tenue sont éventrées, la navigation sur la Scarpe devient impossible, le terrain d'aviation cible principale des chasseurs alliés sera touché à de nombreuses reprises.

Parmi les villageois on dénombre 13 morts et 8 blessés victimes des bombardements.

La libération : Devant l'avance des alliés, fin Août la retraite allemande se fait plus précipitée. Depuis deux jours ils détruisent leurs installations ou terrain d'aviation, les dépôts de munitions, les batteries, leurs cantonnements. Avant de quitter la ville, ils décident de fusiller les 4 prisonniers russes occupés à la DCA. 2 seront abattus dans l'abri, les 2 autres se sauvent, pourchassés par les soldats, l'un sera touché mortellement dans un champ, l'autre quoique blessé réussit à s'échapper. (les 3 victimes seront inhumées dans le cimetière communal)

Le 1 septembre 1944. BREBIÈRES est libéré. A 18ᵐ20 une colonne blindée anglaise est à Brebières, la joie est grande, les drapeaux sortent de leur cachette, les gens s'embrassent, les cris retentissent vive les alliés, vive la France. Les tanks se succèdent sur la nationale filant vers Douai le 3 septembre à 15ᴴ c'est le défilé de la libération, la foule se dirige vers le monument aux morts. Après la Marseillaise visite à la tombe des Russes fusillés par les allemands.

P. Moreau   E. Mocq   M. Debout

Vue Aérienne de Brebières

L'Hôtel de ville

Histoire spéciale:

Pierre MOREAU. 1896-1944 mort en déportation, il était en 1941 responsable intercommunal du réseau de résistance, chef du secteur cantonnal de Vitry, lieutenant FTP. Dénoncé il sera arrêté par la police de Vichy le 8 mai 1943, livré à l'ennemi il sera transféré en Février 1944 à la centrale d'Eyssa, il participera à la révolte de la prison d'Eyssa, le 1 juin 1944, il sera transféré à Compiègne d'où il partira début juillet pour le camp de concentration de Dachau, commando d'Allach transféré au camp de Floёssenbürg le 27 Aout 1944 camp extérieur d'Hersbruck il meurt le 2 décembre 1944

Emile MOCQ. 1914-1945 mort en déportation résistant membre du réseau FTP du secteur de Vitry, il est arrêté par la Feldgendarmerie le 2e juillet 1944, interné à la prison d'Arras puis transféré à la prison de Loos les Lille et déporté en Allemagne par le «Train de Loos» le 1 septembre 1944 vers la KL Sachsenhausen il sera incarcéré au camp de Ravensbrück, transféré au camp de Bergen-Belsen le 24 janvier 1945, il meurt le 20 Février 1945.

Maurice DEBOUT 1914-1944 Prisonnier de guerre, abattu en Allemagne. Mobilisé il rejoint son corps d'armée à Rethel fin Aout, blessé il est fait prisonnier à Charleville le 15 mai 1940, transféré en Allemagne, stalag VII A dans la région de Munich, il forme un noyau de résistance à l'intérieur du camp, et tente de s'évader sans succès. Affecté à un kommando de culture, malade, brutalisé, il se rebiffe et est lâchement abattu par la sentinelle allemande. A la libération designé par le sort il représentera les Fusillés morts pour la France Rapatrié à Paris il repose au Mémorial de la France combattante au Mont Valérien

Hommage au Groupe-Lorraine

Le groupe lorraine célèbre unité des Forces Aériennes Françaises Libres « F.A.F.L » a participé dès la fin 1940 aux opérations de Kouffra d'Abyssinie, d'Erythrée, et de Libye avec la division du Général Léclerc Le 1er Avril 1943 en Angleterre le Lorraine est reconstitué unité française rattaché à la Royal Air Force immatriculé « Squadron 342 » il participera aux opérations du débarquement du 6 juin 1944 et il retrouvera le sol de la France libérée le 15 octobre 1944 sur le terrain d'aviation de Brebières- Vitry. De cette base il participera aux opérations de bombardement outre-Rhin, le 20 avril 1945 il quitte Brebières pour la Hollande et continue ses opérations sur l'Allemagne jusqu'à la fin des hostilités

NOTRE VILLE AUJOURD'HUI

Brebières vit, bouge, évolue se développe En 2016 la commune comptait 4908 habitants, aujourd'hui devenue chef-lieu de canton elle compte plus de 5000 habitants. Brebières bénéficie d'une situation geographique idéale, au cœur de l'Europe du Nord avec un réseau de communication dense, RD950, autoroutes A1, A26, rocade minière 421, ligne SNCF Paris-Lille, TGV lien transmanche, la Scarpe canalisée en liaison du Futur canal Seine Nord-Europe loisirs: à Brebières une trentaine d'associations culturelles, sportives, sociales et de Loisirs anime chaleureusement la ville équipée d'infrastructures de qualité. (complexe sportif, centre-culturel, Espace jeunesse, parc de jeux, etc. Patrimoine historique: célèbre autrefois par son élevage de moutons et ses moulins à eau, les armoiries communales nous montrent deux brebis affrontées à une roue de moulin à eau, symbole de la première activité du village.

- L'Hôtel de ville aménagé dans le château PILAT avec son Jacquemart.
- Le château PRÉVOST et son colombier témoin précieux de l'architecture des 17 et 18e siècle, et de la puissance des anciennes familles.
- L'Église St Vaast, ses fonts baptismaux et ses trois vieilles colonnes.
- La chapelle des chartreux de 1614
- La colonne MADIOT, le Mémorial du Groupe lorraine (Unité des FAFL)
- SIQUIDGAR et RADBODIRODE couple de meuniers immortalisé sous forme de Géants, Figures incontournables du folklore Brebièrois.

Pour plus d'informations sur Brebières, visitez le site officiel de la ville www.brebières.fr

Ces informations ont été préparé par Jean-Pierre Brémard collectionneur passionné d'histoire locale avec l'aide de Jocelyne Cieslak et Jean-Pierre Hecquet Maire de Brebières

87

CORBIE FRANCE

Region: Hauts de France   Pop. 1936: 4,600   1946: 4,000   2020: 6,300

SITING & HERITAGE

Corbie is a small town 15km east of Amiens, in the Somme department, and in the Hauts-de-France region of France. Corbie is located on a site that has been occupied since prehistoric times. The city originated after the conquest of Gaul during the 1st century when a first town was built on the edge of the Anchor river, which was then called La Corbea (the etymological origin of Corbie).

Between 657 and 661, Queen Bathilde, the widow of Clovis II, built a large Benedictine abbey in Corbie, which she bequeathed in its entirety, and with its territory, to future Abbots who became Abbot-Counts. The Corbie Abbey was one of the most important Benedictine establishments in France from the 7th to the 18th centuries. In particular, in the 9th century, under the Abbey of Adhalard, the cousin of Charlemagne, the abbey's influence radiated throughout Europe. Even today, the renowned works of the abbey's scriptorium play a major role in the development of innovative writings (such as the tiny Caroline). The abbey retained great prestige until the French Revolution.

GPS Coord.: N49.9079 E2.5120

OUR TOWN'S OCCUPATION STORY

The Invasion. In May 1940, faced with the fast approach of the German invasion, many residents of Corbie fled the city while many others remained hidden in the cellars of Corbie. One of those was Théodore Roussel who was shot dead a few days after the arrival of the Germans. Refusing to obey when attempting to fetch a bottle for his children, he was shot in the head.

When many of the residents returned to Corbie in June 1940, there was great emotion and great sadness as many houses, factories and businesses had been destroyed by German air strikes, the bombing by French artillery, and the arson and looting of their homes and farms.

Bombardment damage at the Corbie railway station

Entry of the first British tank in Corbie
Lock Bridge, 31 August 1944

Occupation and Bombing. After the invasion, the occupation took place in relative calm. Even if the residents of Corbie are reluctant to accept the enemy's military presence, they still obey the new administration for fear of sanctions and retributions from the German authorities.

The daily life of the inhabitants during the occupation is difficult for the residents. They are forced to only think about the basic supplies they need for their families and are forced to get by with the small ration tickets issued by the administration. Whenever no more tickets are available the residents have to either wait until the following month, barter with fellow residents, or find black market sources.

Fear is part of the daily life of the inhabitants. Night patrols and the rhythmic footsteps of soldiers snapping the heels of their boots on the cobblestones haunt the nights. All residents must respect the curfews and close their curtains at night, under penalty of sanctions.

Worse still, the deafening bombing alerts force them to run for cover, day and night. In August 1944, the Allies decided to bomb the Corbie railway station because it served as an ammunition reserve site for German soldiers. This bombardment is very precise because no explosions were recorded more than 50m from the tracks. However, the explosions caused the violent projection of shards several hundred meters away, killing two civilians and many soldiers.

Resistance. As early as 1940, the Germans tried to control all of city life. However, a passive resistance is quickly put in place, and an active resistance is organized in clandestine networks in 1942.

The Resistance, around the discreet Camille Roland or the FTP of André Foucart, aimed to prepare for liberation by gathering information on the occupation, by hiding Allied soldiers and by organizing sabotage actions. The local resistance fighters derailed two trains north of Corbie, at the Heilly crossing, which enabled residents to recover tons of potatoes that were leaving for Germany.

TWO CORBIE HEROES OF THE RESISTANCE

Camille Roland

Camille Roland *was born April 7, 1896 in Corbie. At eighteen, in 1914, he responded to general mobilization. He went through the entire First World War and participated in the Chemin des Dames battles and then in the Somme fights in 1918 where he was seriously wounded. He became Director of the BVR plant in Corbie in 1932. After the factory fire in June 1940, he began cleaning up and restarting production.*

On January 10, 1942, he joined the Resistance, joining the FFI group Charles de Gaulle, entering the network Zero-France with the rank of Lieutenant. He organized the resistance in the Corbie region in the greatest of secrecy.

On August 31, 1944, the day of Corbie's liberation, Camille was ambushed at the corner of a wall, struck down by a burst of German machine gun fire. Buried on September 2, 1944 with all the honors of the city, he obtained the Legion of Honor posthumously. The street he was killed on is named after him today.

André Foucart

André Foucart *was born in 1906 and, living in Corbie, he was working since 1936 at the Méaulte aviation factory. When war was declared, he was assigned as a special worker and remained in his factory. In 1943, he was contacted to join the Resistance. He joined the Communist Party and enthusiastically joined the movement named the Partisan Francs-Tireurs.*

Andrée then takes part in clandestine meetings in a small cafe in the city, organizing and carrying out sabotage actions on the German communication systems near Corbie. Very involved in the fight against the occupier, his determination earned him to be hated and denounced by the Germans. Finally, André was arrested by the French Militia and the Gestapo on August 4, 1944.

Taken to the Kommandantur in Corbie, he was transferred to the citadel of Amiens where he was tortured before being shot on September 6, 1944. His body was found in the mass grave of Vaux-en-Amiènois. A street in Corbie today bears his name.

LIBERATION & RECOVERY

From mid-August 1944, the German army showed signs of agitation at the advance of the Allies and the increasingly virulent acts of resistance. More arrests are made. Emile Bazin, arrested for sabotage, dies in deportation in February 1945. On August 18, 1944, the Bonnay Resistance Network, 2 km from Corbie, was dismantled. In the debacle, the Germans shot the 18 Resistance fighters on the night of August 28 to 29.

On August 31 at 8 a.m., the last German troops summon able-bodied men to dig defense trenches. The majority of the inhabitants manage to escape them, because of the laxity of the disillusioned soldiers. Around noon, two Resistance fighters (G. Poingt and L. Vivier) defuse the explosive charges of the two bridges at the entrance to the city.

Around 3 p.m. the last SS soldiers machine gun the city and assassinate several people, including Camille Roland, one of the leaders of the Resistance, who was ambushed. The machine gun was destroyed a few minutes later by an English tank. Around 6 p.m., the Allied troops crossed the city distributing cigarettes, chewing gum and chocolates to the people. The joy was immense!

The spectacular Abbey of Saint Peter, Corbie © S. Rondot

The Corbie Town Hall © OTValdeSomme

OUR TOWN TODAY

Today, Corbie is a modern, dynamic town in a beautiful area of northern France cherished by the residents. Corbie is an important town as the headquarters of the community of Communes of Val de Somme which provides many important services to 33 municipalities in the local area.

The city's two architectural gems are the town hall and the remains of the former Benedictine abbey. The town hall is a magnificent 19th century castle, but it is the Abbey of Saint Peter, 55m high, which recalls the prestigious past of the abbey which spread throughout Europe. The tourist office invites you to rediscover this spectacular building, with a history dating to 657 AD and abandoned during the French Revolution, with a virtual reality guided tour.

For those interested in military history, the Sir John Monash Center Museum and Australian National Memorial just south of Corbie offer fans of military history the unique opportunity to experience a commemoration of the Australian servicemen and women who served on the Western Front during the First World war.

*For more information about Corbie and the Val de Somme area, please visit the Val de Somme Tourist Office website **http://fr.valdesomme-tourisme.com/** or the Corbie municipal website: **www.mairie-corbie.fr/** .*

This information was prepared by the Val de Somme Tourist Office, with the help of R. Ossart and R.Godbert, residents passionate about our local history. Photos courtesy of the Commune of Corbie.

DIVES-SUR-MER FRANCE

Region: Normandie   Pop. 1940: 5,300   Pop. 2020: 5,600

SITING & HERITAGE

Dives-sur-Mer is a seaside town along the Normandy coast of France, 20 km northeast of Caen. Immediately adjacent to the D-Day beaches and at the gateway to the fertile Pays d'Auge area.

Besides having a beautiful setting, Dives-sur-Mer has a long and rich history dating back more than 1,000 years. In 1066, William the Conqueror departed the Dives-Sur-Mer harbor with 700 to 1,000 ships and up to 8,000 men for the conquest of England to become King of England.

Dives-Sur-Mer has an important medieval heritage that has been preserved despite the vicissitudes of history, especially its 11th century church. From 1891 to 1986, Dives-sur-Mer hosted a metallurgical industry specializing in the manufacture of copper. For nearly a century, the life of the city revolved around the metallurgical factory, which employed nearly 3,000 people at its peak in 1939.

GPS Coordinates: N49.2866 E-0.1001

OUR TOWN'S OCCUPATION STORY

Occupation. With the arrival of the Germans, the factory closed in June 1940, leaving 1,300 people unemployed. The Germans dismantle the equipment, occupy the factory and 17 casemates (gun emplacements) are installed on the site.

Gaston Manneville, a Communist activist, organized a committee of the unemployed whose actions were closely monitored by the police. In April 1941, 218 unemployed workers were sent to Lorient for the construction of the submarine base but a month later, most returned.

The school premises are requisitioned and occupied by the Germans. The children are divided into different rooms that are made available by the parish or businesses. Passive defense controls are in place every night and no light is allowed to filter through. The breeding of pigeons is prohibited. In Dives, being in the coastal zone, a pass is necessary to move about and fishing is very regulated.

Food is scarce. You have to do your best. The Divais collect wood on the hill for heat. Children steal potatoes or bread. Gardens are organized by the town hall and young people from the youth center grow vegetables to meet the needs of families. In 1942 and 1943, a fair was organized to help prisoners.

Repression. A first roundup in July '41 resulted in the arrest of Communist militants and Russian workers in Dives. Eleven are arrested and brought before a special court in Caen. In October 1941, six Divais were handed over to the Germans as hostages and deportees. Only one will return from the camps.

As early as 1942, men were requisitioned to work on various sites of the Atlantic Wall. They are employed in building blockhouses, cutting down trees for "Rommel's asparagus." At the beginning of 1943, the compulsory labor service (STO) requisitioned men born between 1920 and 1922 and 75 Divais were rounded up. Two did not return. Some hid on farms to avoid the STO.

Nazi and anti-Semitic propaganda is mainly carried out by a branch of the Rassemblement National Populaire (RNP) who collaborated with the Germans. It was created in Cabourg and Dives by Henri Clément dit Thuillier (interpreter at the Kommandantur) and Roger Angelliaume who will be executed on July 6, 1944.

Resistance. The Zero France network, created in 1942 in the north of France, was the result of a Zero network born in Belgium in 1940. Aimable Lepeu, a pharmacist in Dives, organized the local section in October 1943. Made up of around fifty people, the sector practiced primarily intelligence and facilitated the escape of English airmen. It was dismantled in the spring of 1944 by the Gestapo. Aimable Lepeu and about twenty of his comrades were arrested and most of them were deported.

Following the sabotage of trains transporting Germans in May 1942 in Airan (28 soldiers killed) two Communist Divais were arrested and deported to Auschwitz in the so-called 45,000 convoy with 7 Jews from Dives. All will die in deportation.

Arrested for possession of weapons, a retired gendarme also died in deportation.

German soldiers marching in the town
Le Guen Collection

German soldiers at the stadium during the Occupation   Le Guen Collection

Belgian Piron Brigade, August 1944
Piron Brigade Collection

THE DIVAIS COTTAGE RAID

In the very first minutes of June 6, 1944, the British and Canadian paratroopers of the 6th Airborne Division were ordered to attack the area west of Dives. The Red Berets must secure the eastern flank of the Landing.

Under the combined effect of the wind, the artillery, the flak, the night and the fear, many paratroopers found themselves in the marshes surrounding Dives. The Divais are awake, torn between fear and their surprise to see paratroopers fallen in the surrounding marshes and meadows. Without hesitation, some hide them in cellars, in the church steeple or in isolated buildings. During the night, a British Stirling bomber crashed into a hill with 20 soldiers and 6 crew members. No survivors.

On July 4, 1944, the Gestapo d´Argences carried out a large-scale raid in the residential area of Cottage Divais among residents suspected of having hidden paratroopers. Men and women are brutally arrested and taken to Pont-l'Evêque where their torturers await them. Some are released. As for the others, convicted of terrorism, they were murdered a few days later in the woods of Saint-Pierre-du-Jonquet, near Argences, and secretly buried

Return of the bodies from St Pierre du Jonquet, November 1946
Photo: Collection C. David

in a mass grave. The bodies will be discovered in two stages in September 1944 and November 1946. Among the 28 victims, eleven are not able to be identified. The bodies of eight Divais were brought back to Dives for burial.

LIBERATION & RECONSTRUCTION

Liberation. On August 17, when the city of Caen had been liberated a month earlier and the Allies had succeeded in pushing back the Germans during the deadly fighting around Chambois and Falaise, the 6th Airborne Division launched Operation Paddle, which aimed to free the eastern front and go up towards the Seine. The liberation of the coastal zone was entrusted to the Belgians of the Piron Brigade and to the Dutch of the Princess Irene Brigade.

From Sallenelles to Cabourg, progress is difficult and the Belgians have several deaths. On August 21, at dawn, they entered Cabourg. The day before, they heard the explosions announcing the departure of the Germans and their destruction of the bridge.

Guided by a few residents of Cabourg, Dives and Houlgate who remained home, they crossed the Dives, then the canal on boats and rafts hidden by fishermen. Dives, whose inhabitants were evacuated on July 17, is finally released from the grip of Nazi Germany! So many paid for our freedom:

55 civilian victims between March 1, 1944 and December 31, 1945
20 soldiers who died for France inscribed on the war memorial
16 deaths in deportation including 7 Jews
185 deportees returned

Reconstruction. Life is resuming, after months of clearing the ruins and building a new power station. Production at the factory, which became Cégédur in 1942, restarted with 500 workers in the summer of 1945. The city was recognized as a disaster city in April 1947.

The spectacular Church of Notre Dame
en.normandie-tourisme.fr

The serenity of Dives-sur-Mer today
Photo By Michel Dehaye

OUR TOWN TODAY

Dives-sur-Mer is a vibrant seaside town with much to offer. Visitors have the unique opportunity to combine the sea, medieval history and D-Day memories in a relaxing and welcoming seaside setting.

The Port Guillaume marina and residential district is an important part of Dives-sur-Mer because of its setting, its fishing industry, its fish market and its attractiveness to tourists. With its traditional market held in the 15th century Halls and its shops, the historic city center attracts many tourists around the 11th century church and the medieval village.

The Church of Notre-Dame is especially interesting with its connections to William The Conqueror, its unusual leper window and its 400 examples of sailor graffiti engraved on the walls.

The city is dynamic with a thriving commercial zone, 1,200 school children, more than 80 associations, health services and many cultural establishments that include Dive-sur-Mer's well known status as an important center of marionette puppetry.

We invite you to visit our beautiful seaside town where you will always find a warm welcome anytime of the year.

For more information about Dives-sur-Mer visit ***www.dives-sur-mer.fr***. *To learn more about the history of the Dives-sur-Mer area during World War II visit* ***www.ladives1944.com*** *or contact Christime Le Callonec at clecallonec@hotmail.fr.*

Text written and photos collected b y the association "Un fleuve pour l a Liberté, l a Dives". We appreciate their contributions towards creating this commemorative document. Photos courtesy of the Commune of Dives-sur-Mer.

HAZEBROUCK FRANCE

Region: Hauts-de-France   Pop. 1945: 15,000 Pop. 2020: 21,500

SITING & HERITAGE

Hazebrouck is a Flemish city par excellence. Its history goes back to the first millennium when, at the time of the Count of Flanders Charles the Good, monks cleared and dried up a swamp forest that will allow the development of a livestock breeding culture and the beginning of Christianity in our region. First written as "Hasbruc", the name Hazebrouck literally means the marsh (brouck) with hares (Haze).

A strong textile industry developed in the 15th century and by the 19th century, the city's textile factories were well-known far beyond Flanders. The development of a major railway junction during the 19th century reinforced the importance of the city but also made it a coveted target during the last two World Wars. Hazebrouck is full of places steeped in history such as the Convent of the Augustines, the 15th century Church of St Eloi, St James's College and the impressive 19th century Town Hall. Hazebrouck maintains strong ties with its twinning city Soignies, Belgium (see Page 46).

GPS Coordinates: N50.7283 E2.5425

OUR TOWN'S OCCUPATION STORY

Invasion & Occupation. In May 1940, the town of Hazebrouck was hit hard by the German invasion. Following the German offensive of May 10, 1940 on Belgium, the Netherlands and Luxembourg the city sees the arrival of floods of Belgian refugees, leaving their homes.

On May 27, the fighting gained in intensity. The German divisions, after having fought a fierce battle in the communes of Hondeghem and St. Cappel's Eve that same day, struck the symbol of the city, the Church of St Eloi which suffered significant damage. Its spire is partly destroyed which will fall on the night of November 13, 1940 following hurricane-force winds.

Downed German bomber, May 10, 1940

The British 1st Buckimghamshire Batallion, commanded by Major Brian Heyworth (33 years old) retreated to the Orphanage and suffered the wrath of the German armoured vehicles on 28 May. Heyworth was killed at 4.30 pm by a bullet from a German sniper and 84 people were killed in the battle, fought to slow the German advance towards Dunkirk.

That same evening, the German occupier immediately wanted to impose his conditions, taking the Mayor, Joseph Elie Plateel hostage at the Town Hall, forcing him to sleep on a doormat found in the prison that was just behind the town hall. A Kommandantur (military headquarters) was installed which was later moved to 4 Grand Place (now the current cinema).

Kommandantur in Hazebrouck at 4 Grand Place

Julius Bauer. The Organization Todt was an annex group of the Wehrmarcht responsible for the construction of the V-weapon production sites and the famous Atlantic Wall. Its local leader, Julius Bauer, was a colorful, bloodthirsty and impulsive personality, known for his angry disposition and his support of the Germans.

This man, a hotelier in civilian life, could be accommodating. You could go to see him to find work, such as during the construction of the V1 launch site just southwest of Hazebrouck, or to prevent the forced (STO) departure to Germany of a relative or a husband.

However he had a reputation as a king of the black market, making the region a hub of the black market and, among other crimes, he was instrumental in the murder of the Verlycks family by the German military police over some rusty English arms in a nearby barn, left by the retreating British soldiers. After the war he was executed.

Hazebrouck under the bombs. Like the vast majority of French cities, Hazebrouck suffered numerous bombings between June 1941 and August 13, 1944. The worst were two of these bombings. On June 22, 1941, during a religious procession, several projectiles hit near the city slaughterhouse killing 11 civilians and injuring 25 in addition to German casualties on the Rue de Rubecque.

On September 4, 1943, the alert was issued at 6:30 p.m. that about 40 Allied aircraft were approaching the city. At 7:30 p.m., 250 bombs were dropped on the area of the railway station. On this fateful day there were 41 dead and 50 injured, 125 houses were destroyed, 200 railroad cars were destroyed and rail traffic was suspended for 4 days. This was the deadliest bombing of Hazebrouck.

Bombing of June 22, 1941 on the Rue de Rubecque

THE RESISTANCE IN HAZEBROUCK

Like most municipalities in the region, resistance played an important role. Indeed, many Hazebruckois took part in actions against the occupier, through the various local networks established in the region. The networks Sylvestre Farmer, Zero France, La Voix du Nord are names among many others. For Hazebrouck, two names embody the local resistance: Fernande Benoist and Joseph Plateel.

Fernande Benoist was a courageous, committed and determined woman. She rescued several British airmen and then helped them return to England. A Socialist activist and a future Deputy Mayor of the city, she later refused the post of Minister of Education to maintain her local commitment to Hazebrouck. One of the city's colleges was later named after her.

Joseph Elie Plateel was the Mayor of Hazebrouck from 1933 to 1945. At the risk of his own life he systematically opposed the directives imposed by the occupier. A confirmed railway man and trade unionist, he was not a man to be trampled on. His relationship with Julius Bauer was very tumultuous. During a meeting between them, the two men even fight with fists. Afterwards Bauer furiously asked the Germans to remove the Mayor.

Joseph Plateel had to flee the city on June 6, 1944, the day of the Allied Landing in Normandy after the Germans had issued an arrest warrant for him. His Deputy, Jean Frucquet, served as interim Mayor for 3 months until the liberation of the city on September 6, 1944 when he reappeared to the cheers of the people.

The Verlyck Family Massacre. On August 30, 1944, members of the Feldgendarmerie (German military police) went to the Verlyck family home to conduct a search, at 60 rue des Tilleuls (now Rue Verlyck) at midday. They discovered weapons and ammunition, recovered in 1940 after the departure of the English troops, in a building adjoining the house. They have 7 people lined up against a fence wall of the garden: Emile Verlyck 46 years, 4 of his sons and 2 young men of 16 years. All are shot on the spot. Augusta Verlyck , 43 years old and Emile's wife, is arrested and then questioned. Only 7 days before the town's liberation, this crime is hard to understand.

There is every reason to believe that a young Lille man of Greek origin, Pierre Moustafioglou (19 years old at the time of the events), handed over the Verlyck family to the Germans. A few days before, he showed up at the Verlycks' home, meeting his eldest son, Emile (the two young men had met in Germany where they both worked). Emile explains to him that he holds 3 rifles, cartridges and a jammed pistol. Moustafioglou asks to see the weapons, saying he was wanted by the Germans and was a resistant to the STO. Pierre wanted to buy a gun but Emile gives him the gun. But Pierre plays a double game: he actually works for the GHP (Geheime Feldpolizei, the German Secret Police) and came to Flanders to monitor the Verlycks whom he suspected of wanting to set up a resistance network.

THE LIBERATION OF HAZEBROUCK

Liberation. The liberation of the city took place on September 6, 1944, more than 4 years after the arrival of the Germans in the commune. By 4 am, there are no more Germans in town. The day before, on September 5, a group of SS killed Victor Bertrand, father of the owner of the Gauloise Tavern on the Grand Place. He is the last civilian victim of the war.

The joyous celebration of the liberation of Hazebrouck

Women shaved and exhibited on the Kommjandantur balcony

People gather in the Grand Place; the French, British and American flags appear proudly on the windows, we sing the Marseillaise, we kiss, the Church of St. Eloi after four years of silence is heard again and the inhabitants in the surrounding countryside soon realized that Hazebrouck had been liberated. Joseph Elie Plateel then reappeared on the same balcony, and the cheers redoubled when his Deputy symbolically handed him his tricolor scarf. The post-war reconstruction will be long and tedious.

Reconstruction. The main Hazebrouckois buildings were hit hard, such as the railway station, which was destroyed and rebuilt in 1961. The Orphanage, totally destroyed during the events of 28 May 1940, was rebuilt and inaugurated on 24 March 1957.

As far as churches are concerned, the toll is catastrophic. The Church of Our Lady, located in the New World district was totally razed. Reconstruction began in 1956 and the inauguration took place on December 6, 1959. The Church of St Eloi, which was hard hit during the events of May 1940, saw a number of works during the post-war period. The spire will not be rebuilt until 50 years later and will be inaugurated on December 23, 1994.

OUR TOWN TODAY

In 2020, Hazebrouck is a commune of 22,000 inhabitants that has always kept its Flemish authenticity yet has also been able to reinvent itself over the decades. Served by an important rail and road network, the city is at the heart of an active and ever-expanding economy.

The community has much to offer its residents and visitors alike. Traditional food and popular festivals in the company of giants and archers and even pigeon racing establishes the town's identity as a wonderful place to live and visit. The town's commitment to its natural areas, to its history and to sustainability will ensure the future beauty and desirability of our lovely community for generations to come. We invite you to visit and see Hazebrouck's treasures for yourself.

The 15th century Saint-Éloi church and public garden
(Photo By Guillaume Declerck)

For more information about the town of Hazebrouck and the local tourism opportunities visit **www.ville-hazebrouck.fr**.

This text graciously created by Guillaume Declerck, the founder of Historiquement Vôtre, and the wartime photos graciously provided by Jean-Pascal Vanhove, the author of "Hazebrouck 1939-1945". We appreciate their contributions to this commemorative effort.

LAON FRANCE

Region: Hauts-de-France   Pop. 1940: 18,000   Pop. 2020: 25,600

SITING & HERITAGE

The City of Laon is a very unique and beautiful city in north central France surrounded by vast fertile agricultural and forested areas. Laon has been occupied since Roman times and during medieval times Laon became an important town due to the strategic value of the town's 100 meter hill in the city center and the more than 8 km of ramparts surrounding the city center.

Today, Laon is known for its imposing hilltop cathedral, the Notre Dame de Laon, constructed and completed during the 12th and 13th centuries. Its similarity to the Notre Dame cathedral in Paris is no coincidence, as the Notre Dame de Laon church served as the architectural inspiration for the famous cathedral in Paris. Laon suffered significant damage during both World Wars but fortunately the extensive medieval architecture in Laon was spared. Today the Laon area is known for its wine-making and tourism industries.

GPS Coordinates: N49.5642 E3.6199

German military band to greet Hitler at the railway station, June 25, 1940
FRAD002_2FI_0041

OUR TOWN'S OCCUPATION STORY

The Invasion. The German invasion reached the Laon area on May 16, 1940, beginning with the arrival of dive bombers and a powerful force of mechanized equipment and infantry troops, their primary purpose being to destroy all French forces who were opposing their invasion and occupation. The German bombing became continuous, especially at the railway stations. At the Laon station, train wagons loaded with crude oil were bombed, sending up huge plumes of black smoke, destroying homes and killing five civilians.

The residents immediately began evacuating the city. Some trains were still available to the west but most residents were only able to quickly grab a few of their belongings and begin walking on the roads leading south and away from the fierce fighting between the French and German forces. With the roads full of escaping refugees and French soldiers, the German Luftwaffe began a systematic program of strafing civilians and evacuated soldiers with machine guns, killing and wounding many, terrorizing the thousands of refugees and setting the tone for the years of Nazi occupation to come.

The Occupation. Soon after the Germans occupied the city, all of the local and regional transportation options disappeared, making it difficult, if not impossible, for residents to return to the city. Since Hitler had served in the Laon area during World War I he made it a point of visiting Laon on June 25, the day after his visit to the defeated capital, Paris.

Between the fall of 1940 and January 1941, all local newspapers were replaced by Vichy newspapers who began publishing articles about the "dangers" posed by the Jews and soon the Vichy officials began issuing orders required to be followed by all Jewish residents.

By the beginning of 1941, complicated by the winter, food and clothing supplies became critical mostly because most of the railway cars had been sent to Germany, eliminating the possibility of supplies reaching the city. In spite of this, the local residents maintained high spirits and the hope that their beloved France, as they knew it, would someday return.

By the start of 1942 the Mayor of Laon was replaced with a Vichy Mayor and by July, all Jews were required to wear the Star of David on their clothing and soon, entire Jewish families were rounded up for transport east. Using the excuse that they were being "resettled", most of the Jewish people complied with the orders they were issued.

Hitler revisits Laon after his visit to Paris
FRAD002_2Fi_00526

That same month the German officials began the requisitioning of local men to work in German factories and after that, many men were required to leave their families, angering the local residents and forcing many of the men to flee and hide from the German authorities. Shortages of food and shelter continually plagued these men until the liberation.

The Resistance. Most residents of Laon participated in passive, and often, active, resistance efforts against the Nazis. Ultimately, 28 Laon natives were honored with the national Medal of the French Resistance, recognizing their brave contributions during the occupation and especially in the months before, during and after the D-Day invasion. These brave souls continue to be honored today.

The suffering of the residents however was so pervasive and so complete during the Nazi occupation that it is they who deserve the greatest amount of sympathy and remembrance. Every man, women and child was forced to live their daily lives in fear and forced to live each day wondering how they, their families and their friends will survive.

The Cathedral framed by destruction
FRAD002_2Fi_Laon_00480

THE LOUISE MACAULT STORY

Louise Macault was born on July 23, 1921 and in 1935 her family moved to Laon. In 1942 she became a teacher at a school, fell madly in love and became engaged to Robert Aumont but a year later in 1943, Robert was requisitioned by the Germans to work in Dusseldorf under the Compulsory Labor Service directive and is thus forced to leave Laon. Since he was to remain in Germany indefinitely, they are both heartbroken but Robert complies with the order.

Every day each of them writes a letter to the other, trying to stay in touch. Because of the fear of censorship they begin to use invisible ink so that they can share information about the bombings, German troop morale, English radio broadcasts, railway timetables and possible ways Robert might escape. Louise is not a regular member of any resistance group but she shares the news she receives from Robert about Germany with members of the local Laon resistance who she knows well.

There was a friend from Laon that Louise had grown up with who was the daughter of a butcher (Marcel Lamisse), whose home and business had become occupied by the Germans. This butcher became a collaborator and it became known that his daughter, Louise's childhood friend, had denounced her to the Germans. Louise was immediately arrested and interrogated about her correspondence to Robert. The Germans had intercepted letters and so it was that she was found guilty, given a two months' prison sentence and, on September 9, 1943, she was locked up in the Saint-Quentin prison - just when Robert had managed to escape from Germany.

Despite pleas from her parents and others, from there Louise was transported to the Romainville prison, then to the Royallieu camp and then, with 1,000 other women, was sent to the Ravensbruck concentration camp on a train known by the name "Convoy of 27,000". In April, 1944 she was again transferred with a group of women to the Holleischen Labor Kommando in the Sudetenland where she was forced to work 12 hours per day at a Skoda arms factory under terrible conditions. The winter of 1944 was especially brutal.

On May 5, 1945 the camp was liberated by Czech and Polish partisans, two days before the arrival of the American troops. Louise returns to Laon in a state of physical deprivation and only then learns that Robert had escaped almost two years earlier. They were married in August but, due to her deteriorated health, Louise died on August 28, 1946. Louise was only 25 years old.

LIBERATION & RECOVERY

In May 1944 the allies started bombing Laon in anticipation of the D-Day landings but that did not stop the rounding up and deportation of the Jews. Before D-Day, the British and the American air forces increased their bombing raids on German positions throughout northern France and the Laon area was no exception. Laon was pronounced destroyed in the process.

The bombing following D-Day became so extensive it made movement, corresponding and other methods of communicating nearly impossible and there was no telephone service.

On Aug 30 American troops entered Laon and there was great jubilation. On Sept 5 the headlines of the newspapers said "Liberation", "Viva La France" and "Viva America" and they published proclamations from General Eisenhower and articles about the many organizations that had helped in the liberation of France. It was a joyous time!

On August 30, Marcel Lamisse, the collaborating butcher, was executed for his crime of Gross Trafficking with the Germans. The sentence was carried out by an American soldier at the demand of the people.

The spectacular hilltop Notre Dame de Laon cathedral

The medieval caves of Laon

OUR TOWN TODAY

Today, Laon is a vibrant, innovative city that takes great pride in its beauty and historic past. One of the most beautiful cities to approach due to the imposing view provided by the Notre Dame de Laon cathedral, Laon draws tourists from around the world. The view of the hilltop Notre Dame cathedral, lighted at night, is truly unforgettable.

Laon is also known as the City of Flowers with many city parks lavishly and meticulously planted with ornamental shrubs and flower beds. Laon is also known for its local sports associations and its strong representation at national sporting championships.

The wooded town center is surrounded by marshes and ponds and only a few minutes from the city the national forests of Saint-Gobain and Samoussy provide excellent opportunities for hiking, mountain biking and other experiences with nature.

Throughout the year, concerts, shows, fresh air markets, exhibitions, conferences and other events add to the cultural richness of the town for both the residents and visitors alike.

Lastly, visitors must include the fascinating extensive underground quarried caves under Laon in their itinerary. Constructed over centuries, used as prisons during medieval times and comprised of three levels, a 450-meter long portion takes you deep under the most ancient areas of the city.

*For more information about Laon visit **www.laon.fr**. To learn more about the local tourism opportunities and events, please visit **www.tourisme-paysdelaon.com/**.*

We appreciate the assistance provided by Celine Gogny, Director of the Office of Tourism and her staff in preparing this commemorative document. The Louise Macault story is taken from the book written by Joêlle Tourbe. The wartime photos courtesy of the Archives Départementales de l'Aisne.

FRANCE

OYE-PLAGE   FRANCE

Region: Hauts-de-France   Pop. 1940: 4,000   Pop. 2020: 5,500

SITING & HERITAGE

The town of Oye-Plage is a small town on the Pas-de-Calais coast of France that has existed since Roman times when a large number of Roman roads crisscrossed the area. Until the 9th century, Oye-Plage was repeatedly flooded by the sea until the Middle Ages when locks, water-gangs and dikes were constructed and the sea receded leaving clay and sand. During the Middle Ages the Oye-Plage region was continually disputed with England and many battles were fought for control of the area.

In 1872 the arrival of railway service brought Oye-Plage into the modern age and a casino, villas, cafes, restaurants and a hotel established the town as a tourist destination. Over the centuries many of the inhabitants made their living from the sea but agriculture became an important industry, creating many jobs for farm workers, blacksmiths, saddlers and millers, especially for the production of chicory. At one time there were 13 chicory dryers, some of which still exist today, one of which is still in operation.

GPS Coordinates: N50.9776 E2.0433

German soldiers in Oye-Plage

OUR TOWN'S OCCUPATION STORY

The Invasion. Between the initial May 10, 1940 date of the German invasion and May 26, 1940, as a part of the Battle of France, the residents of Oye-Plage witnessed great battles for the Calais area between the invading Germans and the French defenders. Known as the Siege of Calais, these battles played a critical role in delaying the continued movements of German troops and armor, including three Panzer divisions, allowing the French and British Expeditionary Forces to make their way to Dunkirk, making their eventual evacuation to England possible. These constant battles however filled the residents with fear.

The Occupation. When the Germans entered Oye-Plage it was the beginning of four years of occupation. The Saint Médard church was requisitioned, becoming a cinema for the Germans and many other places and private accommodations were seized. The local government officials were replaced by a Kommandantur who established and enforced the new Nazi rules for the community.

The city was bombed during the occupation, but fortunately few victims were reported. However, on October 31, 1941, the bombing resulted in four civilian casualties and all of the stained glass windows of the church were destroyed.

On July 4, 1940 the Germans required all residents to surrender all of their wireless radios at the town hall and all of the coastal dwellings were evacuated and destroyed, including the casino and the villas. The coast is gradually fortified from 1942 with blockhouses, gun emplacements and beach defenses to prevent a possible landing of the Allied forces. The railways through the town of Oye-Plage were used to transport stone, cement, iron beams and water onto the beach sector for the construction of the coastal defensive structures which went on for months.

In February-March 1942, the Germans decided to build a blockhouse and observation tower as a fire control station to direct the fire of 4 casemates that had been constructed. The British Air Force (RAF) flew over the region and bombed a good number of German targets so, to minimize its chance of being bombed, the Germans decided to build the observation tower in a form that would look like a church steeple.

The German observation tower after it had been destroyed by the fleeing German forces

Examples Of Oye-Plage Nazi gun emplacements & fortifications today

LIBERATION & RECOVERY

The Allied Invasion Deception. It is well known that the Allies in England took great effort to confuse the Germans about when and where the Allied invasion of France would occur. The goal of the Allied deception was to convince the Germans that the invasion would occur near our location, the Pays-de-Calais, the nearest point to England. The deception was successful and the Germans concentrated their defenses along our beaches with more than 150,000 troops and the majority of their Panzer divisions.

When the invasion finally occurred on June 6, 1944 these German forces in our area had to be moved west to meet the Allied invasion and the residents were happy to see them leave. The residents of all the towns in the Pays-de-Calais area, including Oye-Plage, were grateful that the invasion did not occur in our area, however it meant that it would be some time before we were able to be liberated. In fact, it would be September before the Allies were able to reach our area.

The Liberation. Little by little, the German soldiers remaining in Oye-Plage left the area but on the eve of September 6, the Germans decided to blow up the observation tower so that the Allies could not use it. However, when the Germans blew up the tower with explosives the charge was not sufficient so the tower ended up leaning like the Tower of Pisa. It took very little time for the Tower to become a curiosity to the locals and today it remains a major tourist attraction.

Celebrating liberation !

The majority of the cities and towns along the north coast and the Pas-de-Calais area were finally liberated between September 1st and September 5th by the combined forces of the British, American, Canadian, Polish and Czech armies, but very fierce fighting, mainly by Canadian forces, was necessary and it wasn't until the end of September that most of the Germans had been removed from the coastal areas. In particular, Dunkirk will remain under siege until May 9, 1945 when Germany capitulated, making it the last French city to be liberated.

Regarding Oye-Plage, the town was liberated by the Canadians on September 6, 1944 between 5 and 6 p.m., the Canadian troops arriving via the Pont d'Oye. The Toronto Scottish Canadians remained in Oye-Plage for about a month before leaving for Holland, with Dunkirk still impregnable.

The Recovery. Following the liberation, the greatest danger to the residents were the thousands of land mines that had been placed by the Germans prior to D-Day. Therefore, a great effort was required to clear all of the mines from the beach and inland areas and this was accomplished with the highest priority as quickly as possible.

Despite the precautions and the training, the accidents were numerous. The number of deaths and injuries during the mine removal efforts is difficult to assess but there were also civilian victims. In 1947, mine clearance was considered complete in France, but in reality many years passed before all the mines had been found and neutralized.

The beautiful & accessible Le Platier d'Oye seaside nature preserve

The endless beaches & marshes of Oye-Plage

Looking towards the cliffs Of Dover

OUR TOWN TODAY

Today, Oye-Plage is known for its natural beauty and calming atmosphere; however, the people of Oye-Plage remember well the years of Nazi occupation and the suffering imposed on its residents by that ruthless and violent regime. Our town treats the many war ruins along our beaches with respect to remember those who were forced to live through those years.

The town has been blessed with a beautiful shoreline along the English Channel and, from a height of 3m above the beach, on a clear day it is possible to see the white cliffs of Dover, the only area between France and England where this is possible.

Many local environmental tours, nature walks and hiking trails are available throughout the area providing a variety of experiences with nature. Nearly 400 plant species, 23 land & marine animals and more than 200 species of birds occupy the local beaches, dunes, wetlands and estuaries and every effort is made to preserve these natural wonders.

Oye-Plage is located adjacent to the Calais airport and only 20 km from the English "Chunnel", offering easy access to visitors and a wide range of accommodations. Less than 10 km from the bustling city of Calais, visitors and residents alike can enjoy the serenity of Oye-Plage yet have access to the many entertainment and cultural amenities of Calais including the Calais Memory Museum, the former Allied Navy Command Post, offering 21 rooms of collections and documents from 1939 to 1945.

For more information about Oye-Plage visit **www.oye-plage.fr**. *To learn more about the Calais Memory Museum, visit* **www.musee-memoire-calais.com/**.

We appreciate the efforts and assistance provided by the Oye-Plage town officials and residents who helped prepare this commemorative document. Photos courtesy of the Commune of Oye-Plage.

RIBEAUVILLÉ FRANCE

Region: Grand Est   Pop. 1940: 4.800   Pop. 2020: 4,900

SITING & HERITAGE

Ribeauvillé is located in the idyllic forested hills of France less than 15 miles from the border with Germany. Archaeological finds have established that the Ribeauvillé area has been occupied since the Neolithic era (6000-2200 BC) making the area important archaeologically. Founded under the name "Ratbaldovilare" in 762, Ribeauvillé has a rich medieval history that is still evident in the old part of town where the streets are lined with 15th to 18th century buildings and decorated Renaissance fountain squares. The town and neighboring hills are dominated by the majestic ruins of the Three Castles of the Lords of Ribeaupierre dating from the 13th century.

Located in the middle of an important French wine production area known as the Alsace, more than 65 wineries produce varieties that include Muscat, Pinot Gris, Rieisiling, Gewurtztraminer and Crémant d'Alsace, a sparkling wine that is mushrooming in popularity.

GPS Coordinates: N48.1949 E7.3191

OUR TOWN'S OCCUPATION STORY

Hitler Youth in Ribeauvillé during the Occupation

The Nazification Of Alsace. From the first weeks of occupation the Nazis published ordinances and gave instructions to replace all traces of French influence and to become German. The new masters strive to make Alsatians good Nazis. In their policy of assimilation they primarily target the teaching of youth. Young people, from 12 years old, are recruited into the Hitler Youth (Hitler Jugend for the boys and the Bund Deutschen Mädel for girls).

By taking full charge of various sporting and cultural activities, the German authorities aimed at the adhesion of this malleable youth to the party's theses. Using both seduction and coercion, the occupant works hard to program the intellect of young boys and young girls.

German programs are imposed on the school and the "Heil Hitler" greeting is introduced, both for teachers and students. In the minds of the authorities, education and cultural life must play a fundamental role in the process of cultural re-education in order to awaken the feeling of belonging to the Germanic culture which is supposed to flourish in every Alsatian.

All civil servants are obliged to declare their allegiance to National Socialism in writing or they are dismissed from the civil service. The change of French-sounding surnames and first names to German-sounding names becomes an obligation, as are the names of certain streets and store signs.

In 1941, a decree incorporating Alsatians aged 17 to 25 into the German RAD (Reicharbeitdienst) was published. In 1942, an ordinance instituting compulsory service in the Wehrmacht was issued and all men 20 to 22 were inducted into the German army, marking the beginning of a nightmare which, for many, will continue in the Soviet internment camps. Of the 100,000 forcibly inducted, 30,000 are dead or missing and 20,000 are injured.

In general, the Alsatian population is watched by the leaders of the Nazi party, spying on conversations and organizing mass demonstrations, including the famous "Kreistag", intended to showcase the power and the benefits of the regime. On days of parades and speeches, the whole population is required not only to participate in it, but also to decorate their homes.

Old Town Ribeauvillé during the Occupation

Life During The Occupation. During the occupation life continues, but with more and more constraints and privations. Some products are replaced by substitutes: Saccharin will replace sugar, wood will be used instead of leather for shoe soles. The inhabitants of villages and small towns like Ribeauvillé however suffer less than those of big cities who are deprived of everything. The wine growers barter wine or schnapps for fabric and people render small services for potatoes or a few eggs.

Women do not lack the ingenuity to make up for the lack of basic necessities. They make soap with beef fat mixed with caustic soda, and with the military blankets they can dye, they make jackets or warm coats.

Beginning in 1943, the German authorities granted each family, according to the number of its members, food and clothing supply cards, however the allotments were meager, encouraging the development of black markets.

American artillery during the Liberation

THE BATTLE OF RIBEAUVILLÉ

The night of December 2, 1944 was relatively calm but at dawn the cannonade resumed. The inhabitants immediately take refuge in their cellars or in the shelters which had been assigned to them. The most daring watch the surroundings from the attic skylights.

The fighting was sporadic but violent because the Germans held several strategic positions around the city: crossroads, heights (Geisberg, Hasaland, etc.) and farms to the east of the city. Around 2:30 p.m., the first Sherman tank descends the Grand Rue and heads for Rue des Pucelles. It was followed by two others and by the first Allied infantry elements.

Rumor circulates like wildfire: "They are here!". The population begins to leave the shelters to observe these soldiers who come from so far. German resistance was short-lived; the firepower of the US tanks quickly overcame the anti-tank batteries located at the intersection of rue Klée and the wine route, and on the Geisberg. Many Germans are taken prisoner.

In the evening the city is completely controlled by American troops. There are 54 tanks, clearing machines and a large number of infantrymen. The enthusiastic population celebrates the liberators. The Americans offer chewing gum, chocolate and cigarettes, and in return the residents take out the best wine bottles and schnapps to celebrate the happy ending.

For a few hours the farms at the eastern entrance to the city continued to be occupied by German troops. The US intended to bomb them in the next few days. French officers intervened with the American authorities to dissuade them from doing so because these dwellings housed Alsatian families being held hostage by residual German troops.

The situation will remain precarious throughout December. It was necessary to welcome and accommodate the refugees from the surrounding villages (Guémar, Illhaeusern, Mittelwihr, Bennwihr and Ammerschwihr) but also an increasing number of troops (American, French, Foreign Legion and Moroccan Goumiers). In addition, the Germans carry out counter-offensives; nightly incursions to the city gates and the bombing of the area create strong feelings of insecurity among the residents.

In fact it was not until the surrender of the Colmar Pocket in February 1945 that the residents were able to recover a semblance of normal life, heal the wounds of these years of war, reconstruct the damage caused and engage in new hopes for a better world.

LIBERATION

As soon as the United States declared war on Germany, the people regained hope. From March 1944 on, the local population regularly saw Allied planes fly over the region. Several flying fortresses crash around the Illhaeusern, St Hippolyte, Bergheim and Houssen areas but others cause major damage to infrastructure or drop leaflets for Alsatians. Unfortunately, many civilian victims will die or be injured during these raids.

Beginning in September, the rumor circulates that the Americans would soon be in St. Dié, approximately 50 km west of Ribeauvillé. Immediately the Germans requisition adolescents and the elderly to dig anti-tank ditches on the road from Ste-Marie-aux-Mines. In mid-November, German civilians fled the district on the run and on November 22 the Burgermeister Michel Fischbach, appointed by the Nazis, hastily leaves the city.

On November 25, Sainte-Marie-aux-Mines was taken over by the American Army 36th Infantry Division, made up mostly of Texans who had fought at Monte Cassino in Italy that spring.

The annual Spring Carnival parade in Ribeauvillé

Idyllic Ribeauvillé and the Alsace hills

OUR TOWN TODAY

.A popular tourist destination, Ribeauvillé has much to offer the visitor. Many wineries can be visited and many recreational opportunities exist throughout the forested Alsace hills surrounding the town.

For more than 30 years the Ribeauvillé Festival has presented very high levels of international programs and entertainment, making it one of the region's most important musical events.

In the well-maintained medieval area of Ribeauvillé, the visitor can find many beautiful examples of medieval architecture and a wide variety of specialty shops, restaurants and accommodations. Since tourism is Ribeauvillé's #1 industry, many efforts have been made to create a multi-lingual atmosphere to accommodate the many international visitors.

Ribeauvillé is a modern community that celebrates its medieval past and remembers the tragedy of the Nazi occupation. The present generations are harvesting the fruits of the sacrifice of the young people who fought for freedom and for the values we wish to be universal.

The commemorations of this event remind us that people from all walks of life can unite their destinies for a cause they considered noble and just

*For more information on Ribeauvillé, please visit the city's official website: **www.ribeauville.fr**. For more information about the history of Ribeauvillé you may contact the email address: **contact@cercle-histor-ribeauville.com**.*

This information was taken from the 2009 publication "65th Anniversary of the Liberation of Ribeauvillé" which was provided by Mr. Bernard Schwach, President of the local Cercle de Recherche Historique de Ribeauvillé et Environs. Photos courtesy of the commune of Ribeauvillé.

VILLERS-BRETONNEUX   FRANCE

Region: Hauts de France   Pop. 1940: 3,400   Pop. 2020: 4,500

SITING & HERITAGE

Villers-Bretonneux is a small town 15km east of Amiens, in the Somme department within the Hauts-de-France region in a rich agricultural area of northern France. The town has existed since Antiquity. "Villers" comes from the Latin Villae, meaning "villa," when the town was a Roman administrative center. "Bretonneux" seems to refer to the barbarians and Celts of the 5th century, arriving from Breton tribes (from Brittany), who invaded the town at the time of the fall of the Roman Empire.

Due to its strategic geographic position as a northern Europe axis of communication and travel, the city has been regularly invaded and occupied: in 853 by the Normans, in 1337-1453 multiple times by the English and Burgundians, in 1636 by the Spanish, in 1815 by the Cossacks, in 1870 by the Prussians, in 1918 by the Germans and in 1940 by the German Nazis.

GPS Coordinates: N49.8684 E2.5180

The Villers-Bretonneux town hall, July 1940

OUR TOWN'S OCCUPATION STORY

The invasion. On May 10, 1940, faced with the German invasion, the evacuation order was given to the residents and many residents fled the city in a hurry. On May 12, the last inhabitants of Villers-Bretonneux note that the agricultural cooperative is full of grain. After the town was overtaken by the German advance, the residents returned to the city in mid June to find that the grain and all the shops and businesses had been looted.

During the invasion, from 24 to 28 May 1940, Villers-Bretonneux served as a rear base for French counterattacks on the Somme, particularly those in the direction of Corbie and Aubigny. The French 4th Colonial Infantry Division was able to hold the city until June 5, 1940 and on June 12 the Germans occupied the city. Two women were found beheaded in the rue d'Hangard on that day.

The Occupation. The occupation is brutal. On July 19, 1940, a war committee took control of the town under the supervision of the Germans. Beginning in December 1940, the German soldiers, helped by the Pétainist militia, embark on a hunt for the Gaullists and the Communists. The arrests follow one another continuously, like Edgard Leroux and Robert Dieu, who were arrested on April 10, 1940 and October 4, 1941 respectively for their political opinions. Living supplies to the city's residents continually become more and more difficult to obtain. After a ration ticket policy is implemented by the Germans, the black market becomes more and more necessary and prevalent.

The Villers-Bretonneux train station is regularly the target of air attacks by the Allies. On September 29, 1943, an English plane machin gunned a train of goods and passengers, leaving two dead and five wounded. A bombing on November 12, 1943 aimed at destroying the locomotive of the freight train, injured one. On May 9, 1944, the national highway was machine gunned, killing two local civilians.

Resistance. From July 1940 on, the Germans try to control all the life of the city. However, active resistance was organized very early on by clandestine networks of different groups of resistance fighters who ultimately grouped into a real organization around Jean Vasseur. Responsible for the Villers-Bretonneux region, he started corresponding with the London General Staff beginning in January 1942.

The passage of English tanks, 31 August 1944

This collection of resistants allows regular acts of sabotage to occur including theft and redistribution of ration tickets, theft and destruction of the occupier's military equipment and the derailment of military trains. The sabotage of the freight trains of July 1 and 11, 1943 resulted in the derailment of 62 coal cars, the destruction of military motor pump trucks and the death of a German soldier.

Faced with the upsurge in these acts of sabotage, the Vichy police and the Occupant decided to tighten their surveillance over the city, launching a campaign of arrests. At the end of July 1943, they arrested 10 members of the Michel Group, who were responsible for the railway sabotage of July 11. They will be condemned to death on August 2, 1943. On August 17, 1943, 23 Bretons are arrested for affiliation to the National Front and 3 more are arrested on August 20 for Gaullist activities.

In response to these arrests, the Resistant organization of Villers reorganized around Marcel Delamotte and Jean Vasseur. They decide on the derailments of two freight trains scheduled for September 18 and 25, 1943, before returning to total anonymity. Sabotage acts on the German forces resumed in the spring of 1944, under the orders of London in anticipation of the D-Day landings.

TWO BRAVE LOCAL RESISTORS

Maurice Seigneugens

Maurice Seigneurgens: Born December 1, 1919, a mechanic adjuster and militant Communist, Maurice lived in Villers-Bretonneux. Beginning in February 1943, Maurice joined the "Michel" group, an organization of FTPFs in the Somme. A very active resistant, he participated in numerous sabotages, including actions that resulted in sabotaging the Amiens-Tergnier railways on March 12, March 17 and April 9, 1943.

Maurice also participated in the attack on the lock at Cerisy-Gailly, which resulted in him being arrested on April 22, 1943. After being injured in an escape attempt and treated at Amiens prison, he was sentenced to death on July 22, 1943 and shot on August 2, 1943. Maurice was only 24 years old.

Marcel Delamotte

Marcel Delamotte: Born December 9, 1922, Marcel lived in Villers-Bretonneux after his father had been appointed deputy chief of the train station. After graduating as an aeronautical engineer in 1942, Marcel quickly went underground becoming a member of the National Front and the FTPF with the rank of second lieutenant, taking part in the clandestine publication of the newspaper "Picardie Libre".

Specializing in the regular theft of ration tickets, Marcel also participated in the recovery of weapons and ammunition parachuted by the Allies, and numerous sabotages between May 1943 and June 1944 that included train derailments and the sabotage of locks and electric pylons. Marcel was arrested on August 1, 1944 in Abbeville and shot during the German retreat at the end of August in the Bois de Gentelles, a few kilometers from Villers-Bretonneux, dying less than 30 days from the town's liberation.

LIBERATION & RECOVERY

At dawn on August 31, one hundred resistance fighters decided to hold the city and prevent the retreat of the German troops. The FFI resistors take up arms and take up positions at the south and west entrances to the city. The fights at the west entrances will be the hardest because the Germans fleeing Amiens, trying to reach Saint Quentin, are forced to take this national road.

Hidden after the first turn between the bridge, rue d'Aubigny, rue des Tavernes and the Tiberghien factory, the FFI took the German troops by surprise. The occupier, unable to cross the city, begins to surrender when the first British troops arrive around 8 a.m. At 11:30 am the fighting stopped, the last German forces withdrew and the Gendarmerie courtyard was full of prisoners. The British Forces finally cross the city from south to north traveling in the direction of Corbie.

Anecdote: During these fights, in the girls' school yard, the school teacher sees an armed resistance fighter come to cry over the body of a man covered with the tricolor flag. He recites a poem by Rimbaud before leaving, saying the words with terrible sadness in his voice and tears in his eyes.

The Villers-Bretonneux town hall © OTValdeeSomme

A view of the Villers-Bretonneux bell tower © Serge Rondot

OUR TOWN TODAY

Villers-Bretonneux is a dynamic town located in a properous agricultural area. The town's industrial past still marks the urban architecture, and thanks to the reconstruction of the city after the First World War, the Art Deco style flourishes along the streets. The rarity of the town's neo-Byzantine style church makes it a must to see and visit.

A visit to the local Franco-Australian museum, recalling the birth of the town's Franco-Australian friendship in 1918, is highly recommended. During World War I, Australian forces fought two major battles at Villers-Bretonneux. Losing the first battle, the Australian Imperial Forces (AIF) won the Second Battle and their victory is viewed as one of the most important turning points in the war against the Germans. After the war the city of Melbourne became a major sponsor of the reconstruction of Villers-Bretonneux. Today, the city of Robinvale, Australia is our sister city.

The museum is an opportunity for the visitor to experience how wonderful relationships can develop and flourish between people who live on opposite sides of the planet.

For more information about the town of Villers-Bretonneux please visit the municipal website: www.villers-bretonneux.com/. For more information about the Val de Somme area, please visit the Val de Somme tourist office website: http://fr.valdesomme-tourisme.com/.

This information was prepared by the Val de Somme Tourist Office, with the help of R.Godbert, a resident passionate about local history. Except as noted, photos courtesy of the commune of Villers-Bretonneux.

Remembering & Honoring The Sacrifices Endured By So Many

French General Charles de Gaulle—1942

Born in 1890, Charles de Gaulle was raised by a devoutly Catholic family in which history and philosophical debates were encouraged and common and, at an early age, de Gaulle developed a keen interest in military strategy and French history. After graduating from France's premier military academy in 1912 as a lieutenant, de Gaulle was soon involved in combatting the invading Germans in 1914. During the next two years of war he was wounded several times and, during the Battle of Verdun, he was taken prisoner, spending the last two years of the war as a prisoner of war at six different camps where he made five unsuccessful escape attempts that resulted in long periods of solitary confinement.

After the war, to a great extent because of his speaking and writing skills, (the 6'5" - 195 cm) de Gaulle rose in the ranks to serve directly under (the 5'7" - 170 cm) Marshall Pétain who supported de Gaulle's advancement. De Gaulle assisted in ghost-writing Pétain's military doctrines but later their relationship became strained and difficult. During the 1930s de Gaulle also became a vocal proponent for armored warfare, making him unpopular with his military superiors favoring the Maginot Line.

When the Germans invaded on May 10, 1940, de Gaulle was commanding a tank brigade but, as soon as Marshall Pétain decided to seek an armistice with Germany, de Gaulle fled to England where he used the power of the BBC radio to exhort the French people to resist the occupier. In response, in absentia, Marshall Pétain's Vichy government sentenced him to death by court martial.

While in exile, de Gaulle concentrated on creating, organizing and commanding the 'Free French Forces', amassing men and equipment primarily at a headquarters he established in the still-free French colony of Algiers. Immediately after D-Day, de Gaulle returned to France, following the advance of the Allies towards Paris where, on August 26, 1944, under sporadic machine gun fire from Vichy loyalists, he led a triumphant parade through Paris and the Arc de Triumph. That evening he was established as the provisional president of France at the Notre Dame Cathedral, brashly ignoring more gunfire inside the church from Vichy loyalists. Charles de Gaulle served as the president of France from 1958 to 1969, passing away a year later at his home in Colombey-les-Deux-Églises.

WORLD WAR II MUSEUMS OF NORTHERN FRANCE

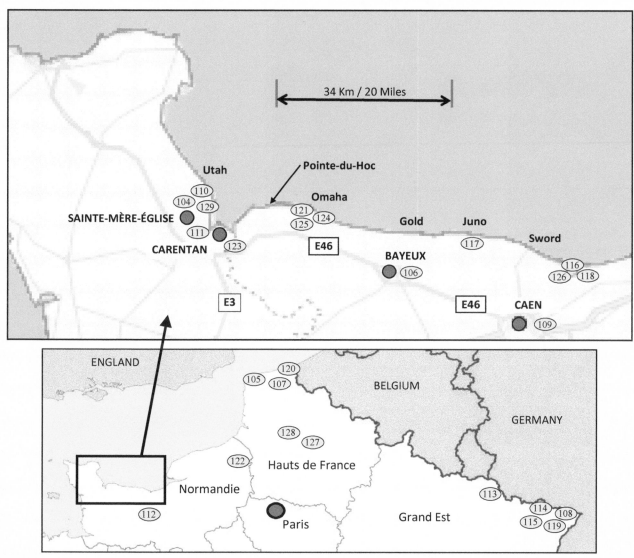

FRANCE

Page	Museum	Municipality	Page	Museum	Municipality
104	Airborne Museum	Saint-Mère-Église	117	Juno Beach Center	Courseulles-sur-Mer
105	Atlantic Wall Battery Todt	Audinghen	118	Merville Battery	Merville-Franceville-Plage
106	Battle of Normandy Museum	Bayeux	119	MM Park France	La Wantzenau
107	Blockhaus D'Éperlecques	Éperlecques	120	Museum Dunkirk 1940	Dunkirk
108	Bunker of Hatten Museum	Hatten	121	Normandy American Cemetery	Colleville-sur-Mer
109	Caen Memorial & Museum	Caen	122	Normandy Resistance Museum	Forges-les-Eaux
110	Crisbecq Battery Museum	Saint Marcouf	123	Normandy Victory Museum	Carentan les Marais
111	D-Day Experience	Carentan les Marais	124	Omaha Beach Museum	Saint-Laurent-sur-Mer
112	Falaise Memorial	Falaise	125	Overlord Museum	Colleville-sur-Mer
113	Fort Hackenberg Museum	Veckring	126	Pegasus Memorial Museum	Ranville
114	Fort Schoenenbourg	Hunspach	127	Picardy Resistance Museum	Tergnier
115	Fort Simserhof	Siersthal	128	Somme Trench Museum 1916	Albert
116	Grand Bunker Museum	Ouistreham	129	Utah Beach Landing Museurm	Sainte-Marie-Du-Mont

AIRBORNE MUSEUM
Sainte-Mère-Église , France

NORMANDIE

GPS Coordinates: N49.4085 E-1.3152

The town of Sainte-Mère-Église is well known to anyone familiar with the movie "The Longest Day". This excellent museum concentrates on the first hours of the D-Day invasion, leaving the visitor with a strong emotional appreciation for those American paratroopers who landed here.

The museum is dedicated to the American paratroopers and glidermen who came on the 6th of June 1944 to free France from the German occupation. By visiting the four buildings of the Airborne Museum, you will understand how the D-Day in Normandy was organized; you can imagine all of the feelings of these men during the D-Day landings.

The Airborne Museum offers you the opportunity to board a real Waco glider, unique in France, or in a C-47 plane as the troops of the 82nd and 101st Airborne Divisions did climbing aboard for the Battle of Normandy.

The museum's collections come alive with realistic scenes. You will have the sensation of jumping from a C-47 plane to land in the heart of the village of Sainte-Mère-Eglise, fight at the Battle of La Fière surrounded by flooded marshes and finally you will become lost during the Battle of Hedgerows.

The film of the museum "The Paths of Liberty" projected in the cinema explains with emotion the fates of the men who arrived at Utah Beach, Omaha Beach, Gold Beach, Juno Beach and Sword Beach as well as the highlights of the aerial assaults and maritime landings.

The museum offers all visitors a tablet to go back in time: the Histopad. With this tablet and its hyper-realistic 3D graphics, you will witness the arrival of the first gliders in Normandy, experience the parachute jump from the plane transporting the famous John Steele who hung by his

parachute from the church steeple just across the street from the museum and witness the battles that made History. **Your immersion is guaranteed!**

For more information about the museum please visit: www.airborne-museum.org. For more information about visiting the Sainte-Mère-Église area, please visit: www.saintemereeglise.fr. Photos courtesy of the museum.

THE ATLANTIC WALL BATTERY TODT MUSEUM
Audinghen, France

GPS Coordinates: N50.8451 E1.6010

Located less than 30 km from the southern coast of England and where the Germans believed the Allied invasion would occur, this was one of the most important defensive positions along Hitler's entire Atlantic Wall. The museum's very rare and impressive K5 railway gun is itself worth the visit.

Constructed as a part of the German plan for the invasion of England at the narrowest point of the English Channel, the intent was to fire on the southeast coast of England and to keep the English Channel free of British warships during the invasion.

Completed in November 1941, Battery Todt consisted of four heavily reinforced bunkers known as Turms, each containing a 380mm (15") gun aimed at England. Constructed by the German Todt Organization and originally named "Battery Siegried", it was renamed "Battery Todt" in memory of Fritz Todt who was killed in a plane crash after a meeting with Hitler just days before the battery's inauguration. The battery fired its first shell on January 20, 1942.

Protected by 3m thick reinforced concrete walls able to withstand attacks from 2,000 lb bombs, the Battery Todt guns were capable of firing 1,800 lb shells at targets more than 50 km away, easily able to reach the southeastern coast of England. Two days after the inauguration, the battery fired to secure the passage of the battleships "Gneisenau", "Scharnhorst" and "Prinz Eugen" through the English Channel. The battery was lively during the year 1942 but less so during 1943. In spire of sustained Allied bombing, each gun continued uninterrupted fire prior to D-Day.

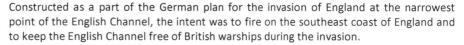

After D-Day and following an intense aerial bombing, the 3rd Canadian Infantry Division, was assigned to attack the Todt battery on September 28, 1944. The attack began at 6:35 am with violent artillery fire, followed by the assault 6:45 am. By 10:30 am white flags were seen everywhere and the battery was captured intact except for Turm #3 which had been flattened by bombs. After the war the four guns were taken by metal scrap dealers.

Today there is a museum in Turm #1 that contains an excellent collection of uniforms, weapons, vehicles and other military equipment. Outside the museum, a rare Krupp K5 280mm (11") railway gun is an impressive sight to see. Used by the Nazis throughout World War II, this is one of only 2 known surviving German railway guns of this size.

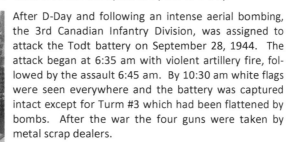

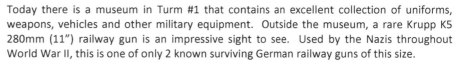

For more information about the museum visit www.batterietodt.com/. For more information about the Calais area, visit: www.calais-cotedopale.com/. Photos courtesy of the museum.

THE BATTLE OF NORMANDY MUSEUM
Bayeux, France

NORMANDIE

GPS Coordinates: N49.2735 E-0.7114

This is a very well appointed museum with many rare and interesting objects. The events of the D-Day invasion are presented in an easy to follow chronological order in multiple languages, leaving the visitor with an excellent understanding of how "The Longest Day" progressed.

The Memorial Museum of the Battle of Normandy in Bayeux devotes 2,300 m^2 to the exhibition of the military operations carried out for the Battle of Normandy during the summer of 1944. Inaugurated in 1981, the museum is located in the very heart of one of the strategic sites of the Battle of Normandy: the city of Bayeux, the first city to be liberated from mainland France on June 7, 1944.

Under the code name Overlord, the great Allied offensive was launched on June 6, 1944 to create a new front and liberate Europe. Its primary objective: the landing of troops and then equipment on the Normandy coast at dawn on June 6. The British troops landing on Gold Beach (Arromanches), liberated Bayeux the next day. The city suffered no damage and became an Allied rear base in the liberated territory, essential for the supply of the advancing armies and the reception of the wounded.

The film "Normandie 44, Decisive Victory in the West" is a 25-minute documentary of archival footage from the National Archives of the Allied countries that is shown in both French and English versions. It traces the major operations of the Battle of Normandy based not only on period films, but also on maps showing the movements of the troops.

An imposing diorama evokes the Falaise pocket and more precisely the junction of the first units of the 90th American Infantry Division with the 1st Polish Armored Division in Chambois, in Orne, in August 1944. One of the most famous episodes of the Battle of Normandy, the diorama symbolizes the meeting of the Allied troops who succeeded in encircling the Germans in a pocket, meeting at the village of Chambois, just east of Falaise.

The tour of the Memorial Museum of the Battle of Normandy in Bayeux offers a chronological visit to discover the military operations carried out on Norman soil the days after the D-Day landings from June 6, 1944 until the end of A ugust. Armament equipment, tanks, uniforms, military vehicles, maps of the advance of the Allied troops, film and archive photos plunge visitors back into the heart of the Battle of Normandy.

Of special interest is the rare British Churchill Crocodile "flame-thrower" tank outside the museum, found in the early 1980s at a scrap dealer in Portsmouth, England.

*For more information about the museum, please visit **www.bayeuxmuseum.com/musee-memorial-de-la-bataille-de-normandie/.** For more information about the Bayeux area, visit **www.bayeux.fr.** Photos courtesy of the museum.*

BLOCKHAUS D'ÉPERLECQUES
Éperlecques, France

GPS Coordinates: N50.8286 E2.1837

This enormous structure was originally constructed by the Nazis to serve as a secret factory to produce liquid oxygen propellant to launch missiles and constructed large enough to also store up to 100 ballistic missiles. You must see this to believe it.

The bunker of Éperlecques is by far the largest bunker in the north of France. Constructed by the Nazi Todt Organization using forcibly conscripted Frenchmen who were supplemented with Belgian, Dutch, French, Polish, Czech and Soviet prisoners of war and citizens. The facility has been open to the public since 1973.

By visiting the Éperlecques bunker, you will discover an authentic German launch pad with its V1 rocket ready for takeoff. From June 1944 to March 1945, 22,384 V1 rockets were launched at England; 10,492 on London alone. In addition, 11,892 V1 rockets were also launched on Liege, Antwerp and some on Paris after the liberation by the allies. Many simply got lost and fell at random. It is estimated that less than 60% reached their targets.

The site of Éperlecques was chosen to build the first completely autonomous V2 rocket launch site. The V2 was designed at the experimental station of the German army at Peenemünde by Wernher Von Braun and then mass-produced in factories. Normally the letter "V" refers to "Versuch" (prototype) but here it meant "Vergeltung", (reprisals/vengeance). Indeed, the V2s were launched to answer allied bombings.

On June 19, 1944, 17 Tallboy bombs fell on the bunker, creating an enormous crater 30 meters in diameter, engendering such shakings and vibrations that major operational equipment components had to be removed and replaced. On July 25, 1944, 15 Tallboys were dropped by the RAF, one of them falling on the bunker roof. The impact is visible on the north side. Starting in January 1945, red flags would be hoisted to warn the inhabitants of Éperlecques that a bombing was coming and to take shelter.

As it was the RAF and USAAC's missions to try out new bombs, they often chose the bunker for bomb trials. One of these was the Disney bomb, invented by Captain Terell of the Royal Navy. Designed to destroy hard-surfaced buildings, it would fall from 20,000 to 50,000 feet, where its electronic ignition propeller was activated to reach the impact speed of 720m/s (which is more than Mach 2).

Outside the bunker, in the surrounding forest, amid bomb craters, are exhibits of military vehicles and equipment appearing to be ready for action. A popular museum, the museum welcomes an average of 50,000 visitors per year to its well appointed visitor's center. We invite you to visit one of the most interesting World War II museums in one of the most beautiful areas of Europe.

For more information about the museum visit: www.leblockhaus.com/. For more information about the Calais area, visit: www.calais-cotedopale.com/. Photos courtesy of the museum.

THE BUNKER (ABRI) OF HATTEN MUSEUM
Hatten, France

A former underground Maginot Line barracks for French soldiers, and located in the center of the popular Alsance region of France, this museum tells the story of the Battle of Hatten, the last western German offensive of World War II.

From January 9 thru 21, 1945, Hatten and the neighboring community of Rittershoffen were the sites of one of the fiercest tank battles in France resulting in 85% destruction and 114 civilian casualties (83 in Hatten and 31 in Rittershoffen).

The battle of Hatten-Rittershoffen was part of Operation Nordwind, Hitler's last offensive on the western front, intended to prevent the US Seventh Army in Alsace from joining in on the Battle of the Bulge. The museum depicts the evacuation of the people of Hatten: their hasty departure from the village in September 1939, their difficult lives as refugees in Chateâuponsac (Haute-Vienne) and their return during the summer of 1940. Near the "Abri", the Memorial Woods is a quiet place dedicated to the innocent civilian victims of the conflict.

GPS Coordinates: N48.8993 E7.9677

The "Abri" is a underground fort, built into the slope and invisible from the surface. The two thick armored doors piercing its massive blank 60 meter-long exposed side were covered by four machine gun positions. Two GFM lookout and machine gun "cloches" (cupolas) located on top of the structure served as observation and defensive positions.

A hall is dedicated to the 130,000 civilian men from Alsace-Moselle who were forcibly drafted into the German Army by the Nazis between 1942 and 1945, during the annexation of the two provinces by the Third Reich. Failure to comply with this totally illegal measure would result in the deportation of their families. Most of the men fought on the Russian front and 40,000 of them died for a cause that was not theirs. Stories and personal recollections will help you understand the fate of these men. You will see a reconstitution of life in the camps and photographs illustrating the living conditions. A section of the exhibit is devoted to Nazi propaganda, which praised the German Army, thus enticing the Alsatians to enlist.

For more information about the museum, please visit www.abrihatten.fr/. For more information about the tourism opportunities in the Hatten area, visit www.visithaguenau.alsace/. Photos courtesy of the museum.

CAEN MEMORIAL & MUSEUM
Caen, France

NORMANDIE

GPS Coordinates: N49.1974 E-0.3840

The Caen Memorial Museum is a relatively new museum, first opening on June 6, 1988. The museum was constructed directly above the accessible and restored 70m long underground command post occupied by the 716th German Infantry Division who was responsible for the defense of the coastline north of Caen prior to D-Day.

From the origins of the Second World War to the end of the Cold War, the Caen Memorial tells the terrible story of the 20th century. Considering the destruction wreaked upon almost three quarters of this martyr city by the bombing during the 1944 summer of Liberation, Caen deserved a fitting tribute for the damage it suffered—the Caen Memorial & Museum.

In addition to the extensive exhibition areas, the film "*D-Day and the Battle of Normandy*" recounts the period from the D-Day landings to the liberation of Le Havre, 50 km east of Caen in September, 1944.

An experience not to be missed, the museum's new immersive film "*Europe Our History*" is presented as a brand new 360° visual and audio experience, providing the visitor an immersive, overall understanding of European history.

A major feature of the Memorial is German General Richter's underground bunker. In this bunker, on June 7, 1944 General Marcks and the commanders of other units around Caen met to organize Field Marshall Rommel's counter-attack plan, thought to be capable of pushing the Allies back to the sea.

The bunker museography guides you along the underground gallery with a dark and oppressive ambiance. After an introduction presenting the historical significance of the bunker and a map showing the initial positions, three successive themes string together: 1) the Calvados Department during the Occupation, 2) the Atlantic Wall and 3) the German Army's 716th Infantry Division that would face the spearhead of the Allies' invasion landing.

*For more information about the museum and online ticketing, please visit **www.memorial-caen.fr**. For more information about the Caen area, visit **www.caenlamer-tourisme.fr/**.*

109

CRISBECQ BATTERY MUSEUM
Saint Marcouf, France

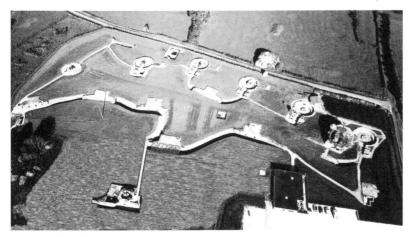

GPS Coordinates: N49.4790 E-1.2958

An important part of Germany's Atlantic Wall system along the Normandy coast, this battery was relentlessly bombed by the Allies prior to the June 6, 1944 D-Day invasion. Imagine the German defenders' initial reactions to seeing thousands of Allied ships appearing just offshore as the sun rose on June 6, 1944. You can imagine it here.

The Crisbecq Battery is near the village of Crisbecq which was chosen for its altitude of 28 meters and its panorama which offers a non-restricted view from the Pointe du Hoc to Saint Vaast la Hougue, covering the entire east shore of the Cherbourg peninsula.

The construction of the battery began in summer 1941 by the organization TODT supervising Russian and Polish prisoners who were lodged in wooden barracks near the castle of Francqueville near Sortosville. Later in 1943 to speed up the work, French workers employed by the TODT organization arrived from Paris and Brittany to work on the site.

Initially, the TODT organization built 5 French 155mm (6") guns. In December 1942 a second phase of construction was undertaken to build shelters and ammunition bunkers. At the end of 1943 the casemates were constructed and soon 210mm (8") guns were installed. With its 210 mm guns, the Crisbecq battery was one of the most powerful of the Atlantic Wall.

Beginning on April 20, 1944, this battery received 2,800 tons of Allied bombs prior to D-Day but was still operational on the morning of June 6. The most violent bombardment took place on the night of June 5 to 6, but, following a spotting error, the Allied planes bombed the village of Saint-Marcouf-De-L'Isle instead of the Battery. As a result of this error, they razed a large part of the village, causing the death of 35 civilians. A naval artillery duel then began between the Crisbecq Battery and the ships off Utah Beach. The guns of the Battery succeed in sinking the American destroyer USS Corry.

On June 8, the Americans arrived in front of the battery compound but were driven off by fire from the neighboring Azeville Battery. On June 10 and 11, the Crisbecq Battery was once again subjected to several bombardments, but, on the afternoon of June 11, the Germans abandoned the battery.

The battery was bought in February 2004 by two history buffs who began the enormous work of clearing all the trees and brambles that had covered everything. Today it is the largest coastal artillery battery on Utah Beach with its 22 underground blockhouses linked by more than a kilometer of trenches where you can imagine the dawn of June 6, 1944.

*For more information about the museum and online ticketing, please visit **www.batterie-marcouf.com/fr/**. For more information about the Carentan area, visit: **https://en.normandie-tourisme.fr/unmissable-sites/cherbourg-en-cotentin/**. Photos courtesy of the museum.*

D-DAY EXPERIENCE
Carentan les Marais, France

GPS Coordinates: N49.3292 E-1.2688

This is truly an impressive D-Day Experience as it combines two museums into one exceptional experience for the visitor. The documentary film at the 3D cinema alone is worth the price of admission.

Spread over more than 10,000 m², our museum complex invites you to live an incredible experience, combining education and entertainment in the heart of a place steeped in history. Here you will experience the D-Day invasion from the view of the soldiers.

Brought to life by our giant (15m x 8m) screen 3D cinema, you will be immersed in the events of June 6, 1944 through a 36-minute documentary about D-Day that focuses on the decisive battle of Carentan.

Then you discover the Dead Man's Corner Museum. Here, the men of the 6th German Parachute Regiment, known as the "Green Devils", fought fiercely for three days against the American paratroopers of the 101st Airborne Division. On June 8, the Germans withdrew to Carentan and the house became the command post of the 502nd PIR of the 101st Airborne.

Dead Man's Corner Museum

Why the strange name? In the village, they say it is haunted; some people now sense wandering souls there and others are uncomfortable. Through the authentic objects that belonged to the German paratroopers, you will discover why Dead Man's Corner was so important in the capture of this city and learn more about the origins of this strange name and the men who clashed with it. The story here is told through the mouth of Major von der Heydte, the commander of the "Green Devils".

When the news of the D-Day landings spread he decided to establish his command post in this house which overlooks the marshes and the road leading to Carentan. Entering the Dead Man's Corner Museum you will discover the chaos that reigns in the German HQ during the morning of June 6, 1944, with the noise of the bombardments and the Major's orders resounding all around you. You are immersed in the skin of a German soldier on the morning of D-Day!

At the D-Day Experience Museum it is Colonel Wolverton who interacts with you, an American paratrooper with a tragic destiny. If you dare, he invites you to relive the mythical crossing of the English Channel on June 6, 1944 aboard his plane, 'Stoy Hora'.

Climb aboard this real C-47 heading for Normandy on this fateful night of D-Day. As soon as your 3D briefing has passed, you are ready to board the plane, take off, and for 10 minutes you are a parachutist in the company of 26 of your comrades, flying over the Channel during a tumultuous flight. The tremors are felt, the smells are everywhere, the noise of the engines is all you hear except for the outside explosions. Everything is done to make you relive what the men of the 101st Airborne, experienced during this legendary crossing. So fasten your seat belts, we're going to take you on a ride!

Colonel Wolverton

For more information about the museum and online ticketing, please visit www.dday-experience.com/. For more information about the Carentan area, visit: www.france-voyage.com/cities-towns/carentan-les-marais-17361.htm. Photos courtesy of the museum.

FALAISE MÉMORIAL - CIVILIANS AT WAR
Falaise, France

NORMANDIE

GPS Coordinates: N48.8942 E-0.2023

This museum is particularly important to the Occupation Stories 2020 commemorative project because it is dedicated to the civilians forced to live through the tragedy of World War II. This new, technologically advanced museum speaks directly to the difficulties, oppression, constant fear and despair suffered by the citizens during the four years of occupation, the heroism of the resistance, the persecution of the Jews, the frightening period that followed the D-Day invasion and then finally . . . the joy of liberation.

Come and visit a new museum dedicated to the lives and survival of civilians during WWII. Its exhibition spaces take visitors into peoples' everyday lives using objects from the period, reconstructed sets, archive film and photographs.

The "Civilians and the Occupation" area is located on the second floor. It deals with the period of occupation in Normandy: daily life of the French population, Norman resistance and the retaliations that followed, Jewish persecution, and the exodus of 1940.

Located on the first floor, the "Civilians and Liberation" area recalls the bombings preceding the liberation. Mostly perpetuated by the Allied forces, the terrible bombings caused many victims among the civilian population. Many Norman towns were destroyed at more than 70% and reconstruction took determination and many years to complete.

The immersive room is on the ground floor where a film, edited from British, German, and French archive footage is shown in a room built at the exact place where there were discovered the remnants of a house destroyed during the successive bombings of Falaise. Famous for being the location of the battle of the 'Falaise Gap', the last battle of the Normandy campaign , Falaise is a marvelous town to visit and explore.

For more information about the museum and online ticketing information, visit: www.memorial-falaise.fr. For more information about visiting the Falaise area, visit: www.falaise-tourisme.com. Photos courtesy of the museum.

FORT HACKENBERG MUSEUM
Veckring, France

GPS Coordinates: N49.3412 E6.3659

Constructed in 1930, this fort was one of the first and one of the largest of the Maginot Line defensive system with the ability to fire 4 tons of explosives per minute. With 10 km of tunnels connecting 19 artillery blocks, the size of this "ouvrage" is almost incomprehensible.

Michael B. Keller/Stars and Stripes

Constructed In 1930, the French believed they had the perfect defense against any future German invasion. They believed that constructing a series of impregnable forts (ouvrages), each with multiple artillery positions, all along France's border with Germany, would deter any frontal attack. This was the "Maginot Line".

Unfortunately they failed to consider how new technology would alter how war is fought. Germany's highly mobilized Blitzkrieg bypassed the Maginot Line entirely, instead attacking through the unprotected Ardennes forest, also thought to be impregnable. Even though the soldiers defending the forts fought ferociously for weeks, the intensive attacks by the German forces quickly overwhelmed the defenders.

The Hackenberg Maginot Fort, with its 19 infantry and artillery blocks and 10 km of tunnels, is the largest of the Maginot forts and one of the first built. A guided tour presents the soldier's life in the fort, the fort's defensive armaments, the magazine where ammunition was stored and, separated from the living areas by an 8-ton blast door, soldier barracks and several kitchen areas where food was prepared for the more than 1,000 soldiers stationed here. You will also be amazed at the electrical generators, all in working order. A military museum of various firearms and military memorabilia and a fully-equipped canteen also occupy a number of these areas.

For the adventurous, it's possible to climb 146 stairs up a steep staircase where a guide can explain the turret's ability to raise, lower and rotate the twin 135mm (5") cannons. For the less adventurous you can take a ride on the electric munitions train through a portion of the underground tunnel system.

Above ground, a marked walking trail allows visitors to see the retractable cannon turrets, machine-gun turrets and the 800 meter-long, 8-meter tall anti-tank wall. At block 8 the visitor sees the heavy exterior damage to the fort that occurred when the fort was finally taken by George Patton's Third Army.

This is a real journey back in time and into the history of one of the most formidable fortifications of the 20th Century. The volunteers and employees of the AMIFORT Association look forward to helping you discover this immense and complex defensive position.

*For more information about the museum and online ticketing, please visit **www.maginot-hackenberg.com/**. For more information about the Veckring area, visit: **www.thionvilletourisme.fr/**. Except as noted, photos courtesy of the museum (AMIFORT Association).*

FORT SCHOENENBOURG OUVRAGE
Hunspach, France

GPS Coordinates: N48.9665 E7.9123

This fort experienced more shelling and bombardment than any other of the Maginot Line forts during the May, 1940 invasion by the Germans. The 3,000 meters of subterranean tunnels are beautifully restored and maintained.

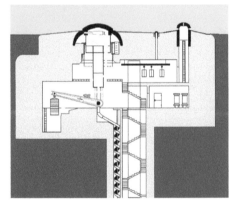

The fortification at Schoenenbourg is the fort (ouvrage) that saw the most combat between September 1939 and June 1940. Over this period, over 17,000 shells were fired from the fort, and it was itself the target of over 3000 shells and 160 bombs. On 19 June 1940, German *Stukas* attacked Schoenenbourg and other *ouvrages*, returning on the 20th and 21st. The attacks on the 21st were joined by a bombardment of 56 shells from 420 mm (16") siege mortars, each shell weighing more than one ton, lasting three days. The bombardment cracked walls, but did not disable the position. Schoenenbourg fired during this period in support of nearby casemates, not seriously affected by the bombardments. Schoenenbourg's turrets were retracted to receive the heavy shells, and raised during the lengthy reloading period for counterbattery fire.

The final surrender of Schoenenbourg was effected on 1 July 1940, in accordance with the terms of the Second Compiègne Armistice. Following the surrender, Schoenenbourg was used as a backdrop for propaganda films and as an indoctrination center for Hitler Youth.

The fort at Schoenenbourg, the most important Maginot Line fortification in Alsace, is listed on the National Register of Historic Places. It comprises 8 blocks for 650 men. You can tour the barracks, the kitchens, the command post, the generating plant and see gun positions, retractable gun turrets and magazines for the ammunition. Documents on the history of the Maginot Line and on military life in a fort are on display. It is open to visitors during the summer months between April and early November.

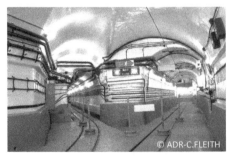

Ignis—Wikimedia Commons

Leon Petrosyan

Lennard Bolijn

© ADR-C.FLEITH

Bert Jans

Matt Hiashn

For more information about the ouvrage, visit: www.lignemaginot.com/. For more information about the local area, visit www.alsace-verte.com/. Except as noted, photos courtesy of the museum.

FORT SIMSERHOF OUVRAGE
Siersthal, France

GPS Coordinates: N49.0587 E7.3710

Located in a beautiful setting of forests and rolling hills, Fort Simserhof is one of the most visited of the Maginot Line forts due to its amenities and historical presentations.

The construction of the Simserhof spread over nearly 10 years, from 1929 to 1939, requiring 2,000 workers working day and night. Equipped with 5 km of subterranean galleries, eight combat blocks, a central power plant and separate ammunition tunnels, it was able to withstand projectiles from giant mortars like "the Big Bertha." With tunnels as deep as 30 meters below the surface, Fort Simserhof was one of the largest, and considered to be one of the most imposing, forts of the Maginot Line.

Following the German invasion of May, 1940, during the month of June, the soldiers of the fort fought heroically, ultimately becoming the last of the Maginot Line forts to surrender to the Germans. The battle for Simserhof lasted 50 days, ending on June 30, 1940 when the French army commanders ordered the fort to surrender.

During the war the Germans occupied the fort, using the underground tunnels for the storage of torpedoes. When the Allies pushed their way east after D-Day, they approached Fort Simserhof in December, 1944. On December 14, 1944, units of the US Seventh Army assaulted the fort with troops and tank destroyers, firing directly into the apertures of the fort. After six days of fighting, bombardment and artillery fire, the fort was finally taken.

Today Fort Simserhof is one of the most visited tourist sites on the Maginot Line. The tour begins with a 12-minute film about the history of the Maginot Line using archival film footage of the construction and battles of the fortress. Visitors then board an automated train to be transported into the ammunition tunnels accompanied by the sounds of the war, special effects and a narration in three languages, presenting life in the fort during the war.

After the tram ride, visitors return to the museum's modern visitor's center where a guided tour takes the visitor down to the barracks, the kitchens, the infirmary and the power plant.

Above ground you can walk a landscaped path through the woods where the fortified concrete entrances and the gun turrets can be seen through the foliage. Afterwards the visitor can enjoy the museum's spacious and comfortable cafeteria, gift shop, restrooms and wi-fi service.

*For more information about the museum, visit **www.simserhof.fr/**. For more information about the local area, visit **www.ville-bitche.fr**. Photos courtesy of the museum.*

THE GRAND BUNKER MUSEUM
Ouistreham, France

GPS Coordinates: N49.2875 E-0.2523

This museum occupies what was the most powerful Atlantic Wall coastal battery along the Normandy coast. Meticulously detailed and restored as it appeared just before D-Day, exploring the five levels clearly shows what life was like for the German soldiers who manned this large and very important coastal defense battery.

The Grand Bunker of the former Shooting Command and Management Station has been completely renovated to house a museum devoted entirely to the Atlantic Wall in Normandy. After having belonged to the Navy, the founders wanted this unique blockhouse to recover its original appearance.

A remarkable piece of construction, all rooms in this Sonderkonstruktion have been remodeled in a remarkable way with an abundance of authentic material. The founders took full advantage of this 17-meter high structure to re-create and present all of the essential functions that characterized the life of the Germans within the defensive positions of the Atlantic Wall before D-Day.

The founders of the Museum wished to offer visitors all 5 levels of this blockhouse which served as the nerve center of the command of the defenses of the estuary of the Orne. Throughout all 5 levels, each area has been restored to like new condition paying perfect attention to all details in order to reconstitute and restore the atmosphere which reigned in this bunker on the eve of D-Day.

Each level will show you how daily life was organized in the Big Bunker. Each room of the Grand Bunker seems to be in full activity as it was on the morning of June 6, 1944. Imagine how life changed instantly for the soldiers that day.

Once inside, you will breathe the air so particular of a blockhouse. You will be able to feel the life behind the concrete, its gas-tight armored doors and its confined spaces. From room to room, from floor to floor, the multiple rooms of the Grand Bunker will allow you to browse and enter all of the internal organs of the Shooting and Command Direction Post.

Just above is the breathtaking 180° degree panorama available to the Germans to monitor all the maritime movements in the Bay of Seine off the coast of Normandy. The rangefinder for measuring distances to targets is always present and, from this high position, you will be able to see how it is possible to sweep the entire area of Operation Overlord—and see the thousands of ships as the sun rose on D-Day.

The Grand Bunker, is the last visible vestige of what was the most powerful coastal battery in the area. Completely renovated to appear as it did on D-Day, we invite you to visit our museum and the beautiful adjacent Plage de Riva Bella beach area.

For more information about the museum, please visit www.museegrandbunker.com. For more information about the Ouistreham / Rivabella coastal area, visit www.ouistreham-rivabella.fr. Photos courtesy of the museum.

JUNO BEACH CENTER
Courseulles-Sur-Mer, France

Photo: © CJB-GWalt

NORMANDIE

GPS Coordinates: N49.3364 E-0.4616

This comprehensive, modern and beautiful museum sits on the sands of Juno Beach as a tribute to the 14,000 Canadian soldiers who landed and fought there to drive the Germans out of France.

On D-Day, June 6, 1944, "Operation Overlord", the long-awaited invasion of Nazi-occupied Europe, began with Allied armies from the U.S., Britain and Canada landing on the coast of Normandy. On D-Day, the 3rd Canadian Infantry Division landed on Juno Beach. The Canadian assault troops stormed ashore in the face of fierce opposition from German strongholds and mined beach obstacles.

The soldiers raced across the wide-open beaches swept with machine gun fire, and stormed the gun positions. In fierce hand-to-hand fighting, they fought their way into the towns of Bernières, Courseulles and St. Aubin and then advanced inland, securing a critical beachhead for the allied invasion. The victory was a turning point in World War II and led to the liberation of Europe and the defeat of Nazi Germany.

Fourteen thousand young Canadians stormed Juno Beach on D-Day. Their courage, determination and self sacrifice were the immediate reasons for the success in those critical hours. The fighting they endured was fierce and frightening. The price they paid was high: the battles for the beachhead cost 340 Canadian lives and another 574 wounded. At the end of the day, its forward elements stood deeper into France than those of any other division and the opposition the Canadians faced was stronger than that of any other beach save Omaha.

Photo: © CJB-Ph.Delval

The Juno Beach Centre is a museum and cultural centre which opened at Courseulles-sur-Mer, France on June 6, 2003. The Centre presents the war effort made by all Canadians, civilian and military alike, both at home and on the various fronts during the Second World War, as well as the many faces of contemporary Canadian society.

The Juno Beach Centre's permanent exhibit draws on photographs, documents, firsthand accounts, multimedia, maps, and artifacts to tell the story of the Canadians who volunteered for military service or mobilized at home to contribute to the war effort. Guided tours of the beach are available.

Primarily, this museum is a tribute to the brave men of the Canadian Army forces who landed here during D-Day. To these people, we owe the freedom that we take for granted. Today an unbreakable bond exists between Canada and Courselles-sur-Mer that is visible throughout the town. Let us never forget their sacrifice. God bless them all.

Photo: © CJB-Ph.Delval

Photo: © CJB-Ph.Delval

Photo: © CJB-Ph.Delval

For more information about the museum visit: www.junobeach.org/. For more information about the Courseulles-sur-Mer area, visit: www.courseulles-sur-mer.com/. Except as noted, all photos courtesy of the museum.

MERVILLE BATTERY MUSEUM
Merville-Franceville-Plage, France

NORMANDIE

GPS Coordinates: N49.2697 E-0.1973

On D-Day, this German artillery battery posed a direct threat to the success of the British forces landing at Sword Beach and thus had to be neutralized as quickly as possible. The task fell to the British parachutists of the 9th Parachute Battalion commanded by Lt. Col. Terence Otway.

Following the visit of Feldmarschall Rommel on March 6, 1944 in Merville, the Todt Organization received the order to significantly accelerate the work to shelter the two howitzers exposed in the open. The last two concrete casemates will be completed in May 1944, only one month before the D-Day landings.

Prior to the June 6, 1944 landings the Merville Battery was heavily bombed but the bombing failed to disrupt the battery's ability to operate. On May 19, 1944, a massive bombardment killed the German commander Captain Karl-Heinrich Wolter, decapitating the command of the Merville Battery.

On the night of June 6, 1944, the C-47s carrying the British 9th Parachute Battalion became scattered as they approached the coast, causing the parachutists to be dropped over a large area, many landing in the flooded marshes surrounding the drop zone. The battalion commander, Lt. Col. Otway was able to collect 150 men by 0250 hours and, with no other option, proceeded to attack the battery. After fierce fighting and many losses on both sides the battery was neutralized.

Lt. Col. Terence Otway

The villagers of Merville these days take great care to ensure that the exploits of the men who fought here will never be forgotten and that future generations will recognize the sacrifices they made for our liberty. There is never a 6th June when the remaining veterans do not come to pay homage to their brothers in arms who fell in Normandy.

The Merville battery and museum form the eastern boundary of the battle of Normandy. Together they comprise a "must visit" place which enables the visitor to understand what really happened at dawn on "the longest day". On a completely preserved historic site, an educational trail invites you to walk between the different blockhouses and discover the history of this important German battery.

 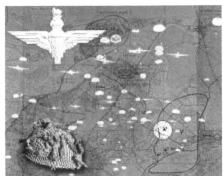

*For more information about the museum and online ticketing, please visit **www.batterie-merville.com/**. For more information about the Merville-Franceville-Plage area, visit **www.map-france.com/Merville-Franceville-Plage-14810/**. Photos courtesy of the museum.*

MM PARK FRANCE
La Wantzenau, France

GPS Coordinates: N48.6658 E7.8091

A new, major museum established in 2017, MM Park France is located on the northern outskirts of Strasbourg. Especially known for its extensive World War II vehicle collection, more than 120 vehicles are displayed in a huge singular room, many of which are rare and one-of-a-kind.

The MMP Park France museum houses thousands of machines and objects, some extremely rare. The displays include tanks, vehicles, equipment and uniforms from the United States, Canada, Belgium, France, Great Britain, Germany and the Soviet Union. All told, the collection includes more than 120 restored and war-worn vehicles, more than 500 uniforms and more than 500 rifles, pistols, machine guns and submachine guns in carefully designed displays.

Large amounts of miscellaneous items such as medical equipment, communication equipment, bicycles and military radios are also displayed. A unique experience, the visitor can also view and board a 20-meter German patrol boat floating in a basin of water within the building.

With more than 7,000 m^2 of exhibition space, MM Park is one of the largest World War II museums in Europe and a 1,500 m^2 expansion is planned for 2021 that will include rooms dedicated to temporary exhibitions plus ancillary improvements that will improve the museum shop, restaurant and children's play areas. There will be a new jumping tower with a height of about fifteen meters from which one can leap straight into the void using a secure system. Another novelty is a 100-meter long zip line outside the building.

A very popular museum, attendance at the museum averages more than 40,000 visitors per year from a wide range of countries. A visit to the museum, combined with a stay in beautiful Strasbourg, provides memories that will last a lifetime.

For more information about the museum, please visit **www.mmpark.fr/**. *For more information about the La Wantzenau area, visit* **www.visitstrasbourg.fr/**. *Photos courtesy of the museum.*

MUSEUM DUNKERQUE 1940 - OPERATION DYNAMO
Dunkirk, France

ENGLAND

HAUTS
DE
FRANCE

NORMANDIE

GPS Coordinates: N51.0462 E2.3813

This museum puts the visitor at the nerve center of one of the greatest feats of mankind when the British nation came together to rescue an entire army from certain defeat and capture. Many civilian mariners stepped forward to help, risking air attacks, submarine attacks and mines to do their duty.

The Dunkirk 1940 Museum - Operation Dynamo invites you to discover Operation Dynamo and the Battle of Dunkirk. With a total exhibition area of more than 1000 m^2, the museum also presents a rich collection of weapons, uniforms and models.

The Dunkirk 1940 / Operation Dynamo Museum is located in the curtain walls of 19th century Bastion 32. Serving as the headquarters of the fortified Dunkirk defense, it was from this location that the orders for the defense of Dunkirk began and where the evacuation of the Allied soldiers by sea were coordinated. The museum is therefore also a symbolic place, playing an important role during the events of Operation Dynamo and the Battle of Dunkirk.

The Museum, renovated and enlarged in 2017, offers an excellent introductory 12-minute video in French and English that dives you into the story of Operation Dynamo. Following the video presentation more than 400 m2 of exhibits showcase an extensive number of period objects, weapons, vehicles, uniforms, photos and maps. All aspects of the Dunkirk evacuation are covered with a special emphasis placed on the naval operations.

The story begins with the explanation of how the British Expeditionary Force (BEF) came to become trapped at Dunkirk ahead of the advancing Germans and why the only option was to evacuate the trapped soldiers by sea. The stories continue about how Operation Dynamo was organized and executed, how the trapped soldiers and rescuers were attacked by the Luftwaffe, how the soldiers were required to reach the rescue boats and the damage and death caused by floating German mines.

Operation Dynamo is the largest military evacuation in history. Often called "The Miracle of Dunkirk", in 9 days, 340,000 soldiers (130,000 French and 210,000 British) were evacuated to England by an instantly-created and determined navy of warships, merchant ships, pleasure yachts and fishing boats. The museum tells their stories but also the stories of the Dunkirk civilians, the Nazi invader and even the Czech liberators in 1945.

The team of the museum and the volunteers of the Memorial Association of Remembrance are committed to sharing the memory of Dunkirk with you and we invite you to discover this episode of World War II, one of the most important events of the war.

For more information about the museum visit: www.dynamo-dunkerque.com/. For more information about the Calais area, visit: www.calais-cotedopale.com/. Photos courtesy of the museum.

NORMANDY AMERICAN CEMETERY
Colleville-sur-Mer, France

NORMANDIE

GPS Coordinates: N49.3590 E-0.8514

Located at Omaha Beach, the American Battle Monuments Commission (ABMC) is responsible for managing and maintaining this beautiful cemetery adjacent to Omaha Beach. No visit to Normandy is complete without a visit to this symbol of American values, pride, patriotism and perseverance.

The Normandy American Cemetery and Memorial in France is located in Colleville-sur-Mer, on the site of the temporary American St. Laurent Cemetery, established by the U.S. First Army on June 8, 1944 as the first American cemetery on European soil in World War II.

The cemetery site covers 172.5 acres and contains the graves of 9,385 of our American military dead, most of whom lost their lives in the D-Day landings and ensuing operations. On the Walls of the Missing, in a semicircular garden on the east side of the memorial, are inscribed 1,557 names. Rosettes mark the names of those since recovered and identified.

The memorial consists of a semicircular colonnade with a loggia at each end containing large maps and narratives of the military operations; at the center is the bronze statue, "Spirit of American Youth Rising from the Waves."

An orientation table overlooking the beach depicts the various landing locations of the multi-national forces in Normandy. Facing west at the memorial, one sees in the foreground the reflecting pool; beyond is the burial area with a circular chapel and, at the far end, granite statues represent the United States and France.

Dedicated in 2007 by the ABMC, the $30 million visitor center includes many exhibits of text, photos, films, interactive displays and artifacts that portray the competence, courage and sacrifice of the Allied forces who landed here on D-Day June 6, 1944. With more than 1 million visitors per year, this is the most visited ABMC cemetery in the world.

For more information about the cemetery, visit **www.abmc.gov/normandy**. *For more information about the Colleville-sur-Mer area, visit* **www.bayeux.fr.** Photos courtesy ABMC/Warrick Page.

NORMANDY RESISTANCE MUSEUM
Forges-les-Eaux, France

NORMANDIE

GPS Coordinates: N49.6131 E1.5473

This museum is dedicated to the French Resistance movement during World War II, the deportation of citizens and how the French people were forced to live their daily lives during the four years of Nazi occupation.

The Normandy Resistance Museum is located in the center of the commune of Forges-les-Eaux, a tourist spa resort in the heart of the Pays de Bray bocage region of Normandie. A very personal museum, the museum is spread over two floors.

On the ground floor, the entrance immediately plunges you into the dark hours of the Nazi Occupation, featuring German mannequins and propaganda posters. The visitor discovers the countless plane crashes that occurred during the war in the heart of the country of Bray and Vallée de la Bresle (Seine-Maritime and Somme). Pieces of planes (B-17s, Spitfires, etc.), photos of pilots and the objects and testimonies of those who lived it retrace the history of each plane. Between 1943 and 1944, plane crashes in the area numbered in the hundreds and every story is different.

On the first floor, the visitor is immersed in the daily life of the French under the Occupation. Ration tickets, a wooden bicycle wheel, a wedding dress made from a parachute and stories about how the Normans adapted their daily life to the war. Among them are the stories of the resistance networks. These men and women in the shadows recover and hide the airmen who have fallen from the sky before exfiltrating them towards England. The museum has an incredible collection belonging to the Cressent family whose father, Roger was one of the heads of these networks in the heart of the Bray region.

An important part of the museum gives the visitor an appointment with the most moving of stories, that of the Deportation, including period outfits and photos of the deportees from all over Normandy. Personalizing these stories are objects (board games made with bread crumbs, Christmas cards, etc.), all made in captivity in the heart of the hell of the concentration camps. The stories of the victims, and in particular those of the women, cannot leave anyone indifferent.

The team from the Museum of Resistance and Deportation is a major player in memory events in our Normandy region. In connection with the French authorities, but also the British, American and Australian authorities, the Museum participates in numerous commemorations and often initiates the creation of monuments in memory of Allied airmen who fell for our freedom.

For more information about the museum visit **www.normandyresistancemuseum.com/index.html***. For more information about the Forges-les-Eaux area, visit:* **www.seine-maritime-tourisme.com/***. Photos courtesy of the museum.*

NORMANDY VICTORY MUSEUM
Carentan-les-Marais, France

NORMANDIE

GPS Coordinates: N49.3046 E-1.1929

This new immersive museum, opened in 2017, is located at the American airfield designated A10 during the battle of Normandy. The visitor can take a ride in an armored vehicle, see a re-creation of the D-Day Utah Beach obstacles and try a re-created American training obstacle course inaugurated by the actors of the Band of Brothers TV series.

The Normandy Victory Museum welcomes you to the heart of the Normandy Cotentin marshes. In about twenty scenes in the midst of more than 10,000 authentic collectibles, our museum invites you on a moving journey alongside those who lived and made history here. Whether they are combatants or civilians, national heroes or everyday heroes, we pay tribute to them.

The Normandy Victory Museum is one of the must-see World War II museums in Normandy because it addresses in detail the battle of the hedgerows which took place during the summer of 1944 in the Normandy countryside. The important and strategic battle of the hedgerows forever marked the memory of the locals and the soldiers involved in this fight. This history is where the museum begins.

As soon as you arrive, the visitor is able to access a section of reproduced landing beach and its German defenses when the first LCVP of the American 4th infantry division reached Utah Beach, including concrete tetrahedra and Czech metal hedgehogs placed to hinder the progress of troops and prevent a landing close to the dunes. In the background, two American barges of the LCVP or Higgins boat type are visible, one of which has been reconstructed, allowing you to see the conditions of the Channel crossing for the young GI's. Inside the museum, professionally staged sounds add greatly to the realism of each of the scenes and dioramas. We invite you to visit our unique museum and our beautiful corner of France.

*For more information about the museum,, visit **https://normandy-victory-museum.fr**. For more information about the Carentan area, visit **https://carentanlesmarais.fr**. Photos courtesy of the Normandy Victory Museum.*

OMAHA BEACH MEMORIAL MUSEUM
Saint-Laurent-sur-Mer, France

Normandie

GPS Coordinates: N49.3670 E-0.8821

This excellent museum is a short walk from the Omaha Beach invasion beach, the marble American Memorial overlooking the beach and the Normandy American Cemetery where more than 9,000 American soldiers rest in peace. This museum is the perfect prelude to visiting Pointe du Hoc at the west end of Omaha Beach.

Extending east from Pointe-du-Hoc for a distance of approximately 10 km, the Omaha Beach sector was the most heavily defended of the five Normandy D-Day invasion beaches and thus it was also the bloodiest sector.

Primarily assigned to the American 1st and 29th Infantry Divisions and the 741st Tank Battalion with their amphibious Sherman tanks, the landings were very difficult. Aerial bombing had been delayed for fear of hitting landing craft and many landing craft ran aground 100 m from the beach, forcing the men to wade in chest-deep water, under fire, to reach the beaches. Of the amphibious tanks, 27 of the 32 sank and were lost in the heavy seas. Pinned down on the beach, the beachmaster halted further landings until a group of destroyers were able to move into the shallow waters to provide artillery support, allowing the landings to resume.

At Pointe-du-Hoc, American 2nd Ranger Battalion units were assigned to scale the 30m vertical cliffs to accomplish the key task of destroying four 155 mm guns able to reach both the Utah and Omaha Beach sectors. At the cost of half their original fighting force, the Rangers accomplished their mission and, in spite of German counterattacks, held out for two days until help arrived.

The Omaha Beach Memorial Museum is located in the center of the Omaha Beach invasion sector and it is the museum's mission to pay tribute to these brave and committed American soldiers who landed and fought here.

Covering an area of 1400m², the Omaha Beach Memorial Museum presents a large and rich collection of authentic and actual WWII uniforms, personal items, weapons and vehicles that have also been incorporated into numerous dioramas of American and German scenes that plunge you not only into the heart of the history of the D-Day landings but also into the daily lives of these men who came here to fight for our freedom. A powerful film is presented that emphasizes the character of these men willing to face death for the freedom of others.

Among the tanks and armaments outside the museum stands the marble American Memorial, peering over the beach and backed by the flags of the Allied nations. The beautiful Normandy American Cemetery also overlooks the beach, containing the remains of 9,387 American military servicemen who died in France during World War II. Naturally, the excellent museum shop is open to all.

*For more information about the museum, visit **www.musee-memorial-omaha.com**. For more information about the Saint Laurent-sur-Mer coastal area, visit **https://bayeux-bessin-tourisme.com**. Photos courtesy of the museum.*

OVERLORD MUSEUM
Colleville-sur-Mer, France

Normandie

GPS Coordinates: N49.3479 E-0.8563

Located only very pleasant 10-minute wooded walk from Omaha Beach and the Normandy American Cemetery, this excellent museum focuses on the period between the D-Day landings and the liberation of Paris. The museum is gaining a reputation for it's very realistic dioramas and excellent equipment collections.

The founder of the Overload Museum was Michel Leloup (1929 - 2011). Michel was born on 19 May 1929 at the small family farm near L'Aigle approximately 120 km west of Paris. The youngest of three children, he began working on the farm from an early age.

As a 15 year old, he observed the battle of Normandy in the skies above where fighter aircraft were wheeling, diving, strafing and crashing. They dropped leaflets and bombed L'Aigle. He listened to the BBC broadcasting from London on a crystal radio set hidden in an old cider barrel, the penalty for being caught doing this under the occupation was death. As the battle moved around and past his home he watched and explored the wrecks of tanks and vehicles that littered the countryside in late August 1944 and soon Michel began collecting artifacts.

Since then the Leloup collection has been built up over half a century of research, salvaging and purchasing historic pieces from the Normandy battlefields. Everything from a reconnaissance plane, V1 flying bomb, more than 10 armored fighting vehicles, 30 soft skin vehicles, artillery pieces, poster, signs, documents and personal objects all bearing witness to the terrible fighting in 1944.

Restoration of many of the vehicles to full running order, accurately equipped and painted have taken many thousands of hours by a dedicated team of skilled specialists. Some of these vehicles that were developed for war are unique as the factories and companies that produced them no longer exist, illustrating the need to preserve the technologies represented by the Overlord Museum equipment collections.

Uniform items found on the battlefield form a complete collection from all of the combatant countries during the 1944 campaign in Normandy. The Omaha Overlord Museum, with the size of the building, the extensive collections and the variety and quality of the equipment on display has become unparalleled in this day and age.

The museum is located less than 1 km from the well-known and beautifully-maintained Normandy American Cemetery where more than 9,000 American soldiers who died during the D-Day landings and the following operations lie in peace.

*For more information about the museum please visit: **www.overlordmuseum.com/**. For more information about visiting the Bayeux-Colleville-sur-Mer area, please visit the local tourism website at: **www.bayeux-bessin-tourisme.com/**. Photos courtesy of the museum.*

PEGASUS MEMORIAL MUSEUM
Ranville , France

Normandie

GPS Coordinates: N49.2424 E-0.2717

Made famous by the film "The Longest Day", the story of the Pegasus bridge is one of the most recognized examples of the difficult Allied airborne operations that had to be carried out during the night before the D-Day invasion. The operating 'bascule' bridge adds a special sense of reality to the visit.

The Pegasus Memorial Museum is dedicated to the 181 men of the 6th British Airborne Division, "the Red Berets" who, on June 5th 1944, arrived in the darkness prior to the main D-Day invasion force with three important objectives designed to prevent the German army from advancing towards the invasion beaches from the east. The division, commanded by Major General Richard Gale, was composed of parachutists and glider borne infantry troops transported in Horsa and Hamilcar gliders.

The three principal missions of the division were: 1) to capture and hold the Ranville bridge over the River Orne and the Benouville (later named Pegasus) bridge over the Caen Canal to enable the seaborne troops from Sword Beach to use them and prevent the German forces from using them, 2) to put the German Merville gun battery out of action to prevent the 100mm calibre guns from firing down onto Sword Beach and the Allied fleet off the coast and 3) to destroy the bridges across the River Dives to prevent German reinforcements from arriving from the east. The high ground also had to be taken and held by the division at each of the three objective locations.

As depicted in the movie "The Longest Day", five of the gliders landed within 50 m of the Pegasus bridge, a great feat in the darkness of the landings. The three missions were accomplished with great success before dawn on D-Day but with heavy losses. Many soldiers paid the ultimate sacrifice and now lie at the Commonwealth War Graves cemetery at Ranville only a few kilometers from the museum.

Inaugurated on June 4th 2000 by HRH the Prince of Wales, the Pegasus Memorial was designed and constructed within a few months by the D-Day Landing Committee, presided over by Admiral Brac de la Perrière. Guided visits, within a thematically laid out exhibition hall, enable the visitors to discover the missions of the division and hundreds of historical objects and photos of the era are presented in the museum. The original Bénouville Bridge, renamed Pegasus Bridge after the liberation, is on display in the park of the museum along with a Bailey Bridge and a full size copy of a wartime Horsa glider. The museum collection constantly increases in size each new year.

*For more information about the museum please visit: **https://musee.memorial-pegasus.com**. For more information about visiting the Ranville area, please visit: **www.ranville.fr**. All photos courtesy of the museum.*

PICARDY RESISTANCE & DEPORTATION MUSEUM
Tergnier, France

GPS Coordinates: N49.6584 E3.3155

Located in Tergnier in the Aisne region, this museum is dedicated to the history of resistance and deportation in Picardy, a geographical area of northern France. This excellent museum has earned the important "Museum of France" designation by the French Ministry of Culture.

At the initiative of Etienne Dromas, former chief of the resistance in the Aisne region with the help of other former resistants, the museum was created in 1986 to trace the period from the Phony War, through the dark period of the Nazi occupation, to the liberation of Tergnier during the Second World War. The museum presents a comprehensive history of the many resistance fighters who continually risked their lives.

Etienne Dromas

A portion of the museum is also devoted to the Nazi deportation of local residents forced to work in the factories of Germany throughout the war and the deportation of Jews, gypsies, resistors and other 'undesireables' to the concentration and death camps, in primarily Germany and Poland.

In the more than 800 m^2 of exhibit space you will discover many archival documents, objects from this period, photographs, maps and posters as well as several vehicles including a Renault R35 tank, a locomotive and a boxcar wagon that was used to transport deportees to the death camps.

A movie theater and the latest temporary exhibitions complete the tour. A library of archived documents is also available to researchers and students on request.

The museum is housed in one of the beautiful Carnegie-style buildings named after the American benefactor who contributed financially to the reconstruction of the city after the First World War. We invite you to visit the museum and our lovely city.

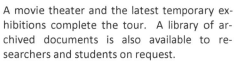

For more information about the museum please visit the museum's website: www.mrdp-picardie.com/musee. For more information about the Tergnier area, visit www.ville-tergnier.fr. Photos courtesy of the museum.

SOMME TRENCH MUSEUM 1916
Albert, France

ENGLAND

HAUTS DE FRANCE

NORMANDIE

GPS Coord.: N50.0039 E2.6483

Located in the heart of the battlefields of the Somme (less than 2 km from the museum), you will live an incredible experience of life in the trenches! This museum is a must for anyone interested in learning why World War 1 was such a terrible conflict.

Located at the heart of the Battles of the Somme (1914-1918), in a tunnel which was converted into an air-raid shelter in 1938, the Somme Trench Museum recreates the life of soldiers in the trenches of the July 1916 offensive, where the allies attacked the positions held by the Germans.

The struggles that took place on the Somme in 1916 were some of the most terrible battles of the First World War. A large number of different nationalities participated and sustained heavy losses in the Battles of the Somme. During the battles, more than 300,000 British, French and German soldiers died.

From the museum entrance hall next to the Basilica (shown above), visitors enter a 250-meter-long tunnel that is 10 meters below the surface. In the tunnel, a series of 15 different alcoves tell the tale of trench warfare in the Somme. Rats, mud and trench reconstructions immerse you in the story of the Battle of the Somme.

The museum also has 25 display cabinets where you can study of all kinds of WW1 artifacts and weaponry. Sound and light effects add to the experience, taking you back to the time of the Great War. The final part of your visit is the Gallery of Heroes, dedicated to nine individuals who distinguished themselves during the war.

As you leave the tunnel you enter an excellent souvenir shop with lots of souvenirs and militaria objects. The museum exits into the public garden of the city where the visitor can discover the Arboretum and the beautiful cascades of the Ancre river.

For more information about the museum visit the museum's website: www.somme-trench-museum.co.uk/. For more information about the town of Albert, visit the town's website at: www.paysducoquelicot.com/. Photos courtesy of the museum.

UTAH BEACH LANDING MUSEUM
Sainte-Marie-du-Mont, France

Normandie

GPS Coordinates: N49.4154 W1.1746

This seaside museum, opened in 1962, is located on Utah Beach where the Americans first landed in Normandy on D-Day, beginning with a major night paratrooper drop amid a dense fog and heavy flak from the coastal guns. The extensive marshes in the area show why the fighting here was so difficult.

Built on the very beach where the first American troops landed on June 6, 1944, the Utah Beach Museum recounts the story of D-Day in 10 sequences, from the preparation of the landing, to the final outcome and success. This comprehensive chronological journey immerses visitors in the history of the landing through a rich collection of objects, vehicles, materials, and oral histories.

Admire an original Martin B-26 Marauder bomber, one of only six remaining examples of this airplane still in existence worldwide, and relive the epic experience of American soldiers through the film "VICTORY IN THE SAND," winner of a CINE GOLDEN EAGLE AWARD 2012 and the 2013 CINE SPECIAL JURY AWARD for best museum documentary. Both English and French versions of the film are available for viewing. Outside, a Sherman Firefly tank and a large American artillery piece can be explored.

The museum focuses on education and has concentrated on developing the exhibits and developing educational programs for elementary through high schools. The young visitors to the museum are continually enticed to learn more.

By the end of your visit, you will understand the strategic choices for the Allied invasion of Normandy and the reasons for the success at Utah Beach. Thanks to your visit, you will also have contributed to safeguarding the site and preserving the memory of the Allied soldiers' extraordinary sacrifices.

For more information about the museum, visit www.utah-beach.com. For more information about the Carentan coastal area, visit www.carentanlesmarais.fr. All photos courtesy of the museum.

WORLD WAR II IN LUXEMBOURG

Saluted by a local policeman, Nazi SS leader Hein-rich Himmler arrives in Luxembourg several months after the invasion, hoping to cajole the Luxem-bourgers to join the Nazi cause. September, 1940.

The aftermath of the Battle of the Bulge battle at Clervaux, December 16-18, 1944 when the Germans attacked the US Army defenders who held and stub-bornly defended their Clearvaux castle position.

A Nazi parade passing by the synagogue in Luxem-bourg City. When the Luxembourgers could not be convinced to join the Nazi cause, the synagogue was ruthlessly destroyed by the Germans in 1943.

Soldiers from Luxembourg training in Britain, 1943. Many of the Luxembourg men escaping to England joined the famous Belgium Brigade Piron, landing at Normandy and fighting until the end of the war.

Under the command of General George S. Patton, American infantrymen of the US Third Army ad-vance in Wiltz on January 25, 1945 forcing the last remaining Germans to flee east towards Germany.

The liberation of Diekirch by the 5th US Armored Divi-sion in 1944. The joyous citizens welcomed the sol-diers with homemade flags secretly stitched together from cut up Nazi swastika flags and parachutes.

THE SMALL TOWN OCCUPATION STORIES OF LUXEMBOURG

THE GRAND DUCHY OF LUXEMBOURG

Luxembourg During World War II.

Luxembourg's Neutrality. In 1867, the "Luxembourg Crisis" occurred when France, Prussia and The Netherlands disputed as to who should control Luxembourg. Because of public opinion in those countries, the political crisis was averted by an agreement that Luxembourg would become a neutral (but autonomous) country (The Treaty of London).

Prior to the start of World War II, Luxembourg did not have the financial resources to construct a defensive system of forts similar to the French and Belgian Maginot Line system. Further, Luxembourg's military only consisted of less than 700 officers, soldiers and policemen and therefore there would not have been enough soldiers to man such a system. Instead, a line of defensive measures (called the Schuster Line) were installed along Luxembourg's border with Germany, only consisting mainly of concrete barriers & barbed wire.

On April 28, 1940, Hitler publicly assured Luxembourg that Germany had no intention of attacking. This proved to be a lie as Luxembourg was ferociously invaded less than two weeks later by the German Wehrmacht along the entire length of the country's German border.

The Invasion. The invasion of Luxembourg, Belgium, France and the Netherlands began in the pre-dawn hours of May 10, 1940. Attacking simultaneously all along Luxembourg's eastern border, the German Blitzkrieg overran and occupied the entire country in one day. By 8 am, Grand Duchess Charlotte abandoned the palace after being told the capital, Luxembourg City, had been surrounded. By noon the capital city surrendered and the invasion was over, the Grand Duchess finally settling in Canada.

The Annexation. The Germans considered Luxembourg to be a Germanic state and immediately began restricting the use of the French language, telling the people they need to return to their Germanic roots and declare their loyalty to Germany. With the support of the right-wing VdB party, and the threat of arrest for any action considered subversive, the people were powerless and Germany officially annexed the country into the Third Reich in 1942. As citizens of the Third Reich, they had the same rights and obligations of all citizens of the Third Reich, including compulsory military service.

The Occupation. After the occupation began, the Germans mandated a survey of the Luxembourg citizens, hoping to show that the people were in favor of joining the Third Reich, but found instead that 95% identified themselves as Luxembourgish. This resulted in severe restrictions and arrests and many were tortured and executed. Many Jews fled the country but, beginning in August, 1941, the German administration under Gustav Simon concentrated on the deportation of all remaining Jews to the death camps. Of these, only 43 survived the war.

The Resistance. Beginning in 1941, the worsening oppression resulted in the increasing formation of resistance groups throughout Luxembourg, much of it being the printing of leaflets, posters and eventually newspapers countering the German propaganda. The increasing forced labor requirements and the German conscription of young Luxembourgers into the German Army (Wehrmacht) resulted in many of these resistance groups meeting the need to protect and keep safe those refusing to serve. Sabotage of German military equipment was rare but the resistance groups actively rescued and evacuated downed Allied airmen and they established communications with the government-in-exile, the Allies and other resistance groups in Belgium and France. Parishes and some households hid and took care of Jewish citizens throughout the war years.

Liberation. Luxembourg had to be liberated twice by the Allies. On September 9, 1944, American forces entered Luxembourg at Pétange. The next day Luxembourg City was liberated, the German troops withdrawing without incident, and by September 12 the Americans occupied 90% of the country. Then, on December 16, 1944, the German offensive known as the Battle of the Bulge began, the Germans attacking the entire northern half of Luxembourg. After fierce fighting and constantly moving frontlines, the last town in the country was finally liberated by General George Patton's US Third Army on February 22, 1945.

As many as 6,000 civilians in Luxembourg died during the war, 2% of the total population. One of the highest losses in any of the western European countries, this would be equivalent to nearly 7,000,000 people dying in the United States today.

LUXEMBOURG

BERTRANGE LUXEMBOURG

Canton: Luxembourg   Pop. 1940: 1,400   Pop. 2020: 8,500

SITING & HERITAGE

Bertrange, a town on the western outskirts of the capital, Luxembourg City, has a hilly topography. The town's origin is Gallo-Roman and there exists the remains of an important Roman villa that was later occupied by the Franks. The town's name comes from a Frankish chief "Bert", associated with "ingen / ange" meaning that this village belongs to the chief Berthe.

Henri de Bertrange built the feudal castle Schauwenburg (1226) and the castle of Colnet-d'Huart (1785) is occupied today by the Luxembourg Red Cross. Grevels Castle (1750) was razed to the ground during the tank battle between the Wehrmacht and the US Army during the liberation of Bertrange on 9 September 1944. The recent transformation of the Bertrange city center into a unique "shared space" meeting area is a great success.

GPS Coord: N49.6111 E6.0511

OUR TOWN'S OCCUPATION STORY

The Invasion. On 10 May 1940, at around 6 am, the very day of the invasion of the Netherlands, Belgium and Luxembourg, long columns of soldiers and vehicles passed through the village in the direction of Paris and Arlon. The school, the large isolated farms and the castles were occupied by the Germans and transformed into workshops for repairing military equipment. An Allied plane attacked German columns and an incendiary bomb set fire to the house dwelling on one of Bertrange's isolated farms.

Parade on the occasion of the funeral of a Nazi collaborator in Bertrange. The young people of the "Hitler Jugend" are at the head of the public procession.

An American tank damaged during the Battle of Bertrange draws a crowd of locals hoping to provide assistance.

The Occupation. To the Nazis, Luxembourg was German soil. A horde of officials from beyond the Moselle invaded the country and the municipality, and they set up an administration based on collaboration and denunciation. In the end, it was about wiping out the Luxembourg nation and integrating the whole of Luxembourg's territory into the German Reich.

From the start of the 1940/41 school year, the school programs were Germanized and modeled on those of the occupant; no more French lessons or religion lessons, and new disciplines such as the study of races and genetics were introduced. All clubs and all local associations were banned and their funds were confiscated. A German employee declared himself head of the village, "the Ortsgruppenleiter" and organized obligatory Nazi propaganda evenings for the inhabitants. The population was terrified and forced to participate in a multitude of ridiculous Nazi organizations. Young people were recruited into the Hitler Youth (HJ), young girls into the German Girls' Union (BDM).

Indigenous civil servants were automatically retrained and put under multiple pressure. Recalcitrant (uncooperative) teachers were dismissed and replaced by Germans or German supporters. All activity was under control; those who opposed were imprisoned, deported or exterminated in concentration camps. Young girls were requisitioned for forced labor services in the country or in Germany. The municipal administrative management was reorganized and moved to the neighboring municipality.

Resistance. With the exception of a few opportunistic or German-born collaborators, almost the entire population of Bertrange was largely hostile to the Nazi occupation. People quickly understood that the slightest refusal to obey had sometimes dramatic consequences. A beating following the refusal to raise the arm in salute to the Nazi flag was commonplace. Nevertheless, passive and active resistance is general. Jewish families or rare German resistance fighters who had fled the Reich got help and their flight through Belgium to the United Kingdon got organized.

The introduction on 30 August, 1942 of compulsory military service for young Luxembourgers triggered a unique strike wave in the country and dozens of strikers were shot by firing squad. The conscription put young people before a cruel choice: join the Wehrmacht or desert while knowing that the deserter's family will be deported to an unknown destination far from their homeland. This decision by the Nazi occupier intensified the resistance of the people and we are witnessing the birth of resistance organizations of smugglers who helped the deserters in their flight to unoccupied allied countries.

Bertrange is crossed by the Luxembourg-Brussels-Manche railway line, and along this railway line major oil companies had set up their fuel depots, so the Germans of course did not hesitate to help themselves. Surprisingly, during the entire period of occupation of the country, these depots were never the object of British or American air attacks.

THE RÉFRACTAIRES.

The occupier's decision to integrate young men born between 1920 and 1924 into the Reich Army significantly influenced the behavior of the population. Young people who did not want their family to suffer from their refusal to join the army were incorporated into the German army and are found in most cases on the eastern front where dozens of young people from Bertrange fell in combat or were injured. Others were taken prisoner by the Russian army and held in camps in Siberia (Tambow) where only the most resilient survived. After the end of the war, it sometimes took more than a year to repatriate them to Luxembourg.

More than a third of the conscripts chose to desert the German army. Or they fled, often to the north of the country, trying, through networks of smugglers, to reach the United Kingdom or to rally groups of deserters who had taken refuge in the Ardennes forests by organizing armed resistance actions. Some got caught and were shot as a deserter.

In Bertrange, a few courageous refractories found, in the immediate family or in certain neighbors, a suitable hiding place to escape the hold of the occupier. These caches, set up in the attics, barns or cellars of houses and farms, must escape the incessant inspections of the occupier. Some spent nearly 2 years in such a hiding place, isolated from the outside world, exposed to the slightest indiscretion and the limits of malnutrition following food rationing.

LIBERATION AND RECOVERY

In the first week of September 1944, traffic intensified on the two main roads through the village but compared to 1940, the direction of travel had changed. Alongside columns of soldiers and all kinds of vehicles, huge herds of livestock stolen along the way were driven towards the German border. Trucks full of Nazi collaborators tried to find refuge in the village. Ammunition depots and trucks laden with explosives were set on fire, the explosions destroying rows of houses.

The Battle of Bertrange. On 9 September, a German rear guard erected barricades, blocking all the main roads. German tanks prepared an ambush on Route de Longwy. Taking shelter at the castle of Grevels under the large trees on the estate, the Germans settled down to wait for the tanks of the 5th Armoured Division, 34th Tank Battalion. A US tank came under fire and the massive American response destroyed the castle and adjoining farm. The blaze lasted 24 hours.

The American air force destroyed houses along Route de Longwy. In the early evening, the last German tanks were annihilated at Helfent, on the outskirts of Bertrange. After this final battle, the City of Luxembourg was liberated on 10 September 1944.

The Battle of the Bulge. While one part of the country was able to celebrate the liberation, the final German offensive – known as the Rundstedt offensive – plunged the north of the country into the bloodbath that became known as the Battle of the Bulge. This counter-offensive lasted until January 1945. More than 10 years were required to complete the full reconstruction of Bertrange.

Grevels Castle in ruins
after the tank battle

US Lt. Martin Pietz, Commander
34th Tank Battalion C34

Aerial view of Bertrange's unique Shared Space Concept

The Shared Space Concept: No pavement markings; no signage; no exposed utilities; complete freedom

OUR TOWN TODAY

Today, Bertrange has a population of 8,500 and is known for its exceptional dynamism and cosmopolitanism. The population includes nearly 100 different nationalities who live in peace and harmony. Many companies in the services sector and the country's largest retail outlets have set up business here.

The availability of municipal infrastructure and administration, schools, sports grounds and halls, the music school, assembly halls and function rooms, the aquatic centre, theatres and concert venues allow a variety of community and cultural organizations to thrive. Over 70 sporting and cultural clubs and associations fill the many modern infrastructures with life throughout the year.

Combining Bertrange's rich medieval history with these many modern amenities makes Bertrange an excellent community to live, work and raise families.

The recent completion of the town's "Shared Space" where schoolchildren, pedestrians, cyclists, bus and car drivers circulate in harmony has breathed new life in the town centre. Shops, retailers, restaurants and sidewalk cafes provide attractive meeting points for one and all. We invite you to visit and experience this innovative public space concept for yourself.

*For more information about Bertrange, visit the town's official website: **www.bertrange.lu**. For more information about Bertrange's history, local castles and medieval heritage, visit the Geschichtsfrënn Bertrange website: **www.geschichtsfrennbartreng.lu** or email the organization at geschichtsfrenn.bartreng@gmail.com.*

This article was prepared by Michel Reuland and Paul Krippler from the association "Les Amis de l'Histoire" in Bertrange. Their contributions are greatly appreciated. Photos courtesy of the commune of Bertrange.

BETTEMBOURG LUXEMBOURG

Canton: Luxembourg   Pop. 1940: 5,300   Pop. 2020: 11,200

SITING & HERITAGE

The Bettembourge Commune is in the south of the Grand Duchy of Luxembourg, just 5 km from the French border. The commune includes the town of Bettembourg and the villages of Abweiler, Fennange, Huncherange and Noertzange, and in 1940 had a population of 5,300 people. Being located next to the Alzette river and having an abundance of fertile pastureland has always made it attractive for settlement.

A motte and bailey castle was located here dating from the 11th century. A château-farm followed in the 12th century, a building which was rebuilt in the 18th century and is now used as the town hall. Modern Bettembourg took shape after 1859 when the railway to France was laid through the territory and a marshalling yard was built. This marshalling yard became an important nodal point that connected the local steel industry to the European rail network.

GPS Coord: N49.5193 E6.1002

OUR TOWN'S OCCUPATION STORY

The German Invasion of Bettembourg. At daybreak on 10th May 1940, Bettembourg's residents were surprised as several German "Fiseler Storch" planes landed in the local countryside. Armed soldiers left the aircraft to occupy parts of the strategically important road and rail network in and around the town. Residents' first panicked reaction was to rush to local shops to secure food supplies to prepare for the highly uncertain future. Germany artillery pieces arrived during the same afternoon as did the artillery of the French army from the Maginot Line 8 km away. These initial skirmishes caused the death of five civilians and considerable material damage.

The evacuation of the residents during the invasion

Evacuation of the Population. Given the intensity of the fighting and the rising number of civilian victims, it was decided to evacuate Bettembourg's population to either the centre and north of the Grand Duchy or behind the French Maginot Line. People brought with them the essentials that they could carry, leaving the rest of their property and livestock to the mercies of the invading army and looters. Bettembourg's mayor and other local government members relocated to Luxembourg City where they sought to organize the flow of refugees. Only after the start of June, after the Nazi troops had advanced into France, were farmers and then residents authorized to return to their looted and badly damaged town. When they arrived, they found that local governance had been assumed by the invading German authorities.

Occupation and resistance. Most residents of Bettembourg reacted with active and passive resistance to the oppression of the German aggressor. In particular they pushed back against efforts to encourage support amongst the local population for the Nazi ideology and a general refusal to join the newly created VdB (Volksdeutsche Bewegung – German National Movement). It was common for people to listen to BBC radio despite this "offense" carrying the death penalty. Railway workers would also sabotage rolling stock at the Bettembourg railway station. Whole families would stage acts of secret resistance, such as by offering hiding places to young people escaping being conscripted into the German army, or helping them to flee abroad. More than 200 young residents of Bettembourg were forcibly conscripted into the Reichswehrmacht (Reich army).

A fake tank of the American Ghost Army

The "Ghost Army" – Operation Bettembourg. The "Ghost Army" was a top secret American army unit which worked to disorient the German forces by faking the massive build-up of troops. This unit used high intensity decoy sounds and optical illusions to simulate movements of military hardware, including inflatable artillery pieces.

The Ghost Army operated in the wooded areas around Bettembourg in September 1944 with 400 GIs simulating the presence of the 6th Armoured Division with its 8,000 men. In fact, the 6th Army was active in France at that time. Thus, the Ghost Army was able to fill a large gap in the allied forces that could have been taken by the German military. This was while General Patton's 3rd Army was moving on the French towns of Metz and Thionville to the south with the goal of this leading to a rapid invasion of German territory. According to Colonel Simenson of the unit, Operation Bettembourg was one of the longest and most risky missions carried out by the Ghost Army during the Second World War.

Bettembourg bombardment of 11 May 1944

The 11 May, 1944 Bombardment of Bettembourg. With the successful Normandy landings planned for the start of June 1944, substantial preparation was required to increase the chances of success. This included the destruction of key railway nodes in the territories occupied by the Germans in order to hamper their ability to send reinforcements.

The attack on the railway installations in Bettembourg began at around 7.30 p.m. on 11 May 1944 by 35 US Air Force Boeing B-17 "Flying Fortresses". The raid saw 234 bombs dropped, weighing a total of 94.5 tons, but with only minimal damage caused to infrastructure and equipment. However, 27 civilians were killed, 40 houses were destroyed, 183 other buildings were damaged, and 281 graves were hit in the local cemetery.

TWO VERY SPECIAL LOCAL RESIDENTS WE CONTINUE TO HONOR TO THIS DAY

Ado Rinnen

Ado Rinnen. *Ado Rinnen, a young deserter from the German Wehrmacht, committed himself to secret anti-Nazi resistance. He assumed the noble, patriotic task of helping more than 200 members of the resistance by finding them hiding places, procuring fake ID papers and helping them escape abroad.*

Tragically, in March 1944 these activities were noticed by German soldiers and Ado was captured. After many months of interrogation and brutal torture he was eventually condemned to death. He was executed by decapitation on 10th August 1944; just a month before the country was liberated by the allies. A commemoration stone to this heroic patriot was erected in Huncherange, the place of his birth.

Valérie Steichen. *A young manager of a haberdashery shore, Valérie showed her patriotism by offering moral and practical support as she sent more than 700 letters and 2,000 parcels of food, clothes and tobacco to those from Bettembourg who had been forcibly conscripted to fight on the eastern front for the Nazis.*

LIBERATION AND RECOVERY

Both in terms of the loss of human life and damage to property, Bettembourg made major sacrifices towards the liberation of the country after World War II. While the first Allied soldiers entered the Grand Duchy on 9th September 1944, Bettembourg was only liberated two days later due to rear-guard action in the south of the country by German forces.

This didn't delay several courageous and impatient patriots, who even the day before the Americans arrived, raised the Luxembourgish flag and played the national anthem on a bugle from the church tower.

The Liberation of Bettembourg

The first jeeps and tanks were welcomed by an enthusiastic crowd, which included the old priest with a bouquet of flowers picked hastily from the church altar.

That afternoon, Lieutenant Colonel J.H. Polk, commander of the 3rd Armored Cavalry Regiment, was officially received at the town hall as liberator of Bettembourg town. He was welcomed by the commune's Council of Aldermen, who resumed their work after having been deposed four years previously by the occupying Nazi regime.

Patton & Polk

The following day, Lieutenant Colonel J.H. Polk established his regiment's command in barracks near Bettembourg that had recently been abandoned by the occupying forces. Located in the place known as "Mosselter", it had been a forced-labour camp (R.A.D. "Reichsarbeitslager") for active opponents of the occupation regime. Later, General George S. Patton, commander of the 3rd Army, would speak with Lieutenant Colonel J.H. Polk at this location.

However, LTC Polk didn't stay long, with he and his forces soon moving east to participate in the invasion of Germany. He never forgot his time in Bettembourg, returning in 1978, this time after having been promoted to the rank of General. Local residents were keen to recognise their gratitude, presenting him with the "Croix de Guerre 1940-1945" medal and naming him an honorary citizen of Bettembourg.

A vigorous programme of reconstruction followed the conclusion of the Second World War. Thus by 1950 war damage had been repaired, restoring Bettembourg's buildings to a state in keeping with this respectable, thriving town.

Bettembourg today – in the foreground the popular "Parc Merveilleux"

The 12th Century Bettembourg town hall

OUR TOWN TODAY

Today, Bettembourg is a modern town with around 11,200 residents keen to maintain the local heritage and a high quality of life for its residents.

The commune is the location of the well-known Parc Merveilleux, a successful tourist attraction attracting each year around 250,000 visitors of all ages where they can enjoy the fairytale atmosphere and the zoo with its collection of local and exotic animals.

The highlighs of the cultural year are the annual LitéraTour, a festival for all who appreciate good writing and the Nuit des Merveilles, a night time event at which artists display their work.

Bettembourg's economy is diverse, ranging from small handicraft businesses to large industrial operations. Many of these enterprises are located in a dedicated business park. Bettembourg is also a multi-modal transport hub that brings rail and road transport together, offering dedicated services across Europe and even as far as China.

For more information about Bettembourg, please visit the town's official website: http://www.bettembourg.lu. For more information about Bettembourg's tourism opportunities please visit https://bettembourg.lu/eis-gemeng/tourisme/ This information was prepared by members of the local historical association Geschichtsfrenn aus der Gemeng Beetebuerg and coordinated by Cyrille Bähr of the City of Bettembourg Public Relations Office. All photos courtesy of the Commune of Bettembourg.

DIEKIRCH LUXEMBOURG

Canton: Diekirch   Pop. 1940: 3,850   Pop. 2020: 7,000

SITING & HERITAGE

Diekirch is situated in the Sauer River valley, marking the geographical border between the southern Guttland and the northern Ardennes. Its medieval core was established on the remains of a Roman villa that was abandoned in the 5th century AD. Diekirch is known as the "City of donkeys." This animal is found in many places in the city and in many forms, recalling the region's essentially agricultural past, when the donkey was the only one capable of helping in the work of the fields on the sloping hillsides surrounding the city, thus contributing to the wealth of Diekirch.

The town supposedly received its name when Charlemagne resettled pagan Saxons in the area and had a church built to convert them to Christianity. This church was known as "Diet-Kirch" ("people's church"). The town was fortified in the 14th century by King John "the Blind" of Bohemia.

GPS Coordinates: N49.8480 E6.0986

Nazi Administrator Gustav Simon in Diekirch

The Nazification of the public square

The city center after the second Liberation

Diekirch war volunteers detained in southern France

OUR TOWN'S OCCUPATION STORY

The Invasion. The first Wehrmacht units entered Diekirch in the morning of 10th May, 1940. During their advance, they shot down a Royal Air Force Fairey Battle light bomber. Among the 3-man crew, Flying Officer Douglas Cameron died at the local hospital due to loss of blood and was buried at the town cemetery. Military authorities over-saw daily affairs until August 1940, when "Chief of the Civil Administration" Gustav Simon, a top Nazi official, arrived in Luxembourg to take charge.

The Occupation: Simon's arrival set the stage for the policy of Germanisation and Nazification. German became the only official language, French was banned and a pro-German collaborationist movement ("Volksdeutsche Bewegung") served as henchmen for Nazi policies. All symbols, institutions, monuments or entities linked to Luxembourgish independence were eliminated. Eavesdropping, political surveillance and repression by the Secret Police (Gestapo and Sicherheitsdienst) were instrumental to instill fear. German laws were enforced and an arbitrary "special justice court" was created to sanction "troublemakers". Meanwhile, active collaboration was rewarded.

Administratively, Luxembourg was reorganized into 4 main districts and Diekirch became one of the 4 regional capitals (Kreisstädte). This meant that the town was to become an important political centre, with many German families arriving to take up the most important positions. All individual, shop and street names were Germanized. For instance, the town's main square was renamed "Adolf-Hitler-Platz".

Nazi party officials, assisted by Luxembourgish collaborators, did their utmost to push the locals to adhere to the "New Order", for example by decorating their houses with Nazi flags, joining propaganda parades or attending the annual Nazi Kreistag convention. Moreover, army barracks were set up in a local hotel and the sinister Gestapo established a regional headquarters in the so-called "Villa Conter". The local schools continued to operate but saw the expulsion of many "anti-German" teachers and students.

Resistance: Students proved indeed most resilient, creating two Resistance organizations in October 1940 who specialized in the clandestine production of propaganda leaflets and false identity papers for a growing number of political refugees and Allied fugitives. After the proclamation of the mandatory conscription into the German Wehrmacht in August 1942, they helped to save thousands of young men, either hiding them in Luxembourg or exfiltrating them abroad. To repress strikes that broke out in protest of forced conscription, the Nazis executed 21 victims, among them young Diekirch citizen Emile Heiderscheid. With the intensification of repression against "political enemies" and draft dodgers, more and more people became targets.

In Diekirch, during the Nazi occupation:

- 100 men and 4 women were confined to prisons and concentration camps. 7 of them were shot, 3 didn't survive brutal torture.
- 15 young men fought in the ranks of Allied armies, 2 died in combat.
- 89 young adults were forcibly conscripted into mandatory labor service and the Wehrmacht. 29 never came back.
- 110 people were deported to the east for "political reasons".
- 35 people died as a result of the Battle of the Bulge .

Three Diekirch Normandy Fighters

Félix Peters and the brothers Jean and Antoine Neven landed in Ouistreham, Normandy on 6 June, 1944 as members of the Free French "Commando Kieffer".

Hoping to reach Great Britain, they had left Diekirch on 19 June, 1941 but were first held in a French labor camp for foreigners. Only on 14 July, 1942 did they reach their destination, having made their way through Spain, Portugal and Gibraltar.

After joining the Belgian Army in the UK, they were sent to the Belgian Congo, but saw their assignment suddenly cancelled because of their Luxembourgish nationality. This prompted the three friends to cross the border into French Equatorial Africa, where they enlisted in the Free French Naval Forces on 16 January, 1943. Returning yet again to Great Britain, they volunteered for the commandos.

On D-Day, they landed on the eastern extremity of Sword Beach as part of "Commando Kieffer", which fought with the British number 4 Commando. Among the first to land on the beaches, their objective was to assault the German forces in Ouistreham, to establish a bridgehead and to join up with other Allied forces. Ouistreham was captured and secured by 11:30 AM. That night they made contact with the British 6th Airborne Division.

The three men survived "the longest day" and went on to fight in Normandy. Félix Peters died in Amfreville, on 17 June, 1944 and Jean Neven was killed during the Battle of Walcheren, in the Netherlands, on 2 November, 1944. Antoine Neven survived the campaign and was able to return to his hometown on Christmas 1945. He died on 23 September 1994, aged 73.

LIBERATION & RECOVERY

Liberation: Diekirch celebrated its First Liberation by American troops on 11 September, 1944. Two days before, the retreating Germans had blown up the main bridge on the Sauer, detonating eight 250-kilo aerial bombs underneath its pillars. The overjoyed local population welcomed the Liberators frenetically and everybody expected that the war would be over by Christmas of 1944.

Known to be situated in a "quiet sector", the town became a "paradise for weary troops" but a bad awakening was soon to follow. When the Germans launched their last ditch surprise attack on December 16, 1944, known as the Battle of the Bulge, seriously outnumbered American forces desperately tried to hold on to vastly overstretched defensive positions. Despite their efforts, Diekirch had to be abandoned on 20 December 1944, not without successfully evacuating more than 5,500 civilians.

For one month, the Germans held on to the town, as it represented a key defensive position on the southern shoulder of their offensive. Located on the front line, under constant shelling and bombardment, Diekirch turned into a ghost town, while a few hundred civilians were still seeking shelter in the cellars. On 18 January, 1945, the Americans launched a daunting counter-offensive known as the Sauer River Crossing. They managed to push the Germans back towards northern Luxembourg, suffering heavy casualties. After heavy fighting, Diekirch experienced its Second Liberation on 20 January 1945.

Recovery: The town was in a truly pitiful state. It wasn't until the early 1950's that most of the damage was repaired. Some traces, like bullet impacts or shrapnel damage, remain visible to this day.

Musée National d'histoire Militaire - Diekirch

Place de la Libération — Diekirch

OUR TOWN TODAY

Diekirch is a picturesque tourist town offering a range of leisure activities, shopping opportunities and entertainment concentrated in the easily accessible, pedestrianized historical centre. Well connected to the national public transport network, the town is ideally situated between the Ardennes and the Mullerthal region (nicknamed "Petite Suisse" or "Little Switzerland").

Diekirch is home to a brewery of national importance bearing its name. It is also known for its lively carnival procession (the Cavalcade) and Al Dikrich, a popular traditional celebration organized around the medieval Saint-Laurent church; and Diekirch holds one of Luxembourg's most ancient archaeological sites, the prehistoric Deiwelselter (Devil's Altar).

The town's mascot is the omnipresent donkey, alluding to the wealth local farmers were able to accumulate in the past on the steep slopes surrounding Diekirch because of the donkey's help. Surrounded by pristine nature in a hospitable environment, the town is a perfect starting point for outdoor activities. When it comes to World War II history, the National Museum of Military History hosts a rich collection centered on the Battle of the Bulge (See page 153).

For more information about Diekirch and the town's recreational opportunities, please visit the town's official website: www.diekirch.lu and www.visit-diekirch.lu.

This information was prepared by Philippe Victor of the Musee National d'Histoire Militaire in Diekich. For more information about the museum please visit www.mnhm.lu. Photos courtesy of the municipality.

ESCH-SUR-ALZETTE LUXEMBOURG

Canton: Esch-sur-Alzette   Pop. 1940: 25,000   Pop. 2020: 36,000

SITING & HERITAGE

Esch/Alzette, in the south of the Grand Duchy of Luxembourg (630,000 inhab.), is the second largest town in the country. Bordering on France, it is the center of a region shaped by industrial culture and immigration. Along with the Lithuanian city of Kaunas, Esch/Alzette has been chosen as the European Capital of Culture in 2022.

For centuries of its past, Esch was a small farming village in the valley of the Uelzecht river until large deposits of iron ore were found during the mid-1850s. Within a few decades, the population grew 10 times, especially after the steel and iron producing company ARBED was founded. This industrial development became a major component of Luxembourg's economic growth during the late 1800s. After the mines and steel production facilities closed in the 1970s, the town has concentrated on redeveloping the industrial areas into a new modern town quarter, now housing many buildings of the University of Luxembourg.

GPS Coord: N49.5010 E5.9861

OUR TOWN'S OCCUPATION STORY

Invasion: On May 10, 1940, the Wehrmacht invaded Luxembourg, violating its neutrality. German paratroopers landed with gliders around Esch, set up roadblocks and laid mines. The first clashes occurred when French troops from Audun-le-Tiche, took up position in Esch. The French army command allowed Esch's 25,000 inhabitants to be evacuated to Burgundy and the south of France. The remaining 2,000 people left on May 13/14 for Luxembourg City or the north of the country. The evacuees were not allowed to return until the end of June 1940.

Demolition of the Esch Synagogue, Esch/Alzette, 1941

Nazi henchmen march in front of Esch townhall, Esch/Alzette, 1940

The Kreisleitung in Esch after the liberation, Esch/Alzette, 1944, Photo F. Jacoby

Esch Under Nazi Occupation: During July 1940, Luxembourg was de-facto annexed by Nazi Germany. The local administration was reorganized on the German model and Esch became the seat of a Kreis (district). The Kreisleiter was both the highest representative of the German administration and of the Nazi party (NSDAP). Three Ortsgruppen (local sections) of the VdB (Volksdeutsche Bewegung – "Movement of ethnic Germans"), a Luxembourgian party collaborating with the new regime, were formed in Esch from July 1940. Local sections of Nazi organizations, like the SS or the Hitler Youth were created as well. Street names were Germanized. German police and security forces, including the Gestapo settled in Esch. Police officers remained at their posts or were transferred to Germany. On October 19, 1940 the "Escher Tageblatt" reappeared as the official newspaper of the VdB.

Resistance and Repression: In August 1942, mandatory military service in the German armed forces was introduced in Luxembourg. As a reaction, strikes broke out throughout the country. In Esch, high school students, apprentices and workers from the local steelworks were involved in the protest movement. The German repression was brutal. Many strikers were arrested and sent to concentration and "re-education" camps in Germany. Some were sentenced to death.

On September 1, a special court, the Standgericht, met in the Esch town hall and pronounced the first death sentences. 21 participants to the strike were executed, including Hans Adam from Esch. The Gestapo was also well informed about the organized resistance. It tried to break them, among other things by raiding the Communist Party or the ALWE RAJE group. The arrested were taken to the Villa Seligmann, the Gestapo headquarters in Esch. There they were interrogated and tortured before being sent to the Hinzert concentration camp or the prisons in Trier or Wittlich.

Jewish Destiny: 380 Jews were living in Esch at the eve of the war. Most of them left for France before the town was occupied; only 60 remained and some returned in June 1940. After France's defeat, the Vichy regime registered foreign Jews and forced them to work. From 1942, Jews were arrested and deported to Auschwitz via Drancy, including some Jews from Esch. 44 of them were killed. In Luxembourg, the Jews were excluded from society. Men were forced to work. German administrations such as the Gestapo or the Kreisleitung in Esch occupied and confiscated Jewish homes. On June 3, 1941 the synagogue of Esch was demolished. From October 1941, the Jews of Luxembourg were deported to the East, 32 from Esch. A total of 113 Jews from Esch were killed.

A SPECIAL STORY OF SURVIVAL

Joseph (called Josy) Schlang was born in Rodange on 5 June 1924. In 1930 he moved to Esch/Alzette with his family. Due to the Nazis' anti-Semitic policies, Josy lost his job by the end of 1940.

On 15 May, 1941 the Schlang family was forced to move to Luxembourg City where Josy and his father Tobias were deployed in the quarries of Nennig where they were required to work as forced labour.

Josy was arrested by the Gestapo in August 1941 for wearing patriotic symbols. For two weeks he was required to report to Gestapo headquarters after work where he was interrogated and mistreated several times. On October 16, 1941 the Schlang family was deported to the Łódź (or Litzmannstadt) Ghetto where Josy was separated from his relatives who were later murdered at the Majdanek concentration and extermination camp.

Josy was detained in various labour camps. In 1943 he was deported to Auschwitz, where he was forced to work at the Auschwitz I, Birkenau, Monowitz and Sosnowitz camps. In January 1945, Josy was forced to take part in death marches to Mauthausen and then to Gusen. He was liberated by the Americans in May 1945 but by that time he weighed only 40 kg.

Josy returned to Luxembourg, became involved in various remembrance associations and spoke at the Musée National de la Résistance until 2011. Josy died in 2013.

LIBERATION & RECOVERY

By the end of August 1944, fearing the Allied advance, the German officials left Esch. On September 1, the Kreisleitung building they abandoned was stormed by the population and the imperial eagle destroyed. The Luxembourg flag was hoisted at the top of church steeples but the celebration of the town's liberation was premature. It was disrupted by the arrival of German troops, who started shooting at the crowd. One person was killed. The Gestapo, the SD and the Kreisleitung re-established themselves in Esch. The alleged ringleaders of the previous day's events were arrested. The Germans finally left Esch for good a few days later. The Wehrmacht retreated via the Esch-Wobrécken neighborhood under heavy fire from American fighter-bombers.

On September 10, American troops liberated Esch, almost without further incident. However, the Delhéischt and industrial schools went up in flames due to detonation. Two days later, Prince Consort Felix and his son and heir to the throne, Prince Jean, visited the city. Meanwhile the Unio'n, a unitary movement of the main Resistance Organisations, had taken over the administration of the town and the other liberated territories, in close cooperation with the US Civil Affairs command.

The Unio'n, who had its own militia, had also started to arrest individuals accused of having collaborated with the Nazi regime. They were interned in the Belval and Katzebierg camps. The already severe housing and food shortages were exacerbated by the flood of refugees sparked by the Battle of the Bulge. Despite its own difficulties, the town of Esch provided direct aid to several villages in the war-torn north for reconstruction.

Memorial of the demolished Synagogue in Esch/Alzette, 2019, Photo Olivier Bouton

Holocaust survivor Gerd Klestadt at International Holocaust Remembrance Day, Esch/Alzette, 2019
Photo Olivier Bouton

OUR TOWN TODAY

Today, Esch/Alzette is the second largest city in the Grand Duchy of Luxembourg. A university town located in the heart of this region of Luxembourg, the population of Esch includes more than 120 different nationalities who all live in inclusive peace and harmony.

Since the decline of the steel industry in the 1970s, Esch has redefined itself to become a city where life is good for all residents. Public and private investments include the University and the Maison de la Grande Région, further underlining Esch's future role as a progressive, forward-thinking small town.

In addition to popular districts such as the "Brill" district, new residential areas continue to emerge, developed to maintain the town's village character. Over half of the municipal area consists of green spaces, parks and forests, maintained to constantly improve public access to these important natural and public park areas.

Each year, numerous ceremonies are held in Esch/Alzette to remember the Second World War, for example the National Commemoration of the Holocaust; the Commemoration for the Victims of Homosexual Persecution; the Commemoration for the Victims of the 1942 General Strike and the Journée de Commémoration Nationale held at the Musée National de la Résistance and at the Place de la Synagogue.

*For more information about Esch-sur-Alzette, visit the Town's Website: **https://esch.lu/**.*

We appreciate the assistance provided by Jérôme Courtoy and Elisabeth Hoffmann of the Musée National de la Résistance in preparing this commemorative document. Photos courtesy of the museum collection.

ETTELBRUCK LUXEMBOURG

Canton: Diekirch   Pop. 1940: 4,500   Pop. 2019: 9,000

SITING & HERITAGE

The city of Ettelbruck is located at the juncture between the country's northern rocky and hilly Ardennes/Eifel region, locally called "Eislek," and the southern gentler landscape of the agricultural and mining "Guttland" (Good land). Today Ettelbruck is a major commercial and agricultural centre. Foire Agricole, the largest agricultural fair in Luxembourg has been held here since 1883.

Ettelbruck's position as a north/south road and railway junction, with key bridges crossing the Alzette and Sûre/Sauer rivers, made it a military asset for logistics and communications and a key point of interest for the Nazis during the war. Today the town is home to the renowned Patton Museum, honouring the American General whose forces liberated the town during the Christmas days of 1944.

GPS Coord: N49.8480 E6.0986

OUR TOWN'S OCCUPATION STORY

Even though the Nazis declared observing Luxembourg's neutrality, the Wehrmacht troops invaded the country on May 10th, 1940. The inhabitants of Ettelbruck suffered from an increasingly repressive occupation. A very effective Nazi organization imposed its influence on the lives of the locals and impacted every aspect of political, social, judicial and commercial life as well as the educational system.

Oppression was present daily, as was the systematic use of propaganda. The installation of a loudspeaker system in Ettelbruck used for "informing" was just one of the measures taken by the occupier. Women and youth organizations (Bund Deutscher Mädel and Hitlerjugend) served as tools of ideological, political and social persuasion.

Active collaboration by some and the risk of denunciation put extremely high pressure on every inhabitant. It was difficult to avoid even unintentional collusion under this severe and systematic repression. The danger of being dismissed from their jobs, the risk of imprisonment, torture, deportation or even death created an atmosphere of ever-present fear for those who refused to conform.

In October 1941, the Nazis held a country-wide registration of civil status, soon called "referendum", that included questions about nationality, mother tongue and ethnicity. Of course, the Nazis expected the answer of "Deutsch" (German) in each case. Because of calls from resistance groups not to abide to the occupier, the Nazis had to note that the results in Ettelbruck as well as in the rest of the country indicated that a stunning 90% + were in favour of Lëtzebuergesch (Luxembourgish). On that they abandoned the effort. This event was even cited in the world press (*New York Times, Pravda*).

Even though the "referendum" fiasco was quickly abandoned, forced Germanization continued unabated. Street names were germanized: the "Grand-Duc Adolphe" street became "Adolf-Hitler-Strasse". Every "French sounding" first name and surname, as well as every trace of "French sounding" words, street or shop names were banned or Germanized. Commonly used French sounding words such as "Merci", were forbidden. Imposing the "Heil Hitler" salute, the forced bearing of Nazi insignia, the compulsory declaration of commitment to the Führer or a prescribed dress code (black pant, white shirt) for official meetings were only some of the other visible aspects of repression.

May, 1940 - German troops enter Ettelbruck

January, 1945—American troops enter Ettelbruck

Still, resistance to the occupier never ceased even though after almost every operation, residents were arrested in retaliation. A "Nazi Honor Gate" was burnt down, Nazi flags on the football/soccer ground were torn down the night before a tournament. A Luxembourg flag was set up on the top of the Nuck, a high point on a hill overlooking the town. Various resistance movements active in the region united under the leadership of Ettelbruck citizen Yvo Kerger who was later shot by the Nazis in the Gusen II-Mauthausen concentration camp. Some inhabitants resisted by helping young Luxembourgers flee in light of the forced enrollment into the Wehrmacht, supplying food, clothes and medicine to those hiding in surrounding villages, farms or forests. Yet others resisted by delivering subversive or non-active civil services. Some, at the risk of their lives, assisted members of a shot-down US aircrew to evade capture. To get information on the course of the war by listening to the BBC radio was risky and if detected, punished with imprisonment.

Some inhabitants did not speak of their activities once the war was over. The stories of other Ettelbruck inhabitants that resisted, whether openly or behind the scenes, are recorded in the country's historical works.

Battle of the Bulge destruction In Ettelbruck

FOUR SPECIAL ETTELBRUCK STORIES

1. During WWII, a major strike movement occurred in the country of Luxembourg on August 31st, 1942. The strike movement followed the declaration of forced enrolment in the Wehrmacht made by Gauleiter Gustav Simon a day earlier. A dozen participants in the strike were arrested in Ettelbruck, amongst them two young railroad workers, Michel Dax and Johann Thull. They were questioned, tortured and transferred to the Hinzert concentration camp, where they were executed on September 5th, 1942.

2. Compulsory labour service or "Reichsarbeitdienst" had already been made mandatory in 1941. After August 31, 1942 the Nazis gradually forced another 153 young men born in the years of 1920 to 1926, to enroll into the Wehrmacht, a process referred to as "Zwangsrekrutierung". Refusing to enlist was at the risk of seeing one's family being deported. The emotional pressure of this cruel dilemma for every affected young man can never be sufficiently acknowledged.

3. Other Jewish families living in Ettelbruck at the end of the 1930s left before the Nazi invasion. Several tried to escape through organized train exodus via France. Of those who chose to stay, most were deported to concentration camps, where many were killed. The Ettelbruck synagogue - one of four in the country, was vandalized by collaborators. The belongings of Jewish residents were confiscated as was the case in so many other places throughout Europe.

4. An interesting interview with a US pilot rescued by the people of Ettelbruck can be viewed at https://www.youtube.com/watch?v=T9yPkhOCOVk.

Public Notice announcing
executions of strikers

LIBERATION & RECOVERY

Nazi troops and collaborators left Ettelbruck as American troops entered the country on September 9th, 1944. Ettelbruck was liberated by US troops two days later. At that time Ettelbruck had barely been subject to destruction.

In December 1944 however, the Nazi war machine launched what came to be known as the "Battle of the Bulge" or "Offensive des Ardennes". On December 19th, the population was called to evacuate. Three quarters of the residents followed the call and the US troops briefly retreated to the south of Ettelbruck. The residents remaining then had to live through a second invasion by the Wehrmacht on December 20th and the town was heavily shelled.

Ettelbruck was liberated the second time during the Christmas days of 1944 by the 318th Regiment of the 80th US Infantry Division under the command of Colonel L. McVickar, part of General Patton's 3rd Army. Col McVickar was killed in action in a nearby forest on January 14, 1945. During the fighting, approximately 20% of the buildings in Ettelbruck were destroyed but many other buildings were damaged, including the bridges in and around Ettelbruck.

The distress of the remaining inhabitants was at its worst as they suffered from insufficient food and heating supplies during this extremely cold winter. The town remained difficult to access until the rebuilding of the bridges began. In February 1945 a contingent of 250 steel workers, (later increasing to 450 men) coming from the southern mining town of Rodange, came to Ettelbruck in order to help rebuild the town.

For more information about the municipality of Ettelbruck, please visit the Municipality's official website: www.ettelbruck.lu. For more information about the municipality's extensive historical heritage please visit www.nordstad.lu & www. patton.lu.

Main referenced authors are Joseph Flies, André Grosbusch, Will Dondelinger, Arthur Muller. This information was prepared by Albert Dondelinger, volunteer on behalf of the GREG/Patton Museum and in the name of the Ettelbruck City Council. See 'Abbes' contribution on Page 5.

OUR TOWN TODAY

Today Ettelbruck is known for its commercial activities, health services and educational facilities. The city also hosts agricultural activities such as a technical agricultural school, an agricultural research laboratory, a slaughterhouse and agricultural fairs. As a regional school center, Ettelbruck operates primary and technical school complexes as well as specialized schools for personnel working with the disabled and/or people with mental illnesses.

Ettelbruck aerial photo by Rol Schleich

Cultural activities take place in Ettelbruck provided by the Centre des Arts Pluriels, and Ettelbruck maintains an excellent Conservatory for musical activities. Sports, indoor and outdoor activities notably in the "Deich" grassland, focus on young and elder people alike, with over 80 clubs including over 20 sports clubs.

Plans for the construction of new railway infrastructure will ensure that the city remains an attractive focal point of the country for economics and tourism. Ettelbruck actively cooperates with surrounding towns and villages to build up a widely-acknowledged regional reputation and a future axis of development in the Grand Duchy of Luxembourg. Ettelbruck is a wonderful place to visit and live.

Town Centre aerial photo by Rol Schleich

NIEDERANVEN G.D. OF LUXEMBOURG

Canton: Luxembourg   Pop. 1940: 1,500   Pop. 2020: 6,300

SITING & HERITAGE

Located just east of Luxembourg City, the Municipality of Niederanven represents the villages of Niederanven, Oberanven, Hostert, Rameldange, Ernster, Senningen, Senningerberg, Waldhof and Staffelter. Today, Niederanven counts about 6,300 inhabitants including more than 80 different nationalities with a foreigners' percentage of about 44 %.

Coming from the Champagne and the Moselle regions, the humans of the stone age penetrated into this Luxembourg area that was rich in sandstone and where ravines and caves offered them a secure protection from the weather, animals and invaders. Numerous archaeological excavations continue to provide information about the municipality's ancient and medieval history.

GPS Coord: N49.6515 E6.2560

Before their retreat, the Germans blew up the trees along the Triererstrasse to make it impossible for the US Army to pursue them

American GIs with a machine gun to defend the Regimental Headquarters in Senningen against enemy aircraft. November, 1944

Three American GIs in front of the school in Senningen with a captured Renault Juvaquatre Nazi car. November 1944

OUR TOWN'S OCCUPATION STORY

The main road from Trier to Luxembourg has always been a major route for war troops. As in Roman times, this was also the case in the 2nd World War. When, on 10 May 1940, in the early hours in the morning, the German troops invaded Luxembourg and crossed Niederanven with their long convoys, the people ran horrified into the street to watch them march through. No one really knew what it all meant, even though most people had the weak hope that they would be spared from the German invasion.

Seeing the German troops with their equipment and the countless vehicles, the armored trucks, patrol cars, field kitchens, etc. was a new, scary world into which the population now had to enter. The people knew little about their destructive ability. Nobody could imagine what devastation it would cause; how many innocent people would fall victim to it and what destruction our country would suffer.

Already in 1939, people of German descent had formed a mlitia in Niederanven who put themselves very early into the service of the Germans and helped them in May 1940 with the quartering of the German soldiers as well as German evacuees in our municipality.

Niederanven was assigned to the district Esch/Alzig in the context of the reorganization of the country carried out by the occupying forces. As in many other villages, the first members of the VdB section (Volksdeutsche Bewegung) and the other hostile groups joined our community quite early. Most of the inhabitants, however, were rather afraid and preferred to keep a proper distance from the occupiers.

The Jewish population had been "encouraged" by the Gauleiter (Nazi Administrator) to leave the country in August 1940. Two Jewish families from Niederanven were deported to extermination camps and killed there.

Life was not easy after the municipalities had been placed under German administration. The French language was banned. In the schools German was taught, the street names and proper names were Germanized. These administrative features changed people's lives a lot. It was demanded of the Luxembourgers that they should integrate into the Reich like Germans. Thus, they were forced to join the Hitler Youth, the Wehrmacht, the VdB or volunteer for the RAD (Reichsarbeitsdienst).

The dairies of Niederanven and Senningen were closed by the German occupiers. The school nurses were dismissed from the Hostert school in February 1941 and replaced by a more German-friendly teacher. The same happened to the town clerk and several other public officials. Some had followed the request of the Gauleiter Simon and volunteered for the Reichsarbeitsdienst, which was introduced in 1941.

The Gauleiter introduced compulsory military service on 28 August, 1942. Of the 92 young men who had to enlist, 18 did not return and fell. Two were shot dead as resistance fighters, 15 hid immediately to escape military service and others did not return to the front after their first home leave, hiding on surrounding farms under great danger for their families, and as a result several families were forced to take on the yoke of resettlement, one family not surviving. In 1943 the local resistance became organized, gradually developing into a effective group, helping these men.

Thank God there was no significant damage in the municipality of Niederanven except for the chapel of Ernster, which was hit by a grenade that caused damage to the roof, choir and church windows. Around noon in November 1944, 38 smaller bombs fell around the village of Senningen, doing little damage except for quite large funnels of smoke.

THE "MOST BEAUTIFUL ACCOMMODATION"

The Senningen Castle

Just like in World War I, the American troops settled in our municipality during World War II, setting up their command in Senningen Castle. Tony Vaccaro, the "soldier with a camera" as he was called, described his stay at Senningen in November 1944 as follows: "The HQ was formerly a hotel in the country, the most stunning digs we had with a fountain outside". Here is a brief history of this "most beautiful accommodation" as Tony Vaccaro describes it.

It is the manor house of the former Lamort paper mill. The manor house was taken over by Ernest Dervaux (1844-1917) after the closure of the factory in 1882 and was converted into a manor house. His son Albert Dervaux (1880-1965) had the first plans to build a luxury hotel from the princely estate in 1934. The project was never carried out and in 1938 Dervaux left the property and never lived in it again.

After the occupation of Luxembourg in 1940, the "Dr. Josef-Goebbels-Stiftung für Kulturschaffende" - the "Goebbels Foundation For Cultural Creators"-confiscated numerous monasteries, castles and stately homes from Jewish and other emigrants and made them available, beginning in 1942, for the recreation of German artists who were creating the new Nazi culture. Fischbach Castle, approximately 15 km north of Niederanven, and Senningen Castle in Niederanven were both confiscated for this purpose.

The Senningen Castle was taken over by the Nazi Administrator in 1941 and then, on the instructions of Reich Minister Dr. Goebbels, beginning on 31 March, 1943 German artists could be admitted to the artists' recreation homes for a three-week free recreation period. The visitors were generally those German artists who were bomb-damaged, war-disabled or widows of fallen members of the Reich Chamber of Culture who were not in a position to pay for a recreational stay with their own means.

The Goebbels Foundation maintained both the Fischbach Castle (put into operation on 2 July 1942 and open all year round) and the Senningen Castle (which only operated during the summer months and was primarily intended to accommodate adults with children). The Senningen facility was opened on May 4, 1943 with great Nazi fanfare with the capacity of 50 adults and children, the latter of whom would be looked after by a "kindergarten teacher".

"D'Amerikaner sinn do!" This was the joyous outcry that went through the Luxembourg population when the first American liberators entered our country. Thus the Castle of Senningen was able to become "the most beautiful accommodation" for the American Army. Today a monument, financed by the Municipality of Niederanven, exists in the memory of the 4th American Infantry Division.

LIBERATION & RECOVERY

Since the liberation of Luxembourg in September '44, there had been no order at that time to proceed further than the Moselle, so the American troops used the time to train their soldiers of the 83rd Infantry Division in attacking and destroying fortifications.

After the 308th Battalion had thoroughly inspected the parts of the Maginot Line located about 20 miles from Senningen, just across the French border, the Americans trained their soldiers there, giving them excellent practice in attacking and destroying bunkers, preparing them for the imminent attack of the Siegfried Line.

On December 6, the American troops finally left our municipality, crossed the border at Steinfort and headed for Hurtgen Forest, from where they later intervened in the Battle of the Bulge.

After the liberation, American doctors temporarily lived in the castle and in private houses, and sick and recovering GI's were accommodated in the village school. Just before the occupation by the Americans, several grenade impacts were recorded at the castle and several windows were broken. Otherwise the liberation went quietly.

During the retreat of the German troops and the passage of the many open lorries with wounded soldiers who drove in the direction of the Reich, many farmers were forced to provide haulage services with their horses. Allied planes attacked these transports on the roads continuously. On one occasion two ammunition cars were shot and set on fire, the fire spreading to two houses in the village.

In order to complicate the progress of the advancing American troops, a concerted effort was made to block the road to Trier in the woods and at the bottleneck near the church, by blowing up forest and chestnut trees in order to create traffic obstacles.

OUR TOWN TODAY

Located in a most beautiful natural setting, Niederanven is known for its many walking paths with targeted educational interpretive signage describing the historical, cultural and environment surroundings along the way.

The increased global awareness of the importance of sustainability coincides perfectly with the living and tourism goals of our community. We encourage you to view a short film about our vision at: www.niederanven.lu/lu/deng-gemeng-entdecken/imagefilm. You will surely enjoy it.

Two views of beautiful Niederanven today

For more information about Niederanven, please visit the commune's official website: **www.niederanven.lu**. For more information about the town's extensive historical heritage please visit **www.gfn.lu**. This information was prepared by the association of local historians © Geschichtsfrënn vun der Gemeng Nidderaanwen, October 2019. Book: Tony Vaccaro, "Soldier with a Camera", ISBN 978-99959-0-315-2 Lions Club Luxembourg Country Luxembourg, Nov. 2017. © Photos: Uli Fielitz, photographer, Niederanven 2019; Tony Vaccaro, Long Island City, NY 11101; Photothèque de la Ville de Luxembourg.

PÉTANGE LUXEMBOURG

Canton: Esch-sur-Alzette   Pop. 1940: 12,000   Pop. 2020: 19,600

SITING & HERITAGE

The Municipality of Pétange is located in the southwestern corner of the Grand Duchy, a tri-state region bordering on France and Belgium. In 1798, after partially belonging to Luxembourg and to the French Duchy of Bar during the Middles Ages, the towns of Pétange, Lamadelaine and Rodange were united under the French administration. In pre-Christian times, a significant Celtic and later a Roman settlement were located on our municipality's territory. According to legend, Rodange was home to St. Amalberga in the 8th century.

In the 19th century, the municipality started booming due to the emergence of the steel industry. Iron ore mines, a steel mill as well as a railway workshop which provided new jobs and many workers settled here to be near their workplace.

GPS Coord: N49.5561 E5.8759

OUR TOWN'S OCCUPATION STORY

The Invasion. On May 10, 1940, the day of the German invasion, at around 5 am, the first German airborne troops touched down at a junction close to Pétange. They arrived by the "Fieseler Störche" (FI-156) aircrafts that carry up to three men and have short field take-offs and landings. 125 well-trained volunteers were airlifted from Trier, a German border town close to Luxembourg.

"Kreistag 1944 Verwundetenehrung"
(Archive Perrard Jos)

American soldiers entering Pétange
9 September 1944

Shortly after 7 am, the first French Cavalry Regiment of the "Spahi" intervened in our region with Frenchmen as well as soldiers from tribes of the French colonies in Northern Africa. Due to German superiority, the French troops were unable to defend our municipality and suffered great losses on the day of the invasion.

The evacuation of 11 May. The southwest of Luxembourg is close to the French Maginot Line and thus was caught in the crossfire. Our region was strongly affected by the fighting, and most inhabitants were evacuated, some leaving for France while others traveled towards the center and the north of the country.

During the evacuation of the population, several members of a local family became the first civilian casualties within the municipality. While attempting to take refuge in a shelter during the bombings, Mr. and Mrs. Hahn, as well as one of their children, were hit by shrapnel on May 11, 1940, in the local schoolyard. In late June, as French troops had retreated inside France and the battles had moved further afield, many citizens of Pétange decided to go home again.

Oppression. German police moved into the premises of the local police station while German customs took control of the borders. The former governing Mayor was divested and replaced by a German Mayor. Political decisions were made by the "Ortsgruppenleiter". Together with his staff, he moved into the "house of the German people's movement" (VDB). Street names were changed to honor important German individuals. Endowed with yellowish uniforms, the collaborators, called "yellow men," participated in exercises and marched through the streets while waving the Nazi flag and chanting military songs. Whoever didn't stop at their passage to salute the flag was beaten up.

Resistance. Many young people joined resistance groups. Here's one example among many. One day, two young men from Rodange blew up a radiator in the "brown house", the local head office of the "VDB". The two men had stolen the explosives in a mine. The Nazis found out who the perpetrators were, interrogated them and punished them by sending them to a labor camp in Silesia, Poland. Upon returning home after the end of the war, both look like walking skeletons. And they were not the only ones. Other acts of resistance by the local population and the founding of "official" resistance groups did not go unpunished either.

Forced recruitment, refractories and smugglers. May 3, 1942, the "Gauleiter" gave a speech in Rodange in which he denied rumors of compulsory military service in the Wehrmacht. Only 4 months later, on August 20, 1942, he introduced the compulsory military service for men born between 1920 and 1924. Those who were conscripted had to make a tough decision: if they obey, their families were protected; if they deserted, hid or fled across the border, they subjected their families to deportation. As the Germans enlisted more and more young men, the number of deserters increased. Networks of people "smugglers" were set up to help these young people escape to France or Belgium. An escape was difficult as the borders were heavily guarded by German soldiers. Due to the geographical situation of our municipality in the tri-state region, these escape helpers ("passeurs" in French) were very busy. If the deserters decided to stay, they had to hide in places like shut-down mines. In 1944, more than 120 young men were hidden for months in a mine close to Rodange. They had to be provided with food by the local population. Many of those brave helpers and "smugglers" were imprisoned, tortured and/or executed.

A SPECIAL PÉTANGE STORY.

The "Greyhound"

Our "Greyhound" Today

The Hyman Josefson Memorial

One of the soldiers riding in the M8 in which Hyman Josefson looses his life is Cyril J. Mayrose. He is 31 years old when he is wounded in Pétange and transported back to the United States to recover. The Battle of the Bulge Veterans' Association found him after a long search.

Thanks to Cyril J. Mayrose, the mystery surrounding the identity of the four heroes of the M8 described below is finally lifted in 1985. Through his testimony, over forty years after the fatal incident, we now know the names of the M8 crew and the Josefson family was able to discover exactly where their ancestor died.

In 1986, Cyril J. Mayrose is awarded the title of Knight of the Order of Chivalry of the City of Pétange while on a visit to Luxembourg. He passes away in February 1991 following a heart attack, a few years after having been to Luxembourg twice and decades after having participated in the liberation of our country.

Accompanied by her son and her daughter, one of Hyman Josefson's nieces visits Pétange quite regularly to commemorate Liberation Day together with the local population.

The Pétange City Hall

The "WAX" Liberation Remembrance Museum "9'44"

OUR TOWN TODAY

Nowadays, Pétange is a cosmopolitan municipality whose population, with its 50% Luxembourgers and 50% citizens from more than 100 countries, lives together peacefully. The iron ore mines were closed, the furnaces were torn down. Only a small rolling mill remains where part of the railroad tracks for the Eurotunnel under the Channel were produced.

On Sundays, vintage railroad cars hauled by a steam engine offer passengers the chance to travel from the station in Pétange to a nearby valley, the Fond-de-Gras, where mine entrances are an integral part of the landscape. At a typical miners' tavern, Bei der Giedel, lunch and dinner are served in a very cozy setting. Visitors may also change trains to take a ride through a closed mine up to Lasauvage, a charming, hardly changed mining village and the only Luxembourgish place where the cemetery is on French soil.

Most buildings and houses in our towns were constructed in the 20th and 21st centuries, with the exception of a flax mill dating back to the 16th century and two neo-Gothic churches from the 19th century.

There are also 20 monuments and squares reminding people of WW2 events. At the scene where the first American soldier lost his life on Luxembourgish soil, a memorial was erected bearing the inscription: "To the first American soldier fallen for the Liberation of Our Country - We shall never forget". The information center 9'44 is located right next to it in the former mill operator's home. Quite a number of Americans touring Europe visit this site to see where their ancestors were fighting.

LIBERATION & RECOVERY

Liberation. On the evening of September 8, 1944, German artillery pieces were placed in various locations, all targeting the road leading to Athus in Belgium. A great number of soldiers took off in the dead of night. The next morning, around nine o'clock, Pétange was on alert. With their gunfire, US fighter planes immobilized steam engines at the train station and once the streets were cleared of German troops, US ground units finally started moving in.

Around noon, the first American reconnaissance vehicle, an M8 armored car, arrived at the mill in Pétange and started firing towards the place where the last German batteries were supposedly located. Suddenly, it was hit by a German anti-tank cannon and immediately went up in flames. Three soldiers, their uniforms on fire, jumped out of the burning vehicle, but the 4th occupant, 2nd Lieutenant Hyman Josefson, didn't make it out on time. He died inside the vehicle and became the first American soldier to lose his life for the liberation of our country. The M8 was followed by other units of Troop A. Their advance was held up by the incident in which the M8 was destroyed.

Relying on the help of Pétange locals, the US soldiers quickly managed to silence the anti-tank cannon. Jubilant people started throwing flowers onto the advancing vehicles, and in the early afternoon, the G.I.s had finally liberated Pétange without any further casualties.

Recovery. During the liberation of Pétange, no serious damage occurred in town. The Germans had planned to destroy a railway bridge as well as the bridge over the Chiers, a stream in Pétange. Both bridges were saved, the railroad bridge for an unknown reason, the bridge over the Chiers thanks to a local sniper who shot the Austrian soldier charged with blowing it up.

For more information about Pétange and the 9'44 museum, please visit www.petange.lu. Text prepared by Roger Klein, Honorary Mayor of the Municipality of Pétange. Text translation by Pia Hansel, Public Relations Manager, Municipality of Pétange. Photos courtesy of the Commune of Pétange.

Remembering & Honoring The Sacrifices Endured By So Many

Charlotte, Grand Duchess of Luxembourg, 1942

Charlotte's sister Marie-Adélaide was the Grand Duchess of Luxembourg during World War I but she was forced to abdicate, in favor of Charlotte, after the war in 1919 because of a perception that she had supported the occupying German forces. Becoming Grand Duchess at the age of 23, Charlotte and her husband, Prince Felix, had five children.

When the Nazis invaded on May 10, 1940, Charlotte called an emergency meeting with her ministers and it was decided they should all seek protection in southwest France. As the Germans advanced further into France, Charlotte and her ministers received permission to cross into Spain provided they did not stop in Spain. Therefore they continued on to Portugal, finally arriving in Great Britain in August, 1940. Once in Great Britain, Charlotte immediately began making BBC broadcasts of encouragement to the Luxembourg people.

She and her family then travelled to the United States, ultimately living in Montreal. In the United States, she helped President Roosevelt campaign across the country against isolationism. During that time, Luxembourg was forcibly incorporated into the Third Reich, thus requiring all Luxembourgers to speak German and making all men liable for conscription into the German army.

In 1943 she returned to London, concentrating on making regular BBC radio broadcasts to the people of Luxembourg where she established herself as an iconic figure representing the resistance groups operating in Luxembourg against the Germans. She and her family again returned to the United States where she lobbied Luxembourg's importance to the Allies, after which they moved back to Montreal, living there until the end of the war. After the war she returned to Luxembourg, continuing her reign as Grand Duchess until she abdicated in favor of her son Jean in 1964.

Credited with significantly increasing Luxembourg's global status during her reign, Her Royal Highness passed away in 1985. She is interned in the Notre Dame Cathedral in the city of Luxembourg.

THE WORLD WAR II MUSEUMS OF LUXEMBOURG

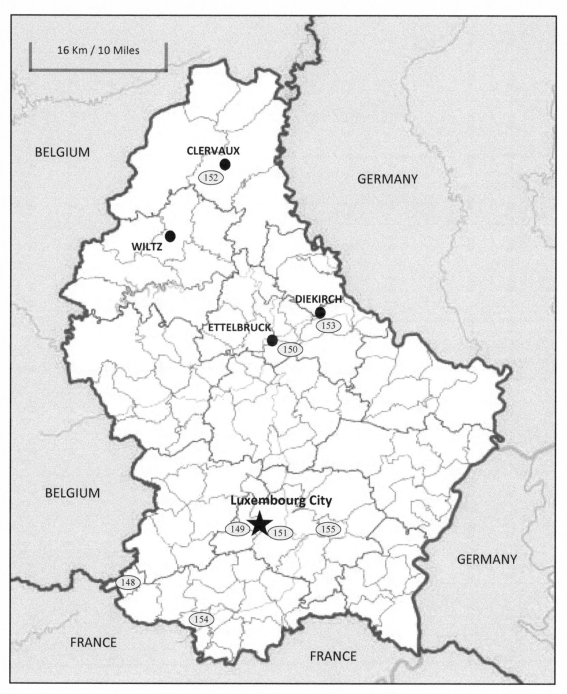

THE GRAND DUCHY OF LUXEMBOURG

Page	Museum	Commune
148	9 '44 Museum	Pétange
149	Deportation Memorial & Museum	Hollerich
150	General Patton Museum	Ettelbruck
151	Luxembourg American Cemetery	Luxembourg City

Page	Museum	Commune
152	Museum of the Battle of the Bulge	Clervaux
153	National Museum of Military History	Diekirch
154	National Museum of the Resistance	Esch-sur-Alzette
155	Sandweiler German Military Cemetery	Sandweiler

LUXEMBOURG

9 '44 WAX MUSEUM
Pétange, Luxembourg

Coordinates N49.5603 E5.8719

Pétange was the first Luxembourg town liberated by the American Army and where, on September 9, 1944 the first American soldier was killed in action, 2nd Lt. Hyman Josefson of the US 1st Army.

Within the Red House at the Pétange WAX facility, the memorable date of September 9, 1944 is explored, the first day American troops entered Luxembourg and the day Pétange was liberated from four years of Nazi occupation. Located on the border between France and Luxembourg, the museum pays special attention to telling the story of the first allied soldier to be killed in action liberating Luxembourg.

The permanent exhibition focuses on three different periods of the Second World War; the invasion, the four years of occupation and finally, the liberation of Pétange. Hundreds of documents and photos present a detailed chronology of events, the actors, the victims, the heroes and the commemorations and monuments that exist today to honor the defenders of freedom who fought in our area.

Through new technologies, the interactivity of the different spaces - either by integrating an iPad into the museum features or by projections on the wall / floor - invites the visitor to become absorbed in the history of a eventful and past.

Within the walls of the old mill on the second floor is the room "Um S päicher". This room is mainly intended for the organization of cultural, artistic and gastronomic activities and can accommodate more than 90 people. The "Moulin-Rouge" stage on the courtyard side is also available for the organization of public cultural and artistic activities. We invite you to visit our lovely WAX facility where there is something for everyone to enjoy and appreciate.

For more information about the museum, visit www.konschtmillen.lu. For more information about the local Pétange area, visit www.petange.lu. Photos courtesy of the museum.

DEPORTATION MEMORIAL & MUSEUM
Hollerich (Luxembourg City), Luxembourg

Coordinates N49.5955 E6.1205

Located in a suburb of Luxembourg City, this railway station was continually used by the Nazis for the deportation of Jews to the death camps and conscripted laborers to serve German industry.

Since 1996, a memorial in the building of the former Luxembourg-Hollerich railway station has commemorated the deportations from the station to the German Reich, which took place between October 1942 and July 1944.

On May 10, 1940, the German Wehrmacht invaded neutral Luxembourg and occupied the country. Adolf Hitler appointed Gustav Simon, the Gau leader of the Koblenz-Trier region, as the new civil administrator of Luxembourg. The occupiers soon began persecuting the Jews. The first deportation train carrying Jews departed from Luxemburg's main station in October 1941 - bound for the Łódź ghetto. Prior to their deportation, Jews were assembled at the Pafemillen (German: Fünfbrunnen) monastery in the north of the country. Until June 1943, six further transports followed to ghettos and concentration camps in occupied Eastern Europe.

In August 1942, Simon introduced the general conscription of men in Luxembourg - by then, Luxembourg had been incorporated into the German Reich. Although the local population protested against these measures, about 11,200 men were drafted for labor service or into the Wehrmacht in the years that followed. Simon had the demonstrations violently suppressed; the conscripts were subsequently transported from the Hollerich station to the east.

Of the 11,200 Luxembourgers forcibly drafted for the Wehrmacht and labour service, over 2,700 did not return. 3,600 Luxembourgian girls were drafted for labour service; 60 of them perished. Beginning 1942, over 4,100 men, women and children were forcibly resettled from Luxembourg to eastern provinces of Germany, about 73 of them died.

The Deportation Memorial was opened in the former Luxembourg-Hollerich railway station in 1996. The memorial contains a permanent exhibition and a memorial to those deported from Luxembourg was erected nearby.

For more information about the museum please visit the museum's website: **www.memorialmuseums.org/eng/denkmaeler/view/1248/Deportation-Memorial-and-Museum-at-Hollerich-Station#.** *For more information about the city of Luxembourg's tourism opportunities, visit* **www.luxembourg-city-com.** *Photos courtesy of the museum.*

GENERAL PATTON MUSEUM
Ettelbruck, Luxembourg

Coordinates N49.8488 E6.1041

Located in the heart of the beautiful Luxembourg Ardennes in the lovely town of Ettelbruck, this is one of the author's favorite WWII museums in Europe. The museum does an excellent job of dissecting the very complex personality of George S. Patton.

The museum, named after US Army General George S. Patton, invites visitors to discover life in Ettelbruck during the frightening years of WWII.

One room specifically honours General George S. Patton, the commander of the 3rd US Army. Remembered for his role in reconquering Luxembourg's territory after the Battle of the Bulge, he is buried at the Luxembourg American Cemetery just east of Luxembourg City. Colonel Lansing McVickar is also remembered for liberating Ettelbruck on December 25, 1944. He was killed in action on January 14, 1945.

Another room in the museum documents the yearly "Remembrance-day festivities" that have been held in Ettelbruck for over 50 years to commemorate the liberation from the Nazis. Various other rooms exhibit a wide range of military items and aircraft remains.

The museum treasures education, especially covering the Nazi occupation between 1940 and 1944, highlighted through documentaries and the many displays of pictures, artifacts, documents. This includes Nazi propaganda, stories about everyday life, collaboration, deportation, the oppression of the Jewish community and local resistance heros. Yvon Kerger, a driving force in uniting several resistance groups around Ettelbruck and Frankie Hansen, a deportee, later a silver star honoured participant in US Army operations are among those honored for their sacrifices in the fight against the Nazis.

*For more information about the museum please visit the museum's website: **www.patton.lu**. For more information about the town of Ettelbruck, please visit the commune's website at: **www.ettelbruck.lu**. Photos courtesy of the museum.*

LUXEMBOURG AMERICAN CEMETERY
Luxembourg City, Luxembourg

Coordinates N49.6129 E6.1860

The American Battle Monuments Commission (ABMC) is responsible for maintaining this beautiful cemetery in the midst of the Battle of the Bulge area. Gazing across this beautiful cemetery conjures emotions that can only be felt at a cemetery such as this.

The cemetery consists of 17 acres of manicured lawn surrounded by 33.5 acres of woods. The visitor center, where information and brochures are available, is to the left as the visitor enters the front gates. Entering through the gates, the visitor will see the impressive Memorial Chapel encompassed by a stone terrace directly in front of them. The chapel includes massive bronze doors embellished with bronze cartouches depicting military "virtues", a sparkling mosaic ceiling and a colorful stained glass window showcasing the Army insignia representing the men and woman that rest in the cemetery.

On the lower level of the terrace, two pylons face each other across a quote by Eisenhower. The pylons display the battle movements in the western European Operations and those of the Battle of the Bulge. On the reverse of the maps, 371 names of those missing in action are inscribed. Twenty-three bronze rosettes identify service members who have been recovered since the inscriptions were made and now rest in known graves.

Sloping away from the terrace is the cemetery where 5,070 American soldiers lie, many of whom lost their lives in the Battle of the Bulge and in the advance to the Rhine River. The cemetery is the final resting place of General George S. Patton.

For more information about this American cemetery, visit www.abmc.gov/Luxembourg. For more information about the history of the area, visit www.citymuseum.lu. Photos courtesy of the American Battle Monuments Commission and Wikipedia.

MUSEUM OF THE BATTLE OF THE BULGE AT CLERVAUX CASTLE
Clervaux, Luxembourg

Coordinates N50.0544 E6.0300

Located within the Eifel mountain range and within the heavily-forested area of the Ardennes known as the "Ösling", Clervaux is one of the most beautiful towns of Luxembourg. A visit to this museum includes plenty of surrounding natural eye candy.

The Ardennes Counteroffensive, also known as the Battle of the Bulge, was the last attempt by the Third Reich to defeat the Allied forces of the West in the winter of 1944-45. On 16 December, 1944, German troops under the command of General von Rundstedt attacked the weakly defended American line along the Sauer and Our rivers. The majority of the population of Ösling was evacuated, but there were nevertheless many victims among the civilian population. General Patton redeployed the Third Army from the Saar to Luxembourg. After intense fighting, he regained the north sector by sector.

The Museum of the Ardennes Counteroffensive commemorates this dark but decisive period of the last century. The Battle of the Bulge lasted almost two months. It was one of the largest and most confusing battles of the Second World War, and ultimately liberated Luxembourg from German occupation. Clervaux was finally liberated on January 25, 1945.

The majestic castle is perched on the slopes of a rocky promontory, the so-called "Lay". The origins of the castle are lost in the mists of time. Some historians believe it was rising on a former Roman fort, while others believe it was built on celtic foundations.

The West wing is the oldest part of the castle, built in the 12th Century upon the initiative of Count Gerhard von Sponheim, a brother of the Count of Vianden. At the beginning of the 15th Century, under the reign of the powerful House of Brandenburg, Clervaux castle was greatly extended. To protect the southern flank of the castle, Frederic I built the massive Burgundy tower which also housed the castle jail. Destroyed December 17, 1944 during the Ardennes Offensive, the castle was acquired by the State and completely restored.

A venerable witness to a prestigious past, Clervaux castle now houses the offices of the municipality of Clervaux, a marvelous collection of models of Luxembourg's fortified castles, the Museum of the Battle of the Bulge exhibiting weapons and souvenirs from the 1944-1945 Ardennes offensive (Battle of the Bulge), and a most remarkable collection of documentary art photography, "The Family of Man" by Edward Steichen.

For more information about the museum please visit: www.visit-clervaux.lu. For more information about Clervaux and the surrounding area, please visit the town's website at: www.clervaux.lu. Photos courtesy of the museum.

NATIONAL MUSEUM OF MILITARY HISTORY
Diekirch, Luxembourg

Coordinates 49.8710 N 6.1590 E

Located in the heart of the beautiful Luxembourg Ardennes near the banks of the River Sûre, this is one of the most significant World War II museums in all of Europe, and one of the most exciting to visit. The collection of vehicles is extensive and accessible for the visitor's close inspection.

In September, 1944, the country of Luxembourg was liberated by Allied Forces. However, on December 16, 1944, the entire northern half of Luxembourg was again overrun by German mechanized forces, beginning the Battle of the Bulge. Terrible fighting between the Germans and the American armies ensued, lasting until February 12, 1945 when George Patton's Third Army was able to liberate the last occupied town in the country. Primarily focusing on the Battle of the Bulge actions in Luxembourg, the Diekirch National Museum of Military History is one of the most impressive World War II museums in all of Europe.

Consisting of more than 3,000 m^2 (25,000 sf) of exhibit space, the museum presents an extensive historical representation of the Battle of the Bulge from all views, American, German and the local civilians. The museum is especially known for its many realistic and well-prepared dioramas such as those shown here.

The museum also contains an extensive collection of restored American and German wheeled and tracked military vehicles, artillery pieces, communications equipment, uniforms, personal belongings, maps and photographs. The museum is located in the 'old brewery' district of Diekirch, a town known for its friendly people, beautiful surroundings and extensive outdoor recreational opportunities. (See Page 136).

For more information about the museum please visit the museum's website: www.mnhm.lu. For more information about the town of Diekirch, please visit the town's website at: www.diekirch.lu. All photos by the Author.

NATIONAL RESISTANCE MUSEUM
Esch-sur-Alzette, Luxembourg

Coordinates N49.4928 E5.9760

The National Museum of the Resistance and Human Rights shows the history of Luxembourg during the Second World War. It is an excellent museum to learn how the citizens of Luxembourg fought to resist the oppression and occupation of the country by the Germans.

The Museum was inaugurated in 1956 at the very center of the city and is situated on the pedestrian zone. Former prisoners of Nazi concentration camps were involved in its conception. The museum focuses on the Luxembourgish population, their reactions towards the Nazi regime (resistance, collaboration) and life under the occupation of the German army, as well as the structure of the Nazi party. It also follows the fate of the Jewish population during WW2 and the daily life in concentration camps.

The defense of Human Rights is one of the cornerstones of the museum's philosophy. By trying to establish links between the past and the present, as well as organizing ceremonies in honor of the victims of Nazism, the museum promotes not only memorial awareness but also political education. The temporary exhibitions (outdoor exhibitions, travelling exhibitions) and events regularly treat current subjects such as the situation of Romani People, the condition of homosexuals or the war fugitive immigration.

In 2016/2017, the local authorities and the Government decreed the renovation and enlargement of the museum. Early 2022 marks the opening of the renovated museum and its new wing. It will offer room to 3 additional exhibition levels (one for temporary shows, two for the permanent exhibition). The existing topics will be completed by a presentation of Human Rights and current civil resistance; the new exhibition will focus on biographies of victims and offenders.

Since the museum is situated in an immigrant neighborhood, one of its aims is the integration of the local population and the creation of participatory projects.

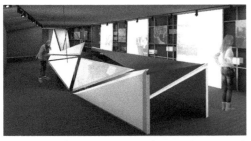

*For more information about the Musée National de la Résistance et des Droits Humains please visit: Site: **www.mnr.lu**; Facebook : Musée National de la Résistance et des Droits Humains ; Phone : 00352 548 472 ; Email : info@mnr.lu. We appreciate the assistance provided by Frank Schroeder and Claudia Lima of the museum in preparing this commemorative document. Photos courtesy of the museum.*

SANDWEILER GERMAN MILITARY CEMETERY
Sandweiler, Luxembourg

Photo By Petra Klawikowski

Coordinates 49.6084 N 6.2032 E

This very large German cemetery is located just east of Luxembourg City and is well worth visiting to pay respect to nearly 11,000 soldiers who died fighting for their country throughout Luxembourg.

Photo By Petra Klawikowski

Photo By Frederic Raffa

During the heavy fighting in the winter and spring of 1945 in the Luxembourg-Belgian and Luxembourg-German border areas, the American burial service recovered its own and German casualties from the combat zone and buried them in two provisional grave fields in its rear army area: the Germans in the area of the municipality of Sandweiler, the Americans on the von Hamm (around 1.5 kilometers apart). After the work by the US Army burial service was completed, the German cemetery counted 5,599 graves.

The first war graves agreement between Germany and a neighboring country was concluded in 1952 between the Luxembourg government and the government of the Federal Republic of Germany.

At that time there were still German soldier graves in 150 places in Luxembourg with a total of 5,286 dead. Most of them were mass graves for which there were only incomplete records. The Volksbund also transferred these dead to Sandweiler. There was enough space here for an extension and thus for the construction of a permanent German war cemetery. The reburial made it possible to identify as yet unknown dead. Around 10,900 war dead have received their final resting place here.

The cemetery is open throughout the year. The Schleswig-Holstein regional association has taken on the sponsorship of this cemetery.

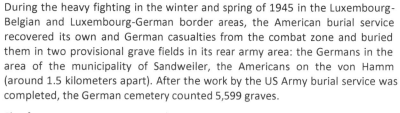

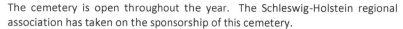

Photo By Frederic Raffa

For more information, visit **www.kriegsgraeberstaetten.volksbund.de/friedhof/sandweiler**. *For more information about the Sandweiler area visit* **www.sandweiler.lu**. *Photos courtesy of the cemetery website.*

WORLD WAR II IN THE NETHERLANDS

The city of Rotterdam after the devastating German bombing of May 14, 1940. Capitulation occurred immediately afterwards to save civilian lives.

Local Eindhoven resistance members, identified by their cloth armbands, with American paratroopers of the 101st Airborne Division, September 1944.

A portion of the more than 35,000 American paratroopers and glider troops landing along the route of Operation Market Garden, September 1944.

An American B-17 bomber drops food and supplies to the people starving and freezing during the '44-'45 Honger Winter food crisis created by the Nazis.

Damage to Arnhem following the Allies' failed attempt to capture the Arnhem bridge over the Rhine river, making it a "Bridge Too Far". September, 1944.

A bugler blows taps at the American military cemetery, Margraten, Netherlands. April, 1945. Nearly 8,300 American soldiers are interred here.

It is worth noting that many stories about the dangers faced by the members of the Dutch Resistance have been memorialized in a number of excellent Dutch movies such as *Zwartnpel (The Black Book), The Resistance Banker, Soldier of Orange, The Reckoning* and many others. You will find the stories to be riveting and the movie productions to be excellent. It is also worth noting that some of the Dutch underground newspapers from the occupation years are still being published today with modern formats including *Trouw, Het Parool* and *Vrij Nederland*.

THE SMALL TOWN OCCUPATION STORIES OF THE NETHERLANDS

The Netherlands During World War II.

The Netherlands Neutrality. *Before World War I, The Netherlands was a neutral country and managed to maintain its neutrality throughout World War I. Even though it was one of the world's largest oil producers because of its colonies in the East Indies and one of the richest, the country's spending was focused on the construction of major public works to control flooding by the sea, not on military defense. In the 1930s, the Great Depression impacted the Netherlands' economy severely, limiting defense spending even further.*

Aggravated by the Depression, right-wing fascist movements developed in the country, notably the NSB socialist movement; however they failed to gain enough support to become an effective political force and in fact, NSB membership dwindled during the late 1930s. In October, 1939, after France and England had already declared war on Germany, Germany issued a statement guaranteeing the Netherlands' continued neutrality. This, of course, was a lie.

The Netherlands

★ **Amsterdam**

Nieuwkoop

Midden-Delfland

Zuidplas

Arnhem

● Rotterdam

Operation Market Garden

Strijen

Noord-Beveland

Oostburg

Reusel

Baarlo

GERMANY

Woensdrecht

Beesel

BELGIUM

100 Km / 60 Miles

The Invasion. *On May 10, 1940, the Netherlands was invaded, without a Declaration of War, by German airborne and land forces at the same time Belgium, France and Luxembourg were being invaded. The invasion was swift and complete with major airborne assaults in the low-lying western part of the country and land assaults along the length of the eastern border. The airborne assault included the bombing of airfields throughout the country and the dropping of large numbers of parachutists, hoping to capture the Dutch government. Queen Wilhelmina was able to escape to England and the Dutch forces fought furiously but a devastating bombing of Rotterdam forced capitulation.*

The Occupation. *Considered by Hitler to be part of the Aryan race, the Germans attempted to coerce the Dutch into joining the Fascist cause, and conditions were at first tolerable. However, soon after, more and more contributions were required to fund the German war effort and the occupier's oppression increased, especially against the Jewish population. Further, all men found themselves to be subject to working in German factories that were being bombed by the Allies, causing many men to go into hiding. During the war, 170,000 Dutch became forced laborers for Germany and 107,000 Dutch Jews were sent to the various death camps, mostly to Auschwitz.*

The Resistance. *Beginning slowly, an increasing number of resistance groups operated mostly independently, forging ration cards, counterfeiting money, publishing underground newspapers, sabotaging phone and rail lines and distributing food to those in hiding. However, as the resistance grew so did the intensity of the Gestapo raids and reprisals, which often ended in the death of uninvolved innocents who were randomly dragged from their homes and executed, the numbers often in the hundreds.*

Operation Market Garden. *One of the most infamous operations of WWII, Eisenhower approved a plan by British General Bernard Montgomery to drive north into the Netherlands from the Belgian border through German-held territory to outflank the northern limits of the German lines, then cross the Rhine and drive deep into the German industrial Ruhr valley, destroy the Germans' ability to manufacture war material and end the war by Christmas. The Germans however halted the Allied advance in Arnhem at "the bridge too far". Except for the liberation of many towns south of Arnhem, the operation failed its mission.*

The Honger Winter. *In September, 1944, the Dutch government-in-exile called for a railway strike to cripple the Germans' ability to move men and material against the advancing Allies. The Germans retaliated by blockading the delivery of all food and supplies to the entire, very heavily populated western half of the country. Occurring during the exceptionally harsh winter of '44-'45 and after a year of bad crops, the results were devastating. With no food and no fuel to heat their homes, more than 18,000 people died of malnutrition and starvation before the Allies were able to air drop food and supplies to provide some relief.*

Liberation. *In spite of the imperative to liberate the western half of the country as quickly as possible because of the mass starvation occurring, stiff German resistance delayed the liberation of most of the country until Germany surrendered on May 5, 1945. The highest per capita death rate in western Europe, more than 300,000 Dutch citizens died during the war, equivalent to 11,000,000 people dying in the United States today. Of those, 107,000 were Holocaust victims. The Nazis were efficient and aggressive in their deportation of the Jews to the death camps. In fact, only 27% of the Dutch Jewish population was able to survive the war, the lowest per capita Jewish survival rate in all of western Europe.*

BAARLO THE NETHERLANDS

Province: Limburg   Pop. 1940: 2,268   Pop. 2020: 6,500

SITING & HERITAGE

Baarlo is located in the southern part of The Netherlands near the Meuse and the German border. The earliest evidence of human occupation dates from the Bronze age (1800 B.C.) and Baarlo is an archaeologically rich area in which 40 tumuli (burial mounds) from that era have been discovered. Archaeological examinations of these many tumuli are continually and currently in progress. Baarlo is also known for the various Roman artifacts that have been found locally.

Three medieval castles and a watermill still exist in Baarlo, along with a fourth castle that was built during the 19th century. A beautifully renovated lavoir (public clothing wash house) is located near the town's historic watermill and town square. Sadly, the town's 19th century church, the old ferry house, some farms, a chapel and two windmills were destroyed during WWII.

GPS Coord.: N51.3302 E6.0951

Baarlo Partisans planning their next mission

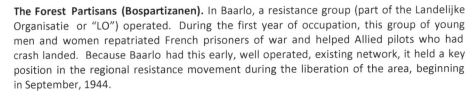

BAARLO'S OCCUPATION STORY

The Invasion. On May 10th, 1940, German troops crossed the Dutch border. Even though the Dutch army had detonated the Maas bridge in the nearby city of Venlo, the Germans built pontoon bridges, crossed the river, and within hours arrived in Baarlo. During the following weeks, German convoys of military vehicles and troops were often seen in the village, moving west to control the occupied territory.

Oppression. Allied forces bombed the nearby Ruhr valley to disrupt the production of the vital weapon and steel industries. Unfortunately, due to inaccuracy and mishap, some bombs were dropped on nearby Baarlo and civilian life became unsafe. Risks in daily life worsened when the German authority proclaimed a Forced Labor Ordinance as a vital part of their economic exploitation of conquered territories, forcing many able-bodied men into hiding. Then, despite the residents' objections, the Germans started confiscating radios, bicycles, fuel, cattle, and horses. German harassment and deportation of Baarlo's men, via *razzia* (labor raids) in 1943/1944 caused essentially all of the local citizens to actively and passively resist. During the *razzia* of October 8th, 1944, 23 men from Baarlo were taken away to Germany. Five of them died.

The Forest Partisans (Bospartizanen). In Baarlo, a resistance group (part of the Landelijke Organisatie or "LO") operated. During the first year of occupation, this group of young men and women repatriated French prisoners of war and helped Allied pilots who had crash landed. Because Baarlo had this early, well operated, existing network, it held a key position in the regional resistance movement during the liberation of the area, beginning in September, 1944.

On September 3rd 1944, three resistance cells in the southern part of The Netherlands (Maas & Waal, Schijndel and Noord-Limburg) were told to gather in Venlo and form a new group, "The Partisans" (Knokploeg). Hearing the code word "Francois" on Radio Oranje, was the signal for these groups to meet. The Squad's role was to aid the advancing Allied Forces by carrying out armed raids and sabotage.

On September 10th 1944, the Partisans were ordered to meet in Baarlo but waited in vain for expected weapons drops. In spite of the lack of sufficient arms they aggressively ambushed, disarmed and detained German soldiers as prisoners of war, holding them on a local farm (Boekenderhof). With the help of local citizens providing food, clothing and other supplies, they soon undertook assaults on larger Nazi groups and vehicles.

Church destroyed by the Germans
November 18, 1944

When the Germans discovered what was happening at the Boekenderhof, it led to the burning of the farm, the fleeing of the Partisans to a hastily developed and well-protected forest base with their prisoners, and the people in the village fearing possible German reprisals. The resistance pressured Baron Weichs zur Wenne (a German aristocrat in Baarlo) to use his position to prevent the detonation of several houses in town and, to the great relief of the population, the threat of reprisals ended.

The Partisans built an underground base in the forest, to wait for the liberation but their situation deteriorated and they were forced to move the captives. On November 19th 1944, the Partisans walked through the front line to Helden with 30 captives where they transferred the prisoners to British forces. Condemned to each other for 66 days, unexpected bonds developed between the Partisans and the captured German soldiers, many of those bonds lasting for years after the war had ended.

Baarlo civilians and British Liberators
November, 1944

A VERY SPECIAL BAARLO STORY

Salomon & Abraham Rosenberg and parents in Amsterdam

The Dutch resistance arranged two hiding addresses in Baarlo to secretly shelter two very young Jewish children from Amsterdam. Unfortunately, they could not save the parents from deportation and Max and Rebecca Rosenberg-de Jongh died on their arrival in Sobibor in 1943.

The resistance however was able to bring their two sons, Salomon Mozes Rosenberg (1942) and Abraham Wolf Rosenberg (1943) to Baarlo in 1943. Salomon was given a safe hiding address with the married couple Neel and Dora Berben-Peeters. Betje and Mientje Gielen, unmarried sisters, took care of Abraham. These foster parents were very moral and courageous, as they risked losing their own lives by taking the children into their homes and they had to constantly stay alert for the Nazis and their local collaborators. The Sicherheitspolizei (Security Police) was notorious for the intense fierceness with which they undertook the hunt to uncover addresses sheltering Jews.

After the liberation, the Commissie Oorlogspleegkinderen (OPK, Commission for War Foster Children) was created. Their tasks included helping all Jewish children without family and completing their adoption within Jewish communities.

Representatives of the OPK visited Baarlo to collect Salomon and Abraham. What followed was a legal conflict that went on for years between the OPK and the foster parents from Baarlo. Eventually, in December 1948, the two boys were legally allowed to stay in Baarlo where they grew up. The four foster parents were honoured by the world Holocaust Remembrance Center, Yad Vashem.

LIBERATION AND RECOVERY

On November 18th 1944, the Germans destroyed the local church and two historic windmills. This was part of their withdrawal strategy since the liberators could use the height of these buildings to easily survey the area and the Meuse. This demolition caused severe pain and anger among the residents of Baarlo.

The center of Baarlo was liberated November 21st by Scotland's Black Watch 1st Batallion C Company 154th Infantry Brigade under the command of Brigadier J.A. Olivier. Until March 1st 1945, the unusual situation existed in which Baarlo was both a liberated village and at the same time a front-line village, under grenade and artillery fire from the other side of the Meuse which was still under German occupation.

Baarlo mourned the death of 24 war victims. The role of Baron Weichs zur Wenne during the war never became fully clear however, as all German property was confiscated after the war; he was expropriated of all his belongings. War damage to houses and the four castles was repaired in the following years and in 1951, the building of a new church was started.

It took the Baarlo residents many years before they could accept the Partisans' actions and the potential dangerous German reprisals these might had caused. The story of the Baarlo Partisans has been documented in books and film for Dutch television and by several local eyewitnesses. Partisans and residents have participated in these projects.

Baarlo: The 13th Century Castle de Borcht

Baarlo: The watermill, church and lavoir

OUR TOWN TODAY

Today, Baarlo is known for its tumuli, four monumental castles, a functioning historic water mill and a beautifully renovated and rare lavoir. The lavoir was of great social importance to generations as residents went there to do their laundry and to hear the latest news and gossip. Tourists visiting Baarlo enjoy its rich history, its collection of castles and the area's surrounding natural beauty. A watchtower on the banks of the Meuse offers visitors a perfect view over the river and the surrounding scenery.

The local tourist office provides visitors with nature walks and historical guided village tours. Visitors interested in military history will particularly enjoy "The Partisans of Baarlo" village tour and there are several war monuments in Baarlo that commemorate WWII. Enthusiasts can also tour the Baarlo PS Aero facility to view, up close, more than 35 historic military planes and helicopters.

Baarlo is not only a village of castles but also a village of art thanks to the world famous Cobra artist Shinkichi Tajiri (1923-2009) who resided in castle Scheres and whose famous "Knots" structure can be seen in Baarlo.

In 2019 multiple artists were invited to create and place sculptures to celebrate the first mentioning of Baarlo in a written document (1219). Each year the Volksfeesten festival is organized in June, attracting thousands of visitors who come to enjoy the food, sports and music.

For more information about Baarlo, visit the town's website: www.peelenmaas.nl. For more information about the town's recreational opportunities, visit www.liefdevoorlimburg.nl. For more historical information about Baarlo, visit http://deborcht.baarlo.com/.

This information was prepared by Herman van Megen, Acting Chairman HWG de Borcht, with the assistance of Jan Wijnhoven of the Historical Working Group de Borcht and the approval of Mayor W.J.G. (Wilma) Delissen-van Tongerlo (Gemeente Peel en Maas). Photos courtesy of the Municipality of Baarlo.

BEESEL THE NETHERLANDS

Province: Limburg   Pop. 1940: 4,900   Pop. 2020: 13,500

SITING & HERITAGE

The Municipality of Beesel lies in a narrow strip of land between the River Meuse and the German border in Limburg, the most southeastern province in the Netherlands. Inhabited since Neanderthal times, this green and rural municipality consists of the villages of Beesel (pop. 2,000) and Reuver (pop. 13,000).

Beesel is the oldest village and is known as the "Dragon Village". Dragon blood is even said to run deep in the veins of the villagers. Since 1736, a week-long Dragon-Slaying spectacle occurs every 7 years in the village to celebrate the legend, the next year being 2023. Signs of the dragon can be found throughout the village.

Slaying The Dragon of Beesel

GPS Coord.: N51.2698 E6.0468

Vehicles being checked by German soldiers
(H. Smeets Collection)

Underground shelter (S. Vintcent Collection, 1990)

OUR TOWN'S OCCUPATION STORY

The Invasion. It was May 10th 1940 when the Germans started their invasion of the Netherlands. This included Beesel and Reuver, although Dutch soldiers had tried to prevent this by using explosives on the Keulseweg road towards the German border. These explosives caused the trees to fall across this entry road from Germany towards Reuver. The German soldiers, however, were not stopped by this and their infantrymen crossed the border. They were soon followed by larger groups of soldiers as well all types of military material such as cannons and tanks. The local people, who had woken up from the noises, felt defeated as they watched the German forces entering and taking over their villages.

At the river Meuse, The Germans were stopped for a short time by resisting forces but, after a short yet heavy battle, the Germans continued their march westward across the river by laying bridges across it. The next days, Beesel served as a main passageway for the German invasion troops and their material.

Resistance. Resistance groups were operating in secret across the entire country during the 2nd World War, including Beesel. In Reuver, the resistance first secretly used a local basement as a reception centre and transit location for fleeing prisoners of war. Later, they extended their activities by supporting Allied pilots and people in hiding from this basement as well. As the war continued, the resistance increased and the basement became the headquarters for the organized resistance group in Reuver.

Somehow the German forces discovered this headquarters and on August 30th 1944 part of the resistance group was arrested and executed. A result of these executions was that the hatred of the people towards the German invaders grew even more intense. Although it never became clear how the location of the resistance was discovered, the remaining resistance force did not stop their fight. The group relocated to nearby Baarlo, which served as the regional resistance headquarters, to continue their resistance from there.

Evacuation. In November 1944 the villages on the western bank of the Meuse were liberated. Due to this, the people of Beesel thought that the liberation of their villages was near, yet the Allied forces did not cross the Meuse. While the liberation was celebrated only three kilometres away, Beesel remained under German occupation for a few more months. In these months, the food rations got smaller and many buildings in Beesel were destroyed by continuous heavy artillery fire and bombers. Other villages in the region were liberated but the people of Beesel continued to have to wait.

In February 1945 the inhabitants of the village of Beesel were forced out of their houses and sent to Brüggen, the closest German village, and the people of Reuver were forced to walk to Kaldenkirchen, another German village on the border. While most inhabitants obeyed the Germans, some families decided to go into hiding and secretly await the liberation in their houses. Eventually most evacuees in Germany were put on trains leaving for the north part of the Netherlands. After three long days of traveling through Germany in cattle wagons, these people finally reached the three northernmost provinces of the Netherlands. They would stay there until the final liberation of the Netherlands in May 1945.

Damaged and plundered homes in Beesel

A SPECIAL BEESEL STORY

Beesel: St. Gertrudis Church

The Russian Girls In Reuver: The power of the German Reich was spread over a large part of Europe. In 1942, after the German attack on the Soviet Union, many young Soviet girls were put on transports to Western Europe. These girls had already been forced to dig trenches for the Germans in eastern Europe and immediately after travelling for days, the girls were put to work. In the Beesel-Brüggen region, the girls had to work in factories. During their work here, many of the Russian girls became friends with the Dutch men who worked in these factories as well. One night, many girls decided to flee across the border together with the Dutch men.

As one of the Russian girls described this night: *"Terrible. Impossible to describe with words, that fear. Fear of being caught by the Germans. Fear of that scary darkness surrounding you. And waiting for the right moment to cross the border. We were used to a lot, to many fears, caused by all the nasty experiences of these last years."*

In Reuver, the other girls went into hiding. This resulted in dangerous situations for both the girls and those who were hiding them. For months the girls and the people who hid them suffered from the continued occupation.

After the liberation of Beesel, many Russian girls decided to stay and start a new life in the Beesel area. Some of them married the man that helped them flee across the border.

Beesel: Nieuwenbroek Castle

LIBERATION AND RECOVERY

Liberation: After the people were evacuated, the deserted villages Beesel and Reuver suffered from the allied attacks on the Germans. Those who secretly stayed behind were too afraid to leave their hiding places during these allied offensives. Once the allied forces captured the German city Monchengladbach, it was clear the liberation of Beesel would not come from the west, but from the east. The German forces were now surrounded and the liberation was felt to be within reach.

On March 1st, the first allied forces arrived in Reuver and Beesel after liberating the nearby city of Venlo. Beesel was liberated without much violence and the allied troops received an enthusiastic welcome from the people. The evacuees that had stayed behind in Brüggen and Kaldenkirchen quickly packed up their belongings and returned home by foot in the next days.

Reconstruction: Although their villages had been destroyed, the people celebrated the liberation from the German Third Reich. 400 inhabitants returned to their damaged and plundered homes in the villages shortly after the liberation. Although most of the cattle had disappeared and homes had been destroyed, the people from Reuver and Beesel were happy to start cleaning the streets and reconstructing their homes, including the homes of those residents who were still in the occupied northern Dutch provinces. The freedom of movement for the people was still very limited due to the 8,000 land mines that had been placed by the Germans around the villages, but the people were relieved. . . . Beesel was free!

OUR TOWN TODAY

Today the Municipality of Beesel is a small, independent municipality in Central Limburg. With only 13,500 inhabitants, Beesel is known for its small scale, the cozy and burgundian atmosphere, and also the extraordinary dragon.

The Dragon Slaying, a week-long, open-air spectacle based on the legend of Saint George and the Dragon, is performed every seven years by volunteers from the village Beesel, the next year being 2023. This centuries-old tradition is recognized on the Dutch National Intangible Cultural Heritage list. While visiting the village of Beesel, the dragon is clearly visible on the streets throughout the town.

The environment of Beesel has plenty of beauty to offer as well. The Beesel area is especially known for the beautiful walking and cycling routes along the River Meuse and through the forests into Germany. The title "Best Cultural Heritage in the Netherlands" was won by Beesel in 2016, recognizing the large diversity of cultural history of the area and Beesel has been named as one of the top 10 most beautiful villages in the Netherlands.

After a walk next to the River Meuse and experiencing the rich cultural history of Beesel, be sure to enjoy some local specialty dishes such as the asparagus or a piece of Limburg flan at one of Beesel's many restaurants and eateries.

For more information about the Municipality of Beesel, visit the town's official website: www.beesel.nl. For more information about the town's recreational opportunities, visit www.vvvmiddenlimburg.nl.

This information was graciously prepared by Shirley Meijers of the Beesel Recreation and Tourism office (info@beesel.nl). Photos courtesy of the Municipality of Beesel.

NETHERLANDS

MIDDEN-DELFLAND THE NETHELANDS

Province: Zuid-Holland   Pop. 1940: 7,890   Pop. 2019: 19,391

SITING & HERITAGE

Midden-Delfland is a sustainable small municipality consisting of the villages of Schipluiden, Den Hoorn, Maasland and the hamlets of 't Woudt and De Zweth. Even though Midden-Delfland is located in the metropolitan region of Rotterdam-The Hague, the area is primarily agricultural and includes 60 dairy farmers. Midden-Delfland contains many important archaeological sites and serves as a designated recreational area for the surrounding metropolitan areas.

The agricultural landscape includes a long history of peat production of national significance, which is now subject to protection requirements. The large De Vlietlanden peat bog area in Midden-Delfland has never settled, so now the area is higher than the surrounding polders (diked reclaimed land areas), a unique situation in the Netherlands. The average elevation of Midden-Delfland is 2 meters below sea level.

GPS Coord.: N51.9545 E4.2883

MIDDEN-DELFLAND DURING THE OCCUPATION

May 10, 1940. "Heavy roaring of aircraft engines, mixed with heavy barking of anti-aircraft guns, disrupted our peaceful environment. It slowly dawned on me that we were at war, that our country now had to fight. We looked with anxious curiosity at all those strange planes that flew low over our village". This is how the war diary of young cattle obstetrician Kees Tetteroo (17 years old) from Schipluiden begins.

Violence. To force the Netherlands to surrender, the Germans surrounded the government city of The Hague. They wanted to occupy the Ypenburg, Ockenburg and Valkenburg airports located there. Only a stone's throw from The Hague, the villages of Midden-Delfland were flooded with war.

"Den Hoorn, otherwise such a peaceful village, received a number of bombs and offered a sad look. Everywhere glass fragments, roof tiles, all shop windows, without exception, were broken. Doors and window frames were splintered on the houses, curtains hung to shreds. The rectory and convent are uninhabitable, the inside of the church is in disarray and the primary school is unusable. No deaths, only some injured."

At that time, the war was mainly fought in the air. "A Junkers full of German soldiers made an emergency landing in 't Woudt and the residents of 't Woudt were driven into their homes by heavily armed soldiers. The night fell over our so unhappy country; a night that would not be forgotten by many and would be the last for many others. The Netherlands is in the War."

After the capitulation, a considerable German defensive force was billeted in our municipality. The damage will be repaired as well as possible here and also in nearby Delft and Westland. Rotterdam is being bombed. "There is no cloud in the sky and yet it is dark. The sun is hiding behind a curtain of soot, ash and paper that floats high through the air from the heat of burning Rotterdam, descending far away."

Sonderausweis (Special Identity Card). Kees Tetteroo has a Sonderausweis because of his work which allows him to go anywhere freely. Although strictly forbidden, he takes photos of crashed aircraft on his way. His Sonderausweis later also gives him the opportunity to perform espionage for the English. Kees is also involved in arms smuggling and bringing crew members of downed Allied planes to safety.

Inundation. Everything is becoming scarce. The church bells are melted into bullets. The freedom of the people is being further and further restricted. The young men from the municipality have to report to the farmers in the countryside and passers-by, often cold and exposed, beg for food. During the course of 1944 a large part of our beautiful lands are flooded to prevent English planes from landing and the remaining polders will be full of posts. The Delft vegetable auction next to Den Hoorn is being bombed flat. The situation becomes dire during the 1944 Hunger Winter (see Page 198). There is no more electricity.

On Sunday, April 29, 1945, food drops occur in our municipality. Many are waving with joy and waving. Would the war really be over?

Source: "My Diary, War Chronicle of Kees Tetteroo"

Trucks in Den Hoorn being taken for
German military purposes. Photo: CT

Kees Tetteroo at the Junker who made an emergency
landing in 't Woudt, 10 May 1940. Photo: CT

Polders are flooded to prevent the
landing of Allied planes. Photo: CT

A SPECIAL TRIBUTE TO BRAVERY

Our town had many resistance heroes and war victims. One example:

Theo van der Stap
Born 1914
Died May 3, 1942

Theo van der Stap grew up in Den Hoorn. He had a pilot's license and was not afraid of the devil or the Germans. Together with others he sabotaged enemy connections, carried out espionage for the English and was involved in arms transport.

On April 27, 1941, Theo was arrested simultaneously with dozens of others. He didn't betray his buddies. At the beginning of 1942 he was transferred to an unknown destination.

Farewell Letter. On May 9, 1942, the parents received a letter from Theo. It was his last. Theo first addressed the letter to his brother, requesting that their parents be carefully informed, if necessary with the help of the Pastor.

Theo writes: "The 11th of April the irrevocable verdict was passed on us: the death penalty. This judgment will now be executed for us 4 o'clock tomorrow morning. " He thanks his father and mother in an extremely impressive way for his good religious education. He asks forgiveness for the grief he has caused to his loved ones.

"I hope that you will not grieve for me because I am now entering a much better life. When I am upstairs, I will pray a lot for you. So be strong in wearing this cross and, in that spirit, for the last time, heartily embraced by Your dearly loving son and brother, Theo. PS: Also ask the family to pray for me.

Tribute: The letter made a huge impression on the residents of the small vil-lage and parts of this letter were quoted at many later commemorations in the church. At the beginning of 2019 a bridge was named after Theo van der Stap so that he and all other war victims, will not be forgotten.

LIBERATION AND RECOVERY

1944-1945 Hunger Winter: In response to a railroad strike ordered by the Dutch government in exile, Germany cuts off all food and fuel supplies to the western provinces of the Netherlands. 4.5 million people are left without supplies; approximately 18,000 Dutch citizens starve, while thousands of others suffer from malnutrition, disease, and exposure but the end was near.

Although the war has been over for a long time, there are still people whose lives are marked by those five years of terror. Many have never really been able to talk about it and they put the memories as far away as possible. After all, the country had to be built up as quickly as possible. The sleeves were rolled up. In this way the Netherlands tried to recover.

In the war diary of Kees Tetteroo from Schipluiden we read: *"Liberation: what tough years we all had behind us. Tension, fear and sadness had made us very different people. Hunger and lack of everything only made us crave for freedom. Do you remember how we regained confidence in the future when we were liberated? "*

And there was a future again. Thanks to the agricultural character of the villages of Maasland, Schipluiden and Den Hoorn, the inhabitants of the valley survived. Yet the years 1940 - 1945 should never be forgotten, they have been too impressive for that. Have we learned from it as a post-war generation? Yes. In Midden-Delfland, the attention for the annual Remembrance Day is growing.

The war memorials in Maasland and Schipluiden bear the names of the residents who fell. It is the toll that Midden-Delfland has paid in the struggle for freedom. *"Liberation also came for our village after five years of occupation. Dear ones have fallen in the underground resistance, as a soldier, as a civilian or as an employee abroad. Our thoughts mainly go to those who were no longer allowed to experience this earthly liberation. They rest in peace! "*

Part of Maasland is a protected townscape

National activities in Midden-Delfland.
In the background 't Woudt

MIDDEN-DELFLAND TODAY

Midden-Delfland was the first Dutch municipality in 2008 to receive the Cittaslow certificate, the international quality mark for small municipalities. Cittaslow is a way of life that chooses its own identity and remains small-scale, where government and residents feel connected, where people look at each other and are committed to the open and green landscape, the cultural heritage and hospitality. In short, where people opt for the quality of life.

The three villages, Maasland, Schipluiden and Den Hoorn, each have their own character and their own village festivals. There is a lot of creativity and activity, ranging from concerts on the water to a rich club life and tasty regional products. The hamlet of 't Woudt is a Protected Village in its entirety and other parts of Midden-Delfland also have this status. Out of respect and reverence for the landscape, the farmers ensure circular agriculture. They prepare environmentally friendly dairy products and meat from their own cows in a traditional way. Sustainability is of paramount importance.

Midden-Delfland is a beautiful green oasis in an urban area. Numerous riding, cycling and hiking trails and an extensive sailing network invite residents of the surrounding towns to come and recreate in the area, seek peace and enjoy the town's welcoming people and local foods.

For more information about Midden-Delfland, visit the town's website: www.middendelfland.nl. For more information about the town's Cittaslow award, visit www.cittaslow.org.

The text and photos for this Midden-Delfland remembrance document were graciously prepared and provided by Gemma van Winden-Tetteroo. We greatly appreciate her contribution. Photos courtesy of the Municipality of Midden-Delfland.

Source: "My Diary, War Chronicle of Kees Tetteroo"

NETHERLANDS

NIEUWKOOP
THE NETHERLANDS

Province: South Holland   Pop. 1940: 4,500   Pop. 2020: 9,000

SITING & HERITAGE

Nieuwkoop is located in the middle of "The Green Heart of Holland" in the west part of the Netherlands along dikes that separate the flooded Plassen areas from the land that has been reclaimed from the water (Polder areas). The first inhabitants settled at the end of the eleventh century, pursuing farming and cattle breeding and using the abundant peat for fuel to heat their homes and buildings.

The serious excavation of peat started around 1300 because there was a great demand in the cities for dried peat for fuel. After the invention of dredging around 1530, the peat below the water level could also be dredged, creating The Nieuwkoopse Plassen (shallow lakes). Now designated as an important natural monument and park, these lakes support many recreational activities. In 1940, Nieuwkoop was a village of approximately 4,500 people, with a small village centre and a traditional church with tower.

GPS Coord.: N52.1502 E4.7773

The stealing of the church bell

The drop team unloading supply containers

A British food and supply drop during the '44-'45 Honger Winter starvation by the Germans

OUR TOWN'S OCCUPATION STORY

The Invasion. On 10 May 1940 it was clear war had started. Because Nieuwkoop is near the Schiphol airport, aerial battles above the town started in the early morning. Several planes, both German and Allied, were shot down or crashed above Nieuwkoop, some of which disappeared in the peat bottoms of the Plassen. A German V2 rocket fell into a pasture, causing a huge blast, but little damage. Several soldiers from the village fell during the first battles around the airports along the coast. Due to its rather isolated location, Nieuwkoop did not experience any intense shelling and bombing, so after the first confusing days of fighting and the Dutch capitulation, everyday life seemed normal again . . . until the consequences of the occupation slowly became painfully clear.

Repression and Persecution. Nieuwkoop was used mainly for quartering German soldiers and for rest after heavy front combat. Residents were subject to nightly blackout and curfew rules and everyone was obliged to carry personal proof of identity (Ausweis). Although Nieuwkoop had few Jewish inhabitants, most of them were arrested and transported to Westerbork camp, but some went into hiding. The area lent itself perfectly to hiding from the Germans because of its many farms, market gardens and large areas of reeds and many survived the whole war by hiding there.

Many men hid to avoid the Germans because young men were arrested at Razzias (raids) and forced into labor for the Germans. Many were sent to Germany, where they endured the bombardments of German industrialized cities by English and American airplanes. Most were able to return home.

Everyday Life. As the war progressed, the Occupation was increasingly felt. Food became severely rationed. Most inhabitants reserved a piece of garden to grow tobacco, not only for their own use, but as an item to trade for extra food. Cars disappeared from the street because they, like the horses, were claimed by the Germans. Radios had to be handed in, and even the church bells were stolen by the Nazis.

Fuel was scarce and many schools were forced to close during the last year of the war and during the winter of 1944, known as The Hunger Winter, the Germans retaliated for a railway strike by cutting off all supplies to western half of the country. Food shortages became so critical that central kitchens had to be set up to feed the people.

The influx of people was a problem because many evacuees from bombed or inundated areas fled to Nieuwkoop. Many of the occupation actions were carried out or coordinated by members of the N.S.B, a political party that collaborated with the Germans. These so-called Landguards were especially active in the control of food and identity documents.

Resistance. Soon after the start of the war, a local resistance movement became active, and later joined with the Allied armed forces. The resistance focused on counterfeiting ration cards and identity documents, hiding people, distributing food, and the printing and dissemination of illegal news magazines. It was dangerous work, and some members of the underground were arrested and sentenced to work punishment in the Vught camp. Some young men who spread illegal newspapers were arrested and put to death.

At the request of the national resistance, a Drop Team was formed in Nieuwkoop. During the last year of the war, they received and distributed weapons, ammunition, money and food that were thrown off at night by parachute from English planes. Secret Agents from London were also parachuted in.

Jos Gemmeke *was a patriotic and courageous young woman who spent the war as an active resistance fighter on the behalf of The Netherlands. At the age of 18 Jos began her resistance activities as a courier distributing illegal newspapers but as the war progressed she became more and more active. Among other things Jos concentrated on transporting radio transmitters from England to the resistance networks.*

Jos Gemmeke In uniform In England

In October 1944 Jos had to cross the lines of battle on bicycle to deliver microfilms for the Special Assignments Office (SAO) in Brussels. On the way she was arrested and interrogated but was able to convince her captors to release her, allowing her to continue. In London, Jos was trained as a secret agent by the Special Operations Executive (SOE) and then parachuted into The Netherlands near Nieuwkoop where she landed in a ditch, suffering a permanent back injury. She was found and treated by members of the local resistance and ultimately was able to complete her mission, bringing the first penicillin to the local hospitals.

Jos continued her dogged resistance until the end of the war and after the war was presented with the Military William Order, the only woman besides Queen Wilhelmina to receive this honor.

LIBERATION AND RECOVERY

The end in sight. Despite the fact that the liberation hung in the air, the surrender of Germany and the liberation of the Netherlands came as a surprise. There were celebrations of dancing and bonfires. The Nieuwkoopse village tower was shaking! But first, order had to be created in the chaos and the Canadian Supreme Command and members of the B.S. (Binnenlandse Strijdkrachten) had to keep order because N.S.B. members, collaborators, black marketeers and girls who consorted with the Germans were being targeted. Soon the peace was restored.

Reconstruction. After the war, the reconstruction of Nieuwkoop took on a dynamic aspect. The City Council took charge of industrialization (employment) and tourism and it didn't take long for the first factories to rise. Many new construction projects also started to satisfy the need for dwellings for the population growth.

Nieuwkoop during the annual Koningsdag Festival

OUR TOWN TODAY

Today, Nieuwkoop is a thriving municipality located in the heart of the South Holland's peat bog areas. Well known for its extensive nature experiences and recreational opportunities, and located on the shoreline of the Noordeinderplas, a large peat bog lake, Nieuwkoop is a major destination for visitors wishing to relax in nature and enjoy the quiet charm of traditional Dutch village life.

The Nieuwkoop Municipality consists of 13 villages each with their own unique combination of local heritage, architecture and quaint peacefulness.

Nieuwkoop is also well known for the area's many cycling, fishing and boating activities in summer and for the area's many skating and ice sailing events in winter, making it a very popular year-round tourist destination. To see why, view Nieuwkoop on Google Earth.

There are frequent markets and festivals in Nieuwkoop, including the Torenschuddersfeest (Tower Shaker Party,) a festival of lighted boats, which is held each September on the Nieuwkoopse Plassen (lake) and each year Nieuwkoop hosts a well-known, three-days Art Tour in May, and its annual Koningsdag (King's Day) festival each year.

Germans leaving Nieuwkoop under Holland flags

Arrested German soldiers, NSB members and collaborators

Today the church bell rings for freedom

*For more general information about Nieuwkoop, please visit the Municipality website: **www.nieuwkoop.nl**. For more information about the area's tourism opportunities, visit the town's tourism website: **www.ontdeknieuwkoop.nl**.*

*The text and photo collection for this document was compiled by Bram Poot, of the Historical Society Nieuwkoop. For more information about the Historical Society please visit **www.hgnieuwkoop.nl**. Photos courtesy of the Municipality.*

NOORD-BEVELAND THE NETHERLANDS

Province: Zeeland   Pop. 1940: 7,500 (4 Municipalities) Pop. 2020: 7,400 (1 Municipality)

LOCATION & HERITAGE

An island, the medieval Noord-Beveland area was flooded by the sea on November 5, 1530 by a storm and was subsequently submerged for nearly sixty years. In 1598 the Oud-Noord-Bevelandpolder area (1731 Hectares) was the first land to be reclaimed and two villages were founded, Colijnsplaat and Kats. Colijnsplaat is a so-called "Front Street" village. There are now six villages in the municipality.

The map of the village is a square and all streets are 120 meters long. Only in 1960 was the village enlarged for the first time, and Noord-Beveland was enlarged by dozens of polders (land reclaimed from the sea). In the twentieth century, Noord-Beveland was permanently linked to the mainland by two dams (1960 and 1961), the Zeeland Bridge (1965) and the Oosterscheldekering (1986).

GPS Coord. N51.5714 E3.7715

THE STORY OF OUR MUNICIPALITY

Canadian troops at the Bouw en Plantlust farm

The Invasion. In May 1940, the German occupation entered Noord-Beveland. The first occupation force was an estimated 200 German-Austrians. The relationship with the population was friendly. In Colijnsplaat there were about thirty German-Austrians billeted in the Hotel De Patrijs. That accommodation was rejected because the officer had his eye on the retirement home Rustoord, demanding that the elderly move to private addresses. As an alternative, Vicar Kluiver suggested the Christian school in the Voorstraat but the school was rejected and the German kept insisting on the retirement home. When Vicar Kluiver said that this would be very bad for the population, a grim look came on the German's face. He did not care about the people because the Germans would be able to get away with it! The German soldiers remained in the Hotel De Patrijs until the end of the war.

Italian Prisoners of War. In November 1943, sixty Italian prisoners of war were sent to the Zeeland capital of Middelburg. Among them were soldiers Gianni Gaia and his two mates. They thought they were in heaven because women wore beautiful traditional costumes and lace hats at the station where the prisoner wagons were opened. During the day they were required to transport heavy bombs from Kamperland to the beach and cook for the Germans who were in the various outposts around Kamperland, where they met a farmer's son named Johan Remijnse. At night they were locked up in the school on the Veerweg in Kamperland. At the end of October the three Italians decided to flee and reach the Allied armies. The second evening after their flight they were picked up again by German soldiers. They were taken to the German Ortskommandant in Kamperland. Gianni Gaia did not understand German, but understood well what he was told: "Tomorrow fruh, Kaputt!" meaning Gianni Gaia and his colleagues would be shot the next day. That same evening they fled again and approached the Bouw en Plantlust farm where the son, Johan Remijnse brought them into safety, where they hid in a shed at the neighboring farm of the family De Kam.

The town welcomes the Canadians in Nov 1944

On the day of the liberation, a large Canadian with a pulled revolver flew into the barn at De Kam, where he had seen a uniform at the window, and pulled the three Italians out of the barn. They were happy that they were found by the Allies and not by Germans. The Canadians also took forty or fifty Germans from the Bouw en Plantlust shed, who had crept into the shed the previous night.

All of the prisoners of war, Germans and Italians, were brought together and held at Stekeldijk near the Remijnse farm. They were then marched off. The Italians walked behind, and they waved goodbye to the residents of Bouw en Plantlust and De Kam because they were very happy that they had survived.

Armenian Prisoners of War. A company of Armenian prisoners of war from the 809th Armenian Infantry Battalion was sent to Noord-Beveland on 8 January 1944 where they were required to perform services for the Germans such as bringing water and loads to the bunkers in Kamperland. Various Zeeland and Noord-Beveland women had relationships with Armenians and children were born. After D-day, the 809th Armenian Infantry Battalion leaves the island of Noord-Beveland and Zuid-Beveland, going to Hoedekenskerke, where they are transferred by boat. Many Armenians were picked up later and placed in labor camps for 25 years because they had worked with the enemy.

Rounding up the Germans, November 1944

Marinus Neerhout
(1902-1966)

Marien Fortuin
(1909-1981)

1st Lt. Ian Jan Haverlaar
Killed In Action

A Special Story. On the night of 24 to 25 November 1944, the first significant action took place after the liberation invasion. German commandos land from Schouwen-Duiveland on the coast of Noord-Beveland near the harbor of Oesterput, west of Colijnsplaat. One of the goals is to blow up the lock at Colijnsplaat. After landing, the Germans walk in the direction of the village and look for a car to carry the many ammunitions. At the first farm they encounter, the De Regt family, farmer Corrie de Regt and Martinus Neerhout, an evacuee from Schouwen-Duiveland, ask what they are doing? The answer is, "We need a car."

When the Germans had left, Neerhout took the bicycle from the Bakster (maternity nurse) Neeltje Kloosterman from Colijnsplaat, who was in the house because of the birth of daughter Anneke de Regt. A bicycle bag hung on the bike and it banged against the spokes of the rear wheel when he was riding, making a rattling noise. Neerhout was afraid that the Germans would hear it so he put the bicycle on his back for about a hundred meters and only then started cycling to Colijnsplaat to warn the Irene Brigade.

In Colijnsplaat, Neerhout tells the Domestic Forces (BS) what is going on. He is taken to the commander of the Irene Brigade. Moments later a BS man comes with Marien Fortuin, a servant at the De Regt farm, who tells the same story. Fortuin runs into the Germans in his way to the farm. They force him to push their car, but the Germans don't pay attention so he takes off. He kicks off his clogs and runs on his stockings through the country back to Colijnsplaat. Because Neerhout also tells the same thing, the situation is taken seriously.

The commander of the Irene Brigade decides to take action. There is a phone call in Colijnsplaat: "Germans have landed and are inside Colijnsplaat". A firefight takes place at the De Valle drainage locks and the Germans retreat towards the Oesterput but it has become low tide so they cannot retreat to Schouwen-Duiveland via the water.

First Lieutenant Havelaar of the Irene Brigade is directed to reconnaissance the homestead Koningsheim of the Van der Weele family on the Wantesweg. They first search the barns to see if there are any Germans. Havelaar then decides with 2 more soldiers to go and have a look at the seawall. Havelaar is fatally shot when looking over the sea dyke. A targeted artillery bombardment by the Irene Brigade followed, during which the German commander died. The Germans then surrender.

LIBERATION

The island of Noord-Beveland is liberated on 1 and 2 November 1944 by the Canadians. Victims at this action: Canadians none. Dutch Resistance 1 man killed, and one civilian injured in Kamperland by mortar fire. The total number of German casualties was: 6 dead and 457 prisoners of war, including 6 wounded and 2 members of the Luftwaffe who were captured on 31 October.

Germans occupied the island of Schouwen-Duiveland until May, 1945. After liberation, the authority and defense of the Island Noord - Beveland is entrusted to the Canadian Reconnaissance Regiment of the 52 Lowland Division. On November 15, 1944, the Recce (Reconnaissance Department) of the Royal Brigade Princess Irene is sent to Noord-Beveland for surveillance and is stationed in Colijnsplaat. They are under the command of the 4th Command, which had relieved the 52 Lowland Division.

The Lt. Ian Haverlaar Funeral. On Sunday 26 November 1944, First Lieutenant Ian Jacob Havelaar is buried with military honor, and with great interest of the population, at the cemetery in Colijnsplaat. After the liberation on 5 May 1945, he is reburied in the family grave at the Hillegersberg Rotterdam cemetery.

In the facade of the Reformed Church in Colijnplaat, a monument to this incident was unveiled on November 25, 1949 and the Dorpsstraat was renamed Havelaarstraat in 1952. The widow Havelaar donates the helmet on November 1, 1992, which is mounted next to the monument. On Friday 19 May 2017, 1st Lt. Havelaar is reburied with military ceremony in Colijnsplaat. The family talks about him "coming home." The circle is complete.

In Memoriam. Each year a ceremony is held in Noord-Beveland to remember Lt. Havelaar. On April 12, 2017, Marien Fortuin and Marinus Neerhout are posthumously honored with a square and a path, the ML Fortuinplein, at a ceremony attended by the two sons, Adrie Fortuin and Adrie Neerhout.

Ceremony remembering
Lt. Havelaar
May 19, 2019

The endless natural experience of Noord-Beveland

OUR MUNICIPALITY TODAY

Noord-Beveland has been one municipality since January 1, 1995, consisting of 6 unique villages where it is good to live and recreate. We call Noord-Beveland an endless island. Endless in the literal and figurative sense. The landscape offers views that you can enjoy walking or cycling. The landscape is characterized by the straight lines. The cycling and hiking trails connect the cores of the island.

The Noord-Bevelander also call themselves Peelander. That nickname originated thanks to the heavy clay soil that is rich in Noord-Beveland. It is precisely on that fertile soil that sugar beets (carrots) thrive like nowhere else. Hence "Peeland". Noord-Beveland is surrounded by three waters: on the sea side lies the wide North Sea beach, in the north the Oosterschelde as National Park, and in the south the Veerse Meer as water sports paradise. We have about fifty kilometers of endless coastline here, just as much as the whole of Belgium. Noord-Beveland just the way it is, no more and no less!

*For more information about Noord-Beveland, visit the official website: **www.noord-beveland.nl**. For more information about the history of the Second World War in Zeeland, visit the official web site of: Liberation Museum Zeeland, Nieuwdorp: **www.bevrijdingsmuseumzeeland.nl/***

This information was prepared by Gerard de Fouw of the Noord-Beveland Municipality Information Department and by Mayor Letty Demmers-van de Geest.

OOSTBURG THE NETHERLANDS

Province: Zeeland   Pop. 1940: 2,900   Pop. 2020: 4,400

SITING & HERITAGE

Oostburg is a very old small town in West Zeeland Flanders. First mentioned in the year 941, a ring rampart originally encircled Oostburg to defend against the threats of invasion by the Normans (Vikings) because Oostburg was a port city with access to both the sea and the grain polders, peat bogs and salt marshes of the Scheldt region. Originally granted city rights in 1237, Oostburg is still allowed to be called a city despite the small number of inhabitants that occupy the ten villages comprising the municipality.

Oostburg is known for "The Tower" because of its water tower that you can see from everywhere in the West-Zeeland-Flemish landscape. Oostburg was completely destroyed during the months of September and October 1944 during the fight to liberate Europe from the Germans.

Coord.: N51.3271 E3.4896

Oostburg town hall barricaded with sandbags.
June 1940

Liberated Oostburg: Top left the town hall
Top right the Reformed Church.

Camouflaged bunker after being bombed
The water tower Is in the background.

OUR TOWN'S OCCUPATION STORY

The Invasion. Nazi Germany invaded the Netherlands on 10 May 1940. Within a few days the Dutch cabinet fled to London with Queen Wilhelmina where the Dutch government remained in exile until the Liberation. Even though Holland capitulated on May 15th, the province of Zeeland continued to resist the invasion because of the French and Belgian troops in the area who had come to the aid of the Netherlands.

However, after a heavy bombing of nearby Middelburg by the German Luftwaffe, the French and Belgian troops were forced to withdraw and on 30 May 1940, Oostburg became the last place in the Netherlands to fall into the hands of Nazi Germany. The French and Belgian troops left a trail of destruction behind so that nothing of military value could be acquired and used by the enemy.

The Occupation. in the early days of the occupation, few changes were noticeable and many of the residents thought that the occupation would not last long. Over time however, this thought changed. A number of buildings were taken over by the Germans to be headquarters or lookout posts and defensive bunkers and trenches were built by the Germans, causing additional resident concerns. In time, the quantities on the food and supply distribution coupons decreased, placing the citizens under severe stress and causing the necessary development of a black market system.

Additionally, those who did not live in Zeeland were not allowed to enter without the approval of the relevant municipality authorities. All of these conditions caused the population to become increasingly against and fearful of the occupier. During the winter of 44/45, the food shortages became critical when the Nazis cut off all food supplies to western Holland in retaliation for a railway strike called for by Queen Wilhelmina (the Honger Winter).

The Resistance. There was a great deal of resistance activity in Oostburg and towards the end of the war the resistance fighters made themselves heard more and more. For example, on the evening of 3 August 1944, the newly-filled safe of the Oostburg distribution office in the former bank building was raided for ration cards and vouchers in order to provide food for people who were living in hiding. The idea came from the Oostburg music teacher Cor Schijve, known to the resistance as "Van Gent". In his home "Viva La Musica", a room had been dug under the floor of the music room where there was room for five people in hiding.

Besides Mr. Schijve, there were other people who helped to ensure that the raid came to a successful conclusion. For example, the safe key was handed over by the police officer who took it to the Marechaussee barracks every afternoon at noon to another person who arranged for the key to reach the craftsmiths teacher at the craft school, who then made a replica of it. After the raid, the booty was hidden in a chicken coop, after which it was sorted in the house "Viva La Musica". A total of 33,892 ration cards and 89,000 ration vouchers were stolen. During the raid, French was spoken to make it seem as if the raid was committed by a Belgian resistance group. On June 27, 1944, a postman was successfully robbed by the resistance to intercept a police report containing the names of resistance members.

TWO SPECIAL OOSTBURG STORIES.

Oostburg, The Nursing Center. *In the Sint Antonius Hospital, wounded civilians and soldiers from all corners of West Zeeland Flanders were received and nursed, especially during the liberation. As the Allies approached in their advance, the hospital also became fuller and fuller. As a result, it was decided to not only nurse victims in the hospital, but the local furniture trade and the Evangelization buildings were also set up as wards.*

After Oostburg had been bombed and shot a number of times, it was decided on 12 October 1944 to transfer all the sick and wounded to the Red Cross village of Groede, a village north of Oostburg. The journey to Groede started with carts and wagons covered with white sheets on which red crosses were painted. A day after everyone was transferred, the hospital became the target of a bombing and artillery fire.

The Oostburg Water Tower. *The present water tower, for which Oostburg is known, was built after the war in 1949/1950. His predecessor, the old water tower, had a hard time in the war and is blown up after just two years.*

In 1939, construction of the old water tower was started in the front part of Breedestraat. Due to the mobilization, construction work was quickly halted and the tower remained in scaffolding for a long time. Only in 1942 did the Germans give permission to complete the construction of the old water tower. The reason for this was that the tower was an ideal vantage point for combating Allied aircraft on their bombing flights to the German Ruhr area.

The Old Water Tower

After a number of rocket bombs hit the tower on September 29 and 30, 1944, the Germans decided to blow up the old water tower on October 1, 1944. This was done because the tower became too dangerous for them as a lookout and observation post. The tower was also a good beacon for the Allies on their bombing flights to the Ruhr area.

At eight o'clock in the evening, the 60-meter-high, barely two-year-old structure went up into the air with an enormous explosion, resulting in a half-collapsed water tower that remained as a ruin.

LIBERATION & RECOVERY

Liberation. The liberation of Oostburg, as part of operation "Swichback", was a terrible struggle. Oostburg was repeadedly bombed on 23, 29 and 30 September and on 6, 11, 13, 17 and 18 October 1944 by the advancing Allies. Oostburg was also regularly under fire during the liberation with long lasting and heavy artillery fire. The entire Oostburg market center was on fire.

Sometimes, after the bombing and shelling, it took days before the recovery of the victims could start. Everything the Germans could hide in the town was destroyed by the Allies, resulting in rubble, rubble and rubble. After it ended, nothing but rubble was left of the centuries-old Oostburg. In addition to all of the material damage, more than 100 local victims were also to be regretted. Oostburg had been totally destroyed.

Recovery. When all the misery was over, the residents started to clean up and build emergency houses, reconstruction was started and Oostburg received a new street plan.

When the war is almost over, Oostburg receives a high visitor. On 13 March 1945, Queen Wilhelmina crossed the border with Belgium and set foot on Dutch soil for the first time in a long time. Along her journey she stops in Oostburg to drink coffee at the notary J. Mijs, after which she continued on her journey. A memorial stone placed at the front door of the house reminds us of this event.

The new water tower of Oostburg today.

OUR TOWN TODAY

Since it was completely destroyed during World War II, Oostburg is a typical reconstruction city and the architecture from the 50s can be seen everywhere in Oostburg. With wide streets and large shops, Oostburg is a small version of a big city, developing over the years to become the centerpiece of the West Zeeuws-Vlaanderen region.

Blessed with an excellent location, Oostburg is less than 10 km from the sea, less than 30 km from Brugge and less than 50 km from Gent. Lying immediately adjacent to the beautiful Zeeland islands and surrounded by natural beauty, Oostburg is an ideal location to visit, live and raise a family. The municipality is making a concerted effort to develop these assets to increase local tourism and to create a healthy environment for businesses to operate and flourish.

Oostburg also places a great deal of importance in protecting and enhancing the natural environment in and around the community and continuing the enhancement of those facilities that are important to the local residents including our hospital, health care and nursing home facilities, our primary and secondary schools and our extensive shopping and entertainment venues.

*For more information about Oostburg, visit the municipal website: **www.oostburg.nl**. For more information about the history of the Second World War in Zeeland, we suggest you visit the official web site of: Liberation Museum Zeeland (please see Page 187) **www.bevrijdingsmuseumzeeland.nl/***

We appreciate the efforts of Thijs Groosman to prepare this information so that this commemorative document could be created. Photos courtesy of the municipality of Oostburg.

REUSEL-DE MIERDEN THE NETHERLANDS

Province: Noord-Brabant   Pop. 1940: 3,000   Pop. 2020: 13,100

SITING & HERITAGE

Since the municipal reorganization in 1997, Reusel-De Mierden has consisted of the town of Reusel and the villages of Hooge Mierde, Lage Mierde and Hulsel. It has an area of 78 km² and is located at an altitude of 30 m. The municipality has a mainly village character, although recent new construction at the end of the 20th century has given the city center a more urban character.

Reusel-De Mierden as a residential center probably originated in the 7th century and historically has had an agricultural past. At the end of the 19th century, more and more companies gradually established themselves in the municipality. Initially these were mainly cigar factories, later textile and agricultural businesses related to them were added.

GPS Coord.: N51.3661 E5.1729

Forced laborers in the camp of Karlsruhe

Destroyed village center with church and Sisters' Convent

1940-1945: THE BATTLE OF REUSEL

The Invasion. In the night of May 10, 1940, the roar of many aircraft over Reusel indicates that the German attack on the Netherlands has begun. By 11 May the Belgian border detachment, which is stationed in Reusel, is forced to withdraw. In a rapid advance, the first German soldiers enter Reusel on 12 May and occupy the area.

Because the Belgian and French troops have entrenched themselves just over the border along the Arendonk canal, the German advance is delayed considerably in the area but, on May 14, after fierce fighting and shelling, the Germans break the resistance, leaving the inhabitants with much fear and damage.

The Occupation. While the Germans continued their attack on Belgium and France, the street scene in Reusel became less and less dominated by German soldiers. When Belgium capitulated, they almost completely disappeared. Day after day, the roar of planes on their way to the front lines could still be heard.

Starting on May 16, 1940, German ordinances and regulations were regularly promulgated and forced onto the residents. They were not pleasant, but they were tolerable, so the occupation was experienced as fairly mild during the first year. However, as the war progressed, the regulations became increasingly strict.

Reusel was also faced with the strict enforcement of the blackout measures, the introduction of the distribution master card and the identity card (Ausweis), and the replacement of Mayors by pro-German Mayors. The Germans adapted their administrative structure efficiently to life in Reusel. Many were drastic measures, of which for Reusel the Arbeitseinsatz (forced labor) was the most drastic.

Compulsory Employment in Germany. All men aged 18 to 35 were required to report for posting to Germany, except for those who worked in agriculture. Many Reusel people tried to get out of employment by registering at the town hall as "indispensable for agriculture", by going into hiding or by forging Ausweis (identity) forms.

As a countermeasure, the occupier set up a new investigative apparatus called the Arbeitskontrolldienst, which regularly held raids. The situation of the people in hiding was difficult and dangerous for everyone. After all, when they and the person hiding them were discovered, they faced severe punishment. However, even that was much better than staying in one of the labor camps. Some residents had to leave their lives in Reusel forever.

Destroyed farm by detonation of landmines in Kerkstraat

Resistance. During the war, there was mainly passive resistance in Reusel, such as the hiding of people and Jewish children, the evasion of the distribution system by clandestinely slaughtering and the withdrawal of agricultural products from the food supply. In addition to helping their own inhabitants and people in hiding, food was collected to help smuggle and provide assistance to crashed pilots and paratroopers.

As far as active resistance is concerned, the resistance group Partizanen Actie Nederland (P.A.N.) operated in Reusel. The Reusel group was part of the De Kempen district. Jan Schuit, a customs officer who was stationed in Reusel at the time, was commander of the P.A.N. Group Reusel.

The group raided the supply distribution office in Bladel and the municipal administration of Reusel passed on relevant data to the Allies about the strength and troop movements of the Germans and brought crashed pilots and paratroopers to safe areas via secret routes. The local population helped the resistance group in this.

The Jewish Oppenheim brothers are hidden in Reusel

THE DEADLY DILEMMA FACED BY AN ENTIRE REUSEL FAMILY.

The Geert Janssen Family

*On September 18, 1944, when Eindhoven is already liberated, the Germans are working hard to consolidate their defensive position in Reusel and they need Reusel manpower. A German officer demands from **Geert Janssen**, who was then Deputy Mayor of Reusel, that he appoint a few hundred men to dig trenches for the Germans. If he doesn't obey his order, he will be shot with his entire family, the threat says.*

Because the Mayor and all civil servants have already gone into hiding and Geert Janssen is the only one who has remained in his post, he is faced with the question of conscience how to respond to this order.

Hundreds of men are now fleeing into the woods. The population of Reusel also wonders in agony how to act. When the German officer repeats his order again and further announces that he will begin the executions at two o'clock if the demand is not met, the panic of conscience has turned into panic among many. Everyone wants to save the Janssen family, but no one wants to help the Germans. The dilemma is great. The fleeing men deliberate again. Finally, 75 young men go to the place designated to report for work. They wait there for a few hours, but the German officer does not show up. Later it turns out that he was dead.

THE BATTLE OF REUSEL & LIBERATION

The Battle of Reusel & Liberation. Reusel-De Mierden was a very strategic place for both the Germans and the Allies. For the Allies, because they needed to prevent the Germans from breaking through the flanks of the Market Garden offensive and they needed to be able to establish control of the supply route from Antwerp as quickly as possible.

For the Germans, because they needed to control the area between Eindhoven and Turnhout to prevent the Allies from using this important road to transport the supply of troops and equipment from the already liberated Antwerp. Moreover, the Germans wanted to keep this escape route open to the north towards Tilburg. That is why the retreating German army offers fierce resistance, despite great losses. In a few days they converted Reusel into a fortress with many barricades.

When the British troops launch their attack, they meet fierce resistance. In the ten days that the Battle of Reusel lasts, the fierce fighting increases from day to day. The population flees and seeks shelter in bomb shelters. Fear, grief and food shortages create dire conditions. More bombs, bullets and grenades are needed to take out the occupiers because their defense is so tough. Hundreds of soldiers are killed, dozens of civilians are killed. After a week of bloody house-to-house, man-to-man, and even inside the church fighting, the pretty village is left with nothing but burning ruins. Besides the church and the two monasteries, many houses and farms have been destroyed or seriously damaged.

When the Germans withdraw, the refugee civilians cautiously return from their hiding places to find that their village and properties have been destroyed or damaged by horrific violence. British soldiers of the Welsh Division describe the fighting in their war reports as "Little Stalingrad". The sacrifice for Reusel's freedom is great but the occupier has been banished from the area. It was October 3, 1944.

The Recovery. After the liberation, the municipality is faced with the difficult task of repairing the destroyed center and the much destroyed and damaged houses. The will is present in the population, but the materials and money are lacking to realize a definitive reconstruction. In the first years, it will be limited to temporary repair work.

The creative mind of some villagers, however, manages to compose a revue. By performing this show, in which the war past is portrayed with a smile and a tear, 43 times, they managed to collect more than 30,500 guilders, with which the church can be somewhat restored. From the summer of 1946 services can again be held in the church. At around the same time, the boys' school can also be reopened. Until that time, one has to make do with spaces in the provisionally restored brother monastery.

The general restoration of the sister monastery did not begin until the early 1950s, and later it was decided to demolish the brother monastery and proceed to a complete new construction. But the scars of the completely destroyed village can still be seen to this day. Only now, in 2020, is a hesitant start being made to completely redevelop the city center.

Reusel church square & town hall today

View of the Dorpsbron area that had suffered a lot of war damage

OUR TOWN TODAY

Nowadays Reusel-De Mierden with its 13,000 inhabitants is a peaceful municipality with lots of space and natural beauty, quietly located on the border with Belgium in the beautiful Kempenland.

The municipality is in full swing and offers many leisure opportunities for both residents and tourists, especially through the extensive international network of equestrian, cycling and hiking trails.

The natural beauty, the good educational opportunities, the favorable employment opportunities and the proximity of the important brainports of Europe makes Reusel-De Mierden a living community that offers its residents excellent living conditions and visitors a wonderful and peaceful place to visit, relax and enjoy the many local restaurants and shops.

*For more information about Reusel, visit the municipal website: **www.reuseldemierden.nl**. For more information about the World War II museum in Reusel and other local tourism opportunities, visit: **www. ipreusel-demierden.nl/**.*

We appreciate the efforts of the Heemkunde Werkgroep Reusel to prepare this information so that this commemorative document could be created. Photos courtesy of the Heemkunde Werkgroep Reusel.

STRIJEN THE NETHERLANDS

Province: South Holland   Pop. 1940: 4,000   Pop. 2020: 6,700

SITING & HERITAGE

A member of the Hoeksche Waard municipality, Strijen is a small town less than 30 km south of Rotterdam. Located along the Hollandsch Diep River where the river is 3 km wide and adjacent to the strategically-important Moerdijk bridge, the residents of Strijen found themselves at the tip of the spear of the Nazi invasion of the Netherlands on May 10, 1940.

The residents of Strijen were first hand witnesses to one of the war's greatest tragedies, the complete destruction of the city of Rotterdam in a matter of days. This is the story of what the residents were feeling when, all of a sudden, their lives and their country were being destroyed and they were about to become occupied by a ruthless and violent German Nazi regime.

GPS Coord.: N51.7450 E4.5535

PREPARING FOR AN INVASION

Molenstraat Strijen Circa 1930

Life in the Netherlands 1939. The Netherlands was a tidy country. It did not interfere with world politics. It was not on the German side, neither on the British or French side: the Netherlands was a neutral country. It approached everything correctly and neatly. The Dutch people were reliable people who worked hard. The Netherlands was a country that smelled of soap and soda: a country where delicate church towers rose above vast polders and where children played games on the 31st of August, the day when the Queen celebrated her birthday. Could a country such as the Netherlands really be attacked? From time to time people looked somewhat anxious in the eastern direction. Something seemed to be going on in the German empire.

Strijen surely noticed some changes. When the Netherlands prepared its army for a possible war, it stationed soldiers in our village. Strijen is not far from the Hollandsch Diep river and the enemy would try to conquer Western Netherlands, which includes the most important cities, as quickly as possible. If the enemy would approach, perhaps they could be held back by a wide river such as the Hollandsch Diep that the enemy would not cross. Additionally, because the Netherlands is a low-lying country, large areas of land could be flooded. In this way, the enemy could be held back and Western Netherlands could be protected. At least, one thought so.

In the context of national defense, Strijen was strategically located. At the beginning of September 1939, the Voluntary Land Storm and Air Observer Corps Strijen worked from the tower of the city hall. This service had the task to control the air situation. At the same time, the 11th Searchlight Department appeared. Its duty was to locate enemy airplanes during the night with the help of strong light beams so they could be shot down. The 11th Searchlight Department used air defence artillery for the shootings. It set up searchlights in the Land van Essche district, at J.J. Overwater's farm, at A.J. Herweijer's farm in the grassland of the village Strijensas and in the village Cillaarshoek. It also installed an air defence artillery near A. Troost's farm along the Langedam road (Nieuw-Bonaventura).

Strijen's city hall staff were very busy with accommodating the Dutch soldiers. The soldiers had accommodation in both farms and ordinary homes. Various military departments spent the winter doing preparedness exercises and expanding defense work. The department of leisure and development tried to combat boredom among the soldiers. They were not able to carry out many field activities due to the severe winter weather in 1939/1940.

In early April, Germany overran Norway and Denmark, which was not very promising for our country. The 23rd field artillery regiment was then stationed in Strijen at A. Voordendag's farm between the roads Morikaanseweg and Strijensedijk. Along the Hollandsch Diep river, two infantry battalions of the 28th infantry regiment were also installed (between the villages Strijensas and 's-Gravendeel). A few years earlier, a modern bunker had been built in Strijensas which they used. The bunker was located more than one kilometre from the bridges of Moerdijk. Considering everything, Strijen had a dynamic mobilization period; busy and pleasant!

Street block at the Boompjesstraat

It seemed that there would be a beautiful Whitsun holiday weekend in May, 1940. When, on Thursday evening, May 9, the sun went down and the clear night seemed to predict a beautiful Friday. No one in Strijen expected that this would be the last evening in the Netherlands as a **FREE** country for the time being.

To keep the center of Strijen dry, a dam was built against the inundation water

THE VIEW FROM STRIJEN.

May 10, 1940. Even before the sun rose, enemy airplanes flew over our country and dropped German paratroopers. Their most important task was to conquer, among other things, the bridges of Moerdijk, less than 5 km from Strijen and the airports around The Hague in order to capture the Queen, the government and military leaders.

At 4 in the morning, Strijen awoke because of the noises of anti-aircraft guns. Dozens of German aircraft, both transport aircraft and bombers, were visible in the sky. Paratroopers came down above the riverbank of Brabant and the island Dordrecht. Along the Hollandsch Diep river, a Dutch army unit bravely defended itself.

May 10, 1940. In our village, many people went out onto the streets − a few of them still wearing nightwear − to see what was going on, witnessing a few air battles, including one above Strijen harbour. They first enjoyed the sight but they were not aware of the danger they were exposed to but soon that first day, the people of Strijensas became anxious and restless. Some found protection in the concrete shelters built along the outer-dike areas. Others left for safer places in the village.

May 11, 1940. The observer corps, stationed near the Strijenschedijk, reported that enemy aircraft were constantly flying above them. The members of the observer corps believed that they had been discovered. Therefore, they moved to an orchard along the Oud-Bonaventurasedijk, which turned out to be a wise decision: on Saturday, May 11, the Germans bombed the abandoned station. Just like the end of the first day of war, the second day began with many rumours. Would France come to the Netherlands to help? There was a lot of commotion in the city hall.

May 12, 1940. On Sunday, May 12, the German troops advanced to the previously conquered bridges of Moerdijk requiring the Dutch soldiers' ammunition to be delivered by ship. On Whit Sunday, an ammunition ship arrived at the outer harbour of Strijensas. The ship was heavily fired upon by the Germans and Skipper Van Meeteren was killed during the shooting. The helmsman, despite being seriously injured, was able to bring the boat into the harbour and after darkness, the local people helped to take the ammunition boxes from Strijensas to Strijen. The tiredness and the lack of sleep contributed to a decrease in the fighting power of the Dutch soldiers.

May 13, 1940. On Monday, May 13, there was a heavy fight with German forces in front of the Grebbeberg mountain and the Dutch troops were forced en masse to leave Strijen. The hopeless situation in the country had become clear. The Queen and ministers decided to move to England to continue to fight from there.

May 14, 1940. On Tuesday, May 14, the city Rotterdam was devastatingly bombed, the Dutch army decided to surrender and the Netherlands fell into German hands. Rotterdam will never forget Tuesday, May 14, 1940, and neither will Strijen. A number of German planes dropped bombs, designated for Rotterdam, on other places, including Strijen and Strijensas. The German bombs damaged the church as well. When the bombing ended, the local people spontaneously started to clean up the mess. Many people rolled up their sleeves. Strijen was at its best!

When the evening fell, people could see a firelight in the distance. It was the firelight of the countless fires in Rotterdam. Due to the wind, the remains of burnt textile, supplies and books ended up in Strijen. After the capitulation, the soldiers, who had survived the war so far, returned to the village, helping to clean up the mess and returning to their homes afterwards.

Five days of war have come to an end. Strijen had experienced a lot in the past few days. Life has suddenly become very strange, completely different. How long would the war last? No one could give a meaningful answer. Germany was so powerful! The people had no idea what awaited them, which was − in retrospect − a good thing.

Four examples of the 14 May 1940 damage in Strijen from that single day of German bombing

LIBERATION.

During October, 1944, the Canadian Army forces fought many major battles to remove the Germans from South Holland but the emphasis placed on Operation Market Garden in eastern Holland combined with Hitler's order that Holland be held at all costs prolonged the war in Strijen.

Strijen remained trapped between two opposing armies throughout the 44/45 winter and, because of the Honger Winter imposed by the Germans which extended throughout all of western Holland, the residents live under starvation conditions even though the Allies were able to parachute food to provide some relief. The Germans doggedly held on north of the Moerdijk bridge throughout the winter and it wasn't until Germany surrendered in May, 1945 that Strijen was liberated.

Rejoicing in the Liberation with the Canadian victors!

OUR TOWN TODAY

Today, Strijen is a charming small town with lots of activities and attractions for residents and visitors alike. Located in an area designated as a National Landscape, the many hiking, cycling and canoeing opportunities throughout the Hoeksche Waard municipality are treasured by the residents and visitors alike.

The Strijen community develops and presents many cultural programs and events throughout the year adding immeasurably to the lives of the residents and the many visitors who come to enjoy them. We invite you to experience the unique combination of natural serenity and vibrant bustling life that is Strijen.

Scenes of Strijen today: One serene; One bustling & lively

*For more information about Strijen, the Hoeksche Waard municipality and the local area visit **www.gemeentehw.nl**.*

Much of the information used to prepare this commemorative document was derived from the Museum Het Land van Strijen document: "Strijen In Wartime, Chapter 2: "Five Scary Days". Photos courtesy of the municipality of Strijen.

WOENSDRECHT THE NETHERLANDS

Province: North Brabant   **Pop. 1940: 11,500**   **Pop. 2019: 21,800**

SITING & HERITAGE

A municipality with a rich archeological and medieval history, Woensdrecht was first mentioned as Wunsdrech in 1249. Today, the Woensdrecht municipality includes the villages of Woensdrecht (1,600), Hoogerheide (8,200), Ossendrecht (5,500), Putte (4,000) and Huijbergen (2,500) and a total population of 21,800.

The landscape in the Woensdrecht area is a unique landscape due to the 'Brabantse Wal' area where the land is as much as 20 m (60 ft) higher than the surrounding natural elevations, much of it beautifully forested, rolling hills. Much of the areas surrounding the Brabantse Wal is below sea level.

Located just north of Antwerp in the Scheldt River basin, the area has always been an important area to control during conflicts between nations because of the area's higher elevations and strategic location. Many sea control structures and dikes exist throughout the area.

GPS Coord.: N51.4293 E4.3047

THE BATTLE OF WOENSDRECHT

During the Second World War, the Woensdrecht area was of great strategic importance for the German occupying forces because of its location on the Brabantse Wal and its proximity to the River Sheldt. In September, 1944, even though the Allies controlled Antwerp, German forces continued to control the Woensdrecht area in order to harass and prevent Allied shipping from reaching Antwerp.

It was also an important village for the Allies because it was the only area that had access to the North Sea islands of South and North Beveland of the Zeeland Province. If the Canadians could conquer the Woensdrecht area, the German forces in the West would be trapped and cut off from all other German forces.

Despite Antwerp's great importance, in September, 1944, the Allies concentrated their major advance into the Netherlands with Operation Market Garden, leaving the front line around Antwerp virtually unchanged for one month. However, by the end of September Canadian troops came into the area to break the German hold on the Woensdrecht area. The first goal was to secure the Scheldt estuary.

On 28 September 1944, the 2nd Canadian Infantry Division crossed the Antwerp-Turnhout Canal and began its attack to liberate the Scheldt. In the beginning it went well until they approached the higher elevations of the Brabantse Wal. On October 7, 1944 the 'Battle of Woendrecht' began.

Canadian troop column on the
Hoogerheide Antwerpsestraatweg

The Germans had superior infantry numbers, made up of veterans of various battles and included the 6th Fallschirmjäger Regiment which was notorious for its fanaticism. Many of the Canadian soldiers were still very inexperienced but the Canadians had the advantage thanks to artillery and air support.

On the night of 7 to 8 October, 'unprecedented heavy' street fighting took place at the beginning of the Raadhuisstraat Street in the village of Hoogerheide, now known as 'the devastated corner'. There were as many as 60 to 70 soldiers killed.

On Friday, October 13th, one of the most bloody battles was fought. The Canadian Black Watch Regiment conducted a frontal attack on an open field against well-prepared German positions. The result was a disaster. The Black Watch lost 183 man, including 56 deaths. Since then, this day is known to Canadian soldiers as Black Friday.

Despite the very heavy losses, the Royal Hamilton Light Infantry was able to conquer the Germans on 16 October under the direction of Colonel Dennis Whitaker. Colonel Whitaker took residence at the local farm of the family van Beek. From the farm, Whitaker prepared and directed the plan for the Battle of the Scheldt and the Battle of Woensdrecht.

The heavily damaged Woensdrecht church and rectory
after the battle between the Germans and the Canadiens

A SPECIAL STORY—THE DUTCH JAMES BOND

Bram Grisnigt – Spy of Orange (1923-2019)

He was called the Dutch James Bond. It is 1941 and The Netherlands is occupied. Eighteen-year-old **Bram Grisnight** cycles towards France to gain freedom and meets Piet Hoekman and the two of them board a ship to Curacao, Venezuela.

On Bram's solo return trip to England, the ship is torpedoed near Jamaica but he is rescued by the US Navy and taken to the US. He soon travels to a military training camp in Canada where he becomes a member of the Princess Irene Brigade. Nineteen months later he arrives in London where he is trained as a secret agent for MI6 and meets the love of his life, Ann.

He returns to the Netherlands as liaison between London and the resistance, continually communicating with his SOE handlers in London and various local resistance groups in The Netherlands. Bram Grisnigt survives many close calls in his dangerous work and he must constantly be on the move to stay one step ahead of the Gestapo. In February 1944 he is arrested and interned in Amsterdam where his stamina is seriously tested.

He survives brutal interrogations by the Gestapo, several concentration camps and a death march during which the cunning Bram escapes, then finds the love of his life Ann and they both move to Curacao, Venezuela where Bram does international work for Shell Oil for more than 30 years. In 1974 they return to the Woensdrect area permanently.

Bram and Ann Grisnigt

After surviving a torpedoing, the Gestapo, concentration camps, a death march and personally seeing his friends die, Bram never speaks of his espionage work after the war. Only his great love Ann knows everything. Shortly after the death of his beloved wife Ann, Bram also passed away on 11 January 2019.

The war story of Bram Grisnigt is recorded in a 2016 book, "Spy of Orange" (ISBN 9789026335396). The book was written for the younger generation so that they know of the occupation and liberation and the sacrifices that were endured, often by young people of their age. To read more about the wartime accomplishments and trials of this remarkable man, please visit the Oorlogs Graven Stichting (War Graves Foundation) website: https://oorlogsgravenstichting.nl/persoon/225539/reijer-abraham-grisnigt

LIBERATION AND RECOVERY

The resulting battles left Woensdrecht and Hoogerheide almost completely destroyed by bombing and door-to-door fighting. It took many years to rebuild these two beautiful villages.

Colonel Whitaker moved to Canada after the war where be became a star quarterback for the Hamilton Tigers of the Canadian pro football league.

Retiring from the Army as a Brigadier General, Whitaker returned to Woensdrect in the 1970's to apologize for shooting the lock off the town hall door to get what he needed to build his command shack. When 100 of the townspeople welcomed him, there was the oak door, long since repaired.

THE RESISTANCE HERO SJEF ADRIAANSEN

In 1939, Hoogerheidenaar **Sjef Adriaansen** was called up for military service. During the mobilization and the war year of 1940, he was active as guardian in the Second Regiment Huzaren Motorijder, After the capitulation, he applied for the military police. In 1942 he decided to leave for England, using the so-called Van Niftik route.

Sjef Adriaansen

In 1943 he received training in England as a secret agent at the Information Office of the Dutch Government. On January 11, 1944, He was dropped in the neighborhood of Princenhage (Noord-Brabant to serve as the liaison between the organized resistance in West Brabant and the Information Office in London.

On July 14, 1944, his station was tracked in Hoeven by the Germans and he was taken prisoner. He was shot on 5 September 1944 in Vught. Partly due to the street in Hoogerheide named after him and the plaque in the municipal hall, his name is forever connected to Woensdrecht. For more information about Sjef's achievements in wartime, visit the website of the Brabant Historical Information Center: www.brabantsegesneuvelden.nl/person/sjef-adriaansen-woensdrecht-1919.

The village center of Woensdrecht today

OUR TOWN TODAY

Today the Woensdrecht municipality is composed of five village centers, creating a thriving municipality with a wide range of facilities, a vibrant business community employing more than 9,000 local residents and a diverse collection of many excellent restaurants and shops.

The Woensdrecht area is known for its agricultural production but even more for the extensive recreational opportunities in the local forested natural areas, especially the many cycling routes. Woensdrecht residents are known for their love of cycling.

Economic development in the fields of aviation, nature and tourism-recreational development are the spearheads of the town's municipal policy. Known for its annual Brabant Wal festival, each year the town holds a remembrance of the suffering the Battle of Woensdrect brought to the residents.

The Hoogeheide-Woensdrecht Monument

The Woensdrecht Sherman Tank Monument

For more information about Woensdrecht please visit the town's official website: www.woensdrecht.nl. For more information about the region's many tourism opportunities, please visit: www.vvvbrabantsewal.nl. Photos courtesy of the municipality of Woensdrecht.

ZUIDPLAS THE NETHERLANDS

Province: South Holland   Pop. 1940: 10,600   Pop. 2020: 43,000

SITING & HERITAGE

Zuidplas is a community whose heritage has been dictated by the deep, extensive peat bogs that covered vast areas of the region for centuries. Zuidplas was largely uninhabited until the Middle Ages when peat, because of a lack of timber, became the most important fuel in Holland and ways were found to harvest peak as much as 3 meters below the water table, resulting in creating deep bog holes that turned into huge lakes with bottom elevations approximately 6 meters below sea level.

The current lowest point in Holland and in fact, the entire European Union was created when the Zuidplaspolder was drained in 1841 which created land surface areas 6 meters below sea level. Protected by an extensive system of dikes and pumping stations, all major land development decisions have, since then, been based on water control and a concern about land subsidence and salt water intrusion.

GPS Coord.: N52.0069 E4.5828

THE OCCUPATION OF ZUIDPLAS

Inlet pipes used by the Germans
to flood the polders

The Invasion. In May 1940, the Zuidplas area began seeing some residents from southeastern Holland arrive who were escaping the invading German army. Fortunately only two men from Zevenhuizen fell between the start of the May 10th German invasion and the Dutch capitulation on May 14, 1944. During that period, a German Junker bomber crashed on the Zevenhuizense Bierhoogtweg and a Dutch pilot had to make an emergency landing on national highway 12 after an aerial fight with a German Fokker.

On 14 May 1940 in Moordrecht, a Dutch military driver, Jan Gaartman, was shot dead by a Dutch lieutenant because he thought he was a spy! The noise and smoke of the bombing of nearby Rotterdam was witnessed by the residents. The bombing brought shreds of paper into the villages and the burning fires could be seen at night. The fires soon brought people into the village who were escaping the flames.

The Occupation. During March 1944, large polder sections were inundated by the Germans in Nieuwerkerk aan den IJssel, Zevenhuizen and Moerkapelle "to prevent the liberation". Quays were built and inlet pipe installed and arrangements were made with the existing pumping stations wherever possible to limit the inundation of areas by the Germans to protect as many properties as possible. There was always the fear that the Germans would blow holes in the protective dikes.

There were a number of local tragedies that occurred during the times just before the Liberation. On 25 February 1945, Nieuwerkerk policeman Rokus Fonkert was robbed and killed for money and food by resistance fighters from the Rotterdam area. On March 19, 1945, the RAF mistakenly bombed a Nieuwerkerk road and eleven people were killed from the De Groot, Steenbergen, Stuit, Pols, Van Bezooyen and Van Herk families. On 11 April 1945, an RAF Stirling E7Y aircraft made an emergency landing in a flooded area near Nieuwerkerk. Thanks to resistance fighters, the crew was rescued and taken to the hunting lodge The Jolly Duck on the Rotte river in the Zevenhuizen area.

In all four Zuidplas municipalities, church tower bells were stolen by the Germans during 1943. A replacement Van Bergen clock, dated 5 May 1945, later became the war memorial in Moerkapelle. The inscription reads: "Our people tormented by German violence, the polder flooded, the clock removed. "The tide has turned, and I have come here, may I praise God."

Resistance. In each of the four villages people were active in the resistance, especially with printing and distributing illegal papers. An 18 year-old teenager from Nieuwerkerk aan den Ijssel, **Tankie Roelofsk** was one of a group of young girls who repeatedly took great risks smuggling, delivering and distributing the newspapers across the Hollandsche Ijssel by boat, cycling long distances to do her assigned tasks.

The horticulturist resistance member **Dirk van den Dool** of Nieuwerkerk was betrayed by a strange person from Dordrecht who was in hiding here, who then left the area. Van den Dool was arrested on New Year's Eve 1944 and was taken to Camp Amersfoort, a German concentration camp in Holland at Amersfoort.

There he was shot as the Germans' revenge for an explosion by the resistance that had occurred on a signal box near the railway station in front of a house in Amersfoort on February 5, 1945. It wasn't until 14 days later that his wife and eight children in Zuidplas learned of his death.

In 1947 a memorial stone was placed at that house in Amersfoort. Van den Dool was Nieuwerkerk's only fallen resistance fighter. In 1957, "Resistance Street" was named to honor his patriotism.

HOFSTEDE 147 ZUIDPLASPOLDER

A painting depicting the flooding of the polders

THE LIBERATION OF ZUIDPLAS

On April 29, 1945, there was a German raid on the hunting lodge The Jolly Duck on the Rotte which was used by the resistance. An American aviator hiding there, a resistance fighter from Zoetermeer and twenty Turkestans who had been forced into compulsery German service were killed.

The German commander had set a trap for them and they could not escape. The Germans then buried them from boats in sacks weighted with stones. A monument was erected in 1995 for the fallen American John E. McCornick and the fallen resistance fighter Jacob L. van Rij.

In reprisal for a national railway strike called for by Queen Wilemena in London, the Germans cut off all food supplies to western Holland and during the winter of 44/45 (the Honger Winter), the people in the large cities were starving. Fortunately, due to the almost entirely agricultural character of the polders in the Zuidplas area, no one died because of famine. In any case, food drops from the Allies did take place at Moordrecht on 1 May 1945.

The Allies advance was halted at the Gouda-Rotterdam national road on 5 May because of the surrender of all German forces to the Allies. Soon after, Canadians arrived at the carpet factory in Moordrecht. One of the Canadian soldiers ultimately married the daughter of the village doctor.

Compared to areas where there was fighting, the Zuidplas villages fortunately suffered little materially. After the liberation, the Red Cross Aid Action (HARK) provided much support for the local population and the inundations because of the dike breaches were quickly repaired.

Liberation parties were organized, a four-day party taking place in Moordrecht from 28-31 August and a two day party in Nieuwerkerk on 5-6 September 1945. In August 1945, the fallen Rotterdam resistance fighter Arie den Toom was reburied in Zuidplas with military honors from the Interior Forces because he was born in Nieuwerkerk.

In Zevenhuizen the two men who died in 1940 were given a monument on 20 August 1945. In Nieuwerkerk on October 20, 1945 a memorial needle was unveiled "for those who fell because of the liberation struggle", especially for the victims of the accidental RAF bombing.

In Moordrecht, a monument was installed to honor the four deported Jews from Moordrecht and three Jews deported from Nieuwerkerk upon which a Star of David with each of their names was added to the memorial needle. In Moordrecht, an information board was also unveiled at a German artillery position in 2013.

Zuidplas memorials to the victims of World War II

The Serene Park Hitland Natural Recreation Area

OUR TOWN TODAY

Today the four villages of the Zuidplas municipality are known for their many small and medium sized businesses with strong local ties and international markets. The extensive horticulture industry in the area supplies vegetables and flowers to the entire world and recreational tourism has become a major part of the local economies.

The municipal vision emphasizes recreation and working together with entrepreneurs and the residents to achieve a more attractive and sustainable Zuidplas. Zuidplas is a green oasis of peace and space where it is pleasant to live and work. It is the vastness of the polders, the cultural history, the greenery and the water that make Zuidplas attractive.

Four mills in the Tweemanspolder   Photo: Jolanda Bakker

The meandering rivers Rotte and the Hollandse Ijssel provide many waterborne activities and the polders are a bird-watchers paradise. There are also various local trailways, all connected to a 900 km trail system. Cycling is especially popular. The regionally popular Park Hitland offers a special mix of cycling, walking, fishing, bird watching, canoeing, riding, skating and golfing opportunities for the visitor.

Of course, the cities of Rotterdam and The Hague are nearby with all the skyscrapers, international entertainment and big city attractions you can ever imagine.

To learn more about WWII in the Zuidplas villages, visit these historical websites: **www.oudzevenhuizenmoerkapelle.nl**, **www.historischeverenigingmoordrecht.nl** *and* **www.hvnweb.nl**. *Text and photos provided by Adri den Boer, secretary of the Historical Association Nieuwerkerk aan den IJssel. Sources: Bram Veerman, Between Light and Dark in Holland's "Green Heart" (1987) and Panc Vink, War and Liberation in Moordrecht (1995). Photos courtesy of the municipality of Zuidplas.*

Remembering & Honoring The Sacrifices Endured By So Many

Queen Wilhelmina of the Netherlands, late 1940s

Wilhelmina Helena Pauline Maria was the longest reigning Queen of the Netherlands in history, reigning from 1890 to 1948, her reign including both World Wars and an economic crisis in 1933 during the Great Depression. During her reign, her business investments, particularly in East Indies oil production, made her the world's richest woman and the world's first female billionaire.

Born an only child, Wilhelmina became queen in 1890 at the age of 10 when her father, King William III, died. She began her reign with her mother serving as regent but in 1898 she was sworn in as Queen. A strong-willed opponent of politicians in general, she ruled with authority, saying that only the people mattered in all decisions of government. In 1901, at the age of age 21, she married the Duke of Mecklenburg-Schwerin but the marriage ended up being an unhappy one. After numerous miscarriages, Wilhelmina finally gave birth to her only child, Juliana in 1909.

During World War I Wilhelmina managed to maintain the neutrality of the Netherlands and after the war she used her vast fortune to help the country build the massive Zuiderzee Works, a project to control the flooding by the sea and create large areas of additional agricultural land.

When Germany suddenly invaded the Netherlands on May 10, 1940, Queen Wilhelmina and her family fled to Great Britain where she set up a government-in-exile and began regular BBC broadcasts to the people of the Netherlands who eagerly looked forward to her late-night broadcasts despite the Germans' penalty of death for doing so. In 1942 and 1943 she traveled to the United States and Canada to address the US Congress and attend the christening of her granddaughter in Ottawa, returning to Britain in 1944 where she was nearly killed when a bomb severely damaged her residence, killing several of her guards.

Following the liberation of the Netherlands, in March, 1945 she returned to the Netherlands where she was warmly greeted by the people. Her failing health conditions forced her to abdicate in favor of her daughter Juliana, in 1948. Queen Wilhelmina died in 1962 at the age of 82.

Occupation Stories 2020

THE WORLD WAR II MUSEUMS OF THE NETHERLANDS

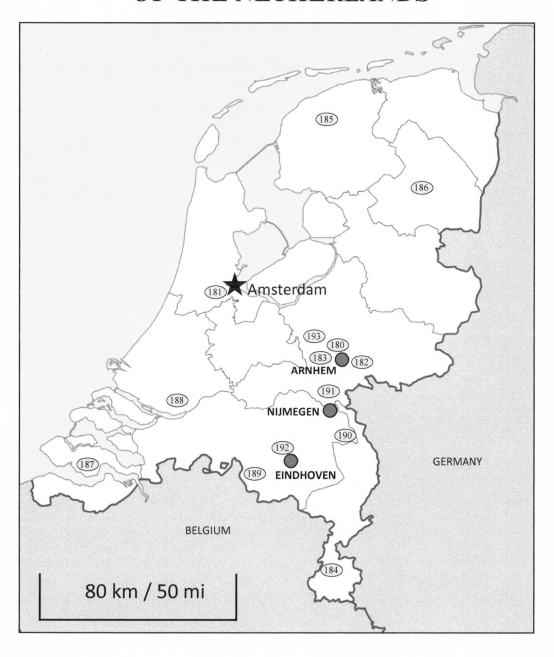

Page	Museum	Municipality	Page	Museum	Municipality
180	Airborne Museum Hartenstein	Oosterbeek	187	Liberation Museum Zeeland	Borsele
181	Anne Frank Museum	Amsterdam	188	Museum 1940-1945	Dordrecht
182	Arnhem War Museum	Arnhem	189	Museum De Bewogen Jaren 39-50	Reusel-de-Mierden
183	Betuws War Museum "The Island"	Heteren	190	Overloon War Museum	Overloon
184	Eyewitness Museum	Beek	191	Vrijheids (Freedom) Museum	Berg en Dal
185	Frisian Resistance Museum	Leeuwarden	192	Wings of Liberation Museum	Best
186	Kamp Westerbork	Midden-Drenthe	193	Wolfheze Glider Museum	Wolfheze

THE AIRBORNE MUSEUM AT HARTENSTEIN
Oosterbeek, The Netherlands

The Airborne Museum at Hartenstein

GPS Coordinates: N51.9878 E5.8328

Recently completely renovated, this innovative, high-tech and very interactive museum is a must-see for anyone interested in the important history of the Operation Market Garden Airborne operations.

Housed in the beautifully maintained Villa Hartenstein constructed in 1865, the Airborne Museum at Hartenstein is the only museum that tells the historical and socio-cultural story of the famous Battle of Arnhem. A center for remembrance, the museum is a place where national and international visitors can reflect on the Battle of Arnhem and on the important role of this battle in World War II.

In September 1944 the Allies launched Operation Market Garden, the largest airborne operation of World War II. They hoped to capture a number of bridgeheads, including the Rhine Bridge in Arnhem, now known as "The Bridge Too Far". On 17 September 1944 thousands of soldiers from the British 1st Airborne Division landed by both parachute and gliders on fields near Wolfheze and north of Heelsum, all at quite a distance from Arnhem. Some of the gliders also transported jeeps and anti-tank artillery to the battlefield areas.

On 18 September another 1900 parachutists landed on Ginkel Heath near Ede and more gliders landed at Wolfheze. Leading the second battalion of the 1st Parachutist Brigade, Lieutenant-Colonel John Frost reached the Rhine Bridge and held it during several days of heavy combat before being forced to surrender. Most of the airborne troops failed to reach the bridge due to German resistance and had to fall back to Oosterbeek. Major General Roy Urquhart was forced to set up his headquarters in Hotel Hartenstein.

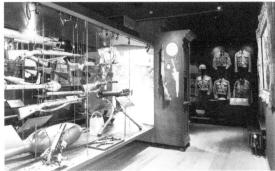

After intense fighting in which many soldiers were killed, wounded or taken prisoner of war, the British troops had to surrender their position. On 26 September Hartenstein was abandoned as the remaining troops retreated across the Rhine. The Allies had lost the Battle of Arnhem, and Hartenstein remained behind in badly damaged condition. Nearly 1,700 Allied soldiers are buried at the nearby Arnhem Oosterbeek War Cemetery.

For more information about the museum please visit the museum's website: www.airbornemuseum.nl. For more information about the municipality of Renkum, please visit the town's website at: www.renkum.nl. Photos courtesy of the museum.

THE ANNE FRANK MUSEUM
Amsterdam, The Netherlands

263 Prinsengracht

GPS Coordinates: N52.3752 E4.8839

One of the best known museums in museum-rich Amsterdam, more than 1.2 million people visit this museum each year. An experience visitors will remember their entire lives, the impact of the Nazis' Jewish racism becomes very personal. A cozy café overlooks a busy canal scene in front of the museum.

Photo: Allard Bovenberg

Photo: Cris Toala Olivares

Photo: Allard Bovenberg

*For more information about the museum and the Anne Frank story, visit **www.annefrank.org**. All photos from the Anne Frank Stichting Photo Collection, Amsterdam.*

The Secret Annex at 263 Prinsengracht, where Anne and her family went into hiding, dates from 1739. An early renovation makes the house suitable for companies that need a warehouse or large workspace and office space. Almost 200 years later, that is what Otto Frank is looking for to house his company Pectacon. In 1940 Otto Frank rents the entire building. The company's workshop is on the ground floor, and the two floors above will be office spaces and storage space.

A new connection is needed between the first and second floor. A new staircase is constructed that ends in the room where the bookcase will later be placed in front of the secret entrance to what Otto called the "Secret Annex".

When Anne's older sister Margot receives a call-up to work in a German camp in July 1942, the entire family immediately decides to go into hiding in the Secret Annex. Hermann & Auguste Van Pels with their son Peter follow a week later. The two families already know each other, Hermann van Pels working for Otto Frank's company. After four months, Fritz Pfeffer, an acquaintance of the Frank family becomes the eighth person in hiding in the Secret Annex. The lower two floors are interwoven with the business premises in the front house so a casual visitor to Prinsengracht 263 will therefore not easily suspect that there is still a whole life behind the bookcase.

Friday, August 4, 1944 is a warm, sunny day in Amsterdam. For the people in hiding, it is day 761 in the Secret Annex. Gestapo detectives suddenly appear at the property at 263 Prinsengracht between 10:30 and 11:00 am with SS-Hauptscharführer Karl Silberbauer in charge. At the warehouse on the ground floor, the agents approach an employee who directs them upstairs, where the office workers are. There is no evidence that the warehouse employees know there are people in hiding in the building.

The office staff is at work when the door suddenly opens. The detectives continue to Director Victor Kugler's office. They question him and take him to search the building. During the inspection, they also enter the room with the revolving bookcase. Even though the fleeting viewer cannot see that there is an entire house hidden behind the cupboard, the detectives find the secret entrance to the Secret Annex and the eight hiding Jews are found.

Helpers Victor Kugler and Johannes Kleiman are arrested together with the 8 people in hiding and the detectives take them away. Taken to Westerbork, they are all soon put on transports to Auschwitz where death awaits. Anne's father Otto is the only person to survive the war.

After the liberation, the building at Prinsengracht 263 is in danger of being demolished but, as the story of Anne in the Secret Annex reaches more and more people, resistance against the demolition grows and demolition is prevented in the mid-1950s. The Anne Frank House is established shortly afterwards, the building is restored and the Anne Frank House is opened on 3 May 1960.

ARNHEM WAR MUSEUM 40-45
Arnhem, The Netherlands

GPS Coord.: N52.0269 E5.8720

Being the location of the infamous "Bridge Too Far" battle during the Allies' failed Operation Market Garden, this museum presents the story from the local perspective plus a great deal of information about life in Arnhem throughout the war.

In addition to a general overview, the Arnhem War Museum gives an accurate picture of what happened in Arnhem and the surrounding area during the years of war. Following Operation Market Garden the city was evacuated and during the last months of the war the Germans looted the city, leaving a devastated city in their wake.

The purpose of this private museum is to keep alive the memory of this important episode in history and to preserve a unique collection of Operation Market Garden uniforms, weaponry and documents for posterity.

The collection has been made possible in no small part by private individuals who have donated many of these items, including many personal items with a direct connection to Operation Market Garden and the Nazi occupation. The museum focuses on preparing exhibits with love and care so these items can be appreciated by a wide audience.

These continuing donations contribute greatly to increasing the public's knowledge of the war years, especially among the young. It is the mission of the museum to ensure that the memory of the Second World War is safeguarded for all future generations to come and that the tragedies of this terrible war are remembered forever.

To obtain more information about the museum, visit **https://en.arnhemsoorlogsmuseum.com/.** *For more information about the tourism opportunities in the Arnhem area, visit* **www.visitarnhem.com.** *Photos courtesy of the museum.*

BETUWS WAR MUSEUM "THE ISLAND"
Heteren, The Netherlands

GPS Coord.: N51.9605 E5.7534

Episode 5 (The Crossroads) of the Band of Brothers TV series occurred just outside this village on October 5, 1944 when Capt. Dick Winters and 35 men of Easy Company of the 101st Airborne encountered more than 300 Germans. The Allies called this area "The Island" because of its location between the Rhine and Waal Rivers where the rivers pass within 5 km of each other. The museum refers to itself as the smallest but the most personal WWII museum in the Netherlands. It is well worth visiting.

In this area (Betuwe) between Arnhem and Nijmegen there was hard fighting between the Allies and Germans. In total, 16 different nationalities competed and 132 planes crashed in this area and more than 60,000 civilians had to be evacuated from the fighting. Between the rivers Rhine and Waal, up to the line Opheusden-Dodewaard, this area was named "Het Eiland" by the Allies in September 1944.

The Betuwe War Museum "The Island" contains a complete overview of this poignant history including Easy Company's heroics. On display are, among other things, five dioramas incorporating all 16 different nationalities, weapons, photo materials and many personal items, most donated over a 45-year period by veterans and residents of this area. Almost every object in the museum has a story, described in a guide as you tour the museum.

As an extra addition to the Betuwe history, there is also a diorama to honor the Dutch army of May 1940 whose position was known as the Betuwe line. There are regularly changing exhibitions in the museum, lovingly prepared by museum staff and visiting experts, insuring the visitor a new experience during every visit.

For more information about the museum, visit www.betuwsoorlogsmuseum.nl. For the complete story of the action at the Crossroads we recommend you visit: www.strijdbewijs.nl/para/crosseng.htm. All photos courtesy of the museum..

THE EYEWITNESS MUSEUM
Beek, The Netherlands

German Paratrooper August Segel

GPS Coordinates: N50.9380 E5.7902

Located in the large home of a former Mayor who, during the war, resigned for reasons of principle in October 1941 and was forced into hiding during 1944. Two SS divisions and senior generals and officers occupied the building during the last months of the war. At this museum, you wil feel the presence of the occupier.

Using 150 life-sized mannequins to depict various wartime scenes in 13 dioramas, the Eyewitness Museum makes the visitor become a first-hand witness of the Second World War in Europe. The dioramas are centered around the war time experiences of German paratrooper August Segel, the fictional main character of the museum whose personal experiences are portrayed through the letters he sent home during the war.

August was a soldier in the First Fallschirmjäger Regiment that later was partly absorbed into the Hermann Göring Division. Enlisting in 1935, throughout the war, he served on many fronts. He served during the invasion in the Netherlands in May 1940 and subsequently he was sent to Russia where he, against all odds, survived. Following his experiences on the Eastern Front he then served in Normandy and Belgium. Finally, August spent the final days of the war in Berlin, suffering all of the consequences of the brutal Russian defeat of the German forces.

Using his story as a framework, the museum offers the visitor deep personal insights into life on the battlefield and the many hardships encountered by the soldiers and the civilians throughout the years of the Second World War.

<u>NOTICE</u>: The museum collection includes many rare and irreplaceable artifacts that have been collected and preserved by the museum founder, Wim Seelen. However, during the night of August 2-3, 2020 a battering ram was used to break down the front door of the museum and in less than five minutes the museum was devastatingly robbed of many of its rare and unique artifacts.

Every effort is being made to identify the perpetrators and retrieve the stolen items including the dissemination of a YouTube video showing the stolen items and asking that the museum be contacted if any of the items on the video have been seen: www.youtube.com/watch?v=JIPN1IVmYyw.

A fund to help with reconstructing the damage has also been established and we encourage you to help with this crucial effort to restore this important museum: www.doneeractie.nl/steuntje-in-de-rug-na-inbraak-levenswerk/-45101 .

*For more information about the museum, visit **www.eyewitnesswo2.nl/**. For more information about the local tourism opportunities in the area surrounding the museum, visit **www.visitzuidlimburg.nl/omgeving/plaatsen/detail/beek/42/**. Photos courtesy of the museum.*

FRISIAN RESISTANCE MUSEUM
Leeuwarden, The Netherlands

GPS Coordinates: N53.1997 E5.7946

In the Fries Verzetsmuseum (Frisian Resistance Museum) you will meet the people who lived in Friesland in the years 1940 to 1945. Frisians and non-Frisians explain how they experienced the war in the Frisian countryside.

There was resistance and persecution, but no 'hunger winter', which meant that refugees and people came from near and far for milk and food. Thanks to objects, photos, film clips and documents, you will discover these personal stories that are passed on from generation to generation.

The Frisian Resistance Museum tells stories that touch, confront and raise questions about people who had to make difficult choices in difficult times. In the museum you will see how the Second World War unfolded and its impact on Frisians. The focus of the museum is on topics such as the air war over Friesland, resistance against the occupier and going into hiding.

Special attention is paid to the spectacular raid by the Frisian resistance on the House of Detention in Leeuwarden on December 8, 1944 when the detention center is raided by the armed resistance, the Knokploegen. Within half an hour and without firing a shot, 51 resistance fighters are freed.

The museum manages a collection of over 50,000 objects including uniforms, arms, daily items, documents, photos and film clips. The museum's excellent presentation of *"Freedom Now"* is the newest exhibition. Ten Frisians from different backgrounds each tell their own story about freedom. Do they feel free to be themselves, to exercise their profession or religion?

The tragedies of the Hunger Winter of 1944-1945 are explored when 20,000 Dutch citizens, mostly elderly men, die of starvation. More than 70,000 hunger winter evacuees were distributed across Fryslân, where food shortages were less acute.

The museum can be visited online via *virtueletour.friesverzetsmuseum.nl*. There you can also virtually visit the exhibition *"Eye to Eye With War"*, which was organized in 2020 by the Fries Museum, of which the Fries Verzetsmuseum is a part.

For more information about the museum, please visit www.friesverzetsmuseum.nl or www.friesmuseum.nl. For more information about the Leeuwarden area, visit www.visitleeuwarden.com/nl. Photos courtesy of the museum.

KAMP WESTERBORK MEMORIAL
Hooghalen (Midden-Drenthe), Netherlands

Photo: Europeanmemories.net

GPS Coord.: N52.9210 E6.5697

This is a very important historical site relating to the Holocaust in Holland. The Kamp Westerbork museum is a dynamic museum, concentrating on the development of educational programs for primary and high schools, sponsoring eyewitness talks about the camp and broadcasting monthly radio programs dedicated to telling the personal stories of the many individuals who passed through the camp.

Photo: Rudi Beuker Aug 2020

Originally constructed to help Jewish refugees from Germany reach England, beginning on 1 July 1942, the Germans established this camp as the assembly and starting point for 93 trains carrying Dutch Jews to the Auschwitz, Sobibor, Theresienstadt and Bergen-Belsen death camps.

To calm the victims, the camp had to function as much as possible like a normal village. A false world. Sports could be played, shopping was possible, the camp had its own money and on Tuesday evenings, revue performances and concerts were performed in the registration barracks.

Children in the camp had to go to school, just like at home so that the youngest camp inmates led a life that seemed as normal as possible during the day but, because teachers would be deported every week, their education depended on the incoming and outgoing transports.

After October 1942, Camp Westerbork was placed in the hands of SS-Obersturmführer Albert Konrad Gemmeker because his predecessors did not deport the Jews as quickly and silently as possible. Gemmeker emerged as a gentleman who treated the Jews correctly but his main concern was meeting the Nazi party's weekly quotas of transported Jews.

93 trains left camp Westerbork for the camps in Eastern E urope. Beginning in July 1942, the first prisoners were deported to Auschwitz: 2,030 Jews, including a number of orphans. In the first months the train departed twice a w eek. It would be announced per barracks who would be deported that day. When you heard your name, you knew what to do. Pack your things in the same suitcase, backpack or duffel bag that you used to come to Westerbork Camp and get on the train. The transports lasted until September 13, 1944. Most Jews were only at the camp for a matter of days, including Anne Frank of Amsterdam.

On April 12, 1945, the Canadian army freed 876 Jewish prisoners in camp Westerbork. On the cry *The Tommy's Are Here!*, everyone rushed out to catch up with the liberators. Many jumped on top of the tanks and rode victorious over the Boulevard des Misères. For the time being, the 876 Jews still had to stay in the camp. The whole of the Netherlands had not yet been liberated and fighting continued further north. Moreover, the risk of infectious diseases was high. First, all camp residents had to be medically examined and the Canadians wanted absolute certainty that no traitors were running free.

Between 1942 and 1945, 107,000 Dutch Jews were deported to the East, mostly via Westerbork. In total, only 5,000 people returned. We invite you to visit the museum and to share in our reverence for the many who did not return.

For more information about the museum please visit the museum's website: **www.kampwesterbork.nl** *or visit* **europeanmemories.net/memorial-heritage/ herrinneringscentrum-kamp-westerbork/**. *Except as noted, photos courtesy of the museum.*

GPS Coordinates: N51.4679 E3.7439

LIBERATION MUSEUM ZEELAND
Nieuwdorp (Borsele), The Netherlands

Located in the municipality of Borsele, the 4,500 m² Liberation Museum Zeeland is the largest museum in the province of Zeeland, occupying 3 hectares and housing more than 40,000 objects relating to the Battle of the Scheldt and the Liberation of the Zeeland Dutch Province.

During the Second World War, when Operation Market Garden failed during September 1944, the need to control the port of Antwerp became critical for the Allies to be able to transport troops and equipment to the armies advancing to liberate The Netherlands and Belgium.

To the Germans, it was imperative to defend their positions to the last man to make sure that the port of Antwerp would not fall into the hands of the Allies.

A Battle of the Scheldt Crossing

Linked to the North Sea by the Scheldt River, five weeks of fierce fighting was necessary by primarily Canadian forces between Antwerp and the North Sea to defeat and remove the German forces, resulting in 13,000 Canadian casualties. Since the village of Nieuwdorp played an important role during the Battle of the Scheldt, it is a prominent focus of the museum.

The museum also focuses on the "Battalion Zeeland" which was formed by local volunteers who, following the liberation of Zeeland, joined the Canadians in the fight to liberate the remainder of the country.

A thread throughout the museum, the story of Kees Sinke, is told to pay tribute to all the fighters who fought in Zeeland for the peace we enjoy today.

After viewing the 4,500 m2 of exhibits and the Bailey bridge example at the 3 hectares museum site, two cozy cafés are available to provide the visitor with snacks and drinks while contemplating the history that has just been experienced.

*For more information about the museum, please visit **www.bevrijdingsmuseumzeeland.nl**. For more information about the municipality of Borsele, please visit **www.borsele.nl**. Photos courtesy of the museum.*

MUSEUM 1940-1945
Dordrecht, The Netherlands

GPS Coordinates: N51.8165 E4.6640

Located just southeast of Rotterdam in South Holland, this museum presents a comprehensive story of Holland's May, 1940 invasion, its struggles during the Nazi occupation, its ultimate liberation by the Allies and the heroism of the local Resistance groups during the occupation.

Museum 1940-1945 lies in Dordrecht, the oldest city in Holland, occupying one of the historic buildings in the midst of the old town area that dates from 1289. Lying along one of the old harbors of the river Oude Maas, this is a beautiful museum to visit.

The position of the city of Dordrecht in May 1940 was unique and of great strategic importance during the German invasion, due to its location and the very important rail and traffic bridges at Moerdijk and Zwijndrecht. The city continued to be strategically important during the German occupation and during the Allies' liberation of the country.

This history was one of the primary reasons for the founding of the *Museum 1940-1945*. The aim was to create a museum that would keep alive the memory of the years 1939 to 1945 and the lessons that must be learned from those years by current and future generations.

The museum collection, which is divided over two floors, can be seen in the many numerous display cases, photo and poster panels, interspersed with numerous old historical uniforms, rifles, small arms, utensils and newspapers supplemented with strategic models that together form a picture of this dark period in Dutch history.

Audiovisual material is presented showing the rise of the Nazis in the 1930s and the four years of occupation, persecution, resistance leading to Holland's eventual liberation. There are also cinemas in the museum showing films from the Second World War, including the critical attack on the Moerdijk bridges by the German parachutists in May of 1940.

Education being a primary focus, children enjoy the treasure hunt designed to hold their interest while they learn about the human suffering endured during the war.

To obtain more information about the museum, visit **www.museum19401945.nl/**. *For more information about the Dordrecht area, visit* **cms.dordrecht.nl**. *Photos courtesy of the museum.*

MUSEUM DE BEWOGEN JAREN 39 - 50
Hooge Mierde (Reusel-De Mierden), The Netherlands

GPS Coordinates: N51.3878 E5.1295

There are many special and rare objects that can be seen at this museum in the attractive village of Reusel-De Mierden southwest of Eindhoven. The creation of John Meulenbroeks, the collection first became a museum on the first floor of his café De Bijenkorf. Today the museum is located near the café and the town square. With a special focus on the September 1944 Battle for Reusel, the museum is open four days each week and by appointment.

Not only does the Museum De Bewogen Jaren 39—50 have a varied and extensive WWII collection, it is one of the few museums that also concentrates on the Japanese persecution of the Dutch people in the Dutch East Indies, adding a poignant additional perspective to the impacts of WWII on the Dutch people.

Continually improving, the museum outlines "a route" through the Second World War in Europe and in our former Dutch East Indies colonies with permanent displays that sketch the course of the war over the years. A detailed guide helps the visitor understand each of the stories presented in the display cases as they are encountered.

This is a dynamic museum focusing on a wide range of local subjects including the Dutch army during the "Blitzkrieg", the French army's battle here on May 12, 1940, the local resistance and escape lines, the air war and crashes during Operation Market Garden and the local persecution during the occupation.

The museum personnel can provide you with extra guidance and if you come with a group, with advance notice, we can provide personal tours. The museum can also combine your visit with a cycling or walking tour or you can have an excellent local meal at the Café De Bijenkorf on the adjacent town square.

The museum promotes and supports the activities of local reenactment associations and schedules frequent lectures about specific events during the war as well as the personal stories of many individuals who faced many fearful times at the hands of the German and Japanese invaders and occupiers.

*For more information about the museum, visit **www.museumdebewogenjaren.nl/**. For more information about the local tourism opportunities, visit **www.tipreusel-demierden.nl/**. Photos courtesy of the museum.*

OORLOGSMUSEUM (WAR MUSEUM) OVERLOON
Overloon (Boxmeer), The Netherlands

GPS Coordinates: N51.5701 E5.9583

Located in the middle of the largest tank battle in Holland during WWII, this important museum was founded in War Museum Overloon is the largest war museum in the Netherlands. The museum was opened on May 25, 1946, making it one of the oldest museums in Europe dedicated to the Second World War.

War Museum Overloon is the largest war museum in the Netherlands. The museum was opened on May 25, 1946, making it one of the oldest museums in Europe dedicated to the Second World War.

The museum is located on the site of the Battle of Overloon, a World War II tank and infantry battle between Allied and German forces that occurred in September and October 1944 in the aftermath of Operation Market Garden. The Battle of Overloon is known as the largest tank battle ever on Dutch soil.

Here, an American Armored Division (7th) and the British Infantry met with the stubborn resistance of the Germans, fighting for 20 days. The Allies had not come up against such hostile opposition since June on the beaches of Normandy. More than 150 tanks from both sides were destroyed in the battle and the town of Overloon was completely destroyed.

The museum is set in 14 hectares of woodland and a major feature of the museum is the large number of military vehicles and equipment on display, both German and Allied, many of which took part in the Battle of Overloon. The military hall (some 2 soccer fields in size) contains over 150 vehicles, aircraft and cannons from WWII.

The museum also presents an extensive overview exhibition of Holland during WWII and a series of personal stories illustrate the problems facing not just the population but also the occupying forces. There are also a large number of special military presentations and dioramas depicting, for instance, German parachutists, as well as dioramas depicting all of the air strikes during WWII.

The museum is known for its "Museum in the Dark" events which are scheduled to occur approximately 6 times per year, leaving the visitor with a lifetime memory of what life was like at night during war.

At the end of your visit, the comfortable museum café is ready to receive you in the attractive restaurant or on the terrace surrounded by peaceful nature.

Photo By Alexander Buschorn — de wikipedia

For more information about the museum, please visit www.oorlogsmuseum.nl/. For more information about the local tourism opportunities in the area of the museum, visit www.visitlandvancuijk.nl/. Except as noted, photos courtesy of the museum.

VRIJHEIDSMUSEUM (FREEDOM MUSEUM)
Groesbeek (Berg en Dal), The Netherlands

GPS Coordinates: N52.9210 E6.5697

The Vrijheidsmuseum (Freedom Museum) is located in the beautiful green, hilly landscape of Groesbeek (now Berg en Dal), just east of Nijmegen. The museum café offers excellent panoramic views of the surrounding hills and forests that include the parachutist landing fields used by the Allies during Operation Market Garden.

The Freedom Museum tells the Story of War and Freedom without Borders in this unique place. This is where the two main operations on the Western Front took place during World War II: Operation Market Garden and Operation Veritable, the beginning of the Allied advances to control the Rhine. Both operations had major consequences for the further course of the war along the German-Dutch border area.

The theme of the permanent exhibition is 'Freedom'. The human dilemmas and unknown stories of civilians and soldiers are portrayed for the visitors from different perspectives. There is never one story and questions arise such as: what do you see when you look at history and how would you have acted? Special attention is paid to developments in the Netherlands, Germany and Europe and their connection with events on the world stage.

The museum immerses you in the Story of War and Freedom without Borders, fully set in the history of the 20th century. The pre-war history and the period after 1945 are important parts of the exhibition and the visitor is challenged to critically reflect on current events: freedom in today's world and, in miniature, in their own life.

The Freedom Museum offers a new and fascinating view of history, full of surprises, interactivity and experience. The many authentic objects, documents and personal stories bring the past very close. Watch the fascinating films, see the impressive photos, interact with the story and experience history and current events.

The Freedom Museum regularly organizes many activities for young and old in and around the museum that include youth programming, field trips in a historic vehicle, lectures, guided tours, etc., provided by more the 120 museum volunteers. With the use of authentic and modern presentation techniques, the museum is ready to serve current and future generations.

The museum also offers the visitor a welcoming café and interesting museum shop.

*For more information about the museum, please visit **www.vrijheidsmuseum.nl**. For more information about the municipality of Groesbeek and the local tourism opportunities, visit **www.bergendal.nl**. Photos courtesy of the museum.*

WINGS OF LIBERATION MUSEUM
Best, The Netherlands

GPS Coordinates: N51.5172 E5.4409

Located in the middle of the Operation Market Garden offensive battle zone, the Wings of Liberation Museum has one of the most comprehensive and extensive collections of Allied and German military equipment in Europe and uniquely, provides battlefield tours in WWII vehicles.

Operation Market Garden is one of the most important military events in Dutch history. In September, 1944 Allied forces used parachutists and glider aircraft to put men and material on the ground in the drop zones adjacent to the present Wings of Liberation Museum. The focus of the museum is to allow the visitor to follow in the footsteps of the heroes of the 101st Airborne Division and relive the events that would result in the liberation of the southern areas of The Netherlands.

The Museum is part of an extensive complex of halls, situation in pleasant woodlands. Learn more about the history of Operation Market Garden and look at unique aircraft, half-track vehicles, jeeps, tanks, gliders, guns and motorcycles that were actually used here at the end of World War II. Then sit down on the terrace at Brasserie Het Boshuys to contemplate what you have seen over a nice lunch, coffee or dinner. For children, we offer a playground with a play castle—and a drawbridge!

The museum offers many different activities that allow you to customize your visit beforehand. If you contact the museum in advance, you can book a tour of the drop zone area in a historic army vehicle and include a visit to the Paulushoef farm, used to guide glider pilots because the name can be seen in large letters on the roof. You can also step into the museum's flight simulator room, sit in one of the original Link trainers or learn how to fly a Dakota aircraft or an F-16 fighter if you prefer!

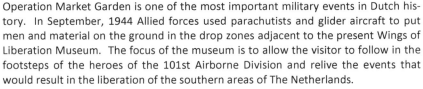

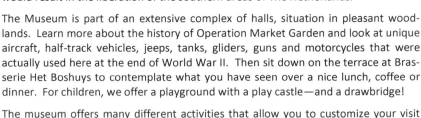

*For more information about the museum, please visit **www.bevrijdendevleugels.nl**. For more information about the municipality of Best and the local tourism opportunities in the area, visit **www.bestbijzonder.com**. Photos courtesy of the museum.*

WOLFHEZE GLIDER MUSEUM
Wolfheze (Renkum), The Netherlands

GPS Coord.: N52.0067 E5.7982

This very unique museum is located just west of Arnhem in an area that witnessed fierce fighting during Operation Market Garden. Within walking distance there is an interesting jeep tunnel under a railroad and a field of defensive foxholes that were used by a platoon of the British 4th Parachute Brigade.

Paul Hendriks has been interested in World War II history since he was a child and became inspired by military objects in his father's shed. In the 1970s Paul and his brother Peter began collecting objects related to Operation Market Garden and the enormous number of Allied gliders that were used to deliver infantry and equipment to the nearby battlefield.

Today the museum houses major components of gliders that were used during Operation Market Garden and in addition to the many glider components, the museum houses a significant collection of uniforms, personal items, maps, recorded personal memories, artifacts and photographs detailing the massive Allied operation that culminated in the Battle of Arnhem.

For more information about the museum, visit www.glidermuseum.nl.https://m.facebook.com/GliderCollectionWolfheze. For more information about the area surrounding the museum, visit www.renkum.nl. Except as noted, all museum photos by Arjan Vrieze.

Remembering & Honoring The Sacrifices Endured By So Many

German Nazi flag, 1935 - 1945
Pop. 1940: 80 million

The flag of Germany, 1945 - Present
Pop. Today: 84 million

LIVING IN GERMANY DURING WORLD WAR II

Several important aspects of life in the small towns of the occupied countries occurred in the opposite order they occurred in the small towns of Germany. Specifically, the people of the occupied countries experienced the greatest amount of fear during the beginning of the war whereas the people of Germany experienced the greatest amount of fear towards the end of the war. Also, as the war went on, the peoples' hope for the future increased in the occupied countries whereas in Germany the peoples' hope for the future decreased. Otherwise, the lives of the people living in Germany and the lives of the people in the occupied countries were not so different in many ways.

For most German citizens, the first two years of the war were reasonably comfortable. The British blockade resulted in some shortages, the war effort consumed many wood and metal materials, but Germany plundered everything possible from the occupied countries, especially manufactured items, essential foods and livestock, reducing those shortages in Germany. Even so, Germans were already familiar with rationing as a rationing program had been in place since August, 1939.

As time went by, more and more items became scarce or unavailable to the German people, especially items that had to be imported from overseas such as coffee. By 1942 Germany's rationing program was tightened, especially with strict limits on all foodstuffs and the penalties for abuse increased to the point where abuse of the rationing program could result in a death sentence. Those classified as essential workers could receive extra rations but if you were of Jewish or Polish descent you could only expect starvation allowances. The situation was made even worse with the need to feed and house the more than 5 million civilian workers and 2 million prisoners of war brought to Germany from the occupied countries to work in Germany's factories.

Of course, the last two years of the war were the worst for the people of Germany. The might of the Allies' air power resulted in bombing raids with as many as 1,000 bombers flying in formation, the greatest danger being in the western industrial areas. Besides the devastation and casualties, transportation, water supply and power supply systems became extremely unreliable.

Worse yet, confidence in Hitler and the German government waned and any hope for a bright future waned along with it. None of the promises made by Hitler about the Third Reich would come true and instead, by the end of the war, the suffering of the German people was just beginning.

Not all Germans believed in the Nazi cause to the end. The following page presents a story about the German village of Voltlage where the bravery of a German soldier saved the village from a terrible bombing by the British in April of 1945.

Voltlage (Volt-la-geh) is the ancestral home of Captain Lester Steinke and his nephew, the author.

VOLTLAGE GERMANY

State: Lower Saxony (Niedersachsen)   Pop. 1940: 1,000   Pop. 2020: 1,700

SITING & HERITAGE

Voltlage (Volt-la-geh) is a small village in northwest Germany less than 50 km from Germany's border with the Netherlands. Lying within an extensive area historically known for livestock, asparagus and grain production, agriculture has been the primary industry in the region for many centuries.

The square tower of the beautiful village church of St. Katharina dates from around the year of 1200. Expanded to its present configuration in 1752, the church continues to be the center of the community. Experiencing destruction from numerous wars since medieval times, Voltlage and the surrounding villages suffered greatly during the Thirty Years War of the early 1600s.

A Voltlage postcard from the 1930s

The St. Katharina church village plaza

A rear view of the St. Katharina church

The St. Katharina church interior

A COMMON THREAD BETWEEN TWO COURAGROUS MEN

During the first week of April, 1945, Montgomery's 2nd British Army crossed the Netherlands border into northwest Germany, only days away from Voltlage. By April 4th, after much fighting and destruction, the nearby city of Osnabrück was captured and, on April 8th, the British army stood at the doorsteps of Voltlage. At Voltlage, a unit of German soldiers had been told by their zealous Nazi commander, Major Grunau, a ruthless and reckless man, that every effort was needed to turn the fate of the Third Reich. The battle was about to begin for Voltlage.

According to British army reports and remembrances of local people, that evening Grunau was killed at about 8 pm, and local people spoke that a mistreated German soldier did it (no name has ever been mentioned). The English stated that Grunau's death and the retreat of much of the German unit spared Voltlage the fate of being bombed to dust, especially after heavy fighting had just occurred south of the village, where more than 40 British soldiers were killed.

The British, supported by tanks and a squadron of Typhoon planes, had to clear, house by house, the last of the soldiers who had come over Voltlage like foreign invaders and taken the village hostage in the name of the Führer. In the end, half the village was on fire, no wonder as there were only half-timbered houses. Fortunately however, the death of Major Grunau spared the village from being bombed and totally destroyed.

Two examples of half-timbered buildings in pre-war Voltlage   A pre-war Voltlage scene

The Common Thread: Voltlage is the village from where, in 1835, the grandfather of Capt. Lester Steinke (see pages 6 & 7) emigrated to the United States. Settling in an area of Ohio almost identical to Voltlage and coming from a family of farmers, he became a farmer in Ohio. As a child, Capt. Steinke remembers that his mother routinely spoke German around the house and that their German last name and their Catholic religion was a source of family pride.

In the Steinke family name for centuries, the original family farm just outside Voltlage is still owned and operated by one of Capt. Steinke's extended family members. A recently recovered village livestock register from 1490 states that the Steinke family owned two horses, five cows and three pigs.

Could it be that St. Katharina intervened so that Capt. Steinke's courage as a P-51 fighter pilot would be shared, giving the German soldier the courage needed to shoot the Nazi major, thus saving Capt. Steinke's ancestral village from a devastating bombing? We like to think so.

OUR VILLAGE TODAY

Today Voltlage is a charming, rather affluent village with many beautiful homes and buildings. Still a major processing point for agricultural goods, the citizens of Voltlage interact as members of an extended family, all enjoying the quiet life of a quaint German village. Surrounding Voltlage, a popular 20 km circular cycling path passes through farmland, orchards and ponds with educational signs about the life of famous resident, teacher and priest Bernard Overberg and other encountered wayside shrines and memorial stones.

For more information about Voltlage, visit the municipal website: ***www.voltlage.de****. We appreciate the information and assistance provided by Norbert Grasbon, Village archivist, St. Katharina archivist and retired Voltlage English teacher. Pre-war photos courtesy of the village of Voltlage. Current photos by the author.*

Remembering & Honoring The Sacrifices Endured By So Many

Flag of the United States, 1912 - 1959
Pop. 1940: 132 million

Flag of the United States, 1959 - Present
Pop. Today: 337 million

LIVING IN THE UNITED STATES DURING WORLD WAR II

Prior to the attack on Pearl Harbor, the majority of Americans were against becoming involved in the European war. This isolationism immediately ended after Pearl Harbor but Americans became fearful that a similar attack might happen on the US coasts, especially the west coast. Curiously, this fear played an important role in motivating every American to do their part to help win the war as quickly as possible.

Everyone joined in. By the end of the war, more than 12 million had joined the military services and by mid-1942, more than 10 million Americans served as civil defense volunteers. Everyone knew that America must become "the arsenal of democracy" and, throughout the country, every effort was made to convert the manufacturing of goods to the manufacturing of war materials. Factories across the country became awash in government contracts, women were encouraged to join the workforce and, when President Roosevelt signed a law banning discrimination in hiring black Americans, black Americans joined the war effort in force. During the war, the unemployment in the US dropped from 17% to 1%.

In 1942, a national rationing program was put in place by the government and coupons were required to purchase many items including sugar, meat and gasoline. In spite of this, a 1943 survey revealed that only 30% of Americans felt that they were having to make 'real sacrifices'. Throughout the country, large collection drives were organized to collect items needed for the war effort, especially metal, rubber, clothing and waste cooking oil and fat for the production of the glycerin needed to manufacture explosives. To reduce copper consumption, the government minted steel pennies and removed the nickel from the 5-cent coins.

Since radio was the primary source of entertainment, most Americans were generally well-informed about what was happening in the war in Europe and, because of the popularity of movie theaters, the US Office of War Information boosted the public's information with a steady stream of 'propagandized' theater news clips designed to boost public morale and optimism.

In spite of all these positive efforts, a black stain on America resulted when the decision was made in 1942 to place all Japanese-Americans into detention camps for the duration of the war. More than 120,000 Japanese were ultimately detained in these camps, ignoring the fact that many Japanese-American men served honorably in the European war and, in fact, the US Army's 100th Battalion, 442nd Infantry Division, a Japanese-American unit, became the most decorated combat unit in US Army history during World War II.

All told, during World War II, America suffered more than 1,000,000 military casualties, including more than 400,000 killed. Indeed, their sacrifices and America's might helped save democracy.

SIDNEY, OHIO

Pop. 1940: 12,000   Pop. 2020: 24,000

The boyhood home of Capt. Lester Steinke, US Army Air Corps *(See Pages 6 & 7)*

SITING & HERITAGE

Sidney, Ohio is a small town located in the western half of Ohio in an extensive agricultural area known for its corn, wheat and soybean production. Named after Sir Philip Sidney, a poet and member of British Parliament, Sidney is located along the Great Miami River in an area that was once the richly-forested hunting grounds of the Shawnee and Miami Indian nations. During the late 1700s and early 1800s Sidney and much of the surrounding areas were settled by farming people primarily of German descent.

In the early 1800s, the construction of the Miami-Erie Canal connected Sidney with the major trade centers, attracting an influx of settlers into the area. The railroads arrived in the mid-1800s and still today Sidney is served by east-west and north-south railroad lines. In the 1950s, Interstate I-75 was constructed through Sidney, linking it permanently to the surrounding major cities.

During the war, the Sidney schools held a series of classes to teach women to operate machine tools.

THE WORLD WAR II STORY OF SIDNEY, OHIO

Following the outbreak of war in Europe and the Pacific, it was critical to focus the hearts and minds of all Americans on one goal: the winning of the war. Shelby County, Ohio needed little encouragement to accomplish what was needed. The local industries quickly converted to making items of war.

The Monarch Machine Tool Company, a defense contractor during World War I, began receiving government orders for lathes even before the disaster of Pearl Harbor and, by midway through the war, Monarch was producing 35% of the country's high grade metal lathes used by the aircraft and early jet propulsion industries. The Ross Products Company and the Stolle Corporation began producing aluminum aircraft parts and when the supply of aluminum became scarce, Wagner Manufacturing developed a new pre-seasoned ironware material as an aluminum replacement.

The rapid industrial expansion in Sidney, already a town with full employment in 1940, created the challenge of providing enough housing for the huge influx of workers. To address this, the city subsidized the construction of hundreds of new homes and the conversion of many of the larger, older homes to serve as multi-unit apartments throughout the war.

The most important impact on the residents was the rationing of goods imposed by the War Production Board or WPB. The shortage of metal resulted in the rationing of anything with metal and ration coupon books had to be used to purchase gasoline, sugar and many other items. To save wool, the WPB even ordered the elimination of vests, patch pockets and cuffs on all new clothing. Scrap drives were especially successful in Sidney. One single drive sponsored by the local farm implement dealers netted 228,000 pounds of iron scrap and another similar drive collected over 109 tons of rubber, an amazing 8 pounds per Sidney resident! Two local scrap dealers received WPB awards for producing enough scrap metal in two months to make 44 of the 2,000 pound bombs used to bomb Tokyo.

Everyone pitched in. Used household cooking grease, oil and fat was routinely saved and more than 800 local volunteers were "home front soldiers" serving as auxiliary policemen, fire watchers, ambulance drivers and air raid wardens. Because of the local war production industries, air raid drills were routinely conducted and Countywide blackout drills were staged on a regular basis.

SIDNEY, OHIO TODAY. Today, Sidney, Ohio is a conservative, growth-oriented community of approximately 21,000 residents that cherishes its collection of historic buildings including the Shelby County Courthouse which occupies a city block in the town center. The Courthouse was recently named one of the "Great American Public Spaces". Known for its outstanding parks and recreational areas, the city established a goal during the 1950s to have a park within 1/2 mile (0.8 km) of every residence and today there are 14 neighborhood parks throughout the city including the 180-acre Tawawa Park nature area.

*For more information about Sidney, visit the municipal website: **www.sidneyoh.com**. The historical information above was taken from a May, 2000 article on **WWII and the Home Front** written by Rich Wallace, a local Sidney attorney and historian.*

DESPICABLE NAZI ACTIONS TO REMEMBER

THE HONGER (HUNGER) WINTER

Throughout the war, Germany viewed the populations of the occupied countries as "useless mouths" who were a drain on the food supplies needed by the German army. Later, as the war went on, the food from the occupied countries became more and more important to the Germans to feed the people of Germany. Thus, food supplies were scarce in the occupied countries throughout the war, especially in the cities.

The people of Holland were forced to endure particularly cruel food and fuel shortages during the winter of 1944/1945. Following the June 6, 1944 D-Day landings at Normandy, the Allied armies fanned out, pushing the Germans back towards Germany. To assist the Allies, Queen Wilhelmina (page 178) called for a nation-wide railway workers strike throughout Holland to cripple the ability of the Germans to move men and material. The Germans retaliated by immediately cutting off all food and supplies to the entire western half of Holland, affecting more than 4.5 million people, most of them living in the cities.

The sad face of famine

That winter of 1944/1945 was especially harsh. Delivery of supplies by boat became impossible and the Germans continued to destroy most of the docks and bridges to slow the advance of the Allies. Food ran out quickly, tulip bulbs were commonly eaten and thousands of people from the city made dangerous treks to the outlying agricultural areas to obtain food. Furniture and houses were torn apart to provide fuel for heating throughout the winter months.

An American B-17 bomber drops food and supplies to the starving and freezing people of Holland

It wasn't until April, 1945 that the Germans agreed to not shoot at Allied rescue planes dropping supplies if the Allies would agree to stop bombing the German positions in the area. The Allies agreed, allowing a constant supply of food and supplies to be air dropped into western Holland the remainder of the war. During the Honger Winter famine, more than 20,000 people died of malnutrition plus there were many more deaths from complications related to malnutrition.

Even for those who survived (including Audrey Hepburn), the experience resulted in the development of many life-long health problems that still continue to be passed from generation to generation. Even today, the epigenetic aspects of the Honger Winter continue to be studied to better understand the impacts of famine on populations throughout the world.

THE STEALING OF THE BELLS

Church bells are made of bronze, a mixture of four parts copper to one part tin and, since the time of Napoleon, church bells have been confiscated by conquering armies to manufacture weapons. To halt this irreverent exploitation, the 1907 Hague Convention treaty prohibited the confiscation of church bells during wartime but this prohibition was largely ignored by the Germans during both World War I and World War II. Beginning in September, 1942, Germany began a concerted effort to obtain as many church bells as possible from the occupied countries to manufacture guns and shell casings. By the end of the war, more than 175,000 church bells had been stolen from the occupied countries, most of them sent to foundries in Hamburg to be melted down.

Thousands of bells at the Hamburg dock

During the war, art historians and museum curators brought this and many other preservation concerns to the attention of President Roosevelt who, on August 20, 1943, established the Monuments, Fine Arts and Archives Division whose members became known as the Monuments Men. These dedicated individuals worked diligently, cataloging missing artifacts as the Allies began the liberation of Europe and then searching for those missing artifacts as each area was cleared of Germans. Their work continued and even accelerated after the German surrender on May 8, 1945.

The Monuments Men were fortunately able to find many sculptures and works of art intact and able to be returned to their rightful owners. That however was not the case with respect to the 175,000 stolen church bells. By the end of the war, more than 150,000 of them had been destroyed, lost forever.

DESPICABLE NAZI ACTIONS TO REMEMBER

FORCED LABOR AND WORKER DEPORTATION

Millions of German soldiers were needed in the *Blitzkrieg* conquest and occupation of northern Europe, creating substantial labor shortages in the German homeland. To keep the *Reich* functioning, Nazi Germany relied heavily on importing labor from the conquered countries, deporting civilians at will to work in Germany. The Germans also routinely forced the residents to work as slave laborers in their own countries, doing whatever work the Germans demanded.

In September of 1942, the German occupiers began issuing Compulsory Labor edicts. All able-bodied men 18-50, and all single women 21-35 were required to register for "any work that the government deems necessary," whether in their own countries or in Germany. Many refused to register or went into hiding, causing the Germans to conduct "raids" to round up men who had not registered. Most of those apprehended were immediately loaded into boxcars and sent to Germany.

French laborers building The Atlantic Wall

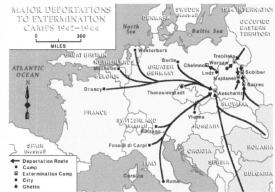

Female forced labor in a Volkswagen factory

Forced laborers were often used in factories that manufactured war materials because the Allied bombings of factories caused a great number of casualties and deaths. Working conditions were hard and 12-14 hour workdays were common. Workers were housed in barracks, were not allowed to move about freely, were poorly fed and received no medical treatment. Some men and women had easier lives if they were assigned to agricultural work or assigned as servants for German officers' families.

During the war, more than 2 million people from Occupied Western Europe were deported to work in Germany. In France alone, 600,000 men were forced to construct the Atlantic Wall. By Sept 1944, 26% of the labor force in Germany were foreigners, most of whom had been deported from their native countries by force. The "Convoy of 27000" forcibly transported 1,000 French female political prisoners to work in German factories (see the story of Louise Macuault, Laon France, page 94).

THE DELIBERATE DEPORTATION & MURDER OF JEWISH CITIZENS

When the persecution of Jews began in Germany in the 1930's, many fled to the countries of the Netherlands, Belgium and France to escape from the Nazis. The German government even encouraged the emigration of Jews until 1941, and an estimated 90,000 left Germany for countries farther west.

When Germany overran and occupied The Netherlands, Belgium, Luxembourg and northern France in 1940, the persecution of Jews did not begin immediately in most of these countries. France was the first country to enact anti-Jewish laws in late 1940 with decrees that all Jews must be identified and denied employment. Similar decrees were issued in the Netherlands in 1940-1941 and Belgium followed suit in 1941. In 1942 the Germans started the wholesale deportation of Jews from northwestern Europe to the Death Camps.

Several concentration camps in northwest Europe were used as collection points from which Jews were then shipped to the Death Camps in Germany and Poland, most to Auschwitz. It is estimated that of the 480,000 Jewish citizens living in Belgium, the Netherlands,

The primary destination of the Jews—Auschwitz

Luxembourg and France at the beginning of the war, 170,000 were murdered by the Nazis. Of the 565,000 Jewish people living in Germany in the 1930s before the war, only 37,000 remained in 1945. This is the greatest war crime of all time. This, the Holocaust, will never be forgotten.

Contributed by Victoria Weals

Occupation Stories 2020

Remembering & Honoring The Sacrifices Endured By So Many

EPILOGUE

THE LESSONS OF WORLD WAR II

The World War II occupation stories compiled for this commemorative project represent the experiences of the many thousands of small towns in these four countries during the more than four years of Nazi occupation. The commemoration of the 2020 75th anniversary of the end of World War II in Europe reminds us all how easily freedom and democracy can be lost when autocratic leaders are given the opportunity to impose their egotistic, bigoted and narrow-minded personalities on a general population.

Personal freedom and democracy for all citizens must therefore always be the unrelenting cornerstone of all government administrations. When judged by future historians, it is only the quality of life and the opportunities able to be provided every citizen that will determine the greatness of any society. Unfortunately, racist beliefs in racial superiority have always been and will always continue to be the main impediment to creating great societies. Racism based on skin color, nationality, religious beliefs and sexual orientations are just a few of the forms of racism that societies must deal with.

Racism is largely based on ignorance and a belief that particular groups of human beings are superior to others. This destructive ignorance can best be fought by educating our youth and one powerful way is to educate them about the tragedies of World War II that were caused by an egotistic, bigoted and narrow-minded autocrat in the name of racism and race superiority.

Young people should be exposed to reading stories such as those in this book and required to visit some of the many excellent World War II museums throughout the world who teach these lessons everyday.

Hopefully our youth will learn the lessons of World War II and, perhaps someday, a truly Great Society will finally be able to be created.

Occupation Stories 2020

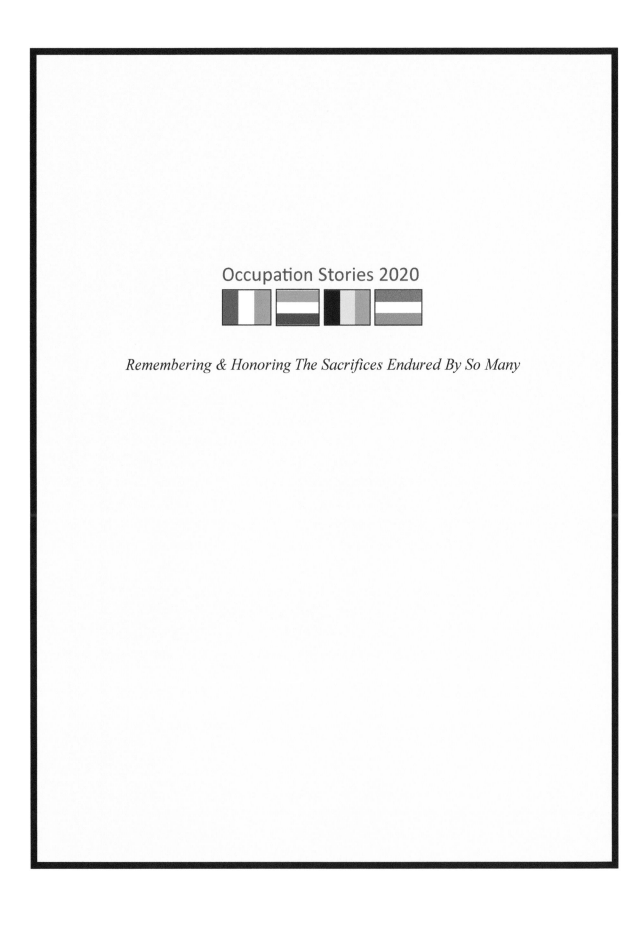

Remembering & Honoring The Sacrifices Endured By So Many

Occupation Stories 2020

Remembering & Honoring The Sacrifices Endured By So Many

ABOUT THE AUTHOR

Steve Carter is a professional civil engineer in Columbus, Ohio. Raised on a working grain farm near the small town of Wapakoneta in northwest Ohio, Steve has been a European Theater World War II history enthusiast since grade school when he first saw photos of his uncle and godfather, Lester Steinke, sitting in the cockpit of a World War II P-51 fighter plane, wearing his very cool aviator sunglasses and crushed officer's hat (see Pages 6 & 7).

As a teenager, Steve often wondered what life would have been like if World War II and the Nazis had come to his small hometown of Wapakoneta. This book answers that question.

A US Air Force Vietnam-era veteran stationed in Turkey and northern California, Steve obtained his civil engineering degree from California State University in Sacramento after which he moved his family back to Ohio, ultimately serving as the Chief Engineer for the Ohio Department of Natural Resources. He subsequently formed TriCar Ltd, a civil engineering consulting firm in Columbus that he has operated for 25 years.

A passionate traveler who firmly believes in the mind-expanding benefits of travel, Steve has traveled to four continents, visiting Argentina, Brazil, Egypt, Mexico, Canada, Saudi Arabia, Greece, Hawaii, the South Pacific islands, Morocco and most all of the countries of Europe several times. Steve has also written "The Guide To Visiting The Amazing World War II Museums of Europe".

An accomplished piano player and guitarist, Steve has been known through the years for his oldies Sing-A-Long events. Today he concentrates his thoughts on his two children Christina and Robb and his four grandchildren, Kendall, Kylynn, Maya and Mason.

ACKNOWLEDGEMENTS

Unquestionably, it is the town and museum officials, the local historians and the residents of these small towns in these four countries who took the time to prepare the information for this commemorative book and who provided the author with constant encouragement throughout the two years required to complete this unique and interesting project who have made this commemorative project possible. We thank each of them profusely.

The extensive editing, proofreading, French translation and constant encouragement provided by Victoria (Vikki) Weals throughout the development of this commemorative book has been critical to the success of the project. Her contributions are greatly appreciated. The translation assistance of Dutch materials provided by Marianne Van Guilijk has also been invaluable and greatly appreciated.

NOTES:

Lightning Source UK Ltd.
Milton Keynes UK
UKHW050002240822
407654UK00002B/80